THE ONE-SHOTS

GAIL SIMONE
BILL MORRISON
WALTER GEOVANI

MARK RUSSELL
MICHAEL MONTENAT

STUART MOORE
FRED HARPER

MARK WAID
LEONARD KIRK

TOM PEYER
GREG SCOTT

ROB LEAN
PAUL LITTLE
ANDY TROY
ROB STEEN

AHOY
COMICS

THE WRONG EARTH
THE ONE-SHOTS

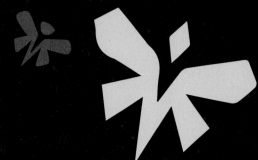

COMICSAHOY.COM   🐦 @ AHOYCOMICMAGS

HART SEELY - PUBLISHER
TOM PEYER - EDITOR-IN-CHIEF
FRANK CAMMUSO - CHIEF CREATIVE OFFICER
STUART MOORE - OPS
SARAH LITT - EDITOR-AT-LARGE
CORY SEDLMEIER - COLLECTIONS EDITOR

DAVID HYDE - PUBLICITY
DERON BENNETT - PRODUCTION COORDINATOR
KIT CAOAGAS - MARKETING ASSOCIATE
HANNA BAHEDRY - PUBLICITY COORDINATOR
LILLIAN LASERSON - LEGAL
RUSSELL NATHERSON SR. - BUSINESS

TRAPPED ON TEEN PLANET

GAIL SIMONE	WRITER
WALTER GEOVANI	PENCILER (PAGES 7–15)
BILL MORRISON	ARTIST (PAGES 16–30)
ROB LEAN	INKER (PAGES 7–15)
ANDY TROY	COLOR
ROB STEEN	LETTERS
PAUL LITTLE	SPECIAL THANKS
JAMAL IGLE	COVER
DAN PARENT	VARIANT COVER B
GENE HA	VARIANT COVER C
TOM PEYER	EDITOR

FAME & FORTUNE

MARK RUSSELL	WRITER
MICHAEL MONTENAT	ARTIST
ANDY TROY	COLOR
ROB STEEN	LETTERS
JAMAL IGLE	COVER
MICHAEL MONTENAT	VARIANT COVER B
GENE HA	VARIANT COVER C
TOM PEYER	EDITOR

PURPLE

STUART MOORE	WRITER
FRED HARPER	ARTIST & COLOR
ROB STEEN	LETTERS
JAMAL IGLE	COVER
JERRY ORDWAY	VARIANT COVER B
GENE HA	VARIANT COVER C
TOM PEYER	EDITOR

CONFIDENCE MEN

MARK WAID	WRITER
LEONARD KIRK	ARTIST
PAUL LITTLE	COLOR
ROB STEEN	LETTERS
JAMAL IGLE	COVER
RICHARD WILLIAMS	VARIANT COVER B
GENE HA	VARIANT COVER C
DERON BENNETT	EDITOR

MEAT

TOM PEYER	WRITER
GREG SCOTT	ARTIST
ANDY TROY	COLOR
ROB STEEN	LETTERS
JAMAL IGLE	COVER
BILL MORRISON	VARIANT COVER B
GENE HA	VARIANT COVER C
SARAH LITT	EDITOR

TODD KLEIN	LOGO
JOHN J. HILL	DESIGN
CORY SEDLMEIER	COLLECTION EDITOR

THE WRONG EARTH CREATED BY TOM PEYER **AND** JAMAL IGLE

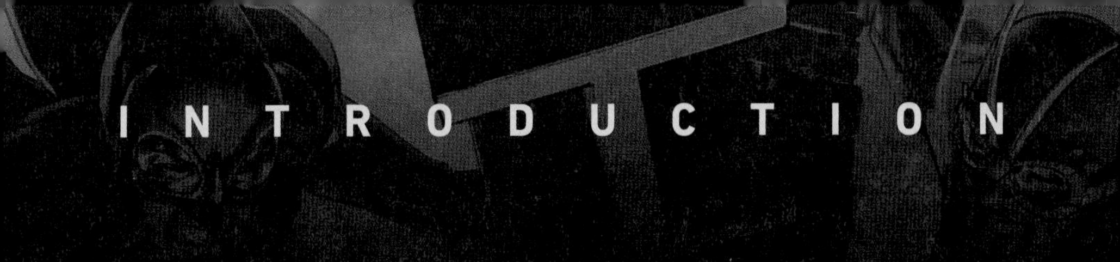

INTRODUCTION

I've long suspected that there were two Earths. Probably more! But at least two.

On the alternate Earth, the one where I (the Bill Corbett writing this) am not, there is another version of me. This Bill Corbett of Earth-Omega is a complete heel: he lies, he cheats, he deliberately farts in inappropriate settings. He makes cutting, sarcastic remarks to toddlers and puppies. He refuses to recycle. Earth-Omega Bill Corbett WILL grab the last slice of pizza, he will not replace a lightbulb or a roll of toilet paper. In restaurants he's a rotten tipper and sneakily steals beer mugs for his "collection." His hygiene is questionable: frankly, he stinks, and gets off on subjecting others to this stinkiness. Man, what an awful creep!

Or...wait. Maybe I, the guy writing this, am the Bill Corbett of Earth-Omega? The awful creep? Maybe there's a BC of Earth-Alpha, that place of relative light and goodness, who is an absolute cornball saint compared to...me. Earth-Alpha Bill Corbett is kind to everyone, his humor is gentle and ultimately uplifting. Inspiring, somehow! He spends 40 hours a week volunteering in soup kitchens, cleaning up litter in the park, reading to puppies and walking toddlers in the baby shelter. He's cheerful as hell, recycles like a damn machine, and is clean as a whistle. Smells vaguely of honeysuckle, but some kinda masculine version of honeysuckle. (Such things are possible on Earth-Alpha!)

Welcome to *THE WRONG EARTH*. But which one is wrong, the Alpha or the Omega? A-ha! That is the question, as some hacky old playwright once said. It's a point-of-view question with no correct answer, but one explored brilliantly by the writers and artists of this *THE WRONG EARTH* collection from AHOY.

One version of our hero, Dragonflyman, is a mid-20th Century costumed do-gooder, selflessly devoted to public safety, good citizenship, Scout's honor, church suppers, and the American Way. He's an old-fashioned, kid-friendly Good Guy who makes sure to brush his teeth and say his prayers every night. His costume might be a bit silly and his name a bit unwieldy, but heck, the man means so well. And he gets results, there on his planetary home turf, Earth-Alpha. Results for JUSTICE.

But the Dragonflyman of Earth-Omega has transcended such kitschy nonsense. Public safety? Bah! Who the hell cares, as long as can pulverize your enemy's bones into dust? And who is your enemy? To quote Brando in *The Wild One*, whattaya got? This grittier version of Dragonflyman has shortened his name to the cooler Dragonfly, made his costume a bit less dorky, and gleefully doles out ultraviolence to anyone in his way. The man will mess you up.

It's the oscillation between these two models of super-heroism, and of the world in general, that makes *THE WRONG EARTH* so much fun. The writers and artists are keenly aware of the last 80-plus years of comic book tropes, styles, retcons, multiverses, etc., and have a creative field

And man, is it a blast. In *Trapped on Teen Planet*, writer Gail Simone and artists Bill Morrison, Walter Geovani and Rob Lean whisk Earth-Omega's Dragonfly to an even more sunshine-y, primary-colors version of Earth which is basically the classic comic book Archieverse. It's hilarious satire, and also a nice sideways commentary on the fact that Archie, Jughead, and the gang have themselves recently been dragged kicking and screaming into a sort of gritty postmodern comics world.

In *Fame & Fortune*, writer Mark Russell and artist Michael Montenat show the two different versions of Dragonfly, Dragonflyman's secret identity, Richard Fame, and how the same humungous rich guy's building project in both worlds may take a slightly different journey, but lead to the same horrible place.

Purple from Stuart Moore and Fred Harper gives us Earth-Kappa, yet another variation of Earth that seems fixed in the 1980s, plus a very satisfying answer to the question "What if Prince were a supervillain?" As you might suspect, music is key.

Confidence Men, by Mark Waid and Leonard Kirk, dives into the fraught world of superhero sidekicks, and well, what the hell is that all about? They toggle between worlds for a sharp exploration of the relationship between Dragonfly(man) and his young helper Stinger.

And finally, *Meat* by Tom Peyer and Greg Scott explores superhero loneliness and grief, even in the much more brutal universe of Earth-Omega. It is also incredibly funny, introducing one of my favorite quirky bad guys ever: Dr. Meat. The name alone cracked me right up.

This collection is smart, sometimes poignant, and hysterically funny at times. I'm glad I got to bounce between these wrong worlds and experience some of the most creative people in comics at their peak.

OK 'bye folks, gotta take out the recycling! Or maybe not. I mean, why should I???

Bill Corbett
August 2022

Bill Corbett is a writer and actor best known for Mystery Science Theater 3000 *and* Rifftrax. *He's also a playwright, screenwriter, and voice actor. Once he even wrote a comi*

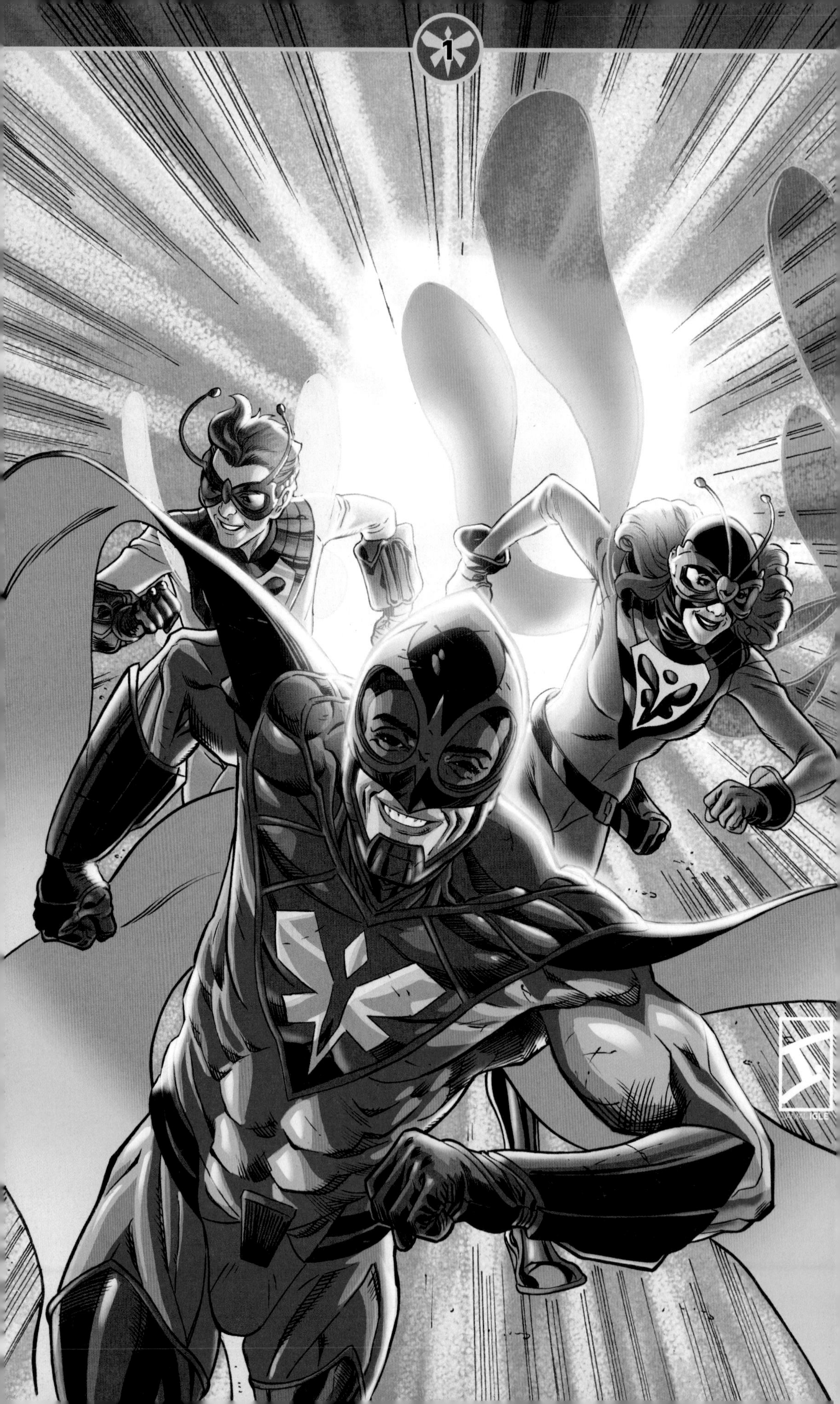

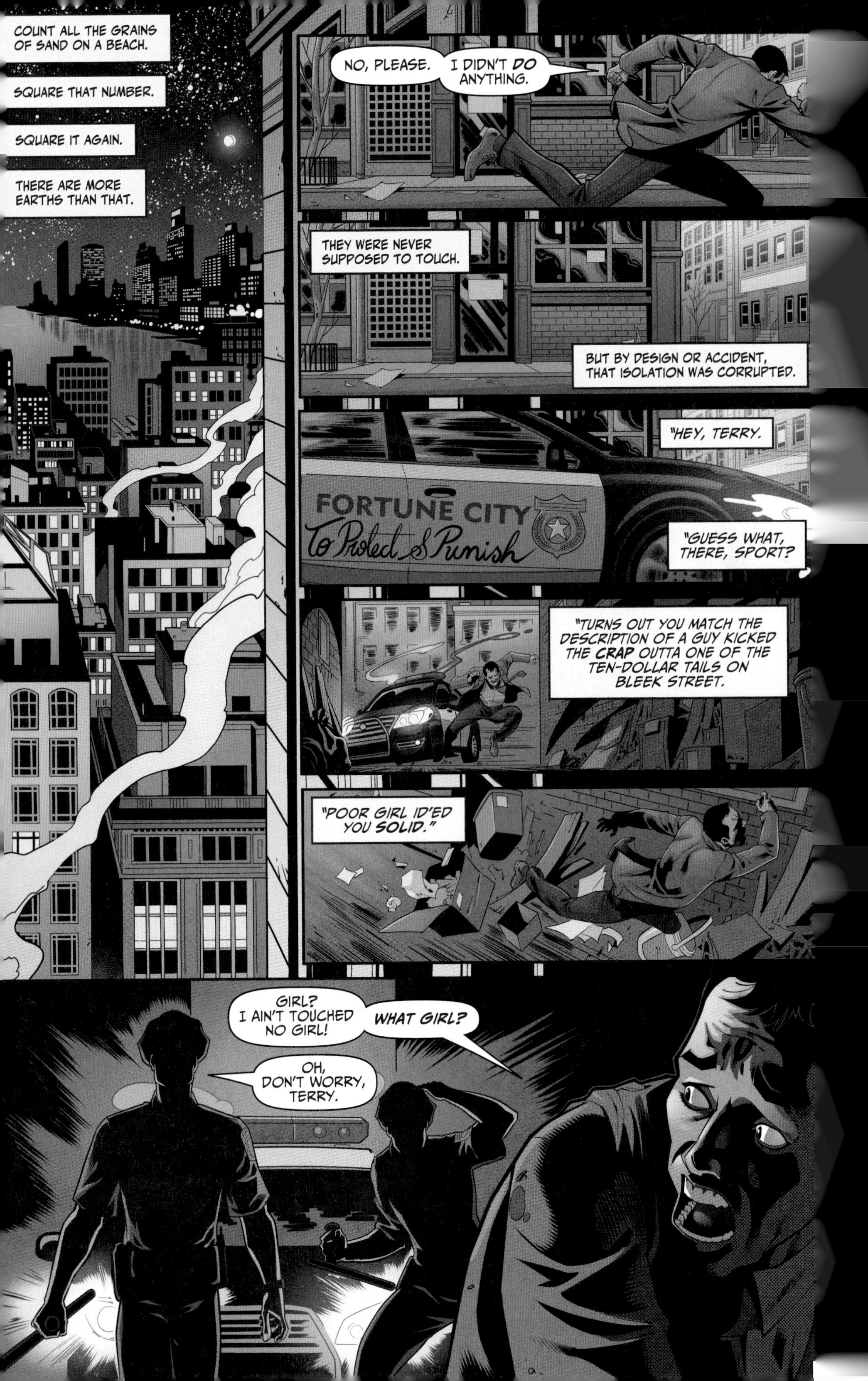
COUNT ALL THE GRAINS OF SAND ON A BEACH.
SQUARE THAT NUMBER.
SQUARE IT AGAIN.
THERE ARE MORE EARTHS THAN THAT.
NO, PLEASE.
I DIDN'T DO ANYTHING.
THEY WERE NEVER SUPPOSED TO TOUCH.
BUT BY DESIGN OR ACCIDENT, THAT ISOLATION WAS CORRUPTED.
"HEY, TERRY.
FORTUNE CITY
To Protect & Punish
"GUESS WHAT, THERE, SPORT?
"TURNS OUT YOU MATCH THE DESCRIPTION OF A GUY KICKED THE CRAP OUTTA ONE OF THE TEN-DOLLAR TAILS ON BLEEK STREET.
"POOR GIRL ID'ED YOU SOLID."
GIRL? I AIN'T TOUCHED NO GIRL!
WHAT GIRL?
OH, DON'T WORRY, TERRY.

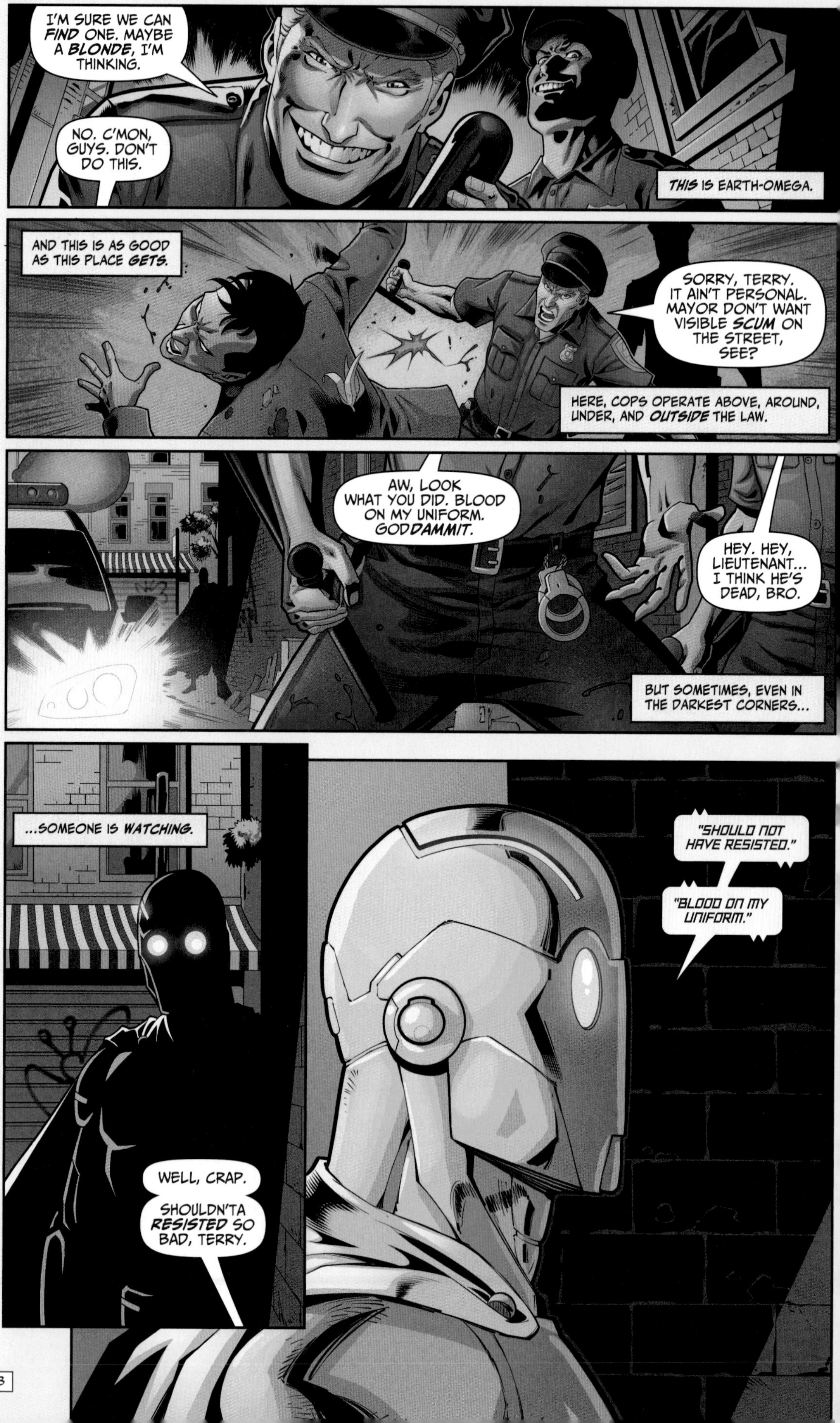

I'M SURE WE CAN FIND ONE. MAYBE A BLONDE, I'M THINKING.
NO. C'MON, GUYS. DON'T DO THIS.
THIS IS EARTH-OMEGA.
AND THIS IS AS GOOD AS THIS PLACE GETS.
SORRY, TERRY. IT AIN'T PERSONAL. MAYOR DON'T WANT VISIBLE SCUM ON THE STREET, SEE?
HERE, COPS OPERATE ABOVE, AROUND, UNDER, AND OUTSIDE THE LAW.
AW, LOOK WHAT YOU DID. BLOOD ON MY UNIFORM. GODDAMMIT.
HEY. HEY, LIEUTENANT... I THINK HE'S DEAD, BRO.
BUT SOMETIMES, EVEN IN THE DARKEST CORNERS...
...SOMEONE IS WATCHING.
WELL, CRAP.
SHOULDN'TA RESISTED SO BAD, TERRY.
"SHOULD NOT HAVE RESISTED."
"BLOOD ON MY UNIFORM."

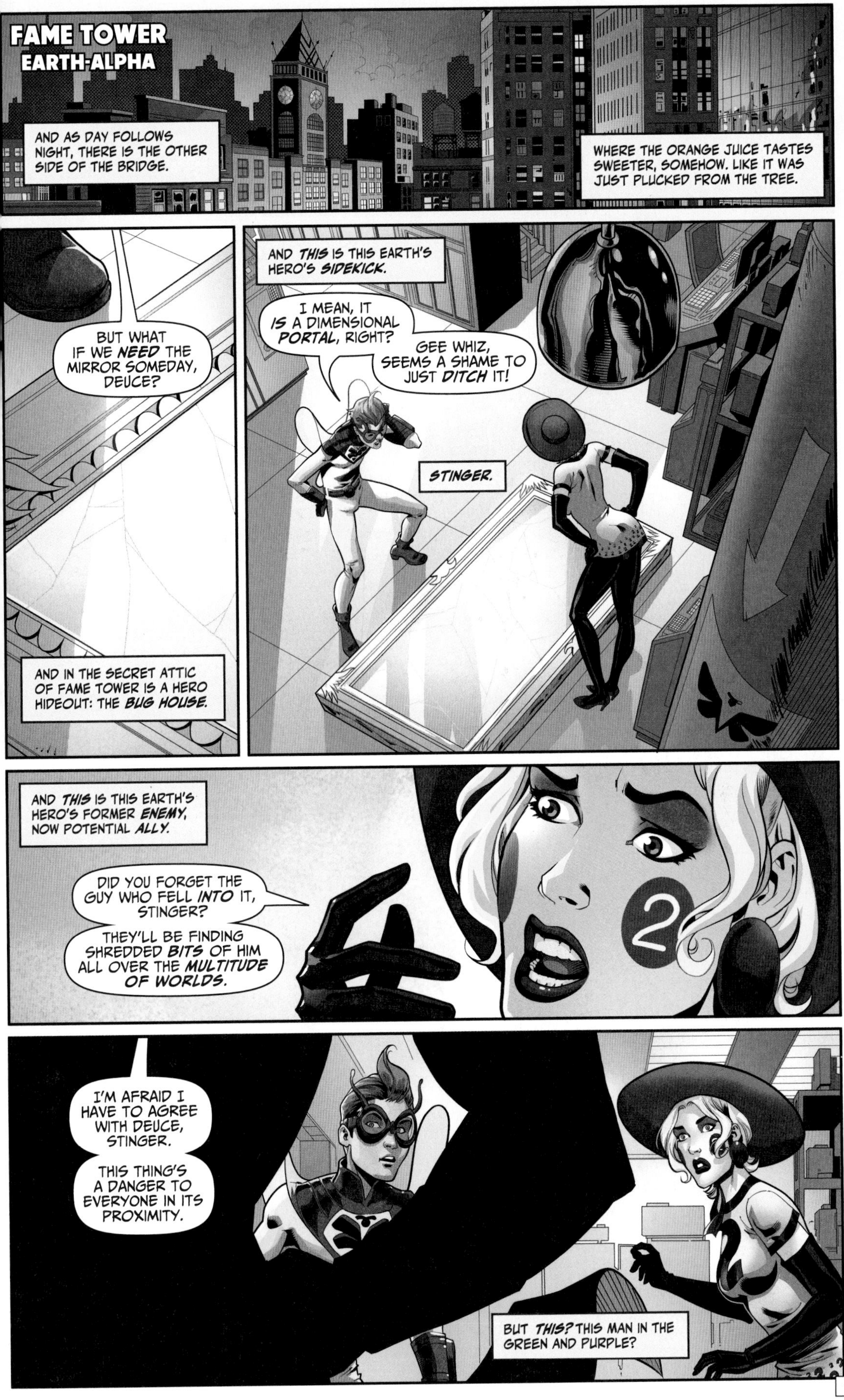
FAME TOWER
EARTH-ALPHA
AND AS DAY FOLLOWS NIGHT, THERE IS THE OTHER SIDE OF THE BRIDGE.
WHERE THE ORANGE JUICE TASTES SWEETER, SOMEHOW. LIKE IT WAS JUST PLUCKED FROM THE TREE.
AND IN THE SECRET ATTIC OF FAME TOWER IS A HERO HIDEOUT: THE BUG HOUSE.
BUT WHAT IF WE NEED THE MIRROR SOMEDAY, DEUCE?
AND THIS IS THIS EARTH'S HERO'S SIDEKICK.
I MEAN, IT IS A DIMENSIONAL PORTAL, RIGHT?
GEE WHIZ, SEEMS A SHAME TO JUST DITCH IT!
STINGER.
AND THIS IS THIS EARTH'S HERO'S FORMER ENEMY, NOW POTENTIAL ALLY.
DID YOU FORGET THE GUY WHO FELL INTO IT, STINGER?
THEY'LL BE FINDING SHREDDED BITS OF HIM ALL OVER THE MULTITUDE OF WORLDS.
I'M AFRAID I HAVE TO AGREE WITH DEUCE, STINGER.
THIS THING'S A DANGER TO EVERYONE IN ITS PROXIMITY.
BUT THIS? THIS MAN IN THE GREEN AND PURPLE?

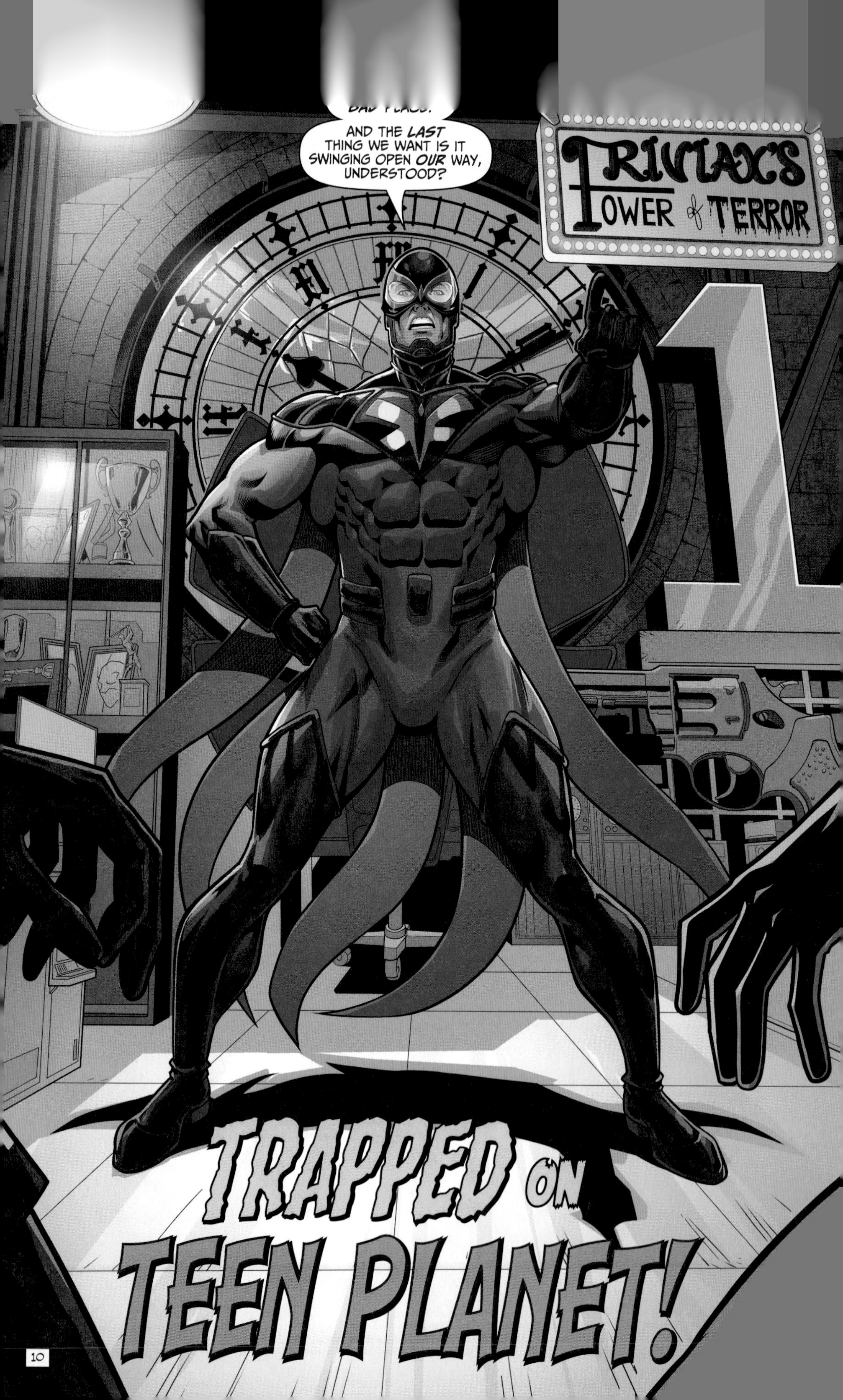
AND THE *LAST* THING WE WANT IS IT SWINGING OPEN *OUR* WAY, UNDERSTOOD?
TRIVIAX'S TOWER of TERROR
TRAPPED ON TEEN PLANET!

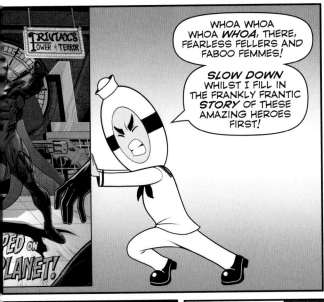

WHOA WHOA WHOA *WHOA*, THERE, FEARLESS FELLERS AND FABOO FEMMES!

SLOW DOWN WHILST I FILL IN THE FRANKLY FRANTIC *STORY* OF THESE AMAZING HEROES FIRST!

HEY, *AHOYAGERS!!* YOU ALL KNOW ME, I'M *CAPPY COMICS*, THE *KING OF KAPTIONS!*

AND I'VE BEEN BRINGING YOU THE *LOOPY LOWDOWN* ON ALL OUR *MIND-MELTIN'* *MAG*S SINCE 1957!

OKAY, SEE, IT'S LIKE *THIS*.

EARTH *ALPHA* (THE NICE ONE) AND EARTH *OMEGA* (THE *NOT-SO-NICE-BUT-FAR-BETTER-SELLING* ONE)...

USED TO NOT EVEN *KNOW* EACH OTHER EXISTED!

UNTIL FREAKY *TELEPORT-MIRRORS* STARTED OPENING *DOORWAYS BETWEEN* 'EM!*

AND *DRAGONFLYMAN* FROM ALPHA GOT *SWAPPED* WITH *DRAGONFLY* FROM *OMEGA!*

GOT IT? MAKE SENSE?

WHAT? NO?

YOU'RE *STILL* CONFUSED?

LOOK. THERE'S *TALK*, ALL RIGHT?

SOME OF THE *EDITORS* SAY THEY DON'T *NEED* CAPPY ANYMORE.

THAT I'M *CORNY* AND--

WAIT! *WAIT!*

YOU DON'T UNDERSTAND. I *NEED* THIS GIG!

ALL RIGHT. *ALL RIGHT.*

DO YOUR *OWN* &^%$ CAPTIONS, THEN!

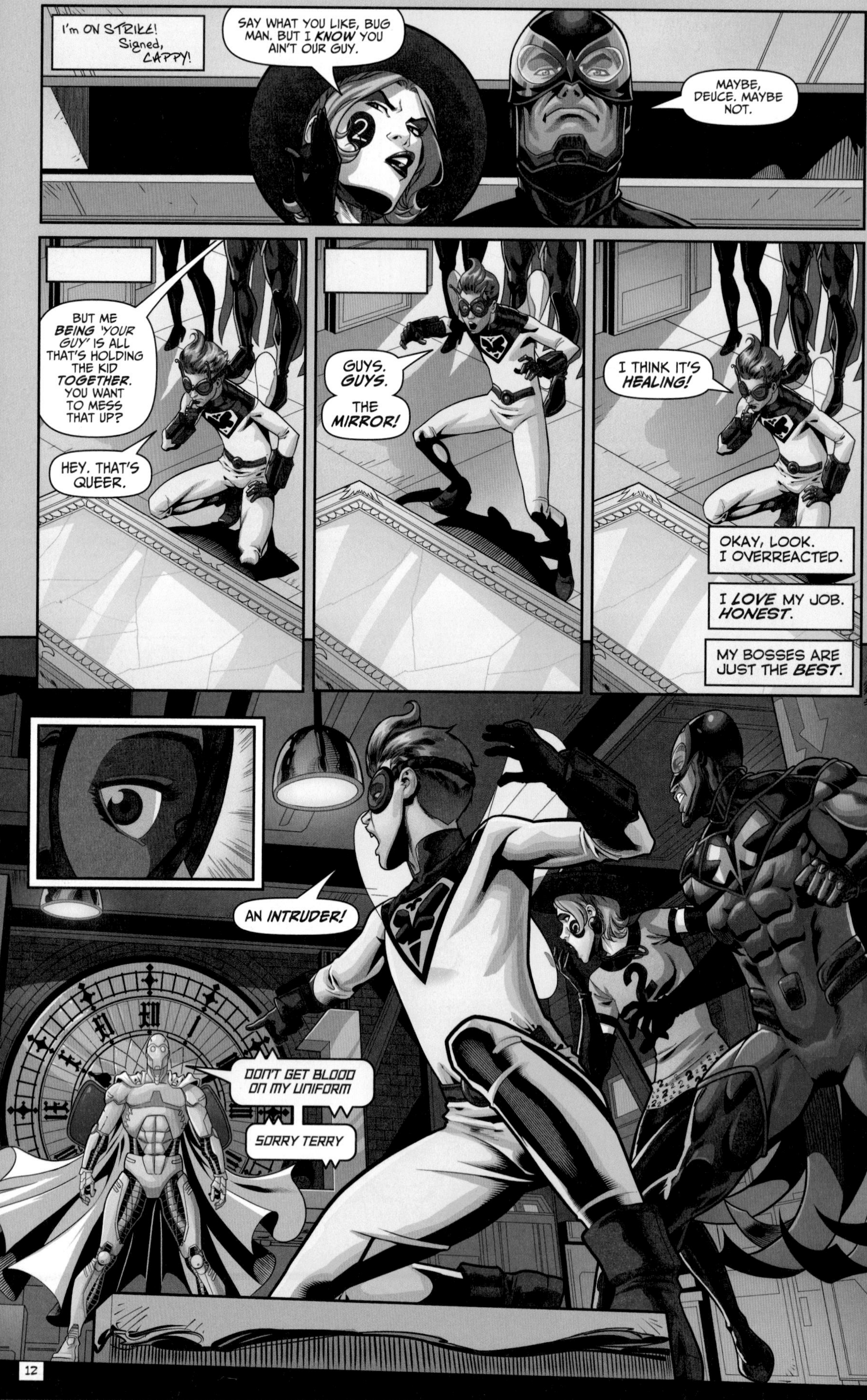

I'm ON STRIKE! Signed, CAPPY!
SAY WHAT YOU LIKE, BUG MAN. BUT I KNOW YOU AIN'T OUR GUY.
MAYBE, DEUCE. MAYBE NOT.
BUT ME BEING 'YOUR GUY' IS ALL THAT'S HOLDING THE KID TOGETHER. YOU WANT TO MESS THAT UP?
HEY. THAT'S QUEER.
GUYS. GUYS.
THE MIRROR!
I THINK IT'S HEALING!
OKAY, LOOK. I OVERREACTED.
I LOVE MY JOB. HONEST.
MY BOSSES ARE JUST THE BEST.
AN INTRUDER!
DON'T GET BLOOD ON MY UNIFORM
SORRY TERRY

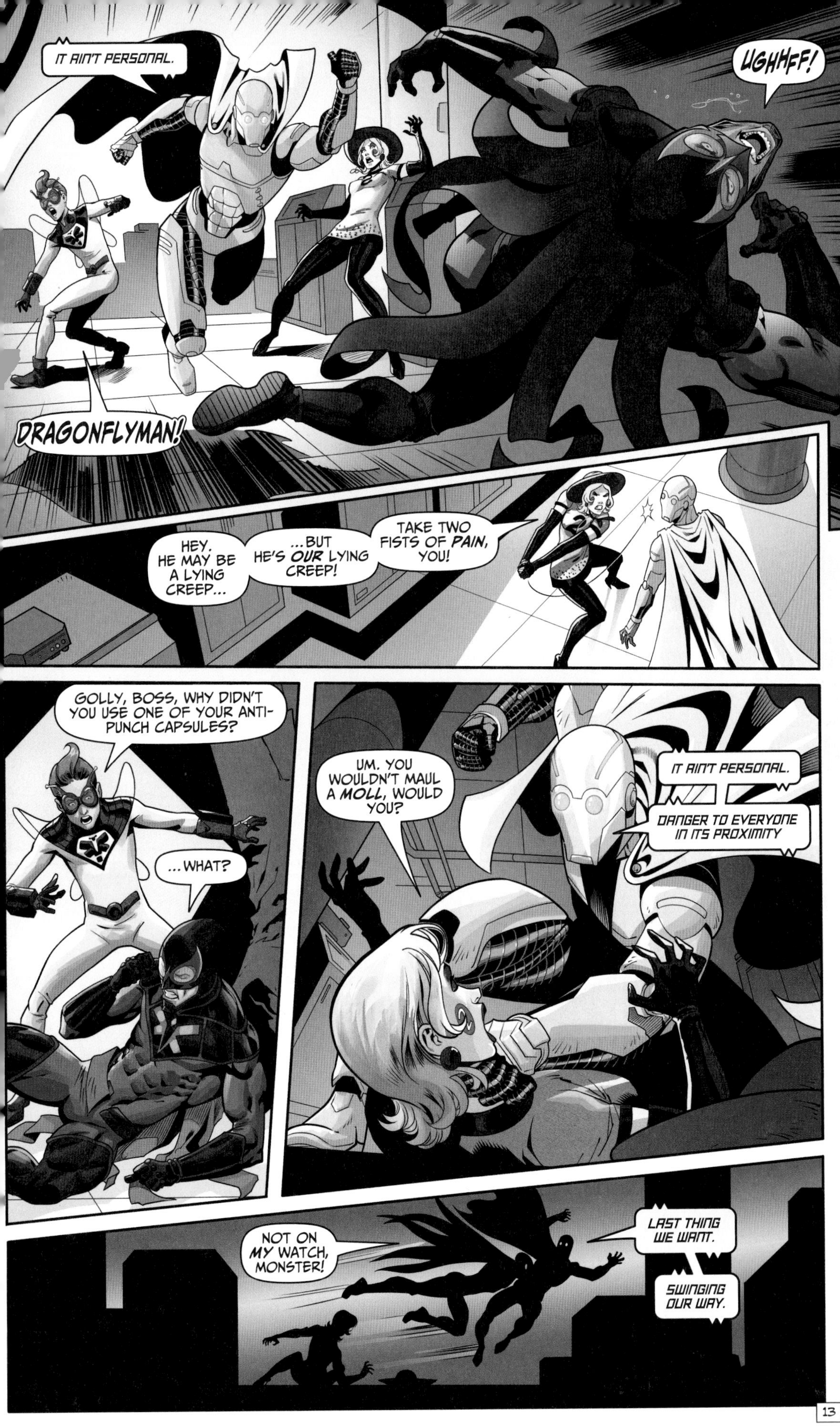
IT AIN'T PERSONAL.
UGHHFF!
DRAGONFLYMAN!
TAKE TWO FISTS OF PAIN, YOU!
HEY. HE MAY BE A LYING CREEP...
...BUT HE'S OUR LYING CREEP!
GOLLY, BOSS, WHY DIDN'T YOU USE ONE OF YOUR ANTI-PUNCH CAPSULES?
...WHAT?
UM. YOU WOULDN'T MAUL A MOLL, WOULD YOU?
IT AIN'T PERSONAL.
DANGER TO EVERYONE IN ITS PROXIMITY
NOT ON MY WATCH, MONSTER!
LAST THING WE WANT.
SWINGING OUR WAY.

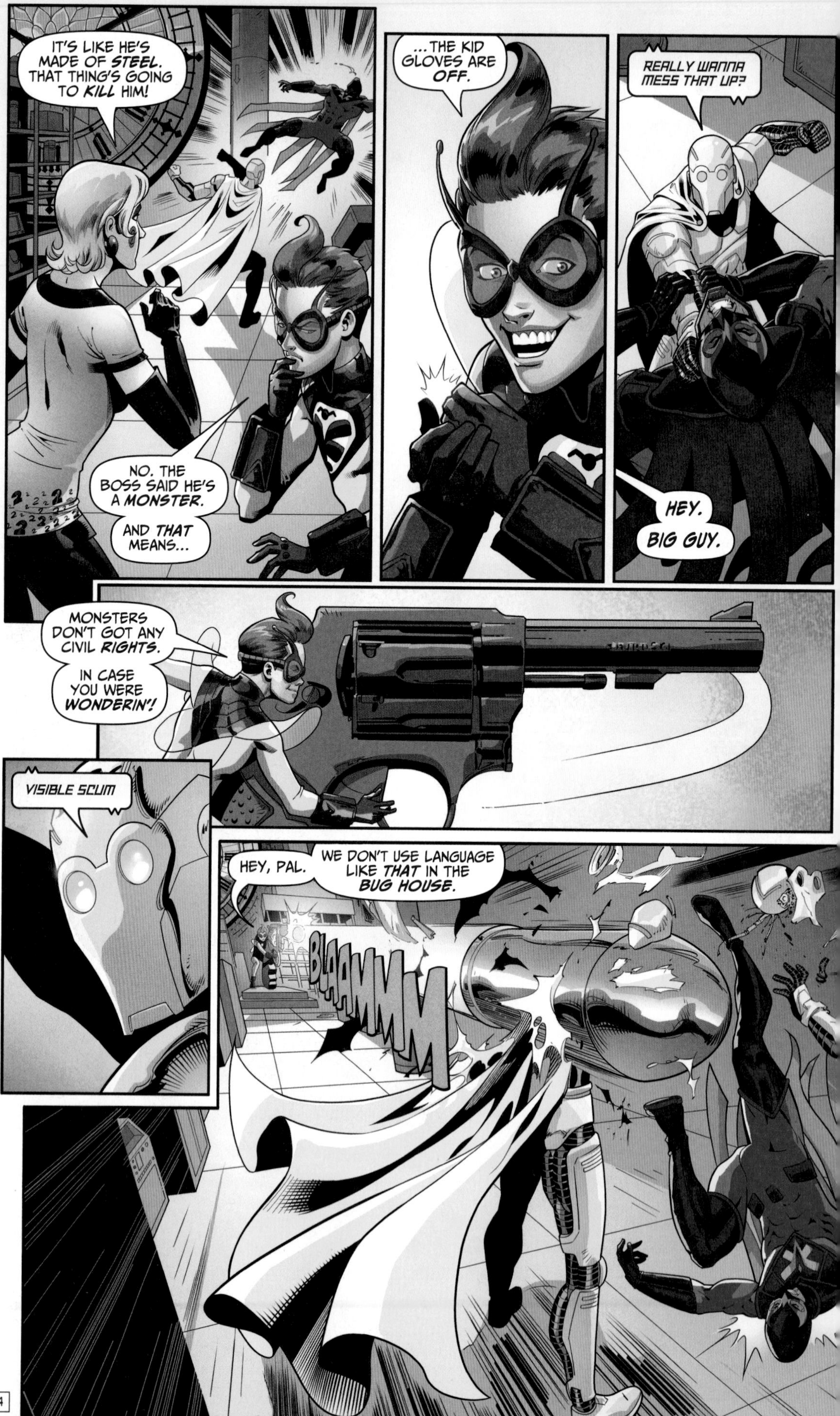
IT'S LIKE HE'S MADE OF STEEL. THAT THING'S GOING TO KILL HIM!
NO. THE BOSS SAID HE'S A MONSTER.
AND THAT MEANS...
...THE KID GLOVES ARE OFF.
REALLY WANNA MESS THAT UP?
HEY. BIG GUY.
MONSTERS DON'T GOT ANY CIVIL RIGHTS.
IN CASE YOU WERE WONDERIN'!
VISIBLE SCUM
HEY, PAL.
WE DON'T USE LANGUAGE LIKE THAT IN THE BUG HOUSE.
BLAAMMM

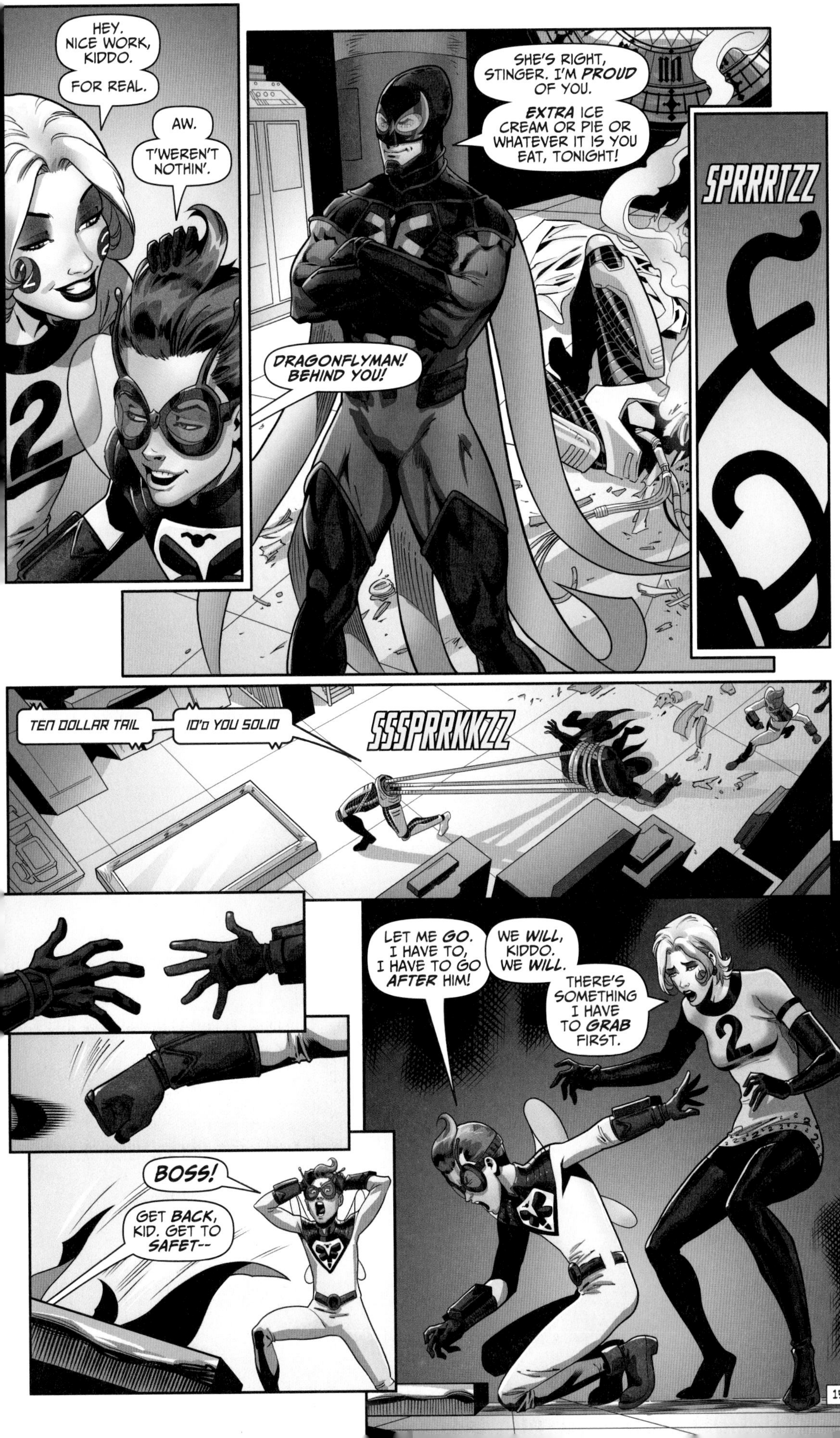

HEY. NICE WORK, KIDDO.
FOR REAL.
AW.
T'WEREN'T NOTHIN'.
SHE'S RIGHT, STINGER. I'M PROUD OF YOU.
EXTRA ICE CREAM OR PIE OR WHATEVER IT IS YOU EAT, TONIGHT!
DRAGONFLYMAN! BEHIND YOU!
SPRRRTZZ
TEN DOLLAR TAIL
10'D YOU SOLID
SSSPRRKKZZ
BOSS!
GET BACK, KID. GET TO SAFET--
LET ME GO. I HAVE TO, I HAVE TO GO AFTER HIM!
WE WILL, KIDDO. WE WILL.
THERE'S SOMETHING I HAVE TO GRAB FIRST.

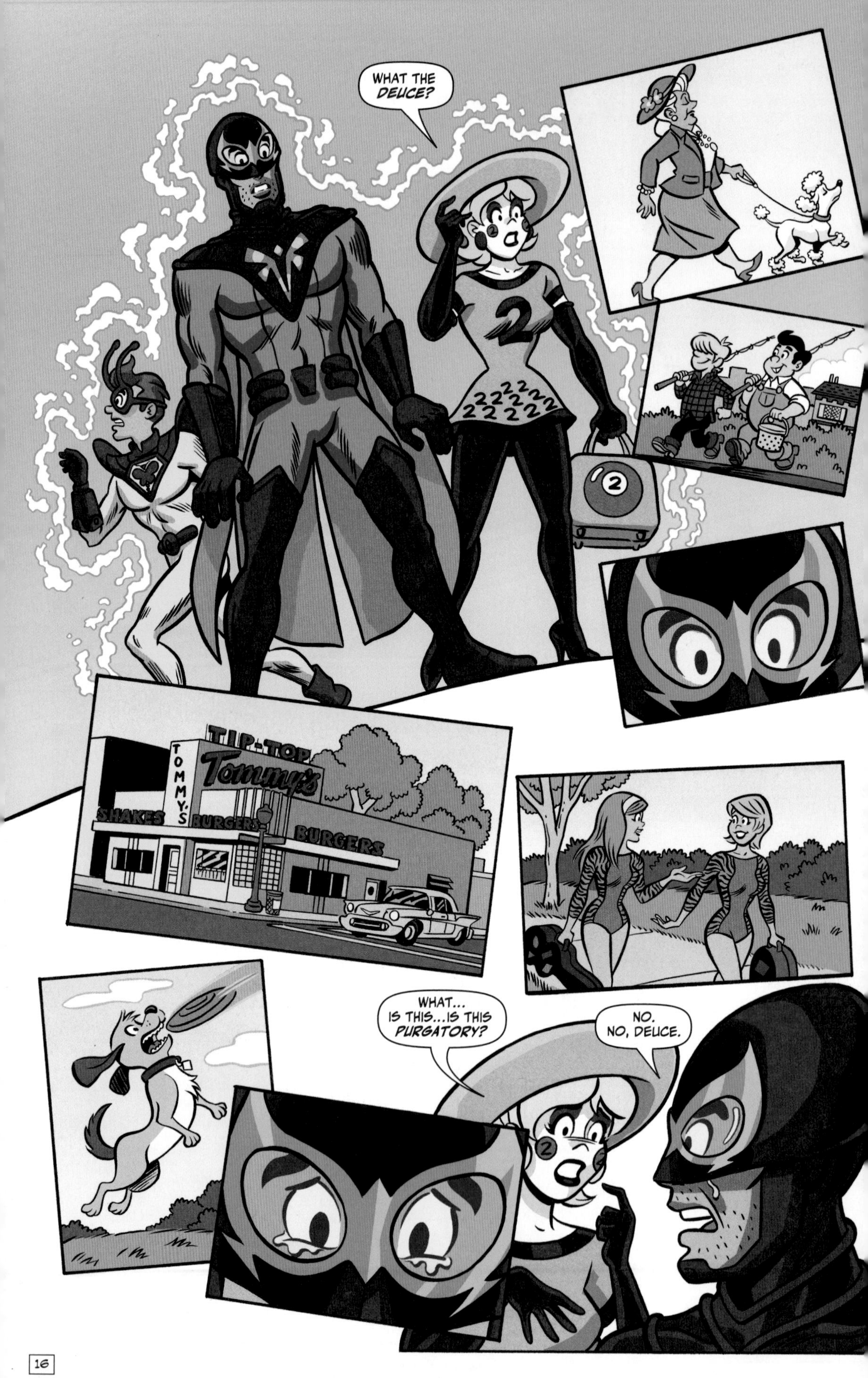
WHAT THE DEUCE?
TIP-TOP
TOMMY'S
Tommy's
SHAKES
BURGERS
BURGERS
WHAT... IS THIS...IS THIS PURGATORY?
NO. NO, DEUCE.

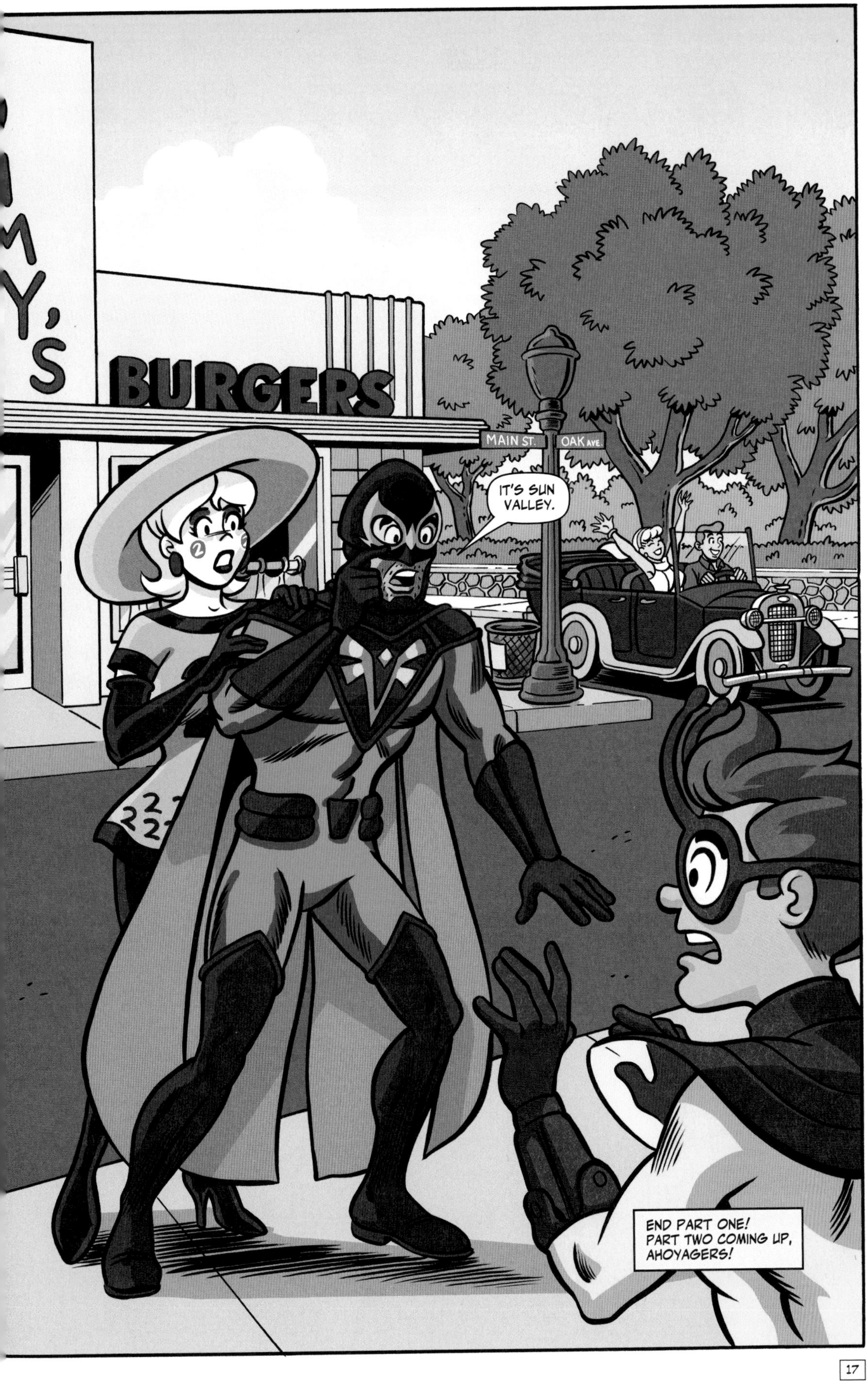
MY'S
BURGERS
MAIN ST.
OAK AVE.
IT'S SUN VALLEY.
END PART ONE! PART TWO COMING UP, AHOYAGERS!

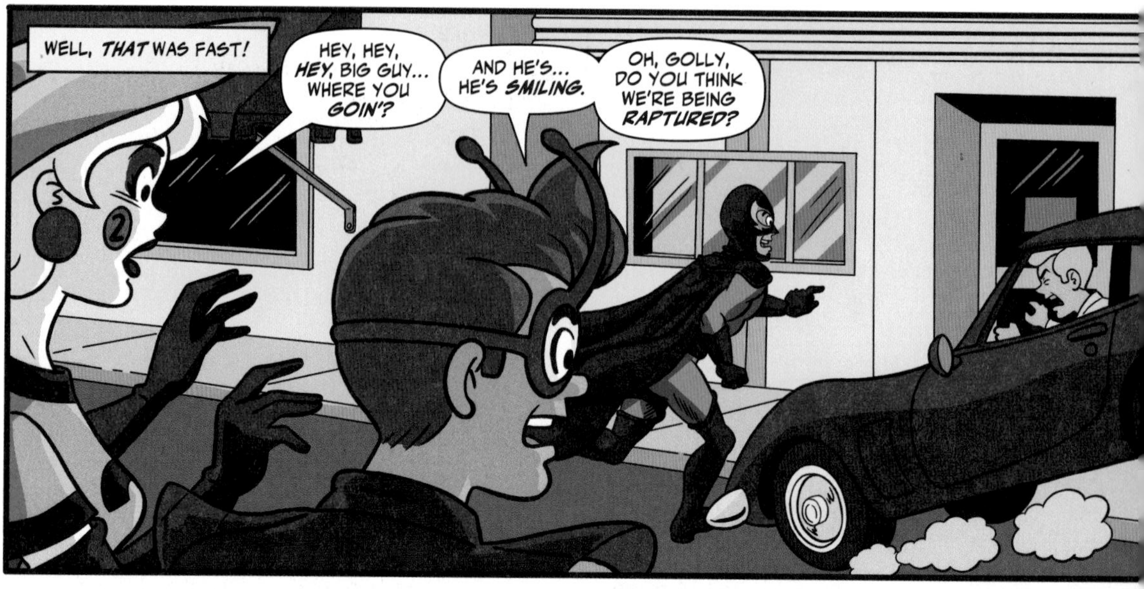
WELL, *THAT* WAS FAST!
HEY, HEY, *HEY,* BIG GUY... WHERE YOU *GOIN'?*
AND HE'S... HE'S *SMILING.*
OH, GOLLY, DO YOU THINK WE'RE BEING *RAPTURED?*

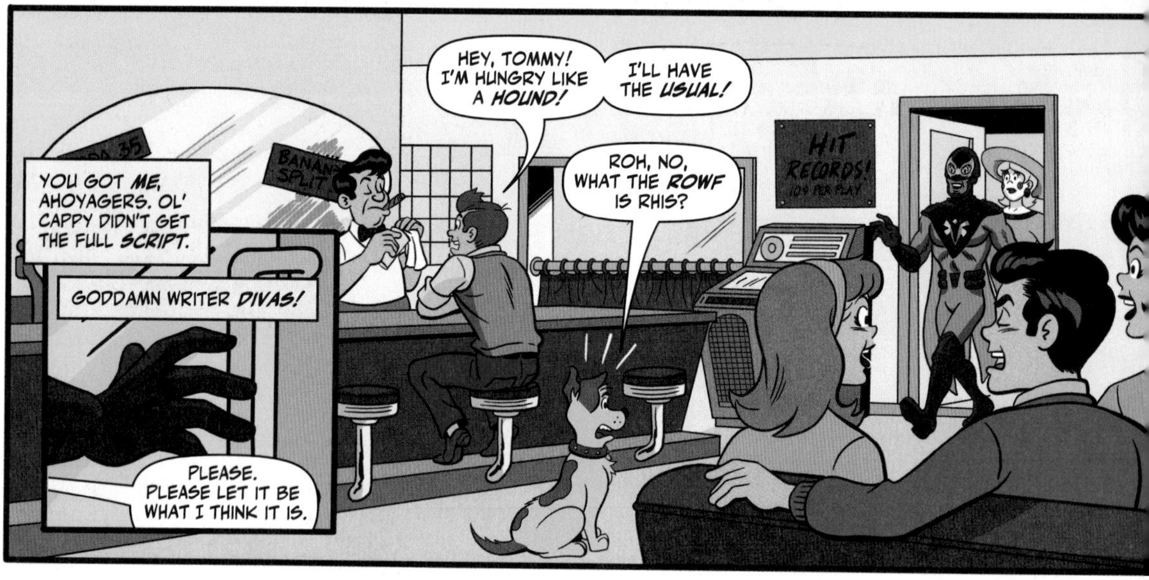
YOU GOT *ME,* AHOYAGERS. OL' CAPPY DIDN'T GET THE FULL *SCRIPT.*
GODDAMN WRITER *DIVAS!*
PLEASE. PLEASE LET IT BE WHAT I THINK IT IS.
HEY, TOMMY! I'M HUNGRY LIKE A *HOUND!*
I'LL HAVE THE *USUAL!*
ROH, NO, WHAT THE *ROWF* IS RHIS?
HIT RECORDS!
10¢ PER PLAY

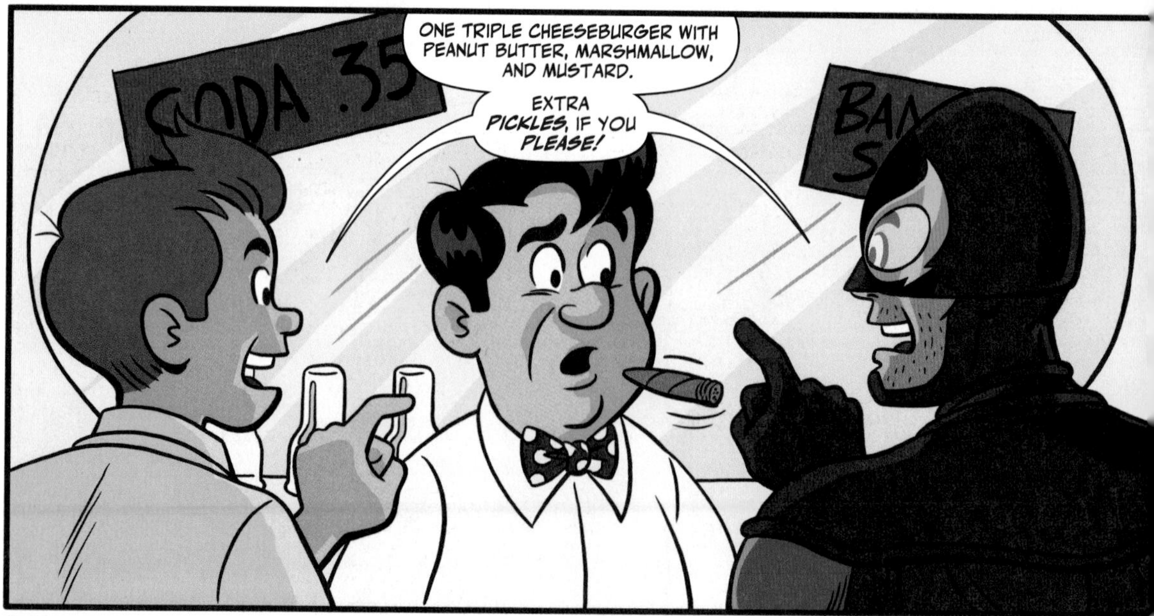
SODA .35
ONE TRIPLE CHEESEBURGER WITH PEANUT BUTTER, MARSHMALLOW, AND MUSTARD.
EXTRA *PICKLES,* IF YOU *PLEASE!*

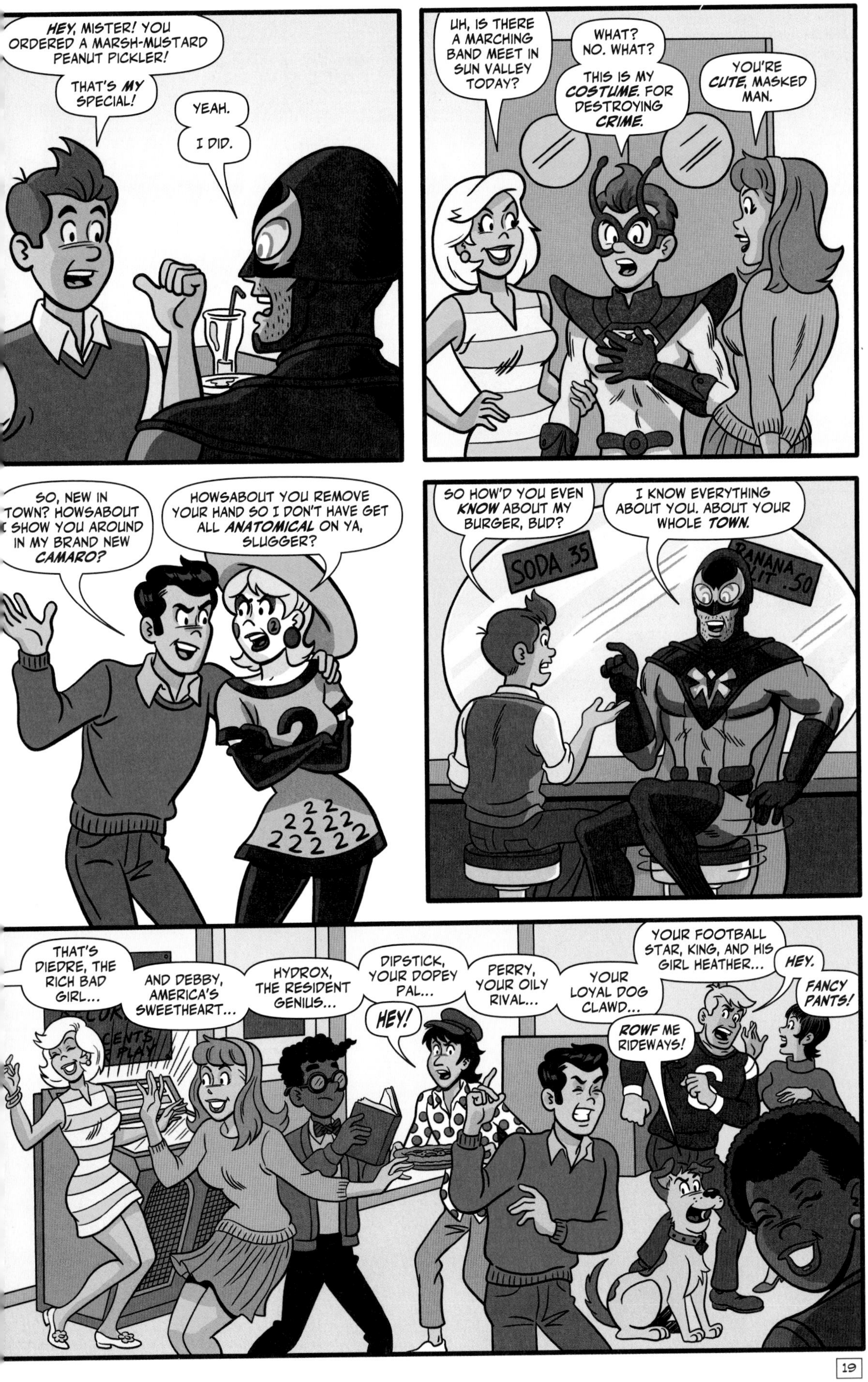
HEY, MISTER! YOU ORDERED A MARSH-MUSTARD PEANUT PICKLER!
THAT'S MY SPECIAL!
YEAH.
I DID.
UH, IS THERE A MARCHING BAND MEET IN SUN VALLEY TODAY?
WHAT? NO. WHAT?
THIS IS MY COSTUME. FOR DESTROYING CRIME.
YOU'RE CUTE, MASKED MAN.
SO, NEW IN TOWN? HOWSABOUT I SHOW YOU AROUND IN MY BRAND NEW CAMARO?
HOWSABOUT YOU REMOVE YOUR HAND SO I DON'T HAVE GET ALL ANATOMICAL ON YA, SLUGGER?
SO HOW'D YOU EVEN KNOW ABOUT MY BURGER, BUD?
I KNOW EVERYTHING ABOUT YOU. ABOUT YOUR WHOLE TOWN.
SODA .35
THAT'S DIEDRE, THE RICH BAD GIRL...
AND DEBBY, AMERICA'S SWEETHEART...
HYDROX, THE RESIDENT GENIUS...
DIPSTICK, YOUR DOPEY PAL...
HEY!
PERRY, YOUR OILY RIVAL...
YOUR LOYAL DOG CLAWD...
ROWF ME RIDEWAYS!
YOUR FOOTBALL STAR, KING, AND HIS GIRL HEATHER...
HEY.
FANCY PANTS!

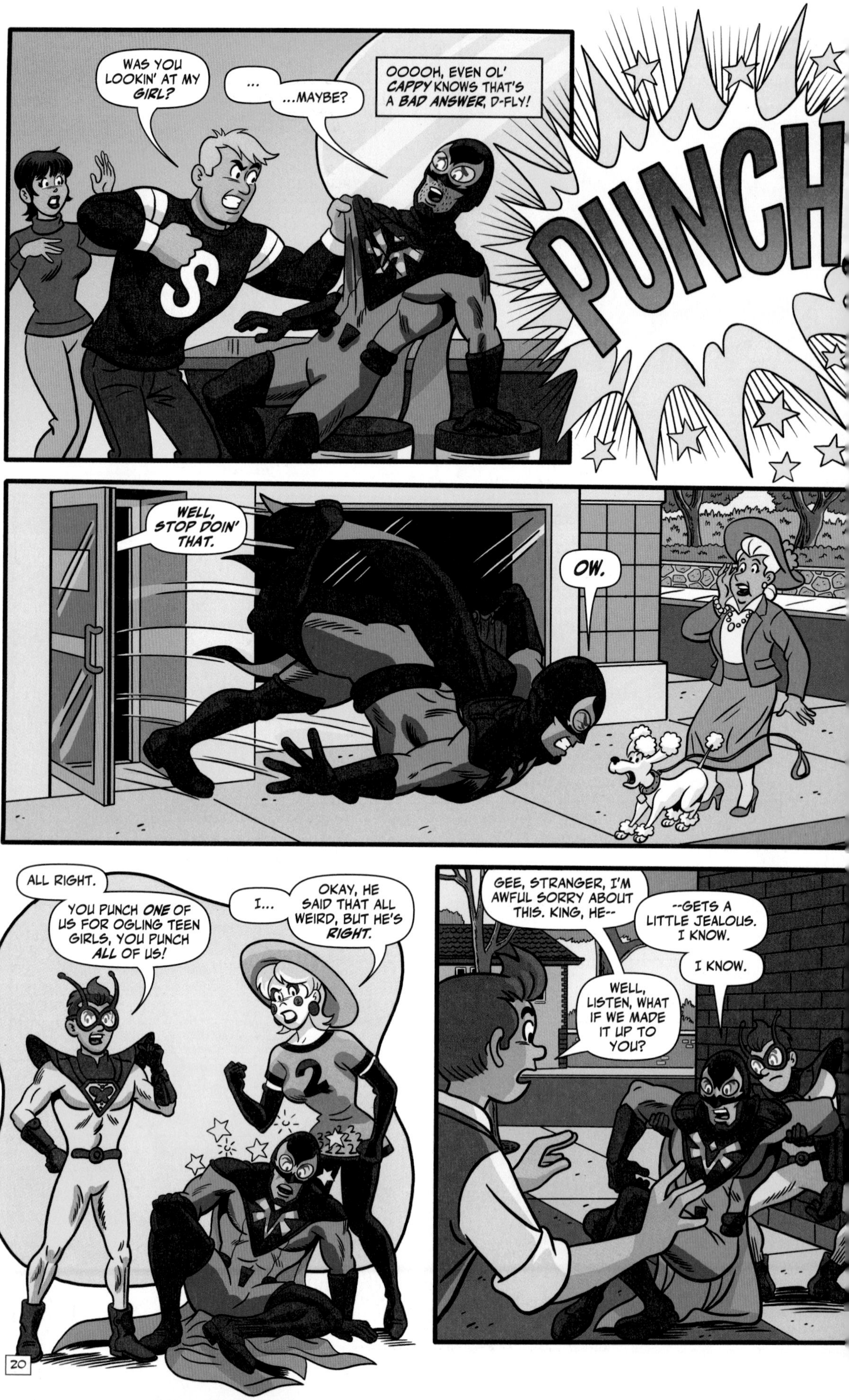
WAS YOU LOOKIN' AT MY GIRL?
...
...MAYBE?
OOOOH, EVEN OL' CAPPY KNOWS THAT'S A BAD ANSWER, D-FLY!
PUNCH
WELL, STOP DOIN' THAT.
OW.
ALL RIGHT.
YOU PUNCH ONE OF US FOR OGLING TEEN GIRLS, YOU PUNCH ALL OF US!
I...
OKAY, HE SAID THAT ALL WEIRD, BUT HE'S RIGHT.
GEE, STRANGER, I'M AWFUL SORRY ABOUT THIS. KING, HE--
--GETS A LITTLE JEALOUS. I KNOW.
I KNOW.
WELL, LISTEN, WHAT IF WE MADE IT UP TO YOU?

SUN VALLEY'S HAD TROUBLE, WE GOTTA BLOW OFF STEAM. COME TONIGHT? AS MY GUEST?

TONIGHT ONLY
AT THE HIGH SCHOOL GYMNASIUM
THE SUN VALLEY SOCK HOP!

The PECAN SANDYS!

WITH SPECIAL GUESTS PEGGY AND THE ZEBRA DOLLS

FUN! REFRESH-MENTS!

ROLL MUSICAL NUMBERS!

OH, MAN, I FEEL IT COMING. IT'S DEFINITELY HAPPENING!

AND HERE IT IS!

THE *OBLIGATORY MULTIVERSE CROSSOVER HANDSHAKE OF MUTUAL RESPECT!*

SEE YOU THERE, BUD, ALL RIGHT?

YES. YES, YOU WILL. *"BUD."*

TA TA FOR NOW, BUG BOY.

I'M NOT A *BUG.* I'M A... *STINGING THING* OF SOME SORT!

HEY. HOT GIRL!

LEAVE THE KID ALONE, BEFORE YA JUMPSTART HIS *PUBERTY!*

GOLLY, HOW *DO* YOU KNOW EVERYTHING ABOUT THIS NOWHERESVILLE TOWN?

... MY DAD, HE--

HE WAS A DRUNK. A DRUNK WHO LIKED TO HIT THINGS.

WALLS. ANIMALS.

HIS *SON.*

"BUT I HAD COMICS. COMICS ABOUT SUN VALLEY. I READ THEM A THOUSAND TIMES, BETWEEN BEATINGS.

"SANDY, HE WAS AMERICA'S FAVORITE BOY.

"AND THE KIDS HERE, THEY--

"--THEY WERE MY FRIENDS."

Sand

OU NEED EXTRA MONEY?

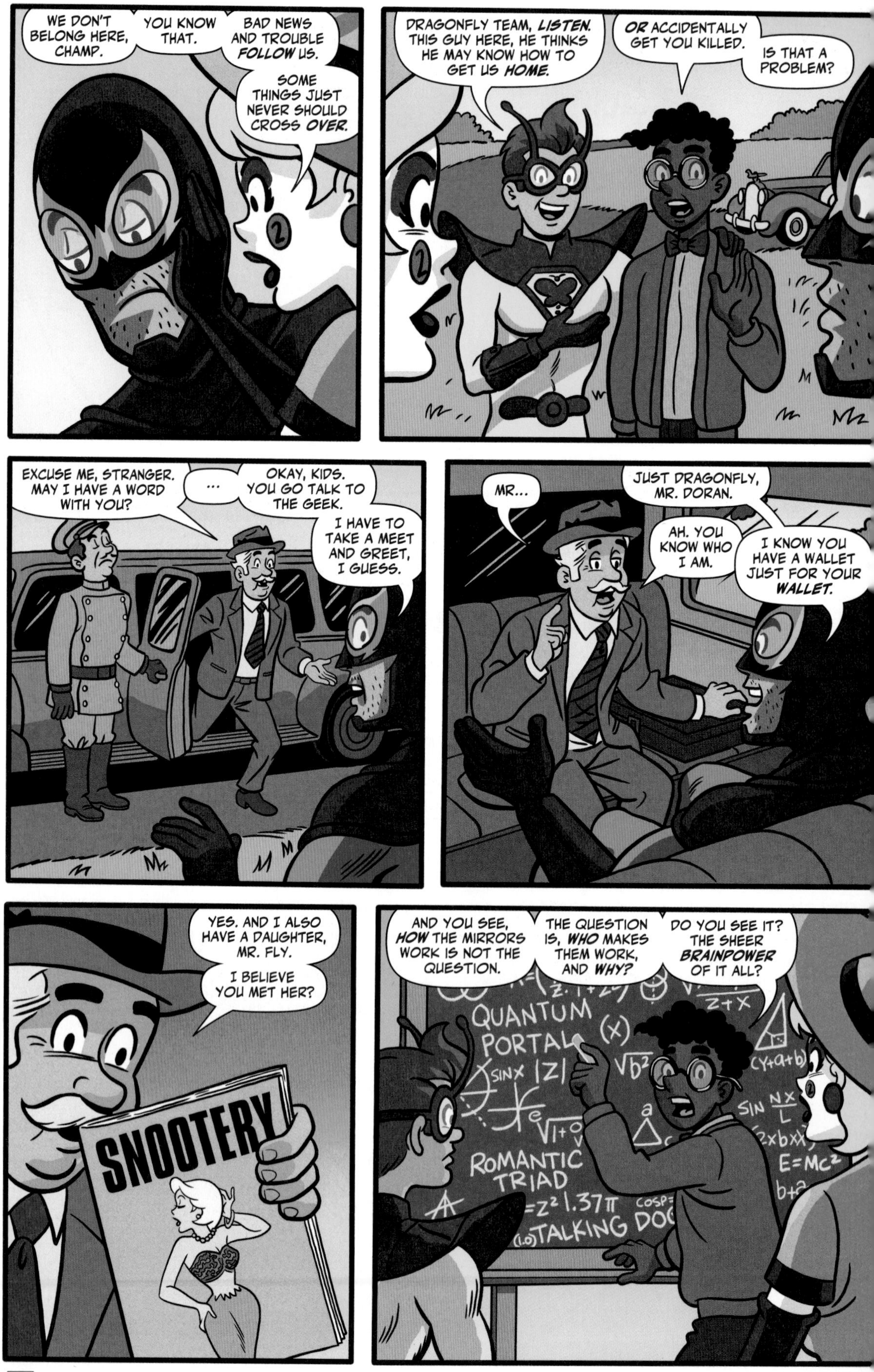
WE DON'T BELONG HERE, CHAMP.
YOU KNOW THAT.
BAD NEWS AND TROUBLE FOLLOW US.
SOME THINGS JUST NEVER SHOULD CROSS OVER.
DRAGONFLY TEAM, LISTEN. THIS GUY HERE, HE THINKS HE MAY KNOW HOW TO GET US HOME.
OR ACCIDENTALLY GET YOU KILLED.
IS THAT A PROBLEM?
EXCUSE ME, STRANGER. MAY I HAVE A WORD WITH YOU?
...
OKAY, KIDS. YOU GO TALK TO THE GEEK.
I HAVE TO TAKE A MEET AND GREET, I GUESS.
MR...
JUST DRAGONFLY, MR. DORAN.
AH. YOU KNOW WHO I AM.
I KNOW YOU HAVE A WALLET JUST FOR YOUR WALLET.
YES. AND I ALSO HAVE A DAUGHTER, MR. FLY.
I BELIEVE YOU MET HER?
SNOOTERY
AND YOU SEE, HOW THE MIRRORS WORK IS NOT THE QUESTION.
THE QUESTION IS, WHO MAKES THEM WORK, AND WHY?
DO YOU SEE IT? THE SHEER BRAINPOWER OF IT ALL?
QUANTUM PORTAL
ROMANTIC TRIAD
TALKING DOG
E=Mc²

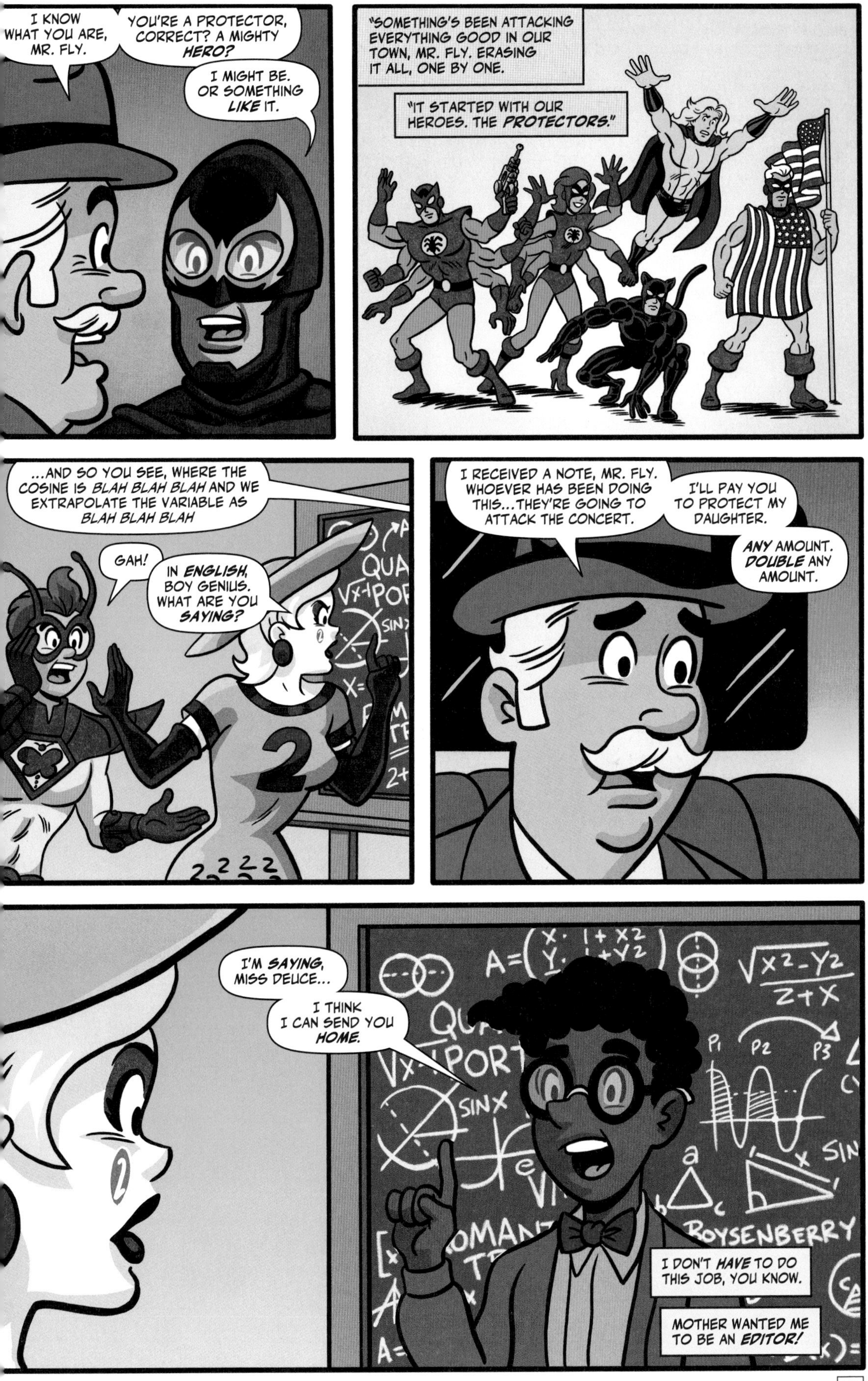

I KNOW WHAT YOU ARE, MR. FLY.
YOU'RE A PROTECTOR, CORRECT? A MIGHTY *HERO?*
I MIGHT BE. OR SOMETHING *LIKE* IT.
"SOMETHING'S BEEN ATTACKING EVERYTHING GOOD IN OUR TOWN, MR. FLY. ERASING IT ALL, ONE BY ONE.
"IT STARTED WITH OUR HEROES. THE *PROTECTORS.*"
...AND SO YOU SEE, WHERE THE COSINE IS *BLAH BLAH BLAH* AND WE EXTRAPOLATE THE VARIABLE AS *BLAH BLAH BLAH*
GAH!
IN *ENGLISH,* BOY GENIUS. WHAT ARE YOU *SAYING?*
I RECEIVED A NOTE, MR. FLY. WHOEVER HAS BEEN DOING THIS...THEY'RE GOING TO ATTACK THE CONCERT.
I'LL PAY YOU TO PROTECT MY DAUGHTER.
ANY AMOUNT. *DOUBLE* ANY AMOUNT.
I'M *SAYING,* MISS DEUCE...
I THINK I CAN SEND YOU *HOME.*
BOYSENBERRY
I DON'T *HAVE* TO DO THIS JOB, YOU KNOW.
MOTHER WANTED ME TO BE AN *EDITOR!*

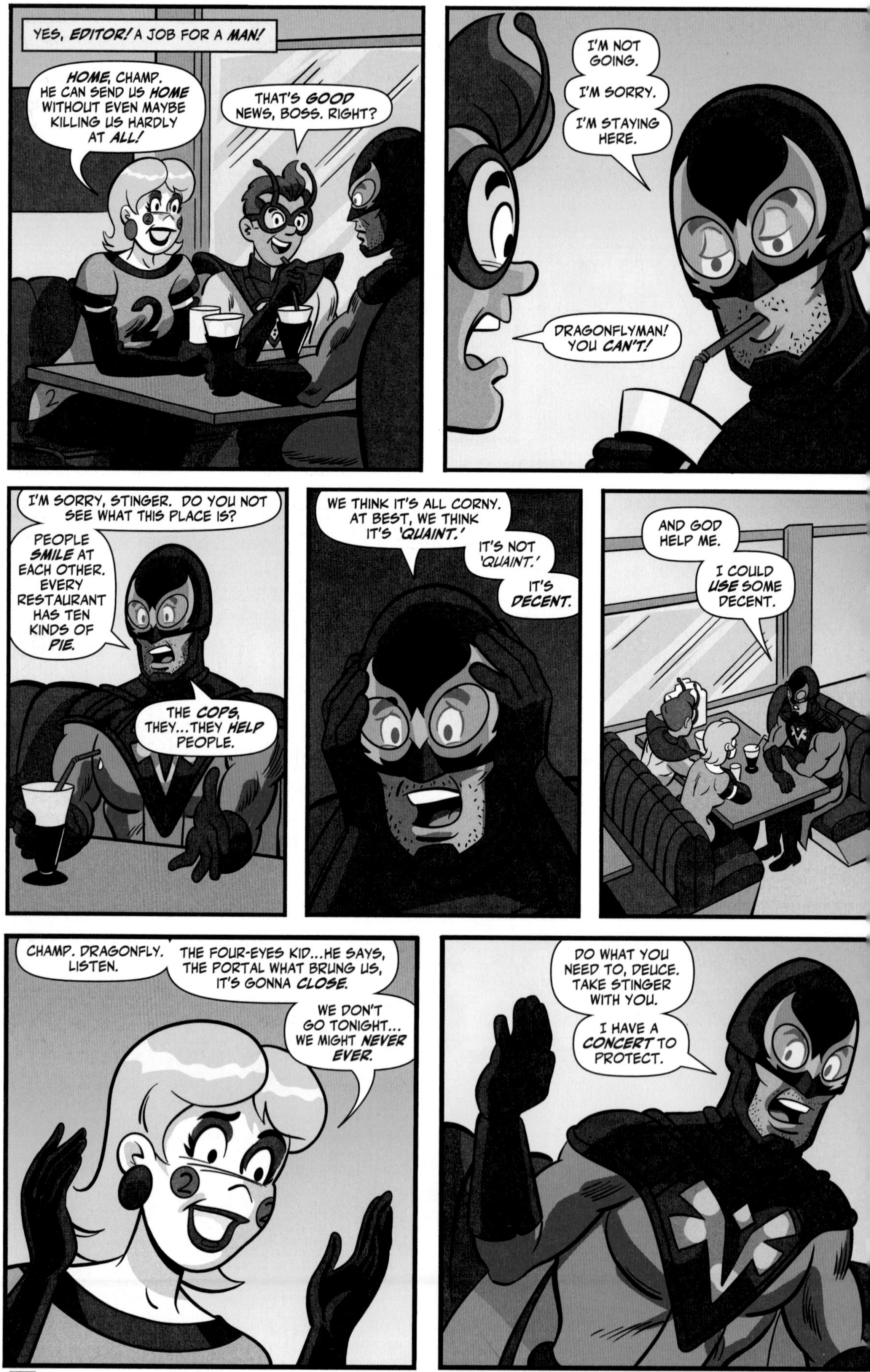
YES, EDITOR! A JOB FOR A MAN!
HOME, CHAMP. HE CAN SEND US HOME WITHOUT EVEN MAYBE KILLING US HARDLY AT ALL!
THAT'S GOOD NEWS, BOSS. RIGHT?
I'M NOT GOING.
I'M SORRY.
I'M STAYING HERE.
DRAGONFLYMAN! YOU CAN'T!
I'M SORRY, STINGER. DO YOU NOT SEE WHAT THIS PLACE IS?
PEOPLE SMILE AT EACH OTHER. EVERY RESTAURANT HAS TEN KINDS OF PIE.
THE COPS, THEY...THEY HELP PEOPLE.
WE THINK IT'S ALL CORNY. AT BEST, WE THINK IT'S 'QUAINT.'
IT'S NOT 'QUAINT.'
IT'S DECENT.
AND GOD HELP ME.
I COULD USE SOME DECENT.
CHAMP. DRAGONFLY. LISTEN.
THE FOUR-EYES KID...HE SAYS, THE PORTAL WHAT BRUNG US, IT'S GONNA CLOSE.
WE DON'T GO TONIGHT... WE MIGHT NEVER EVER.
DO WHAT YOU NEED TO, DEUCE. TAKE STINGER WITH YOU.
I HAVE A CONCERT TO PROTECT.

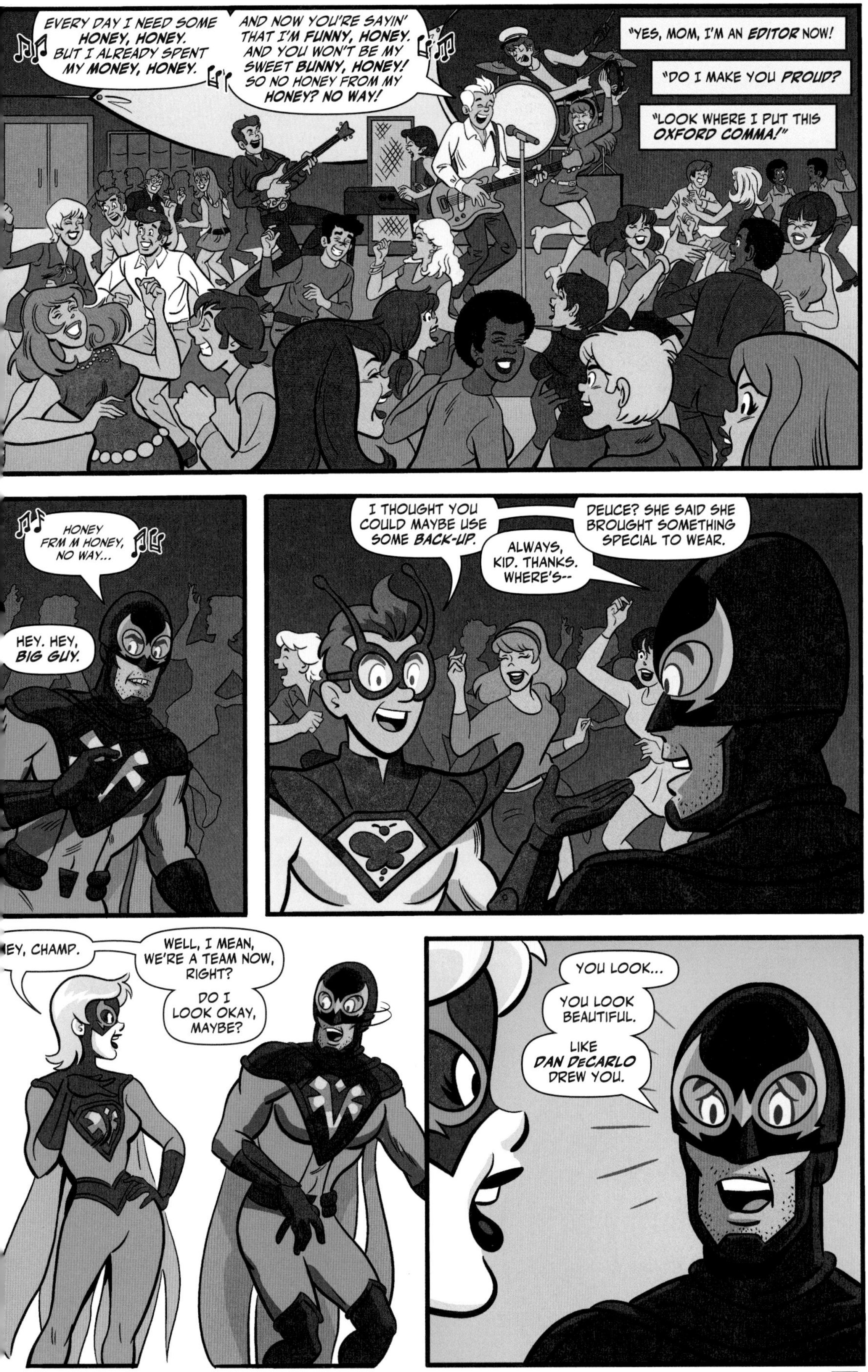
EVERY DAY I NEED SOME HONEY, HONEY. BUT I ALREADY SPENT MY MONEY, HONEY.
AND NOW YOU'RE SAYIN' THAT I'M FUNNY, HONEY. AND YOU WON'T BE MY SWEET BUNNY, HONEY! SO NO HONEY FROM MY HONEY? NO WAY!
"YES, MOM, I'M AN EDITOR NOW!
"DO I MAKE YOU PROUD?
"LOOK WHERE I PUT THIS OXFORD COMMA!"
HONEY FRM M HONEY, NO WAY...
HEY. HEY, BIG GUY.
I THOUGHT YOU COULD MAYBE USE SOME BACK-UP.
ALWAYS, KID. THANKS. WHERE'S--
DEUCE? SHE SAID SHE BROUGHT SOMETHING SPECIAL TO WEAR.
EY, CHAMP.
WELL, I MEAN, WE'RE A TEAM NOW, RIGHT?
DO I LOOK OKAY, MAYBE?
YOU LOOK...
YOU LOOK BEAUTIFUL.
LIKE DAN DECARLO DREW YOU.

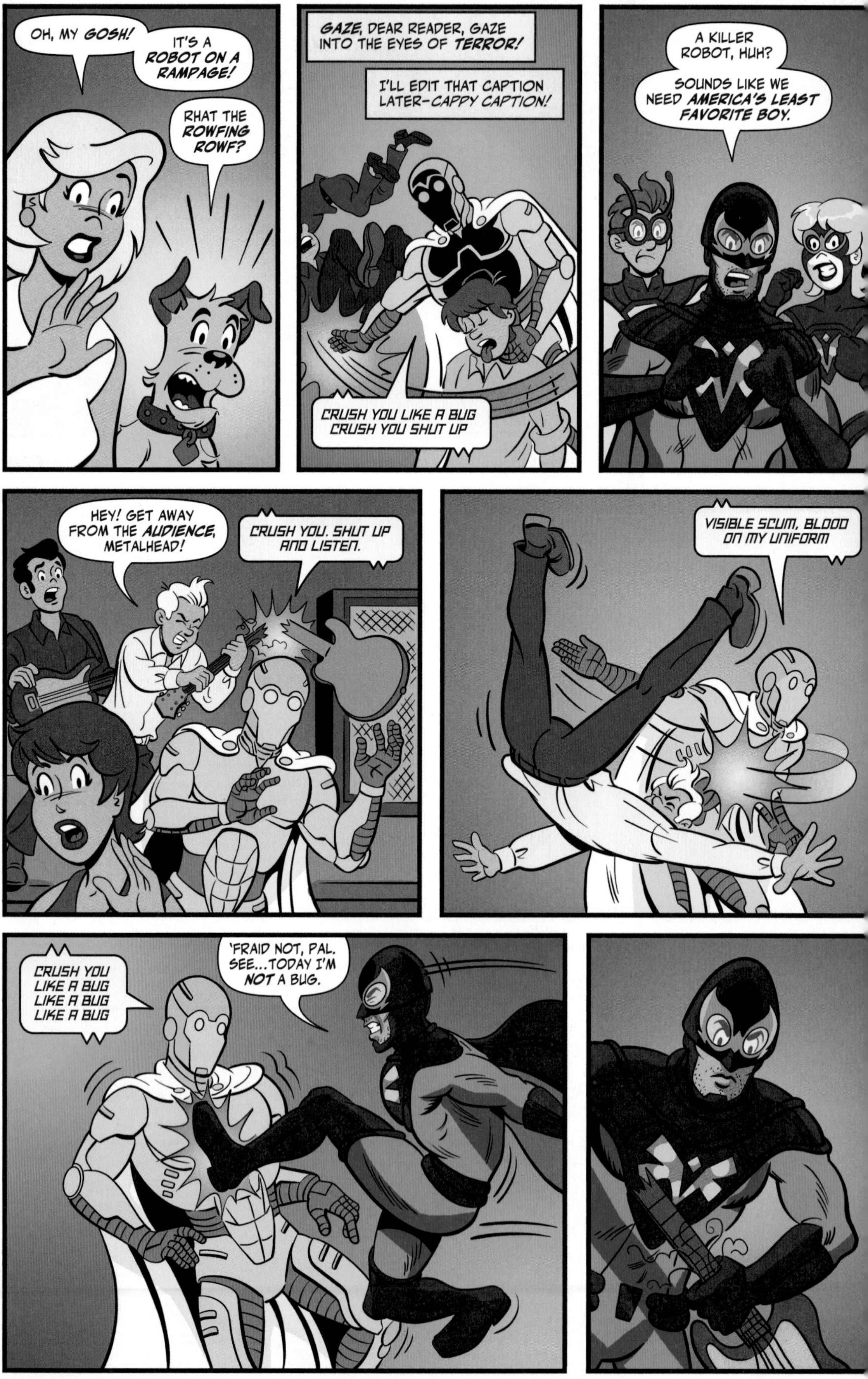

OH, MY GOSH!
IT'S A ROBOT ON A RAMPAGE!
RHAT THE ROWFING ROWF?
GAZE, DEAR READER, GAZE INTO THE EYES OF TERROR!
I'LL EDIT THAT CAPTION LATER—CAPPY CAPTION!
CRUSH YOU LIKE A BUG CRUSH YOU SHUT UP
A KILLER ROBOT, HUH?
SOUNDS LIKE WE NEED AMERICA'S LEAST FAVORITE BOY.
HEY! GET AWAY FROM THE AUDIENCE, METALHEAD!
CRUSH YOU. SHUT UP AND LISTEN.
VISIBLE SCUM, BLOOD ON MY UNIFORM
CRUSH YOU LIKE A BUG LIKE A BUG LIKE A BUG
'FRAID NOT, PAL. SEE...TODAY I'M NOT A BUG.

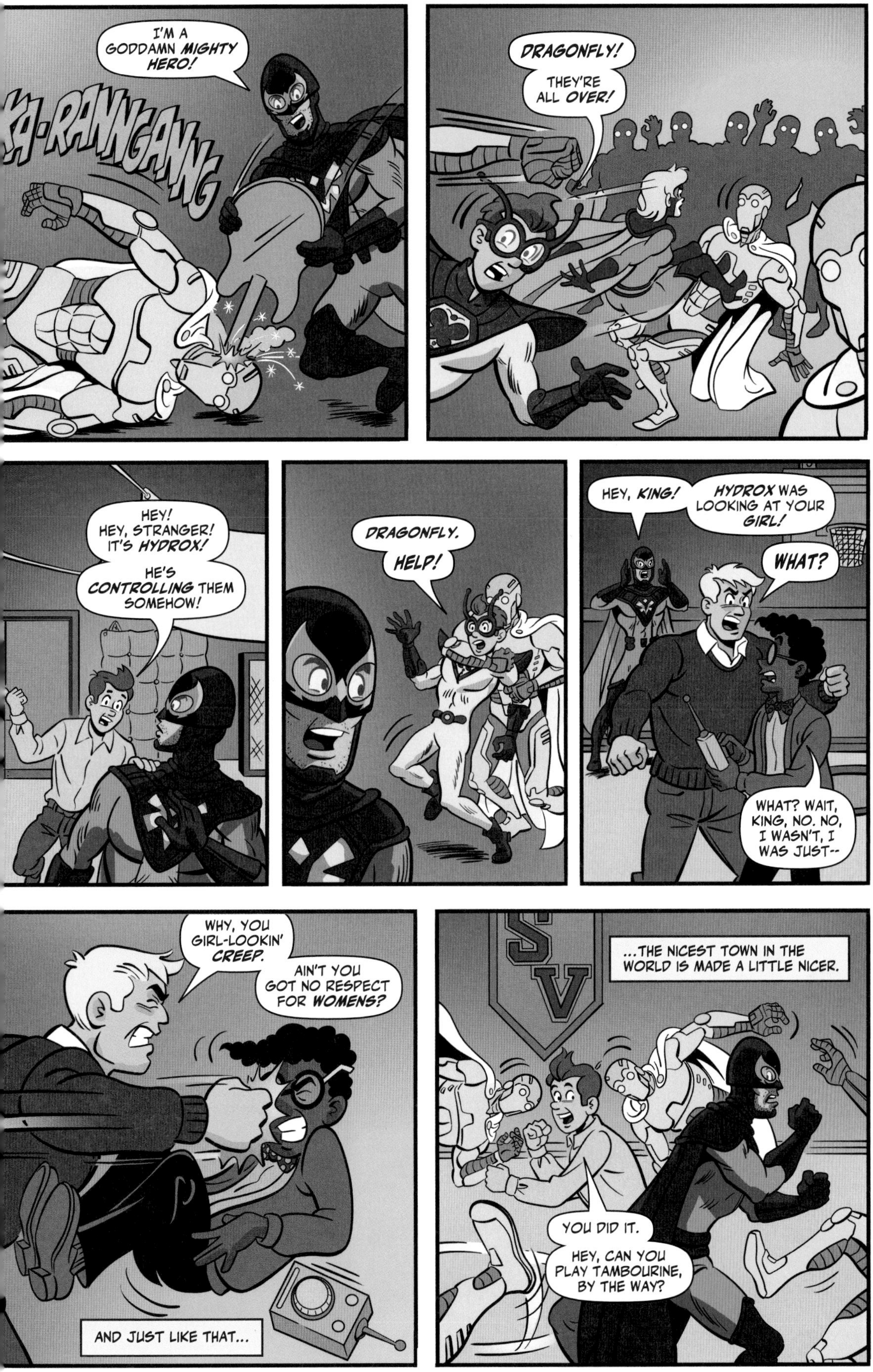
I'M A GODDAMN *MIGHTY* *HERO!*
KA-RANNGANNG
DRAGONFLY!
THEY'RE ALL *OVER!*
HEY! HEY, STRANGER! IT'S *HYDROX!*
HE'S *CONTROLLING* THEM SOMEHOW!
DRAGONFLY.
HELP!
HEY, *KING!*
HYDROX WAS LOOKING AT YOUR *GIRL!*
WHAT?
WHAT? WAIT, KING, NO. NO, I WASN'T, I WAS JUST--
WHY, YOU GIRL-LOOKIN' *CREEP.*
AIN'T YOU GOT NO RESPECT FOR *WOMENS?*
AND JUST LIKE THAT...
...THE NICEST TOWN IN THE WORLD IS MADE A LITTLE NICER.
YOU DID IT.
HEY, CAN YOU PLAY TAMBOURINE, BY THE WAY?

NO POINT HOLDING OUT, YOU KNOW THAT, RIGHT?

HYDROX ALREADY RATTED YOU *OUT*. SAYS YOU PLANNED THE WHOLE *THING*.

BUT FOR GOD'S SAKE *WHY*?

WHY? YOU ASK ME *WHY*?

WE'VE BEEN CHASTELY *CELIBATE* FOR *EIGHTY YEARS* AND YOU ASK ME *WHY*?

"WHEN HE SHOWED ME THE WORLDS OUT THERE, I KNEW I HAD TO SEE THEM.

"BUT I NEEDED *KNOWLEDGE* AND *FUNDING*.

MANTIC TRIAD $A+B^2=C^2$ $\frac{3-4}{5 \cdot 7}$ $2 \bigcirc$ $x+4$ $\therefore -3$

$\pi=3.14$

QUANTUM PORTAL $\triangle$ $\sqrt{9}$

$\pi=3$

$\frac{3-x}{4}$ $\sqrt{9}$

$(1+x)^2$

$5x-2x$ $6x$ $\sqrt{x}$

y^2

"YOU THREE WERE JUST MY *LAB RATS*, TO MAKE SURE I'D *SURVIVE* THE *JUMP*.

YOU KNOW THE THING ABOUT BEING THE *'NICE ONE?'*

EVERY SMILE FEELS LIKE *ACID* ON MY *FACE*.

AND GUESS WHAT? I'M *STILL* THE HOT ONE.

HAHAHAHA.

WOW. HOW *DELUDED* SHE IS.

YOU SAID IT, THINKING *SHE'S* HOTTER THAN THE *BRUNETTE*?

PLEASE.

WE BETTER HURRY IF WE'RE GONNA CATCH THE PORTAL HOME--

--TEAM.

WE'RE GOIN' HOME? FOR *REAL*, CHAMP?

YEAH. TURNS OUT...

...THIS TOWN IS A REAL ROWFING *CLUSTER-ROWF*.

THAT'S *ALL*, ROWFS!

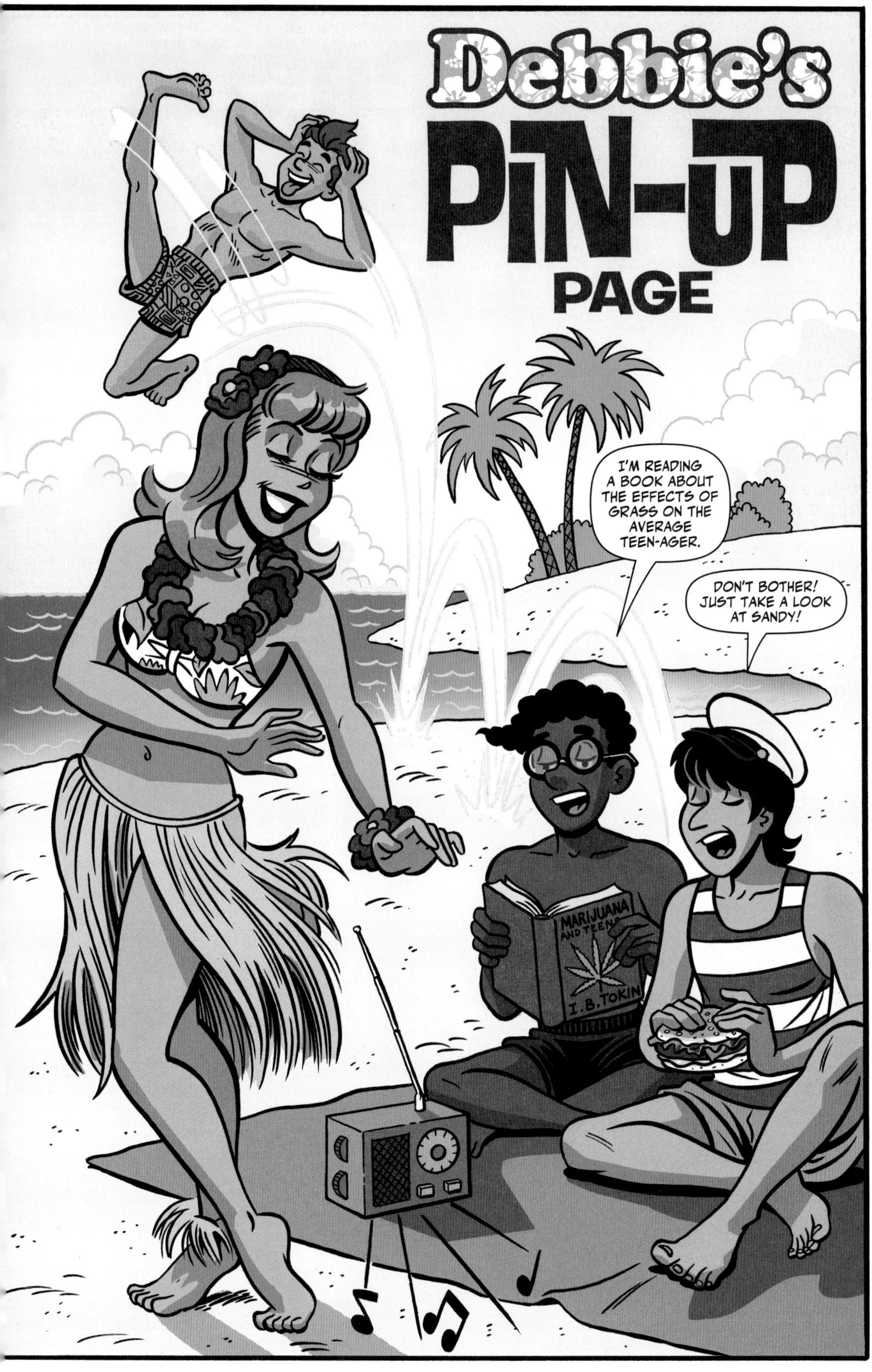
Debbie's
PIN-UP
PAGE
I'M READING A BOOK ABOUT THE EFFECTS OF GRASS ON THE AVERAGE TEEN-AGER.
DON'T BOTHER! JUST TAKE A LOOK AT SANDY!
MARIJUANA AND TEENS
I. B. TOKIN

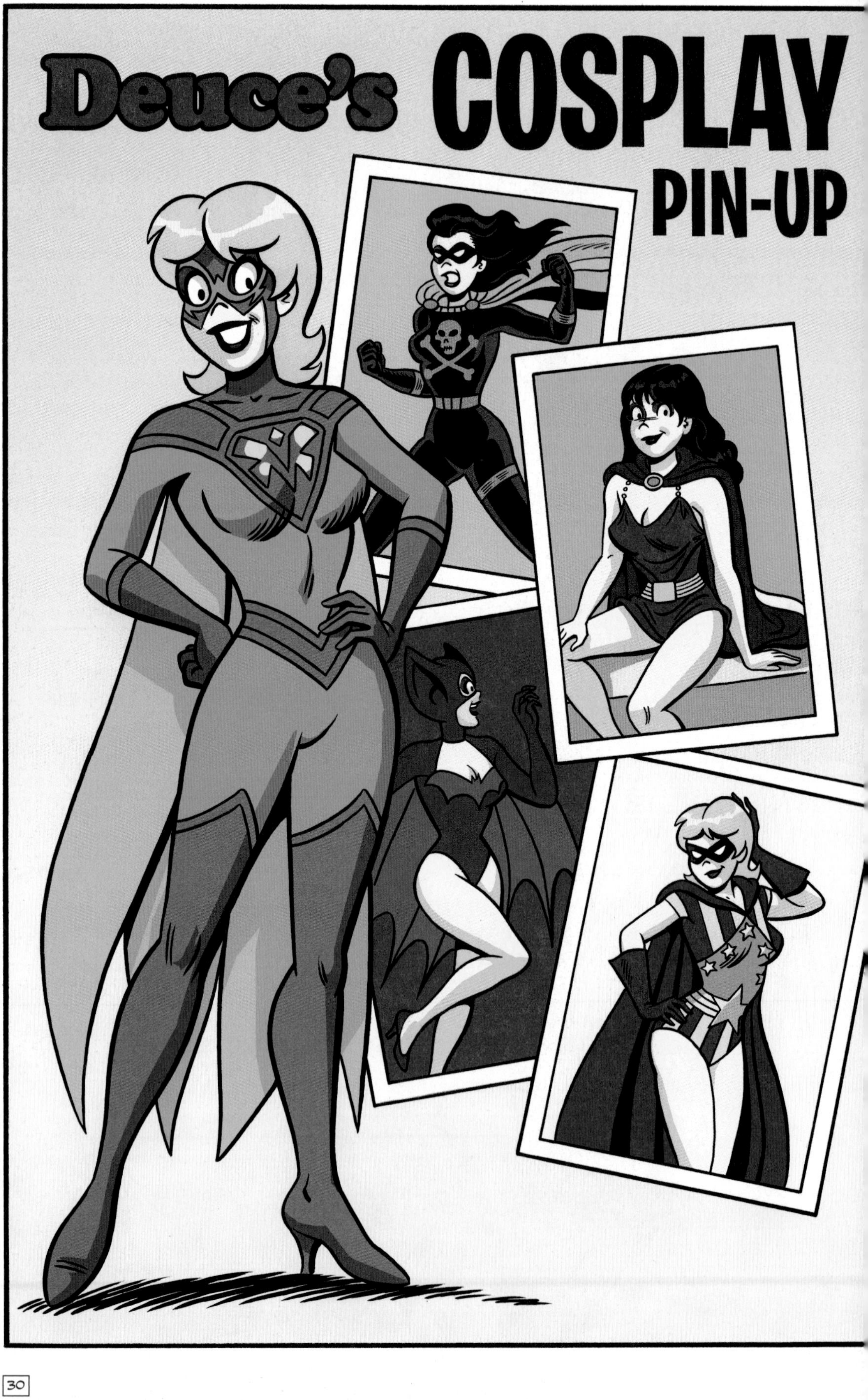

Deuce's COSPLAY PIN-UP

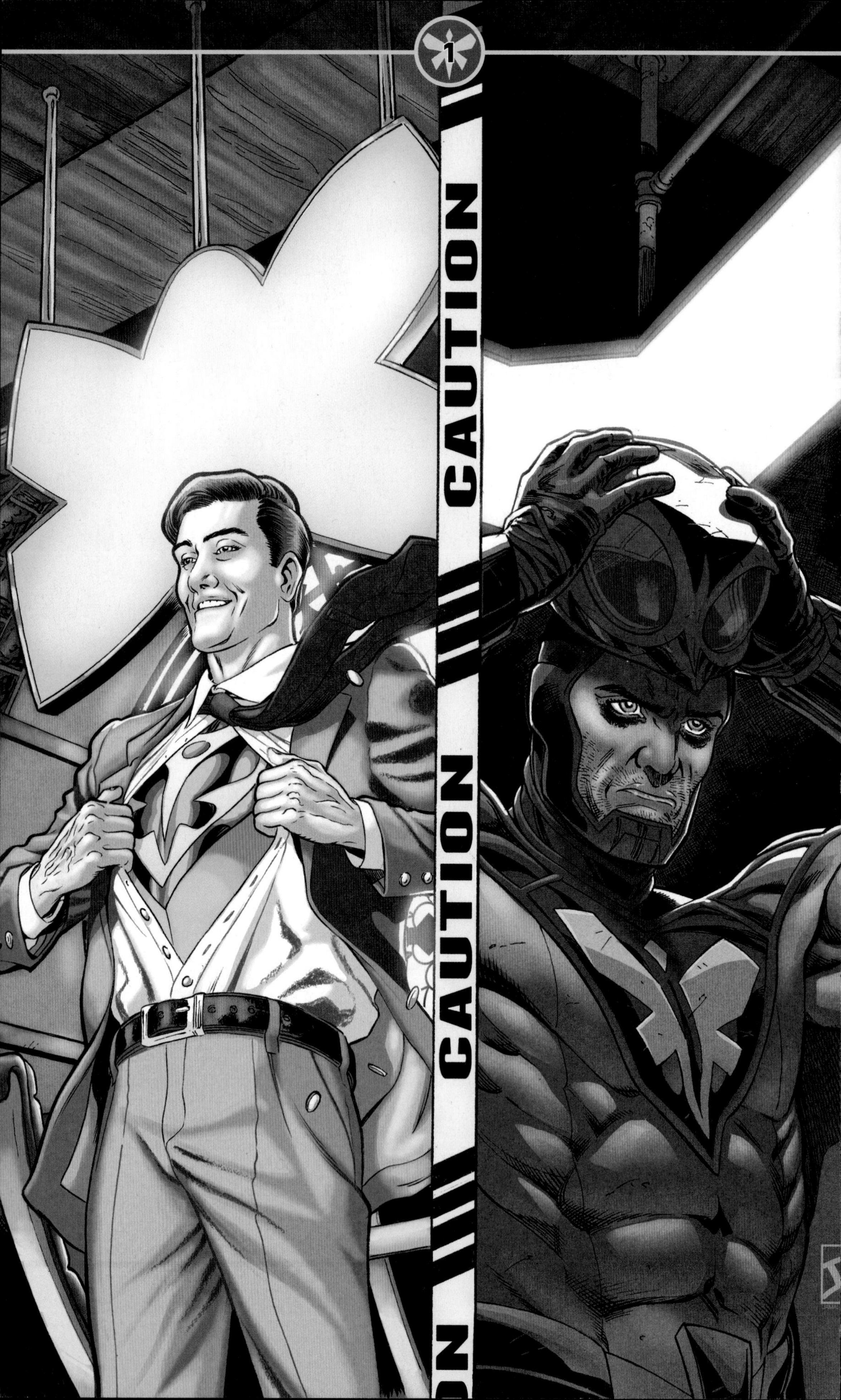
1
CAUTION
CAUTION

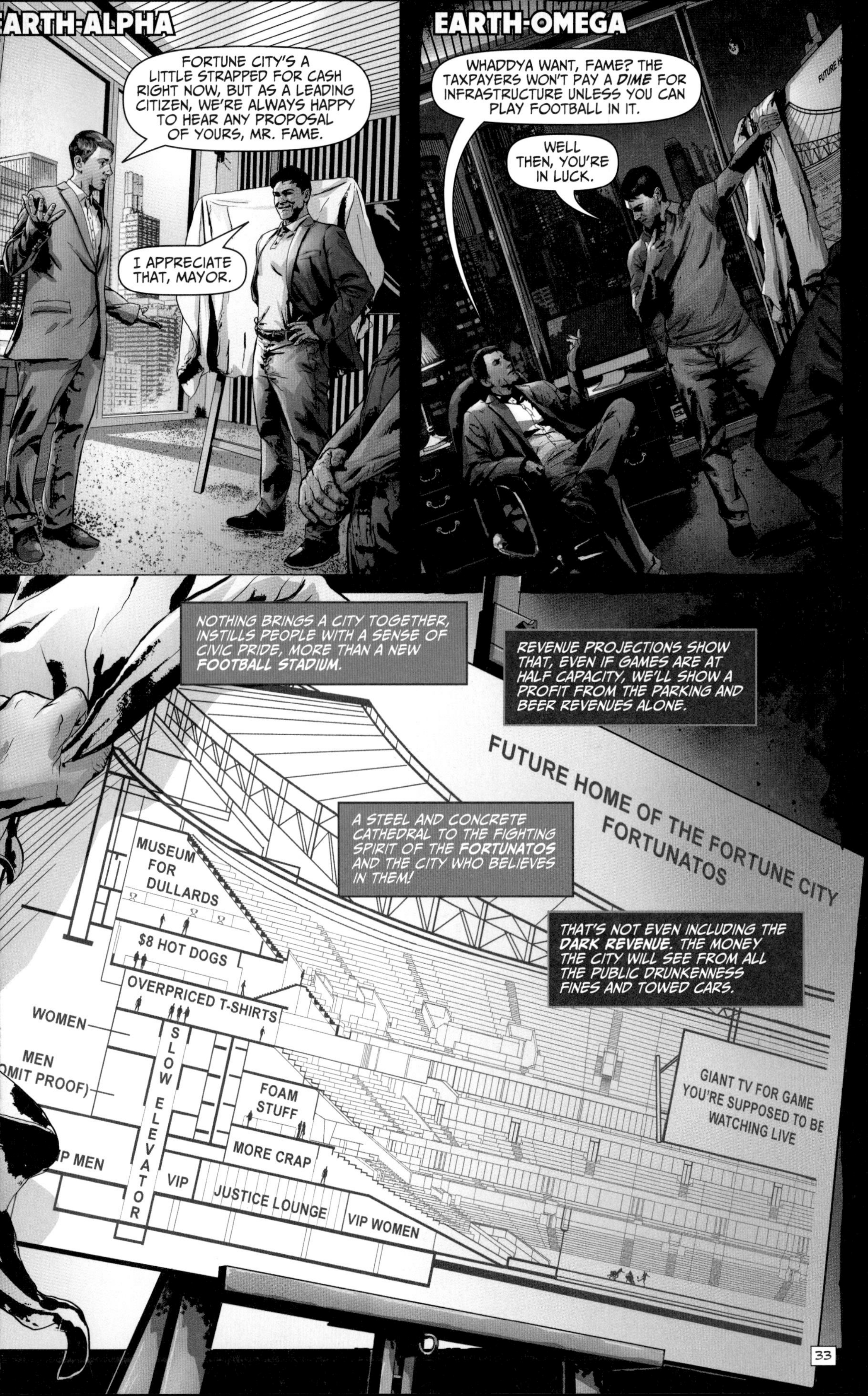
EARTH-ALPHA
FORTUNE CITY'S A LITTLE STRAPPED FOR CASH RIGHT NOW, BUT AS A LEADING CITIZEN, WE'RE ALWAYS HAPPY TO HEAR ANY PROPOSAL OF YOURS, MR. FAME.
I APPRECIATE THAT, MAYOR.
EARTH-OMEGA
WHADDYA WANT, FAME? THE TAXPAYERS WON'T PAY A DIME FOR INFRASTRUCTURE UNLESS YOU CAN PLAY FOOTBALL IN IT.
WELL THEN, YOU'RE IN LUCK.
NOTHING BRINGS A CITY TOGETHER, INSTILLS PEOPLE WITH A SENSE OF CIVIC PRIDE, MORE THAN A NEW FOOTBALL STADIUM.
REVENUE PROJECTIONS SHOW THAT, EVEN IF GAMES ARE AT HALF CAPACITY, WE'LL SHOW A PROFIT FROM THE PARKING AND BEER REVENUES ALONE.
FUTURE HOME OF THE FORTUNE CITY FORTUNATOS
A STEEL AND CONCRETE CATHEDRAL TO THE FIGHTING SPIRIT OF THE FORTUNATOS AND THE CITY WHO BELIEVES IN THEM!
THAT'S NOT EVEN INCLUDING THE DARK REVENUE. THE MONEY THE CITY WILL SEE FROM ALL THE PUBLIC DRUNKENNESS FINES AND TOWED CARS.
MUSEUM FOR DULLARDS
$8 HOT DOGS
OVERPRICED T-SHIRTS
WOMEN
MEN
MIT PROOF)
SLOW ELEVATOR
FOAM STUFF
MORE CRAP
P MEN
VIP
JUSTICE LOUNGE
VIP WOMEN
GIANT TV FOR GAME YOU'RE SUPPOSED TO BE WATCHING LIVE

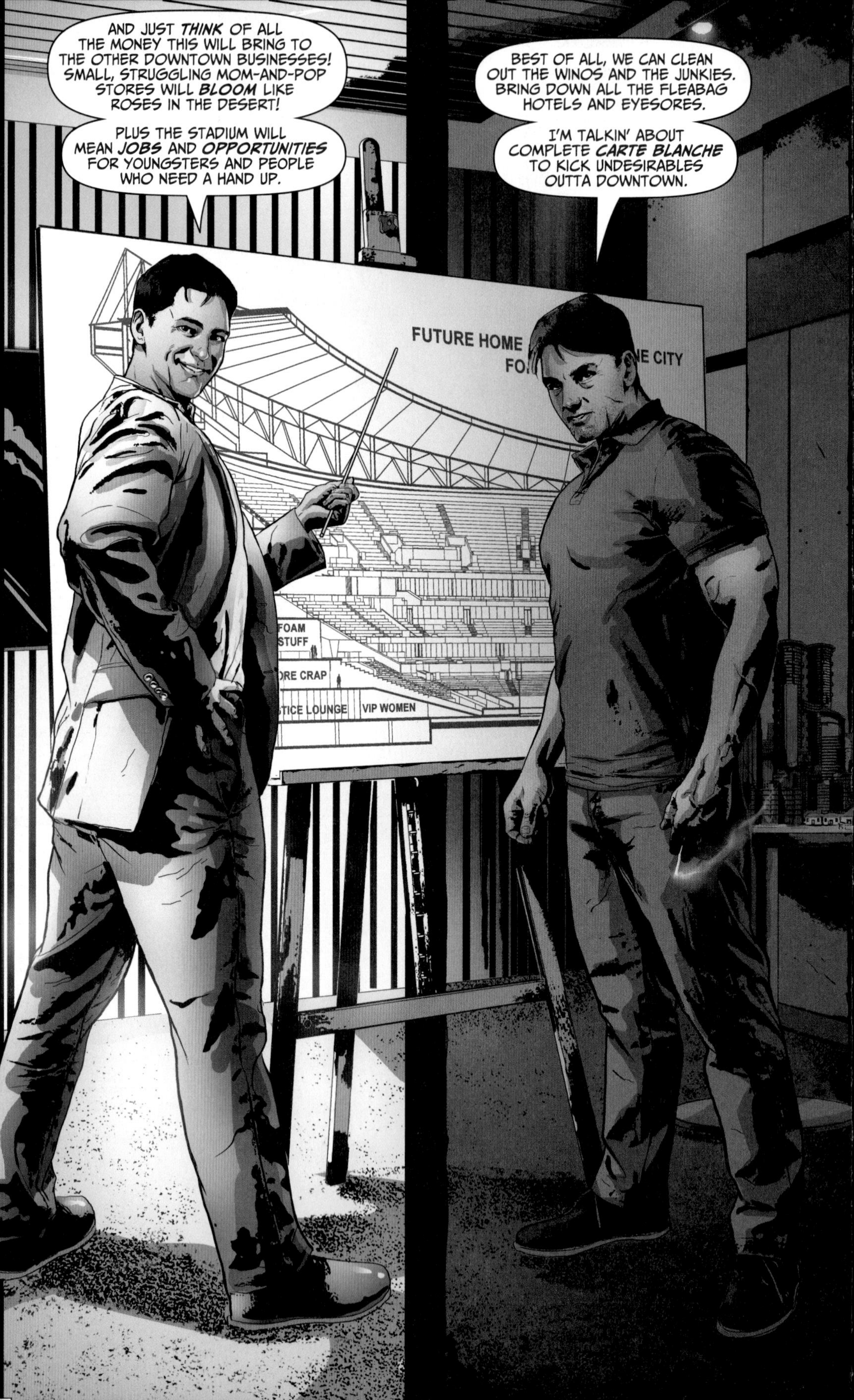
AND JUST THINK OF ALL THE MONEY THIS WILL BRING TO THE OTHER DOWNTOWN BUSINESSES! SMALL, STRUGGLING MOM-AND-POP STORES WILL BLOOM LIKE ROSES IN THE DESERT!
PLUS THE STADIUM WILL MEAN JOBS AND OPPORTUNITIES FOR YOUNGSTERS AND PEOPLE WHO NEED A HAND UP.
BEST OF ALL, WE CAN CLEAN OUT THE WINOS AND THE JUNKIES. BRING DOWN ALL THE FLEABAG HOTELS AND EYESORES.
I'M TALKIN' ABOUT COMPLETE CARTE BLANCHE TO KICK UNDESIRABLES OUTTA DOWNTOWN.
FUTURE HOME
FOAM STUFF
ORE CRAP
STICE LOUNGE
VIP WOMEN

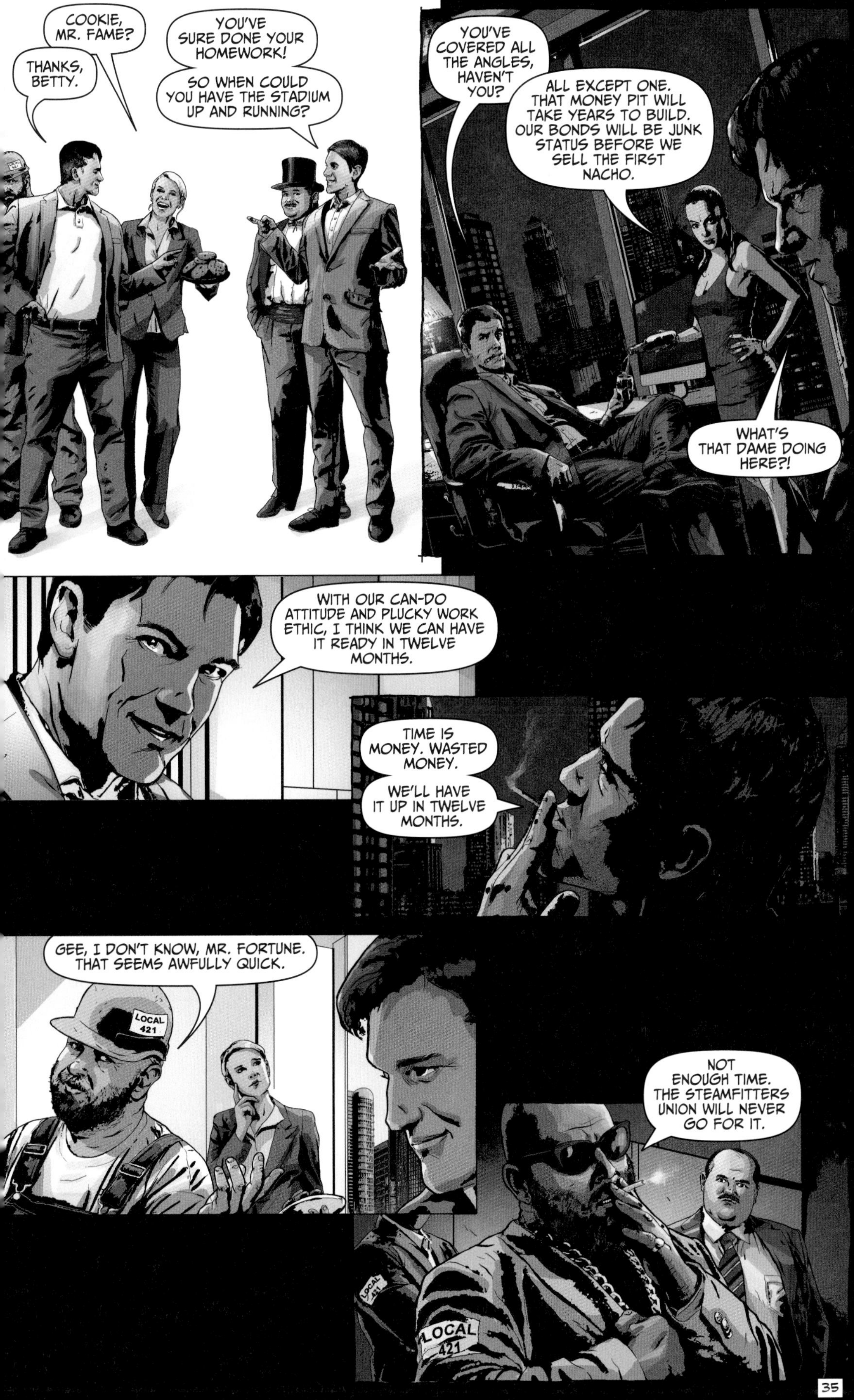
COOKIE, MR. FAME?
THANKS, BETTY.
YOU'VE SURE DONE YOUR HOMEWORK!
SO WHEN COULD YOU HAVE THE STADIUM UP AND RUNNING?
YOU'VE COVERED ALL THE ANGLES, HAVEN'T YOU?
ALL EXCEPT ONE. THAT MONEY PIT WILL TAKE YEARS TO BUILD. OUR BONDS WILL BE JUNK STATUS BEFORE WE SELL THE FIRST NACHO.
WHAT'S THAT DAME DOING HERE?!
WITH OUR CAN-DO ATTITUDE AND PLUCKY WORK ETHIC, I THINK WE CAN HAVE IT READY IN TWELVE MONTHS.
TIME IS MONEY. WASTED MONEY.
WE'LL HAVE IT UP IN TWELVE MONTHS.
GEE, I DON'T KNOW, MR. FORTUNE. THAT SEEMS AWFULLY QUICK.
LOCAL 421
NOT ENOUGH TIME. THE STEAMFITTERS UNION WILL NEVER GO FOR IT.
LOCAL 421
LOCAL 421

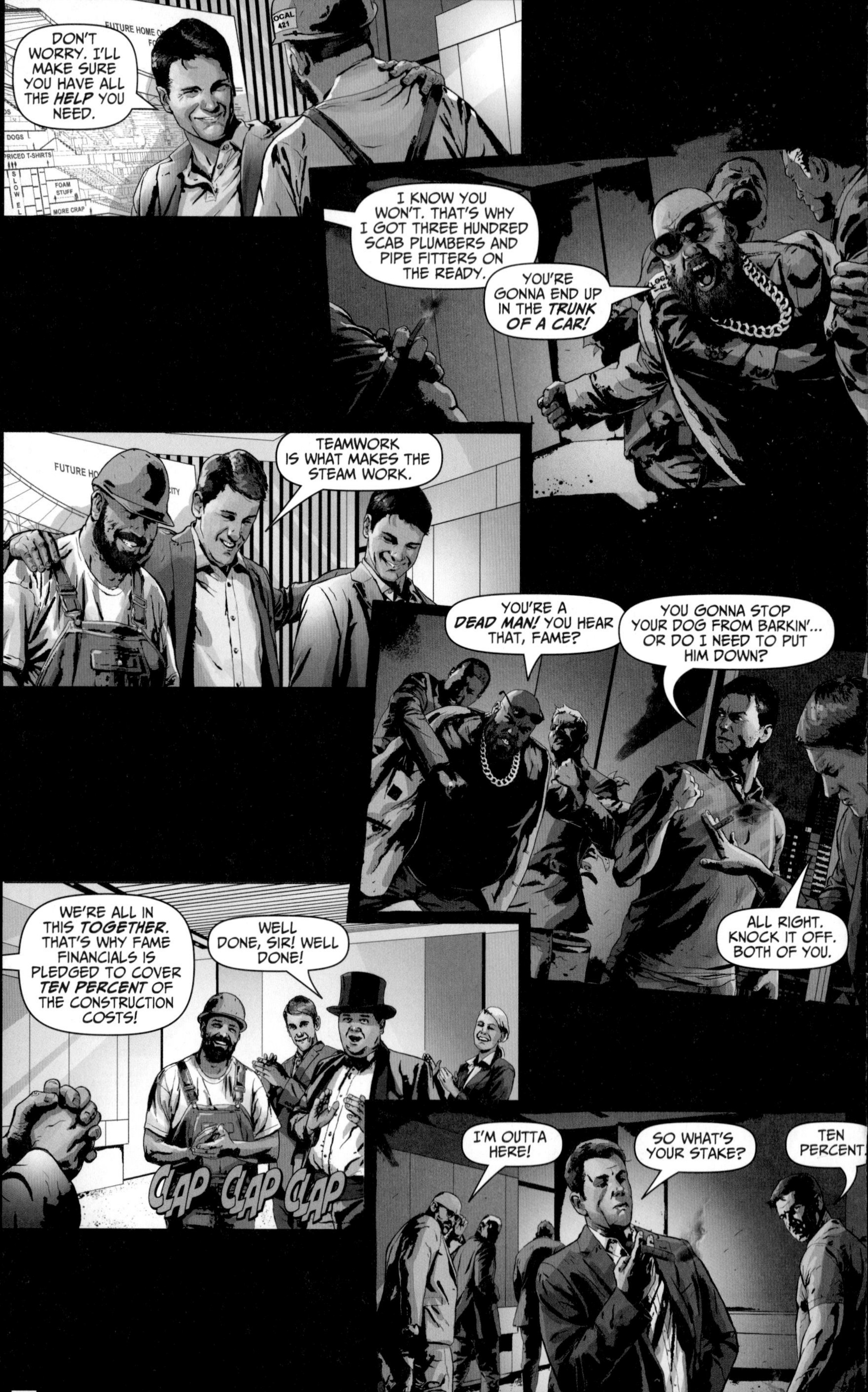
DON'T WORRY. I'LL MAKE SURE YOU HAVE ALL THE HELP YOU NEED.
I KNOW YOU WON'T. THAT'S WHY I GOT THREE HUNDRED SCAB PLUMBERS AND PIPE FITTERS ON THE READY.
YOU'RE GONNA END UP IN THE TRUNK OF A CAR!
TEAMWORK IS WHAT MAKES THE STEAM WORK.
YOU'RE A DEAD MAN! YOU HEAR THAT, FAME?
YOU GONNA STOP YOUR DOG FROM BARKIN'... OR DO I NEED TO PUT HIM DOWN?
ALL RIGHT. KNOCK IT OFF. BOTH OF YOU.
WE'RE ALL IN THIS TOGETHER. THAT'S WHY FAME FINANCIALS IS PLEDGED TO COVER TEN PERCENT OF THE CONSTRUCTION COSTS!
WELL DONE, SIR! WELL DONE!
CLAP CLAP CLAP
I'M OUTTA HERE!
SO WHAT'S YOUR STAKE?
TEN PERCENT.

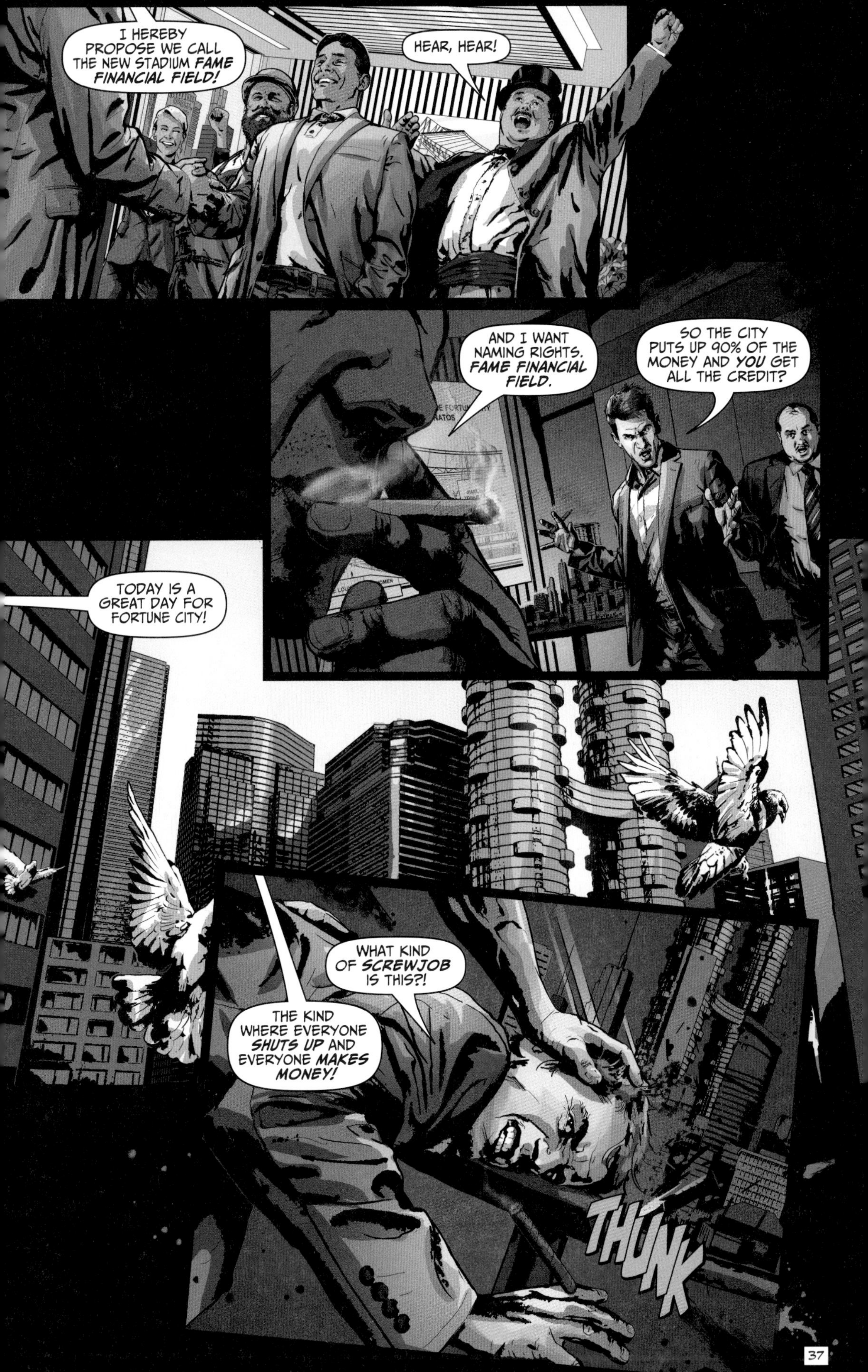
I HEREBY PROPOSE WE CALL THE NEW STADIUM FAME FINANCIAL FIELD!
HEAR, HEAR!
AND I WANT NAMING RIGHTS. FAME FINANCIAL FIELD.
SO THE CITY PUTS UP 90% OF THE MONEY AND YOU GET ALL THE CREDIT?
TODAY IS A GREAT DAY FOR FORTUNE CITY!
WHAT KIND OF SCREWJOB IS THIS?!
THE KIND WHERE EVERYONE SHUTS UP AND EVERYONE MAKES MONEY!
THUNK

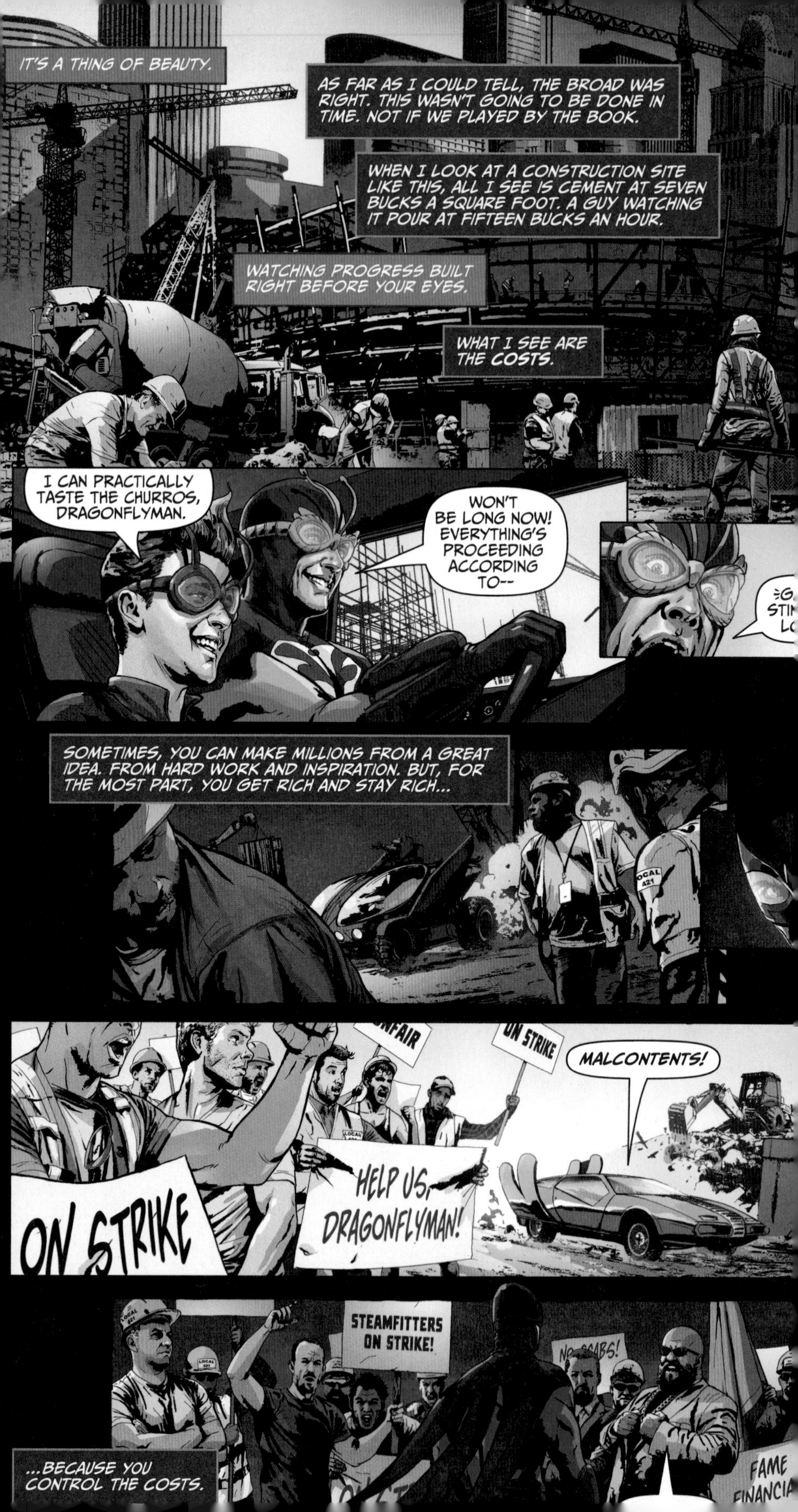

IT'S A THING OF BEAUTY.
AS FAR AS I COULD TELL, THE BROAD WAS RIGHT. THIS WASN'T GOING TO BE DONE IN TIME. NOT IF WE PLAYED BY THE BOOK.
WATCHING PROGRESS BUILT RIGHT BEFORE YOUR EYES.
WHEN I LOOK AT A CONSTRUCTION SITE LIKE THIS, ALL I SEE IS CEMENT AT SEVEN BUCKS A SQUARE FOOT. A GUY WATCHING IT POUR AT FIFTEEN BUCKS AN HOUR.
WHAT I SEE ARE THE COSTS.
I CAN PRACTICALLY TASTE THE CHURROS, DRAGONFLYMAN.
WON'T BE LONG NOW! EVERYTHING'S PROCEEDING ACCORDING TO--
SOMETIMES, YOU CAN MAKE MILLIONS FROM A GREAT IDEA. FROM HARD WORK AND INSPIRATION. BUT, FOR THE MOST PART, YOU GET RICH AND STAY RICH...
ON STRIKE
MALCONTENTS!
ON STRIKE
HELP US, DRAGONFLYMAN!
STEAMFITTERS ON STRIKE!
...BECAUSE YOU CONTROL THE COSTS.
FAME

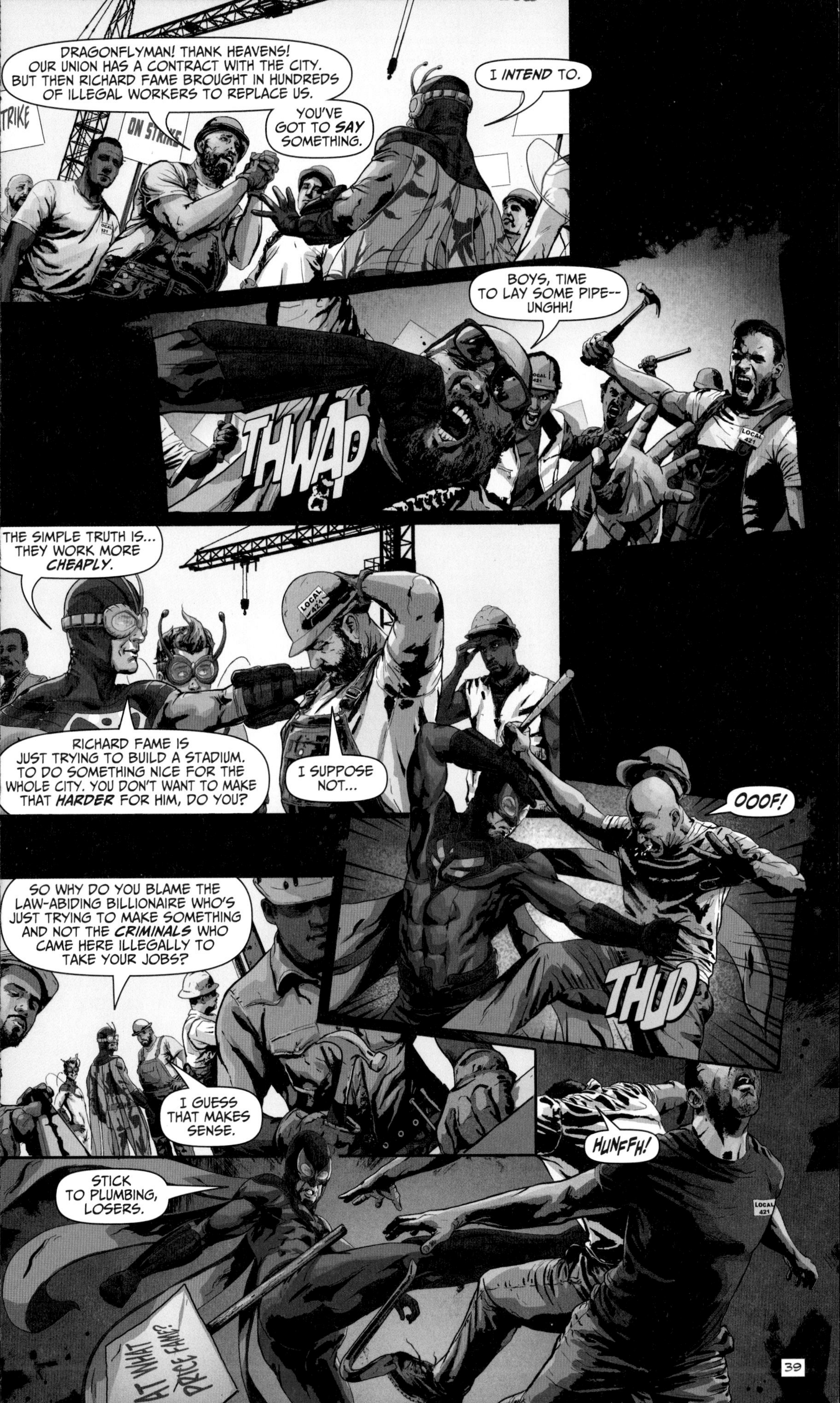
DRAGONFLYMAN! THANK HEAVENS! OUR UNION HAS A CONTRACT WITH THE CITY. BUT THEN RICHARD FAME BROUGHT IN HUNDREDS OF ILLEGAL WORKERS TO REPLACE US.
YOU'VE GOT TO SAY SOMETHING.
I INTEND TO.
ON STRIKE
BOYS, TIME TO LAY SOME PIPE-- UNGHH!
THWAP
LOCAL 421
THE SIMPLE TRUTH IS... THEY WORK MORE CHEAPLY.
RICHARD FAME IS JUST TRYING TO BUILD A STADIUM. TO DO SOMETHING NICE FOR THE WHOLE CITY. YOU DON'T WANT TO MAKE THAT HARDER FOR HIM, DO YOU?
I SUPPOSE NOT...
OOOF!
THUD
SO WHY DO YOU BLAME THE LAW-ABIDING BILLIONAIRE WHO'S JUST TRYING TO MAKE SOMETHING AND NOT THE CRIMINALS WHO CAME HERE ILLEGALLY TO TAKE YOUR JOBS?
I GUESS THAT MAKES SENSE.
HUNFFH!
STICK TO PLUMBING, LOSERS.
AT WHAT PRICE FAME?

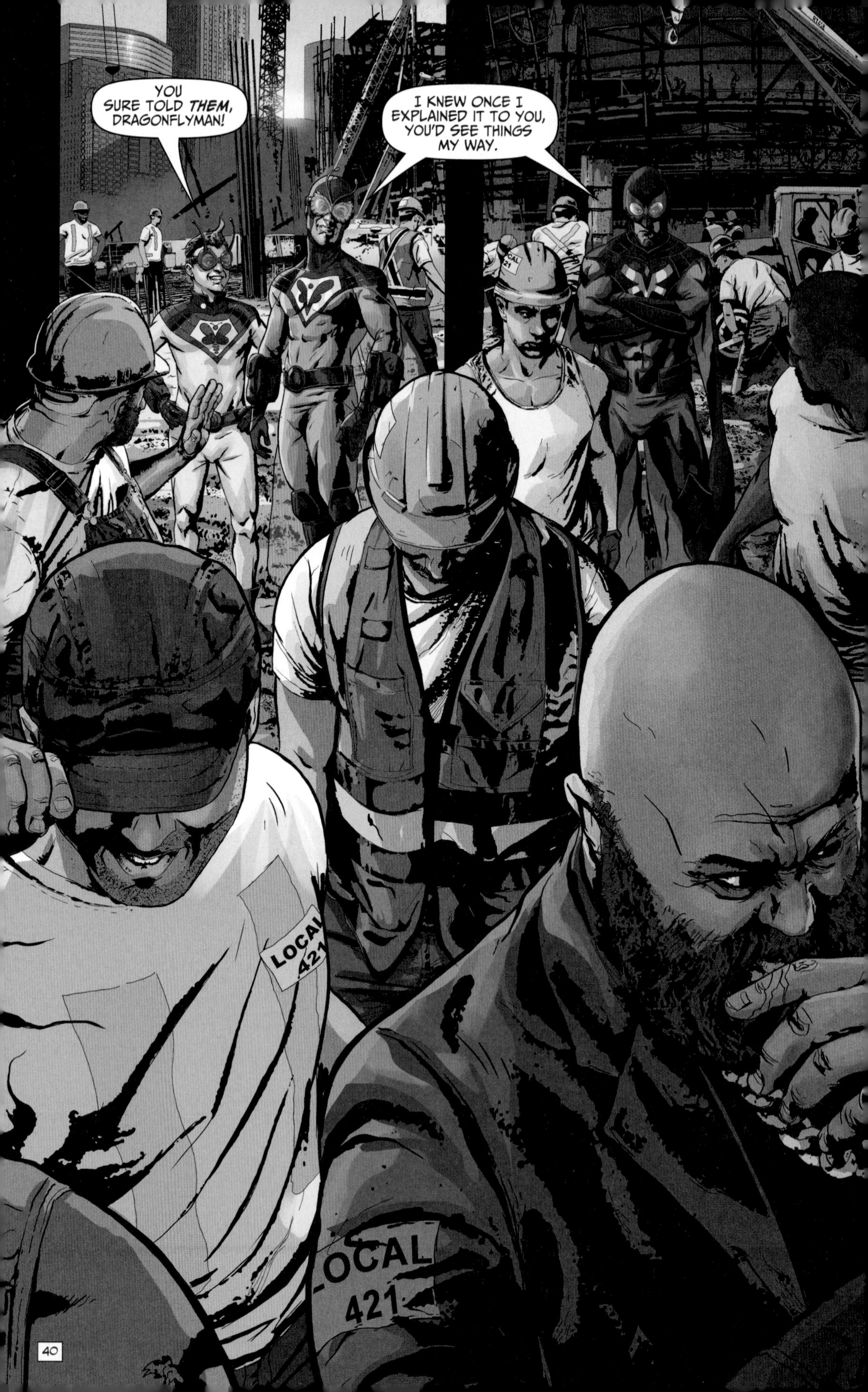
YOU SURE TOLD THEM, DRAGONFLYMAN!
I KNEW ONCE I EXPLAINED IT TO YOU, YOU'D SEE THINGS MY WAY.
LOCAL 421
LOCAL 421
LOCAL 421
LOCAL 421

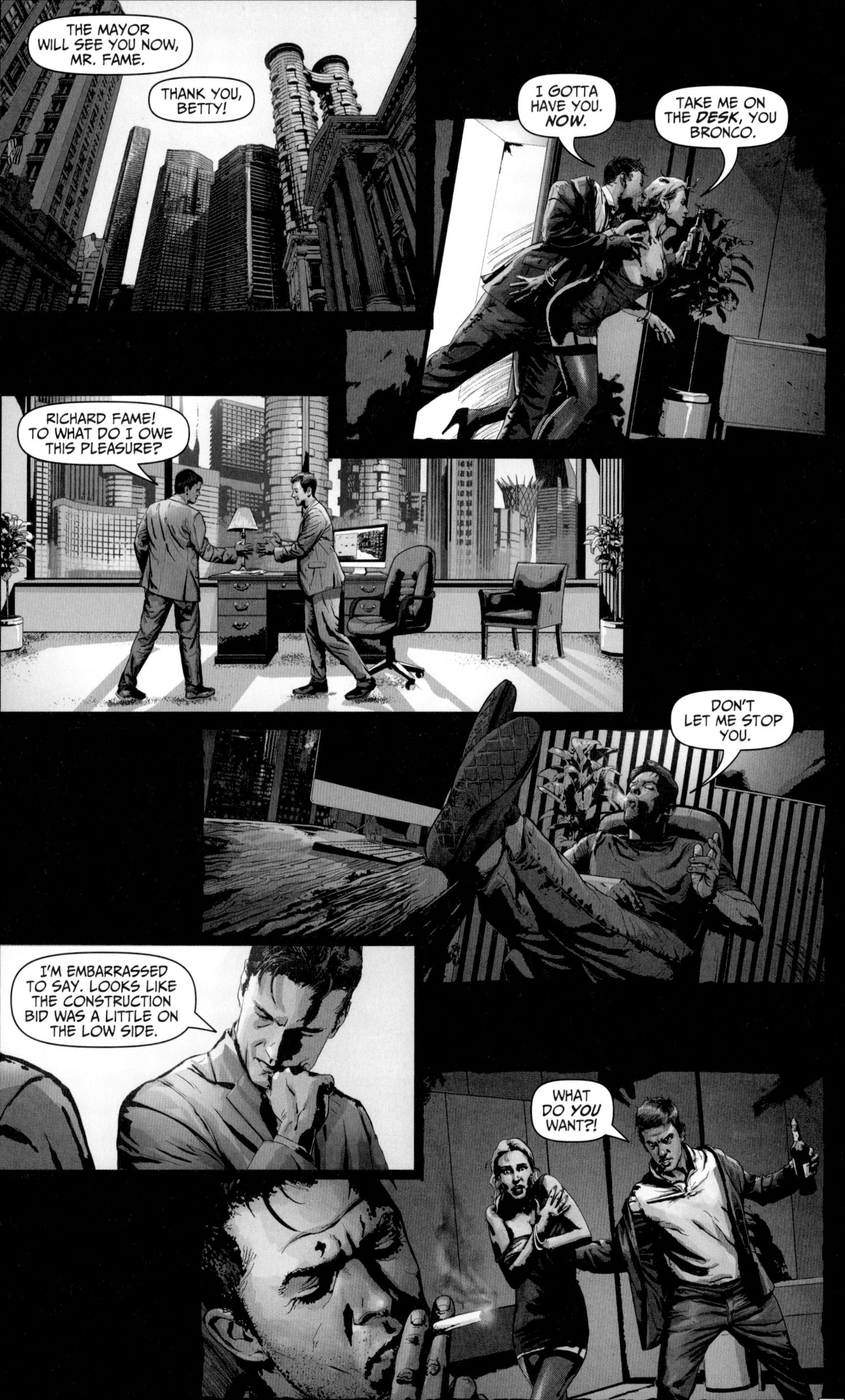
THE MAYOR WILL SEE YOU NOW, MR. FAME.
THANK YOU, BETTY!
I GOTTA HAVE YOU. NOW.
TAKE ME ON THE DESK, YOU BRONCO.
RICHARD FAME! TO WHAT DO I OWE THIS PLEASURE?
DON'T LET ME STOP YOU.
I'M EMBARRASSED TO SAY. LOOKS LIKE THE CONSTRUCTION BID WAS A LITTLE ON THE LOW SIDE.
WHAT DO YOU WANT?!

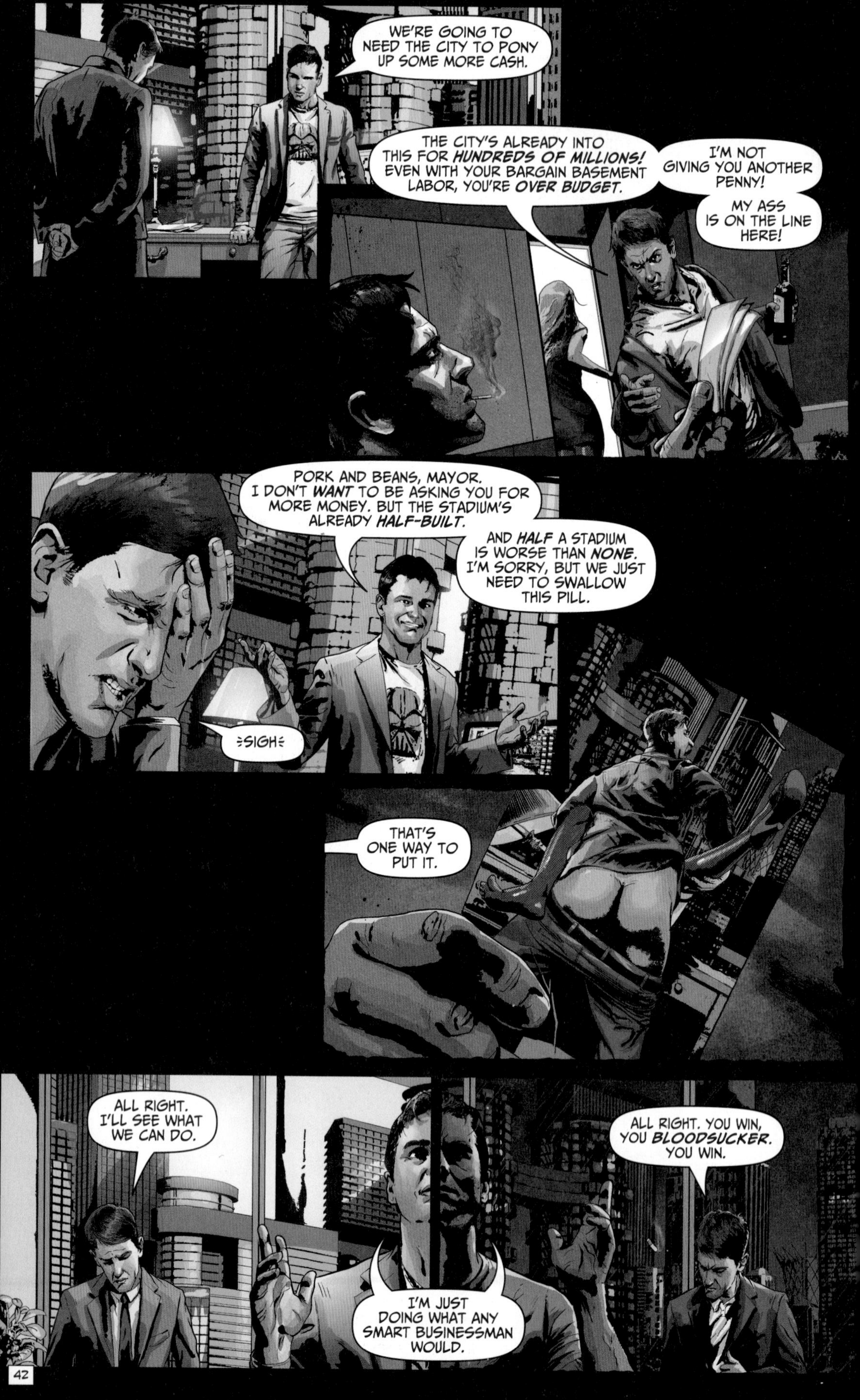
WE'RE GOING TO NEED THE CITY TO PONY UP SOME MORE CASH.
THE CITY'S ALREADY INTO THIS FOR HUNDREDS OF MILLIONS! EVEN WITH YOUR BARGAIN BASEMENT LABOR, YOU'RE OVER BUDGET.
I'M NOT GIVING YOU ANOTHER PENNY!
MY ASS IS ON THE LINE HERE!
PORK AND BEANS, MAYOR. I DON'T WANT TO BE ASKING YOU FOR MORE MONEY. BUT THE STADIUM'S ALREADY HALF-BUILT.
AND HALF A STADIUM IS WORSE THAN NONE. I'M SORRY, BUT WE JUST NEED TO SWALLOW THIS PILL.
SIGH
THAT'S ONE WAY TO PUT IT.
ALL RIGHT. I'LL SEE WHAT WE CAN DO.
I'M JUST DOING WHAT ANY SMART BUSINESSMAN WOULD.
ALL RIGHT. YOU WIN, YOU BLOODSUCKER. YOU WIN.

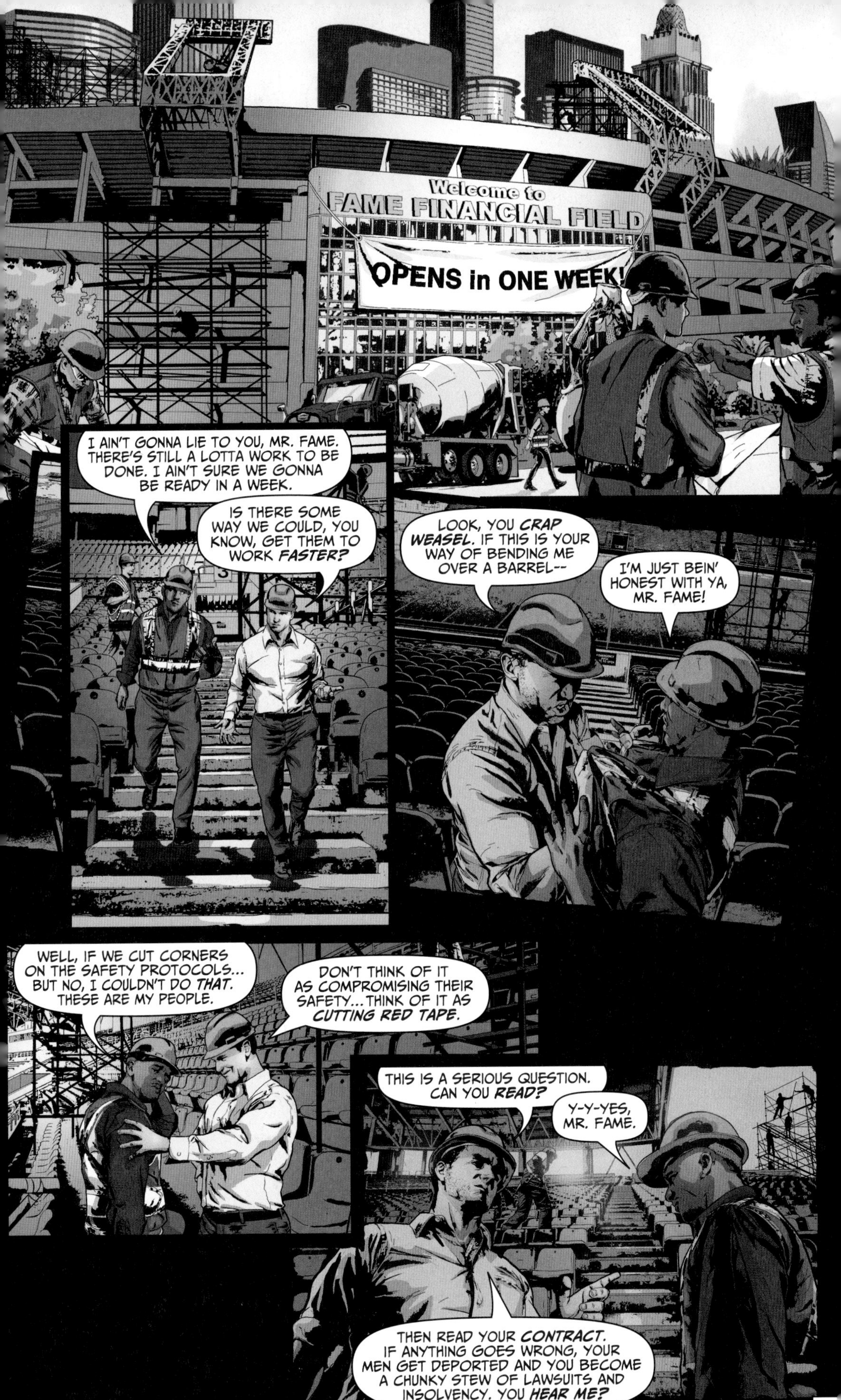
Welcome to
FAME FINANCIAL FIELD
OPENS in ONE WEEK!
I AIN'T GONNA LIE TO YOU, MR. FAME. THERE'S STILL A LOTTA WORK TO BE DONE. I AIN'T SURE WE GONNA BE READY IN A WEEK.
IS THERE SOME WAY WE COULD, YOU KNOW, GET THEM TO WORK FASTER?
LOOK, YOU CRAP WEASEL. IF THIS IS YOUR WAY OF BENDING ME OVER A BARREL--
I'M JUST BEIN' HONEST WITH YA, MR. FAME!
WELL, IF WE CUT CORNERS ON THE SAFETY PROTOCOLS... BUT NO, I COULDN'T DO THAT. THESE ARE MY PEOPLE.
DON'T THINK OF IT AS COMPROMISING THEIR SAFETY... THINK OF IT AS CUTTING RED TAPE.
THIS IS A SERIOUS QUESTION. CAN YOU READ?
Y-Y-YES, MR. FAME.
THEN READ YOUR CONTRACT. IF ANYTHING GOES WRONG, YOUR MEN GET DEPORTED AND YOU BECOME A CHUNKY STEW OF LAWSUITS AND INSOLVENCY. YOU HEAR ME?

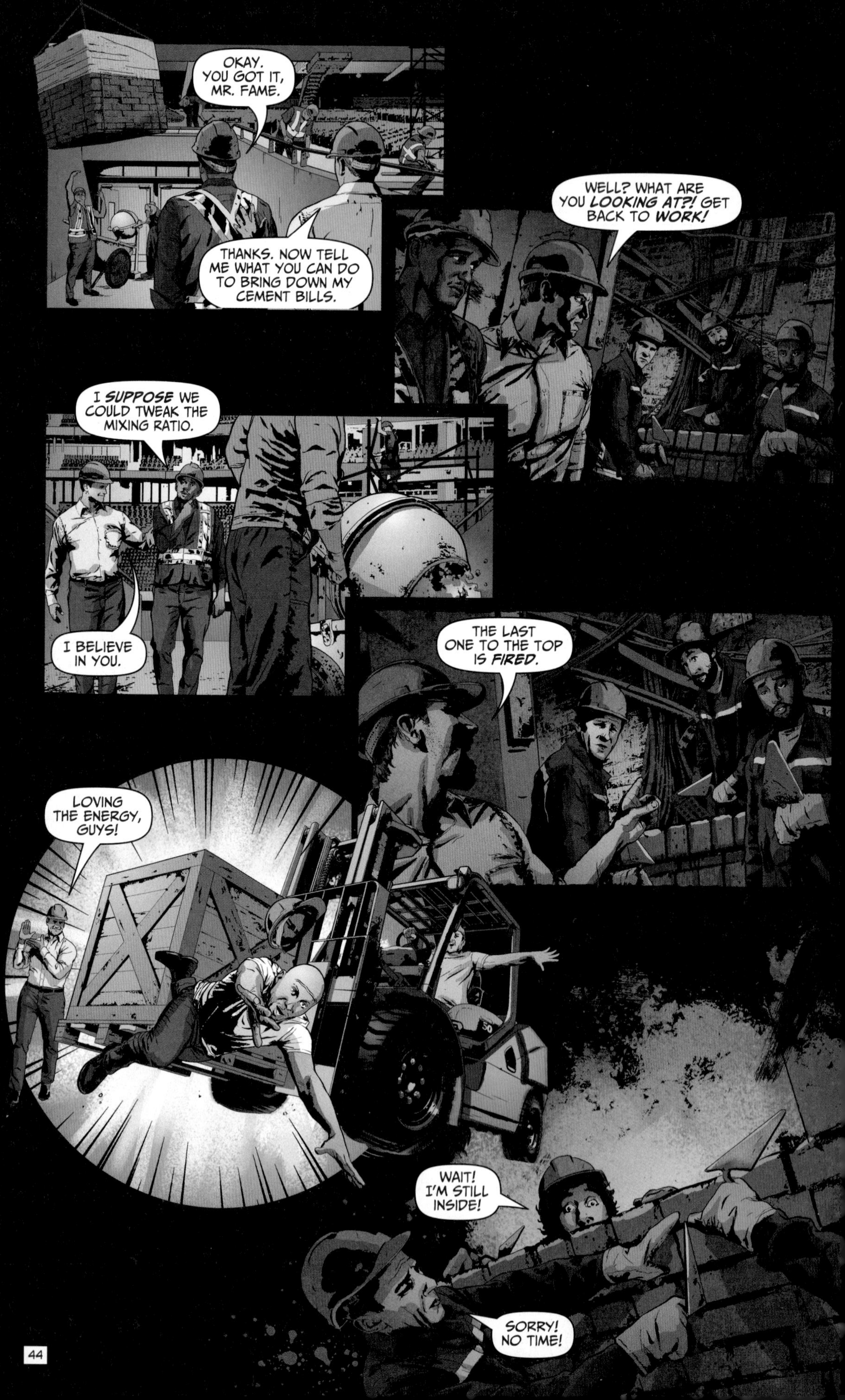
OKAY. YOU GOT IT, MR. FAME.
THANKS. NOW TELL ME WHAT YOU CAN DO TO BRING DOWN MY CEMENT BILLS.
WELL? WHAT ARE YOU *LOOKING AT?!* GET BACK TO *WORK!*
I *SUPPOSE* WE COULD TWEAK THE MIXING RATIO.
I BELIEVE IN YOU.
THE LAST ONE TO THE TOP IS *FIRED.*
LOVING THE ENERGY, GUYS!
WAIT! I'M STILL INSIDE!
SORRY! NO TIME!

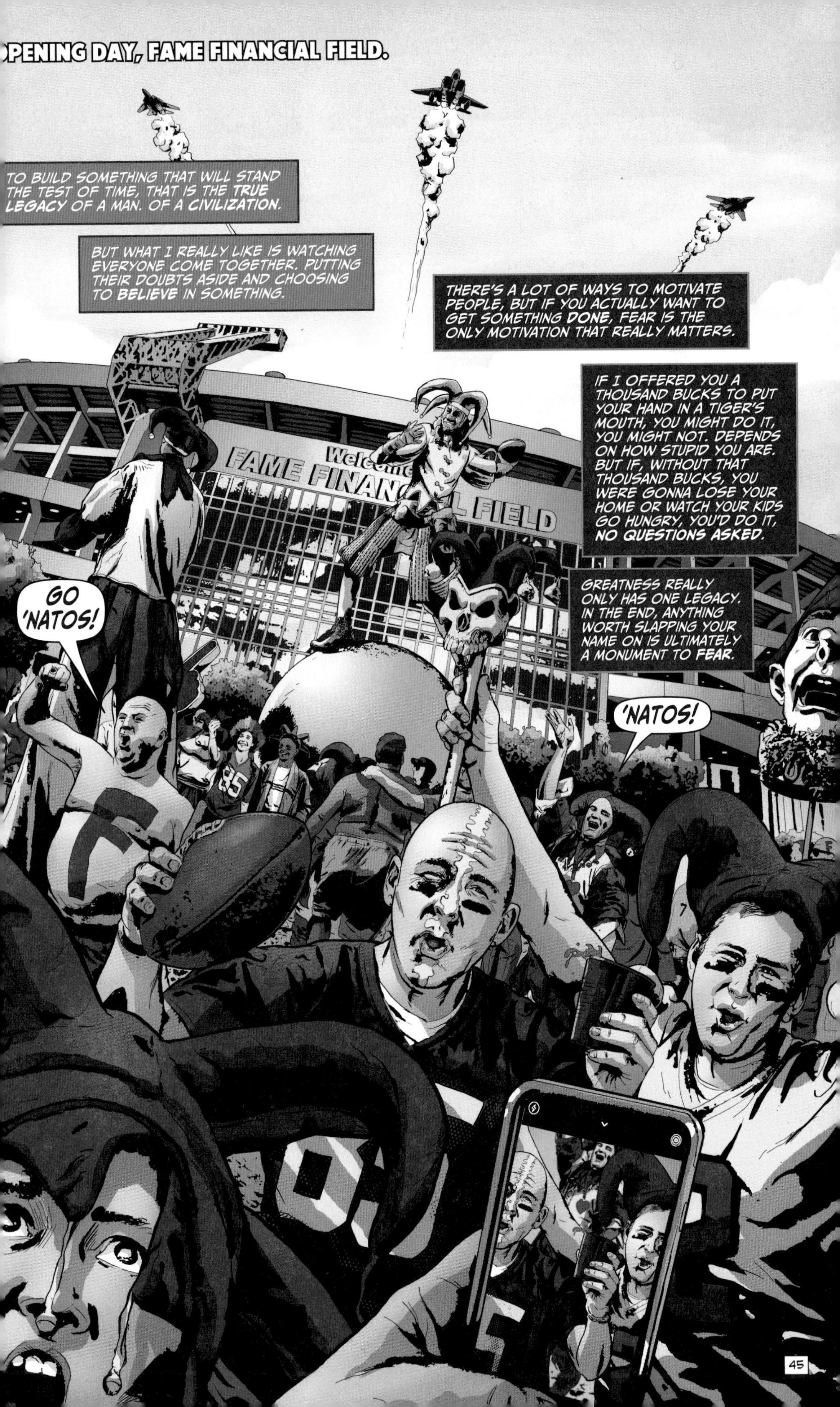
PENING DAY, FAME FINANCIAL FIELD.
TO BUILD SOMETHING THAT WILL STAND THE TEST OF TIME, THAT IS THE TRUE LEGACY OF A MAN. OF A CIVILIZATION.
BUT WHAT I REALLY LIKE IS WATCHING EVERYONE COME TOGETHER. PUTTING THEIR DOUBTS ASIDE AND CHOOSING TO BELIEVE IN SOMETHING.
THERE'S A LOT OF WAYS TO MOTIVATE PEOPLE, BUT IF YOU ACTUALLY WANT TO GET SOMETHING DONE, FEAR IS THE ONLY MOTIVATION THAT REALLY MATTERS.
IF I OFFERED YOU A THOUSAND BUCKS TO PUT YOUR HAND IN A TIGER'S MOUTH, YOU MIGHT DO IT, YOU MIGHT NOT. DEPENDS ON HOW STUPID YOU ARE. BUT IF, WITHOUT THAT THOUSAND BUCKS, YOU WERE GONNA LOSE YOUR HOME OR WATCH YOUR KIDS GO HUNGRY, YOU'D DO IT, NO QUESTIONS ASKED.
GREATNESS REALLY ONLY HAS ONE LEGACY. IN THE END, ANYTHING WORTH SLAPPING YOUR NAME ON IS ULTIMATELY A MONUMENT TO FEAR.
GO 'NATOS!
'NATOS!

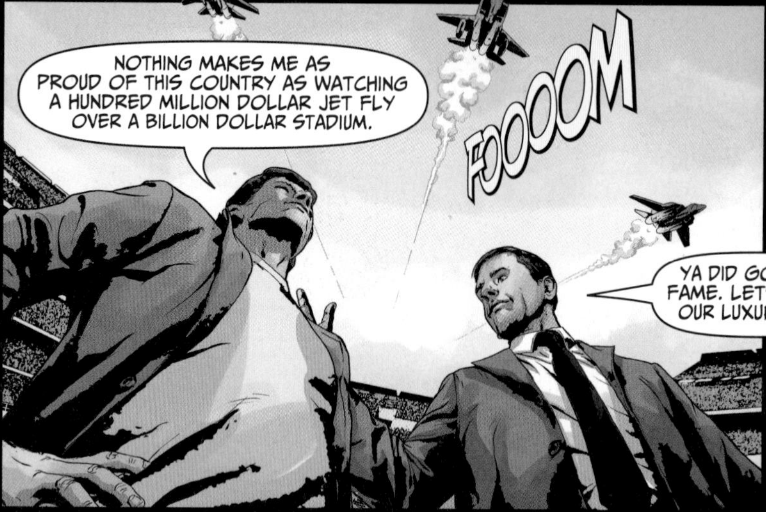
NOTHING MAKES ME AS PROUD OF THIS COUNTRY AS WATCHING A HUNDRED MILLION DOLLAR JET FLY OVER A BILLION DOLLAR STADIUM.
FOOOOM
YA DID GOOD, MR. FAME. LET'S GO TO OUR LUXURY SUITE.

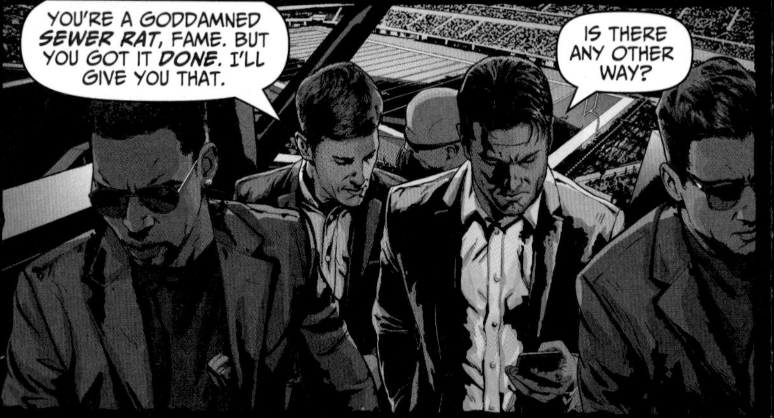
YOU'RE A GODDAMNED **SEWER RAT**, FAME. BUT YOU GOT IT **DONE**. I'LL GIVE YOU THAT.
IS THERE ANY OTHER WAY?

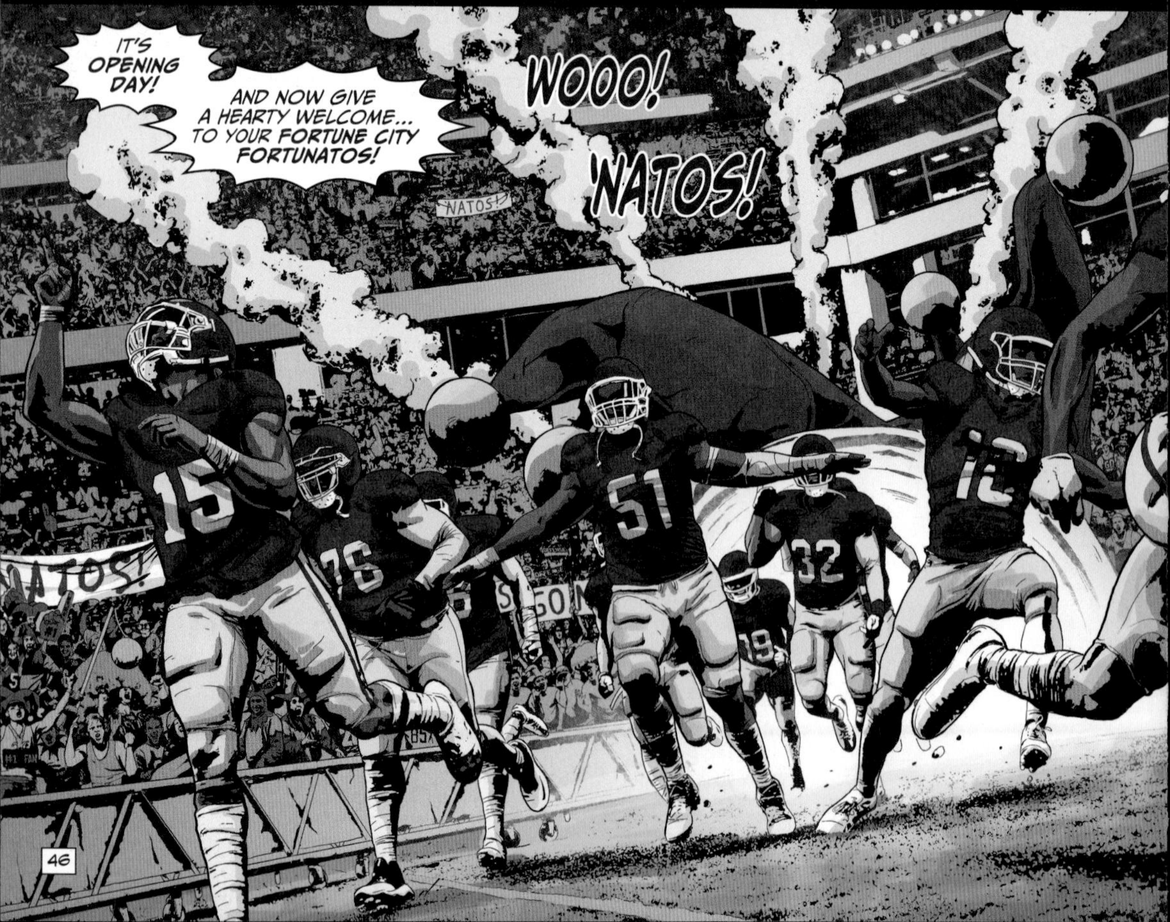
IT'S **OPENING DAY!**
AND NOW GIVE A HEARTY WELCOME... TO YOUR **FORTUNE CITY FORTUNATOS!**
WOOO!
'NATOS!
'NATOS!

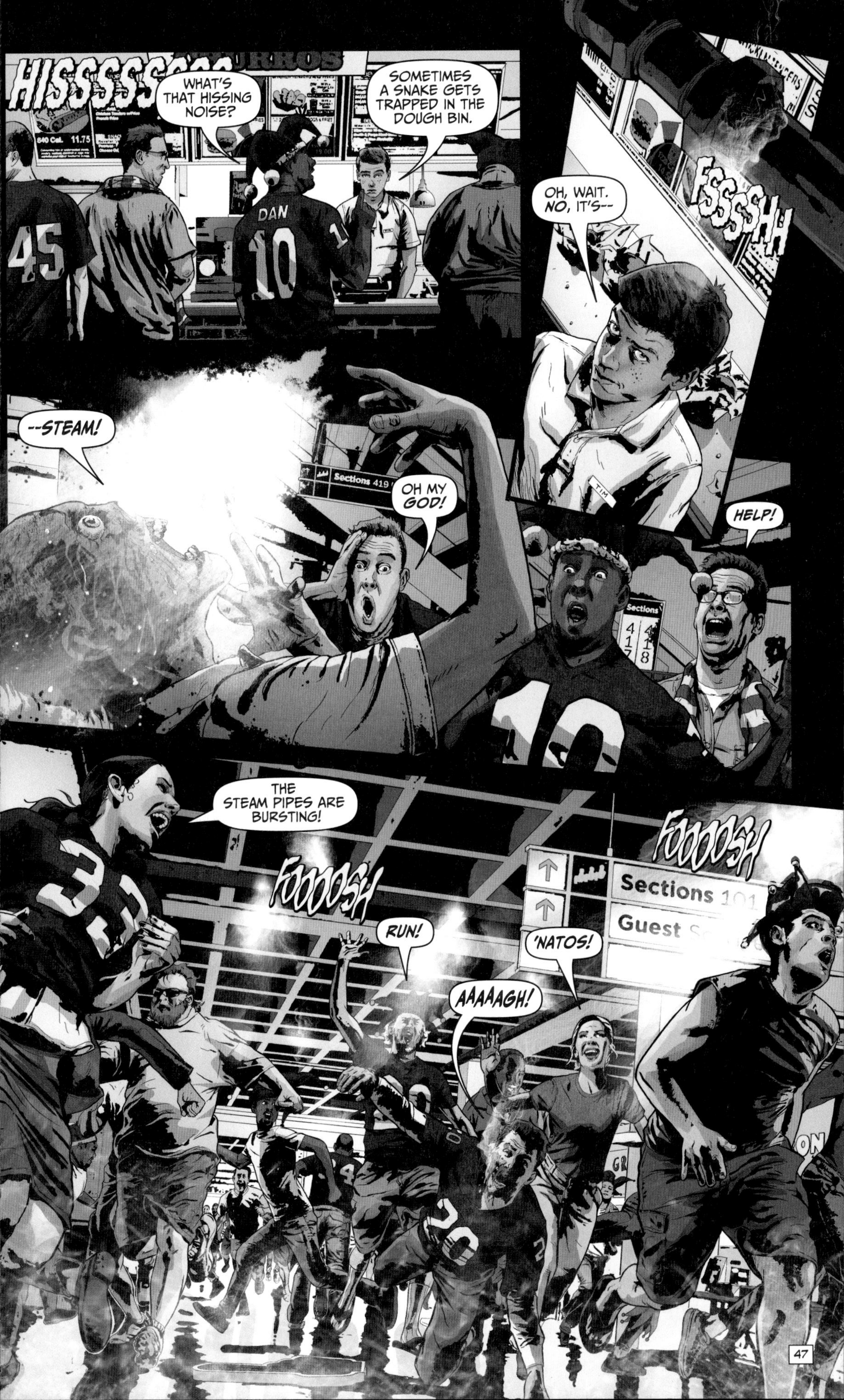
HISSSSSSSSS
WHAT'S THAT HISSING NOISE?
SOMETIMES A SNAKE GETS TRAPPED IN THE DOUGH BIN.
OH, WAIT. NO, IT'S--
FSSSHH
--STEAM!
OH MY GOD!
HELP!
THE STEAM PIPES ARE BURSTING!
FOOOOSH
FOOOOSH
RUN!
'NATOS!
AAAAAGH!

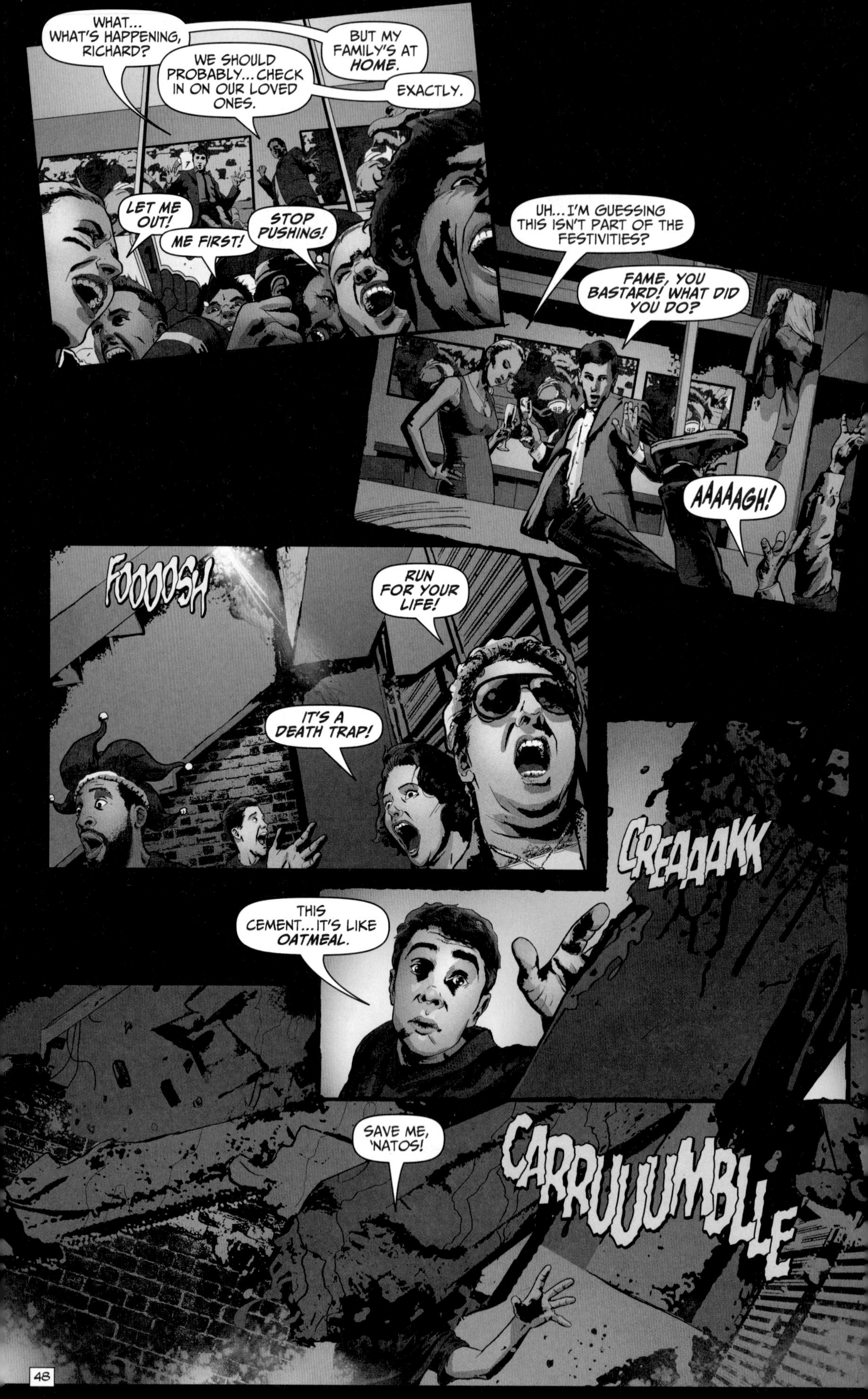

WHAT... WHAT'S HAPPENING, RICHARD?
WE SHOULD PROBABLY...CHECK IN ON OUR LOVED ONES.
BUT MY FAMILY'S AT HOME.
EXACTLY.
LET ME OUT!
ME FIRST!
STOP PUSHING!
UH...I'M GUESSING THIS ISN'T PART OF THE FESTIVITIES?
FAME, YOU BASTARD! WHAT DID YOU DO?
AAAAAGH!
FOOOOSH
RUN FOR YOUR LIFE!
IT'S A DEATH TRAP!
CREAAAKK
THIS CEMENT...IT'S LIKE OATMEAL.
SAVE ME, 'NATOS!
CARRUUUMBLLE

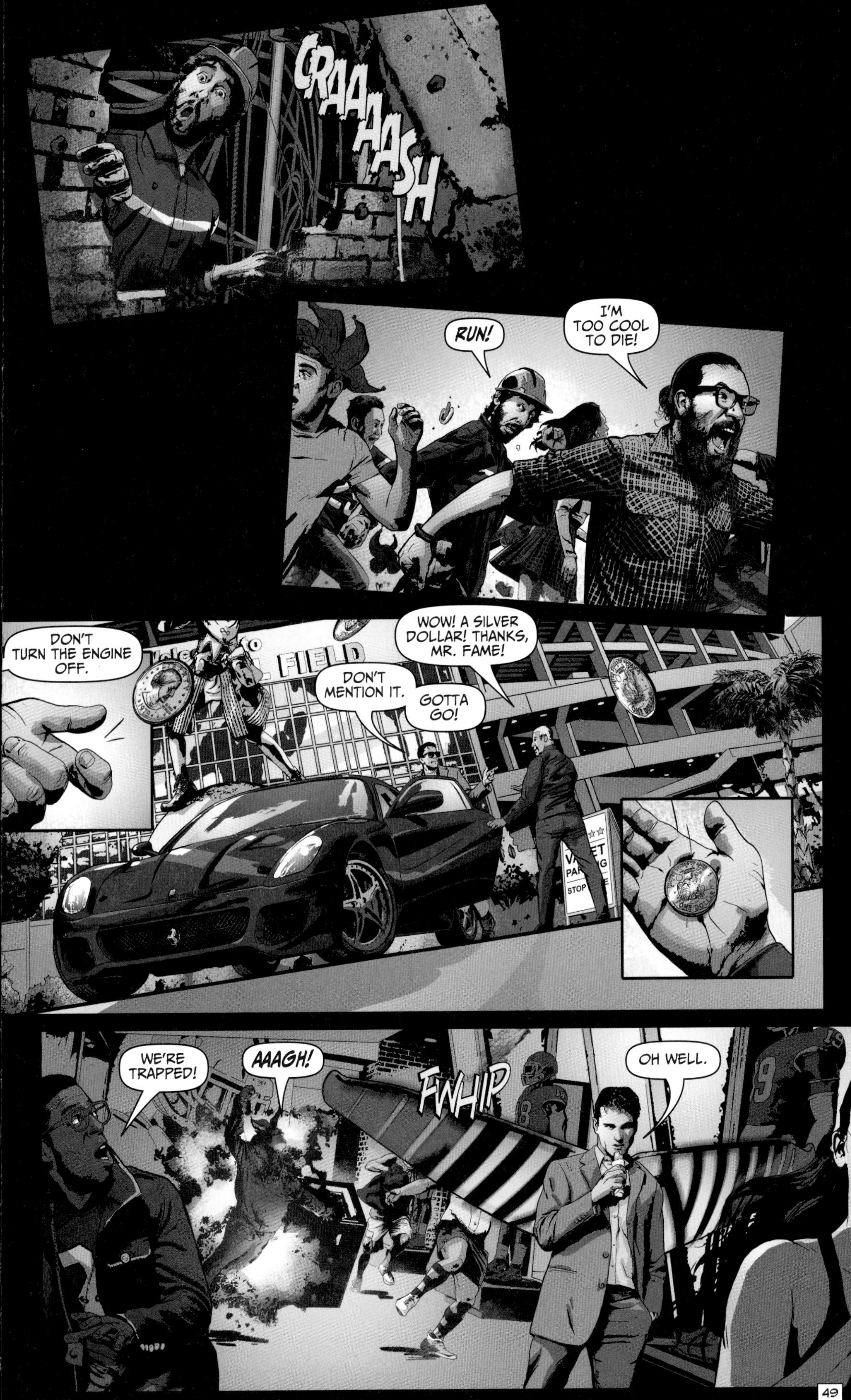
CRAAAASH
RUN!
I'M TOO COOL TO DIE!
DON'T TURN THE ENGINE OFF.
WOW! A SILVER DOLLAR! THANKS, MR. FAME!
DON'T MENTION IT.
GOTTA GO!
WE'RE TRAPPED!
AAAGH!
FWHIP
OH WELL.

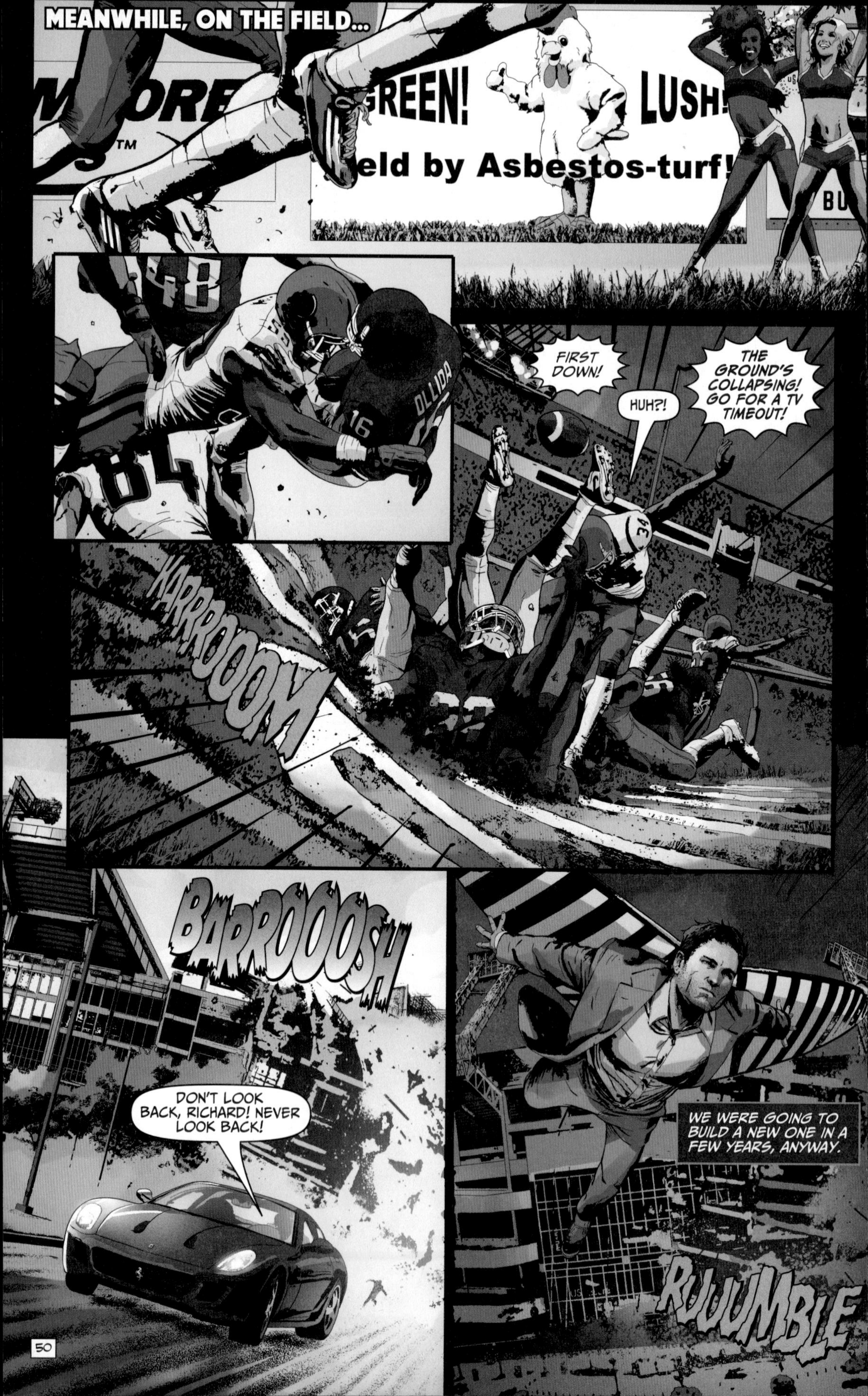
MEANWHILE, ON THE FIELD...
GREEN!
LUSH!
eld by Asbestos-turf!
FIRST DOWN!
HUH?!
THE GROUND'S COLLAPSING! GO FOR A TV TIMEOUT!
KARRROOOM
BARROOOSH
DON'T LOOK BACK, RICHARD! NEVER LOOK BACK!
WE WERE GOING TO BUILD A NEW ONE IN A FEW YEARS, ANYWAY.
RUUUMBLE

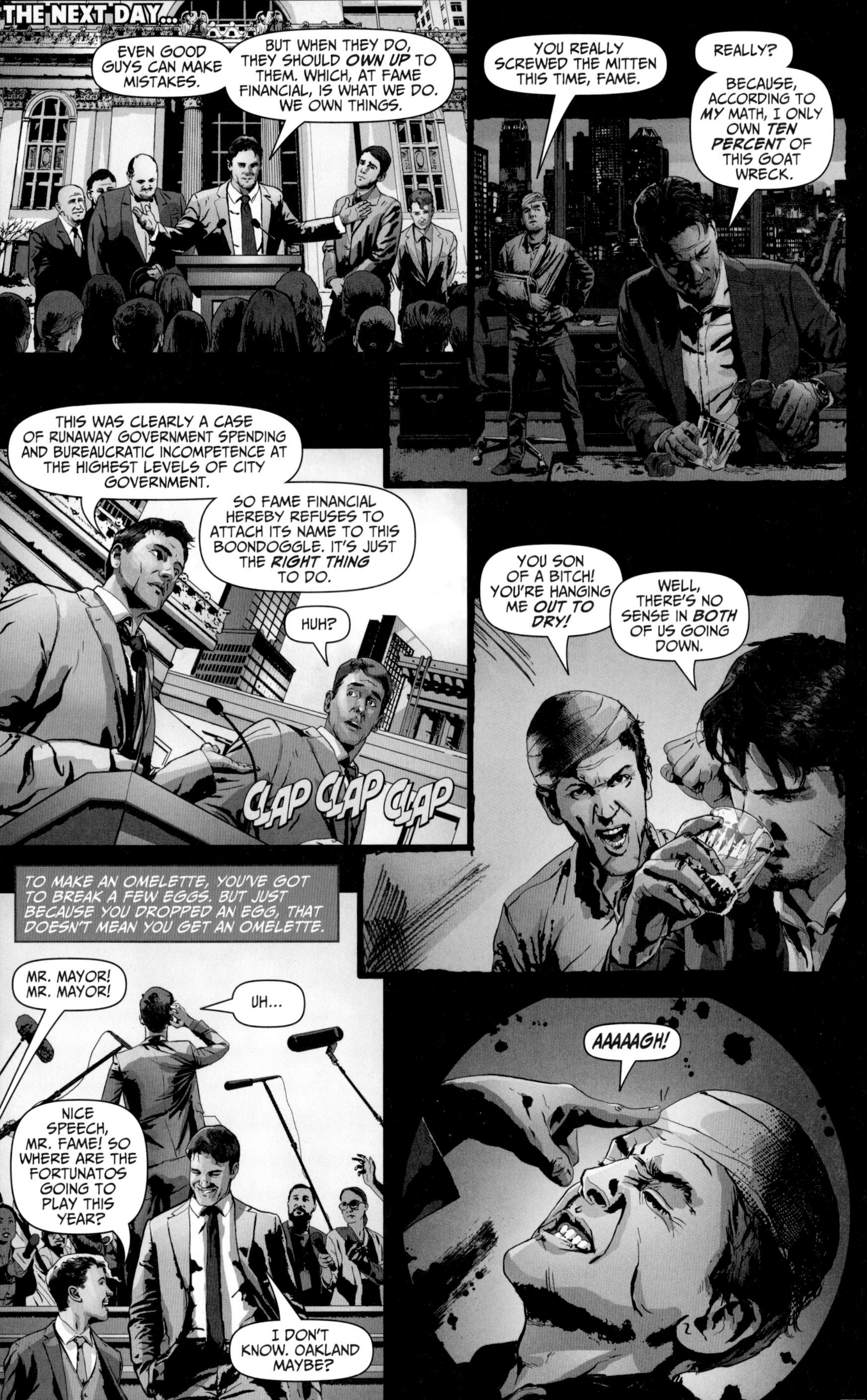
THE NEXT DAY...
EVEN GOOD GUYS CAN MAKE MISTAKES.
BUT WHEN THEY DO, THEY SHOULD OWN UP TO THEM. WHICH, AT FAME FINANCIAL, IS WHAT WE DO. WE OWN THINGS.
YOU REALLY SCREWED THE MITTEN THIS TIME, FAME.
REALLY?
BECAUSE, ACCORDING TO MY MATH, I ONLY OWN TEN PERCENT OF THIS GOAT WRECK.
THIS WAS CLEARLY A CASE OF RUNAWAY GOVERNMENT SPENDING AND BUREAUCRATIC INCOMPETENCE AT THE HIGHEST LEVELS OF CITY GOVERNMENT.
SO FAME FINANCIAL HEREBY REFUSES TO ATTACH ITS NAME TO THIS BOONDOGGLE. IT'S JUST THE RIGHT THING TO DO.
HUH?
CLAP CLAP CLAP
YOU SON OF A BITCH! YOU'RE HANGING ME OUT TO DRY!
WELL, THERE'S NO SENSE IN BOTH OF US GOING DOWN.
TO MAKE AN OMELETTE, YOU'VE GOT TO BREAK A FEW EGGS. BUT JUST BECAUSE YOU DROPPED AN EGG, THAT DOESN'T MEAN YOU GET AN OMELETTE.
MR. MAYOR! MR. MAYOR!
UH...
NICE SPEECH, MR. FAME! SO WHERE ARE THE FORTUNATOS GOING TO PLAY THIS YEAR?
I DON'T KNOW. OAKLAND MAYBE?
AAAAAGH!

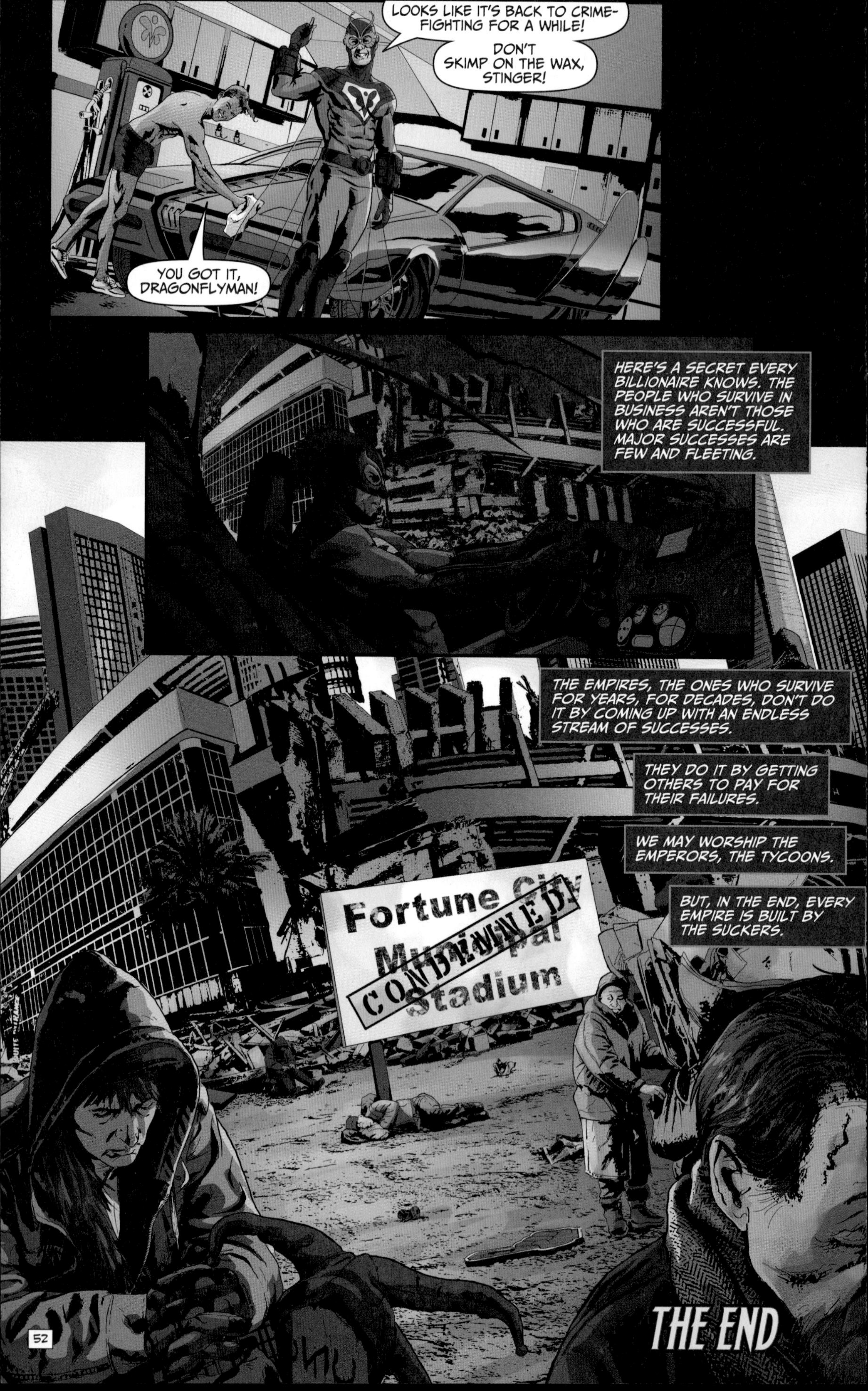
LOOKS LIKE IT'S BACK TO CRIME-FIGHTING FOR A WHILE!
DON'T SKIMP ON THE WAX, STINGER!
YOU GOT IT, DRAGONFLYMAN!
HERE'S A SECRET EVERY BILLIONAIRE KNOWS. THE PEOPLE WHO SURVIVE IN BUSINESS AREN'T THOSE WHO ARE SUCCESSFUL. MAJOR SUCCESSES ARE FEW AND FLEETING.
THE EMPIRES, THE ONES WHO SURVIVE FOR YEARS, FOR DECADES, DON'T DO IT BY COMING UP WITH AN ENDLESS STREAM OF SUCCESSES.
THEY DO IT BY GETTING OTHERS TO PAY FOR THEIR FAILURES.
WE MAY WORSHIP THE EMPERORS, THE TYCOONS.
BUT, IN THE END, EVERY EMPIRE IS BUILT BY THE SUCKERS.
Fortune City Municipal Stadium
CONDEMNED
THE END

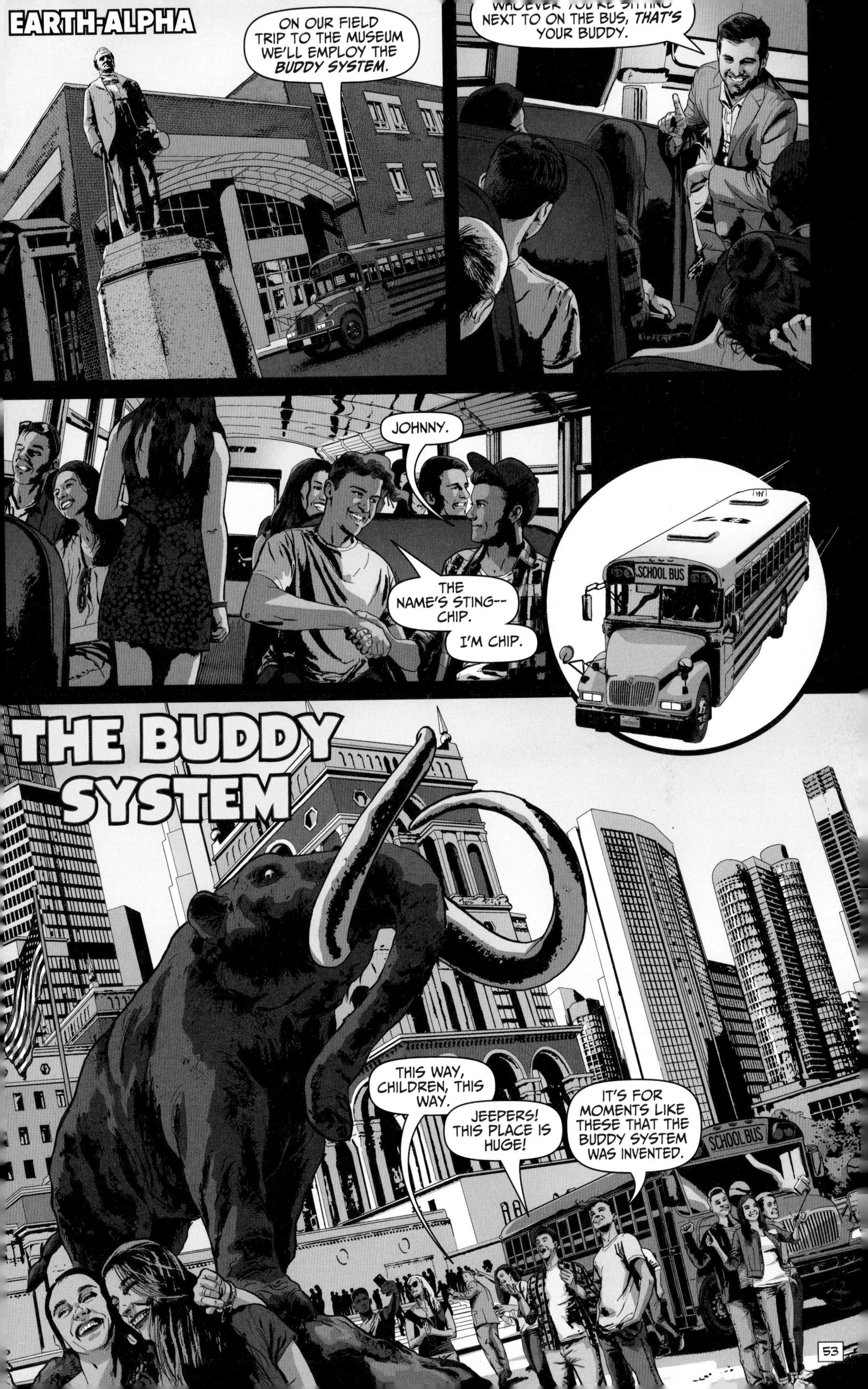
EARTH-ALPHA
ON OUR FIELD TRIP TO THE MUSEUM WE'LL EMPLOY THE *BUDDY SYSTEM.*
NEXT TO ON THE BUS, *THAT'S* YOUR BUDDY.
JOHNNY.
THE NAME'S STING-- CHIP.
I'M CHIP.
SCHOOL BUS
THE BUDDY SYSTEM
THIS WAY, CHILDREN, THIS WAY.
JEEPERS! THIS PLACE IS HUGE!
IT'S FOR MOMENTS LIKE THESE THAT THE BUDDY SYSTEM WAS INVENTED.
SCHOOL BUS

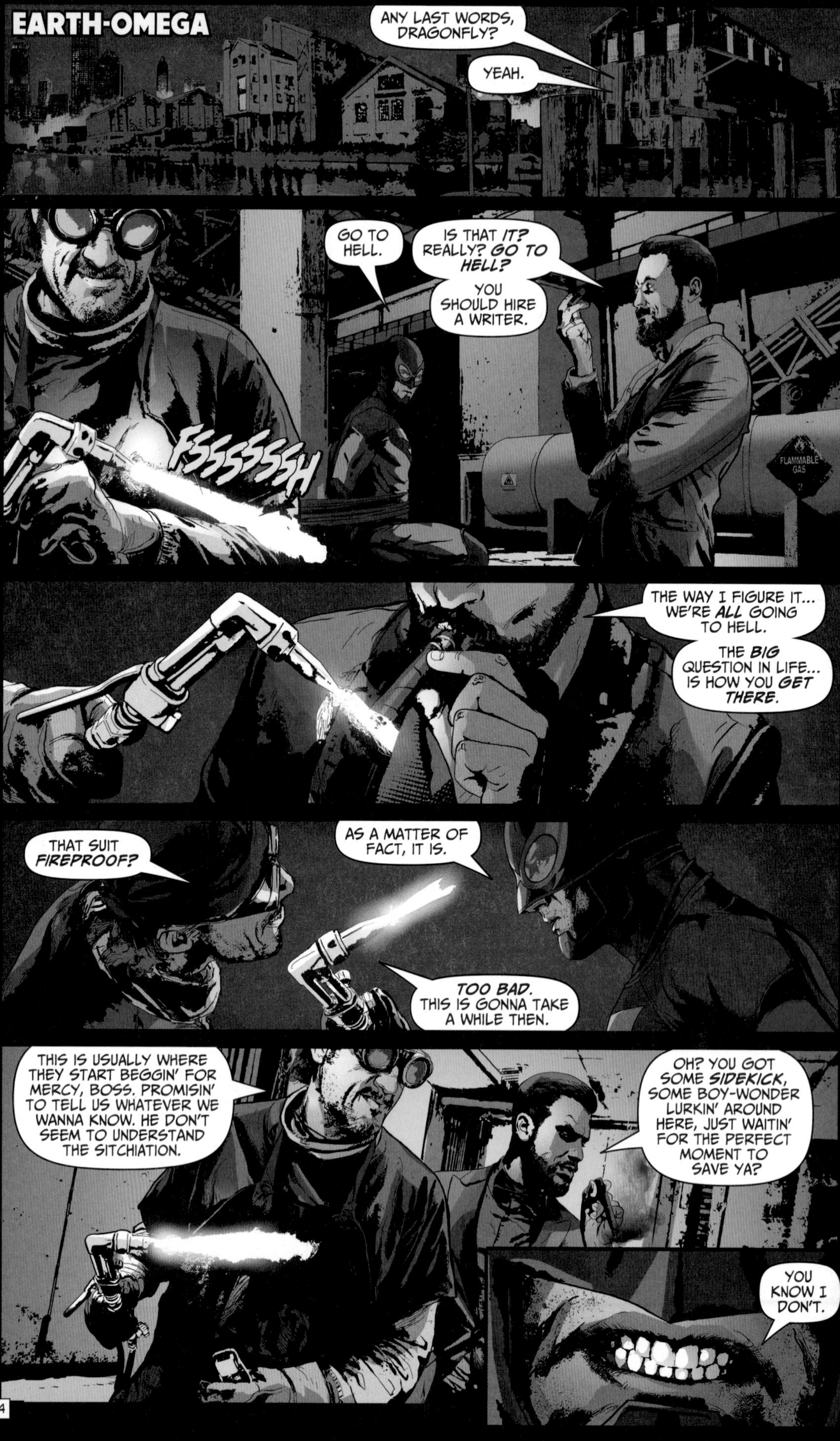
EARTH-OMEGA
ANY LAST WORDS, DRAGONFLY?
YEAH.
GO TO HELL.
IS THAT IT? REALLY? GO TO HELL?
YOU SHOULD HIRE A WRITER.
FSSSSSSH
THE WAY I FIGURE IT... WE'RE ALL GOING TO HELL.
THE BIG QUESTION IN LIFE... IS HOW YOU GET THERE.
THAT SUIT FIREPROOF?
AS A MATTER OF FACT, IT IS.
TOO BAD. THIS IS GONNA TAKE A WHILE THEN.
THIS IS USUALLY WHERE THEY START BEGGIN' FOR MERCY, BOSS. PROMISIN' TO TELL US WHATEVER WE WANNA KNOW. HE DON'T SEEM TO UNDERSTAND THE SITCHIATION.
OH? YOU GOT SOME SIDEKICK, SOME BOY-WONDER LURKIN' AROUND HERE, JUST WAITIN' FOR THE PERFECT MOMENT TO SAVE YA?
YOU KNOW I DON'T.

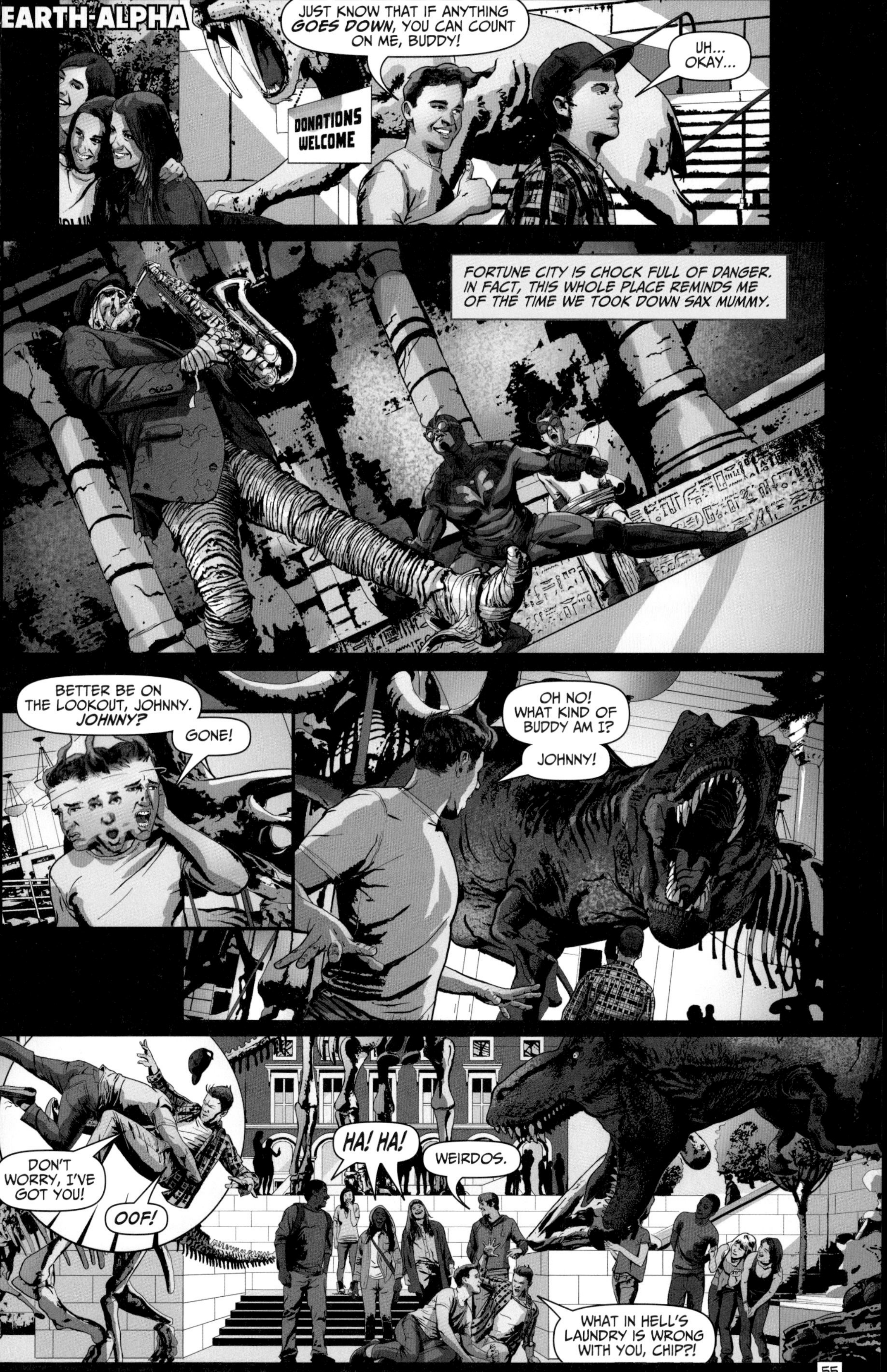
EARTH-ALPHA
JUST KNOW THAT IF ANYTHING GOES DOWN, YOU CAN COUNT ON ME, BUDDY!
UH... OKAY...
DONATIONS WELCOME
FORTUNE CITY IS CHOCK FULL OF DANGER. IN FACT, THIS WHOLE PLACE REMINDS ME OF THE TIME WE TOOK DOWN SAX MUMMY.
BETTER BE ON THE LOOKOUT, JOHNNY. JOHNNY?
GONE!
OH NO! WHAT KIND OF BUDDY AM I?
JOHNNY!
DON'T WORRY, I'VE GOT YOU!
OOF!
HA! HA!
WEIRDOS.
WHAT IN HELL'S LAUNDRY IS WRONG WITH YOU, CHIP?!

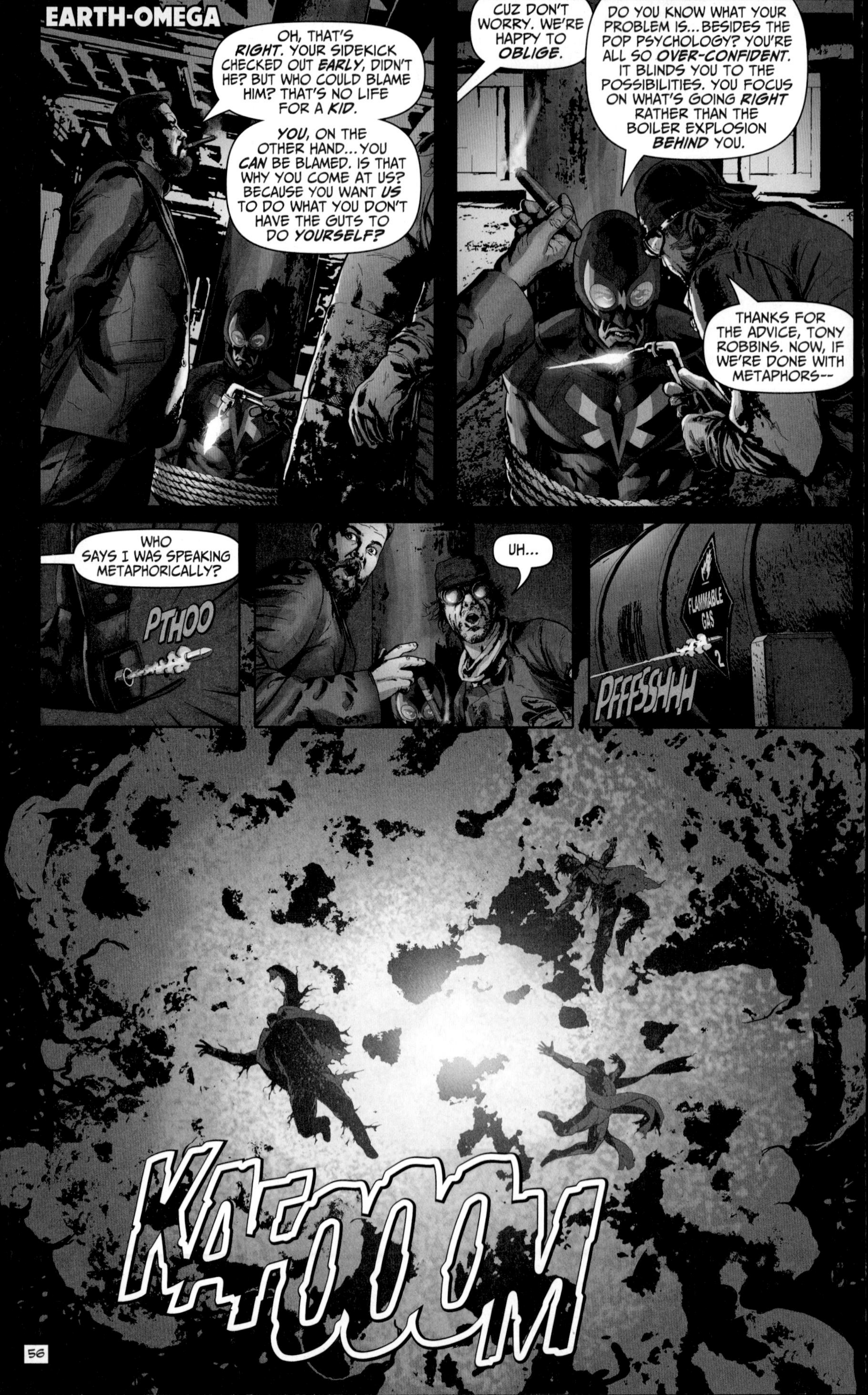
OH, THAT'S RIGHT. YOUR SIDEKICK CHECKED OUT EARLY, DIDN'T HE? BUT WHO COULD BLAME HIM? THAT'S NO LIFE FOR A KID.
YOU, ON THE OTHER HAND... YOU CAN BE BLAMED. IS THAT WHY YOU COME AT US? BECAUSE YOU WANT US TO DO WHAT YOU DON'T HAVE THE GUTS TO DO YOURSELF?
CUZ DON'T WORRY. WE'RE HAPPY TO OBLIGE.
DO YOU KNOW WHAT YOUR PROBLEM IS...BESIDES THE POP PSYCHOLOGY? YOU'RE ALL SO OVER-CONFIDENT. IT BLINDS YOU TO THE POSSIBILITIES. YOU FOCUS ON WHAT'S GOING RIGHT RATHER THAN THE BOILER EXPLOSION BEHIND YOU.
THANKS FOR THE ADVICE, TONY ROBBINS. NOW, IF WE'RE DONE WITH METAPHORS--
WHO SAYS I WAS SPEAKING METAPHORICALLY?
PTHOO
UH...
FLAMMABLE GAS
2
PFFFSSHHH
KATOOOM

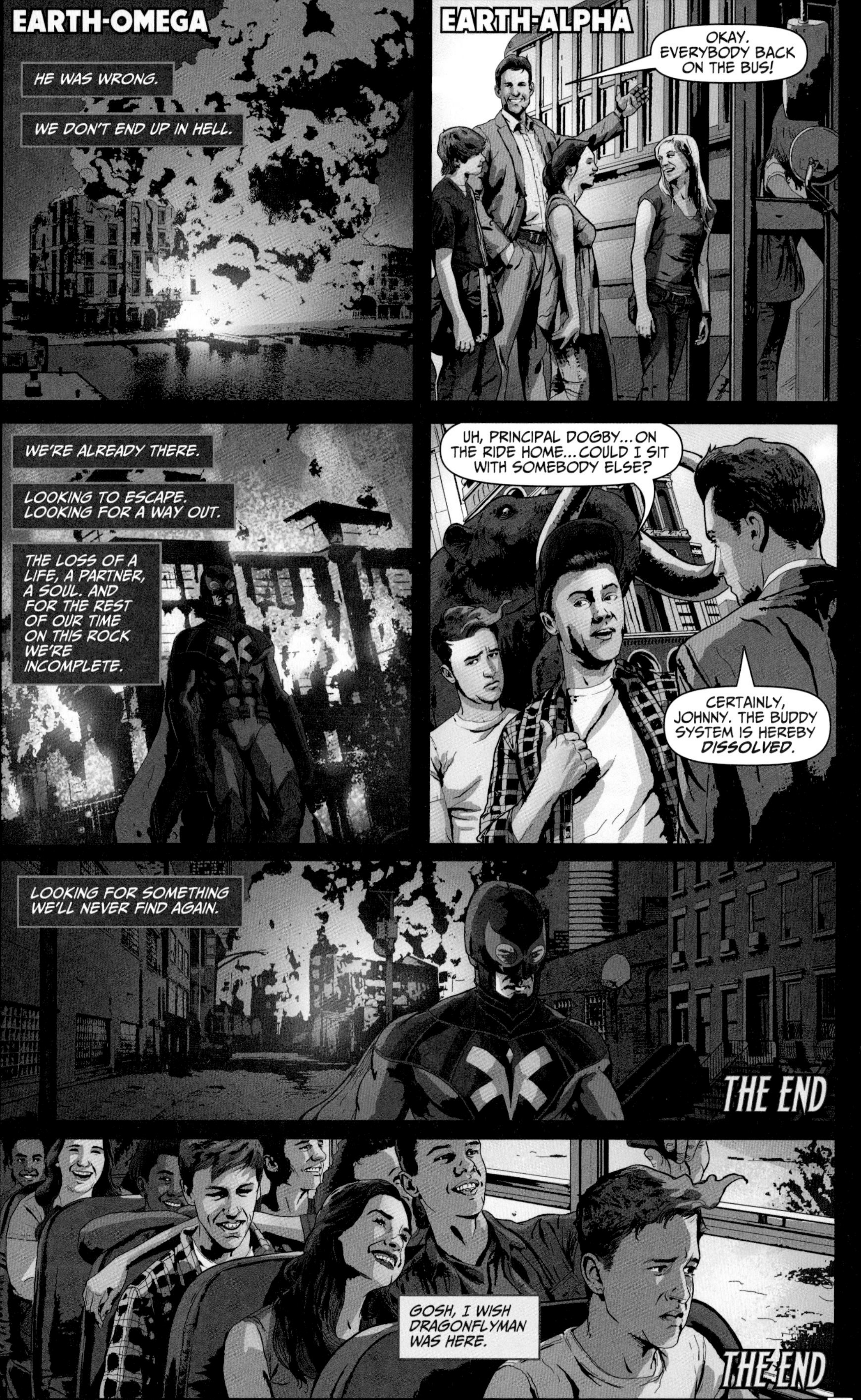
EARTH-OMEGA
HE WAS WRONG.
WE DON'T END UP IN HELL.
EARTH-ALPHA
OKAY. EVERYBODY BACK ON THE BUS!
WE'RE ALREADY THERE.
LOOKING TO ESCAPE. LOOKING FOR A WAY OUT.
THE LOSS OF A LIFE, A PARTNER, A SOUL. AND FOR THE REST OF OUR TIME ON THIS ROCK WE'RE INCOMPLETE.
UH, PRINCIPAL DOGBY... ON THE RIDE HOME... COULD I SIT WITH SOMEBODY ELSE?
CERTAINLY, JOHNNY. THE BUDDY SYSTEM IS HEREBY DISSOLVED.
LOOKING FOR SOMETHING WE'LL NEVER FIND AGAIN.
THE END
GOSH, I WISH DRAGONFLYMAN WAS HERE.
THE END

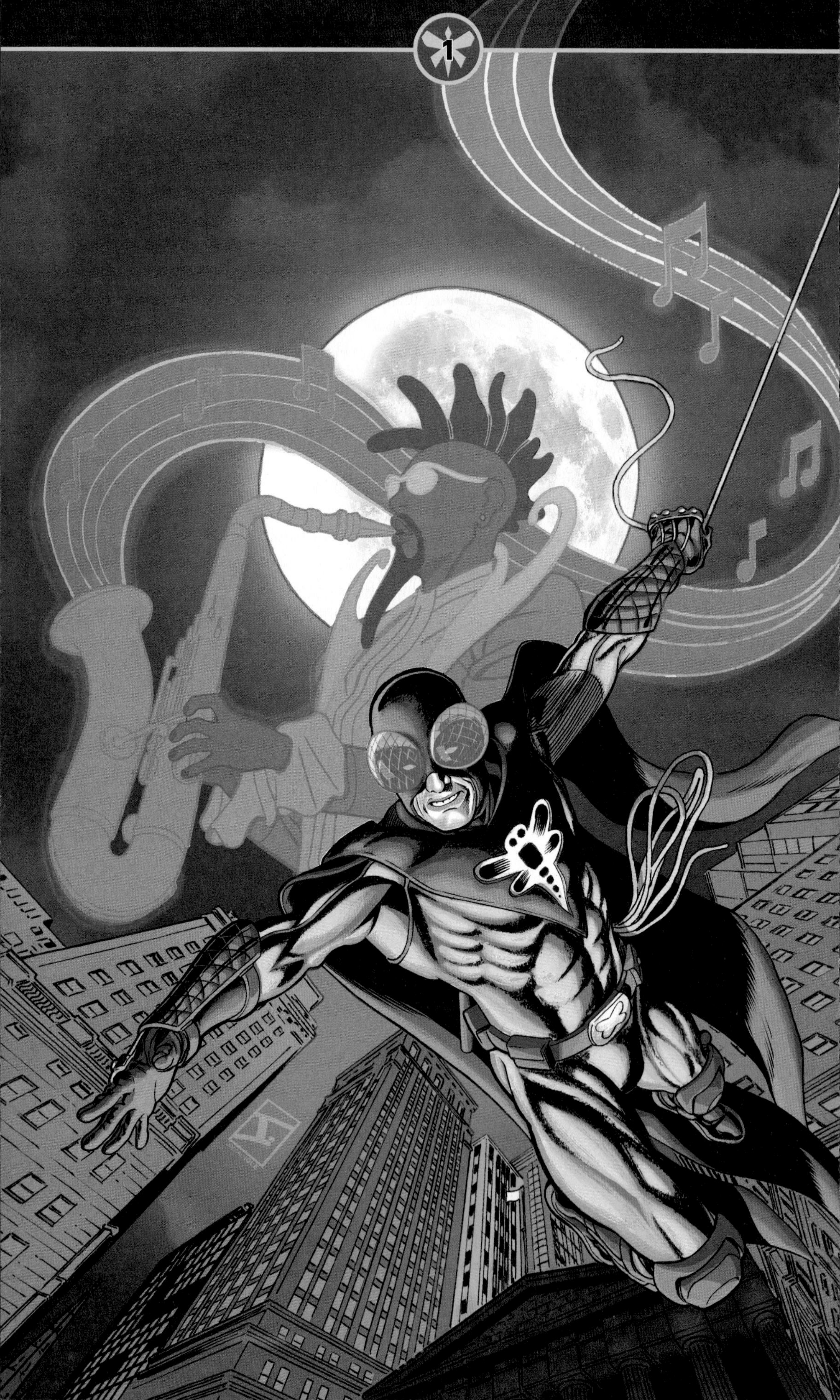
1

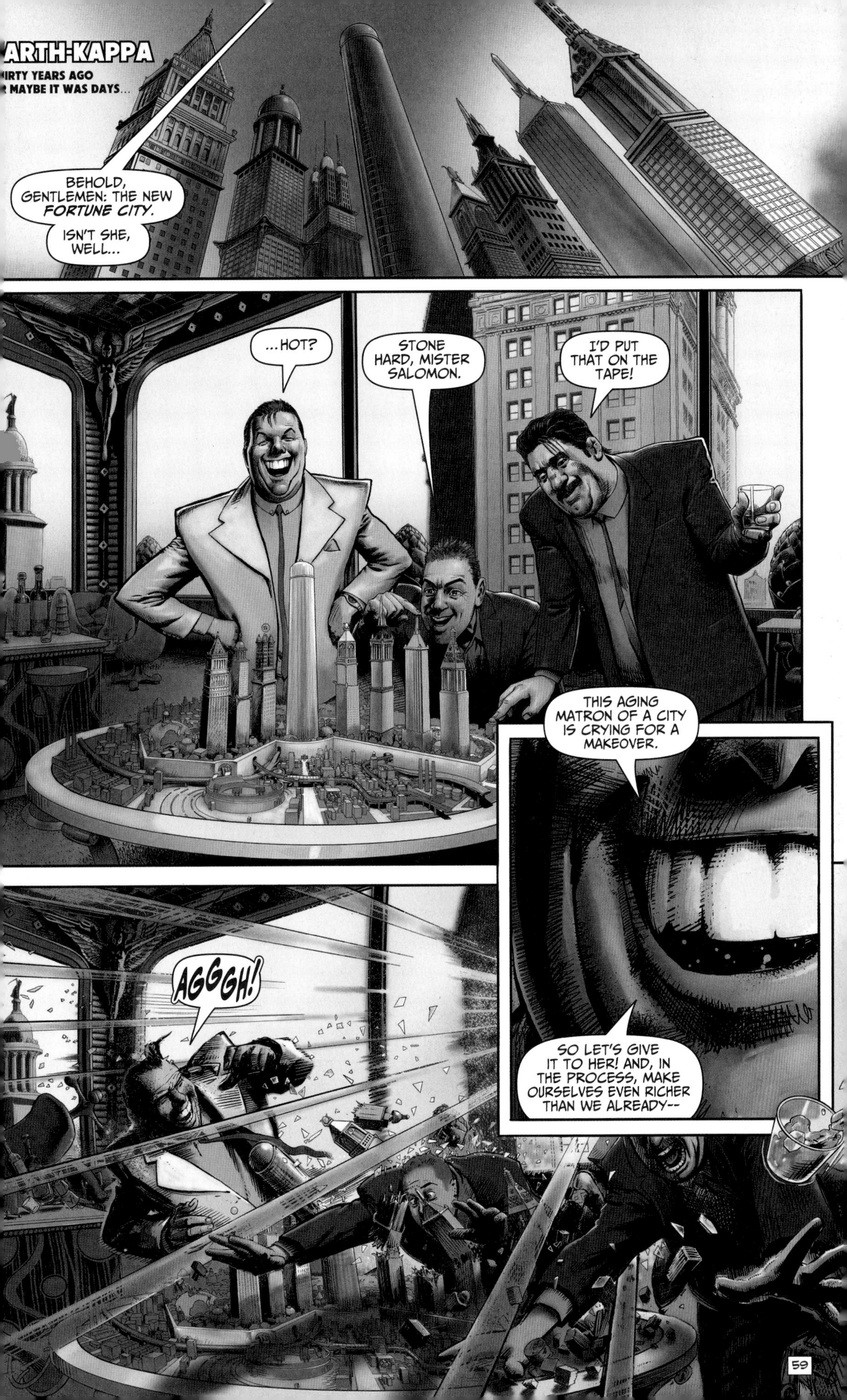

ARTH-KAPPA
IRTY YEARS AGO
R MAYBE IT WAS DAYS...
BEHOLD, GENTLEMEN: THE NEW FORTUNE CITY.
ISN'T SHE, WELL...
...HOT?
STONE HARD, MISTER SALOMON.
I'D PUT THAT ON THE TAPE!
THIS AGING MATRON OF A CITY IS CRYING FOR A MAKEOVER.
SO LET'S GIVE IT TO HER! AND, IN THE PROCESS, MAKE OURSELVES EVEN RICHER THAN WE ALREADY--
AGGGH!

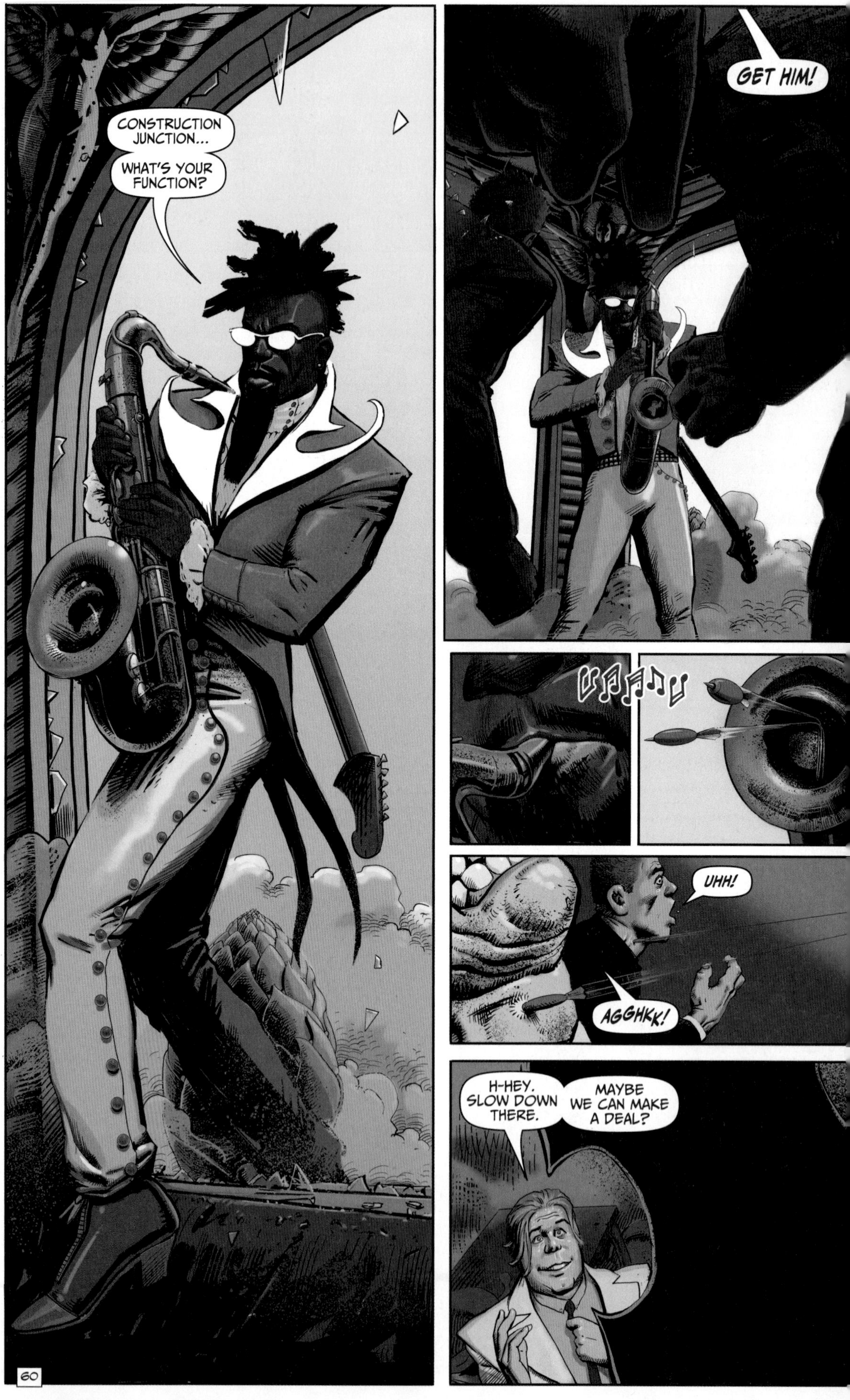
CONSTRUCTION JUNCTION...
WHAT'S YOUR FUNCTION?
GET HIM!
UHH!
AGGHKK!
H-HEY. SLOW DOWN THERE.
MAYBE WE CAN MAKE A DEAL?

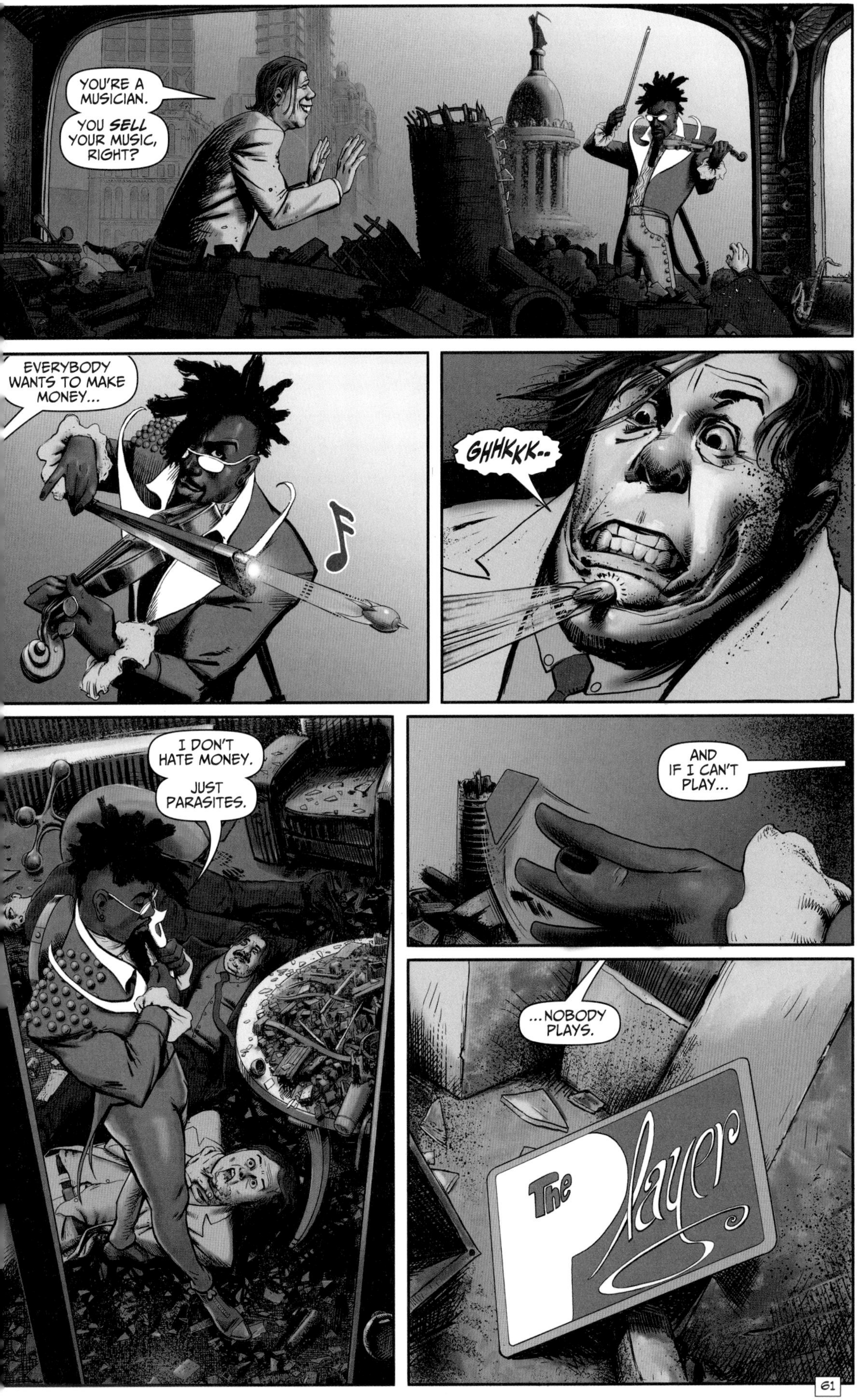
YOU'RE A MUSICIAN.
YOU SELL YOUR MUSIC, RIGHT?
EVERYBODY WANTS TO MAKE MONEY...
GHHKKK..
I DON'T HATE MONEY.
JUST PARASITES.
AND IF I CAN'T PLAY...
...NOBODY PLAYS.
The Player

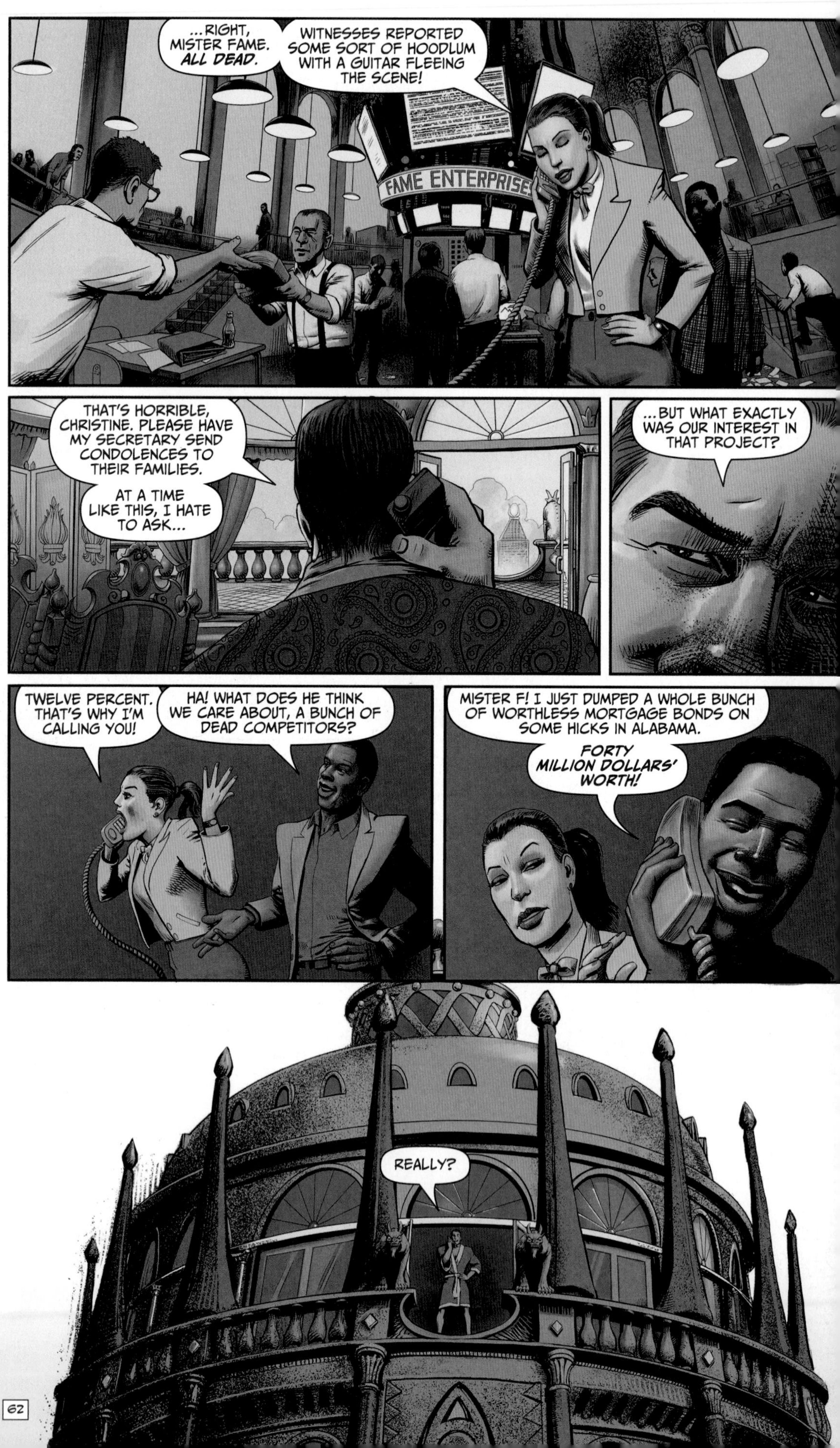
...RIGHT, MISTER FAME. ALL DEAD.
WITNESSES REPORTED SOME SORT OF HOODLUM WITH A GUITAR FLEEING THE SCENE!
FAME ENTERPRISES
THAT'S HORRIBLE, CHRISTINE. PLEASE HAVE MY SECRETARY SEND CONDOLENCES TO THEIR FAMILIES.
AT A TIME LIKE THIS, I HATE TO ASK...
...BUT WHAT EXACTLY WAS OUR INTEREST IN THAT PROJECT?
TWELVE PERCENT. THAT'S WHY I'M CALLING YOU!
HA! WHAT DOES HE THINK WE CARE ABOUT, A BUNCH OF DEAD COMPETITORS?
MISTER F! I JUST DUMPED A WHOLE BUNCH OF WORTHLESS MORTGAGE BONDS ON SOME HICKS IN ALABAMA.
FORTY MILLION DOLLARS' WORTH!
REALLY?

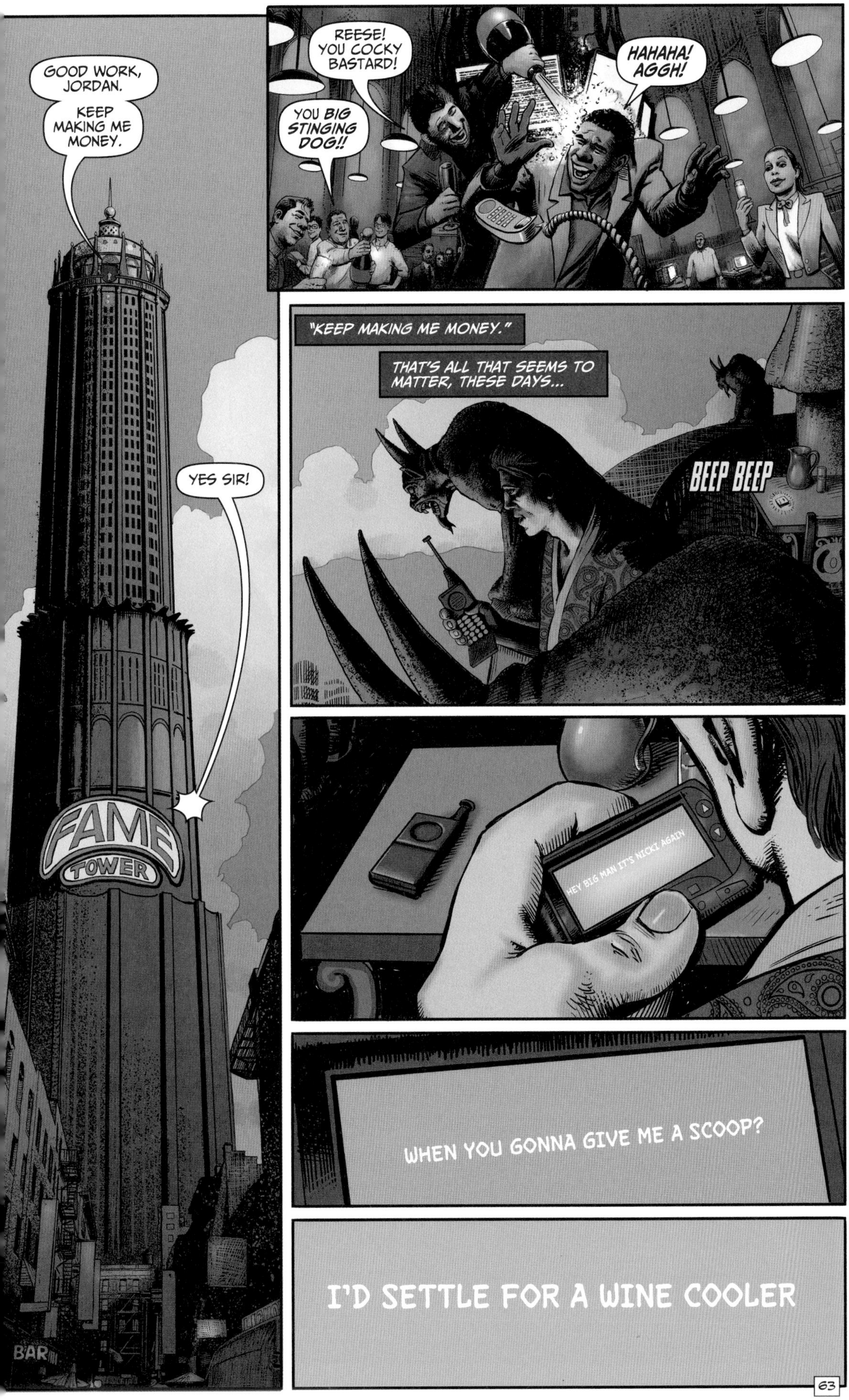
GOOD WORK, JORDAN.
KEEP MAKING ME MONEY.
YES SIR!
REESE! YOU COCKY BASTARD!
YOU BIG STINGING DOG!!
HAHAHA! AGGH!
FAME TOWER
BAR
"KEEP MAKING ME MONEY."
THAT'S ALL THAT SEEMS TO MATTER, THESE DAYS...
BEEP BEEP
HEY BIG MAN IT'S NICKI AGAIN
WHEN YOU GONNA GIVE ME A SCOOP?
I'D SETTLE FOR A WINE COOLER

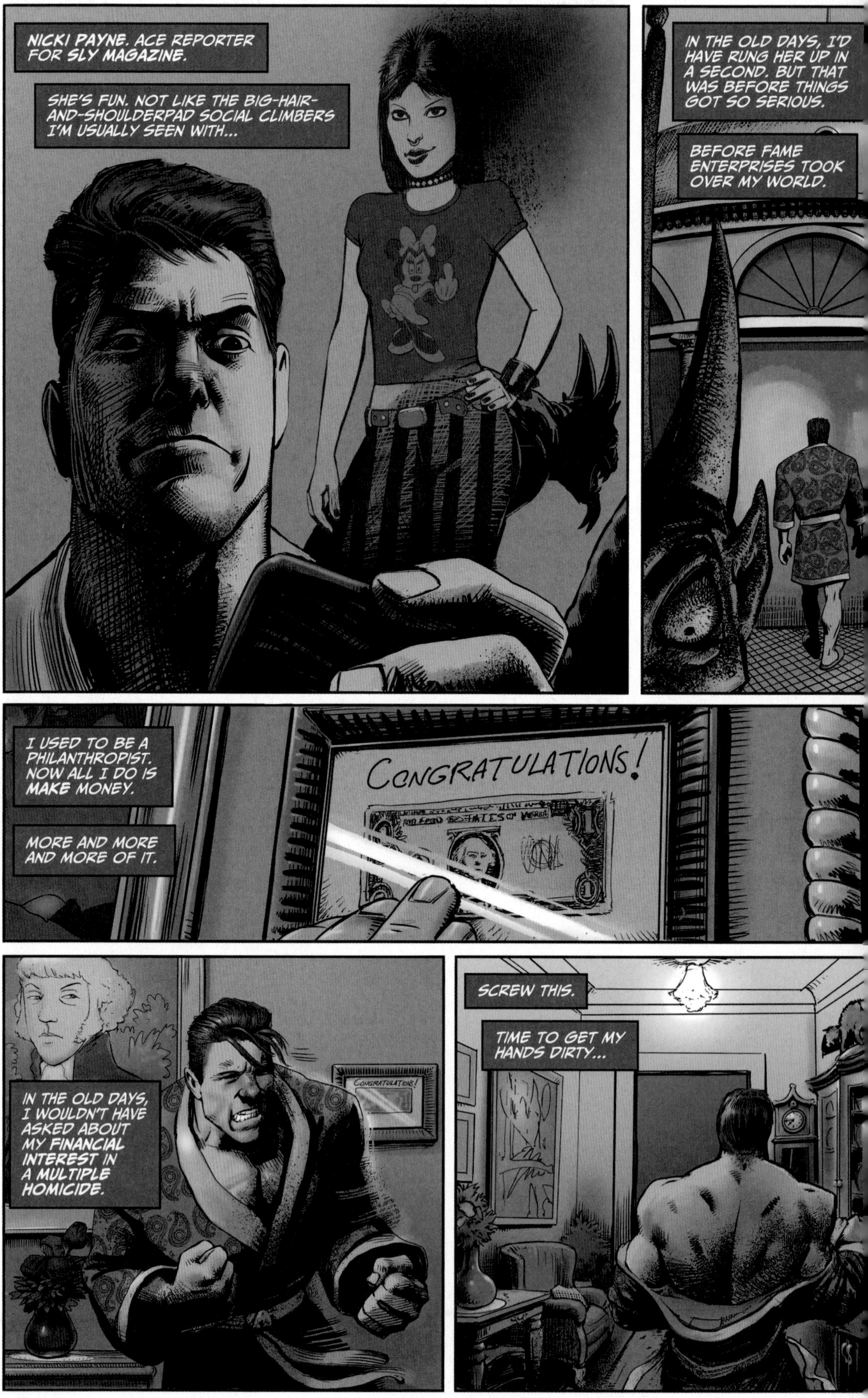
NICKI PAYNE. ACE REPORTER FOR SLY MAGAZINE.
SHE'S FUN. NOT LIKE THE BIG-HAIR-AND-SHOULDERPAD SOCIAL CLIMBERS I'M USUALLY SEEN WITH...
IN THE OLD DAYS, I'D HAVE RUNG HER UP IN A SECOND. BUT THAT WAS BEFORE THINGS GOT SO SERIOUS.
BEFORE FAME ENTERPRISES TOOK OVER MY WORLD.
I USED TO BE A PHILANTHROPIST. NOW ALL I DO IS MAKE MONEY.
MORE AND MORE AND MORE OF IT.
CONGRATULATIONS!
IN THE OLD DAYS, I WOULDN'T HAVE ASKED ABOUT MY FINANCIAL INTEREST IN A MULTIPLE HOMICIDE.
CONGRATULATIONS!
SCREW THIS.
TIME TO GET MY HANDS DIRTY...

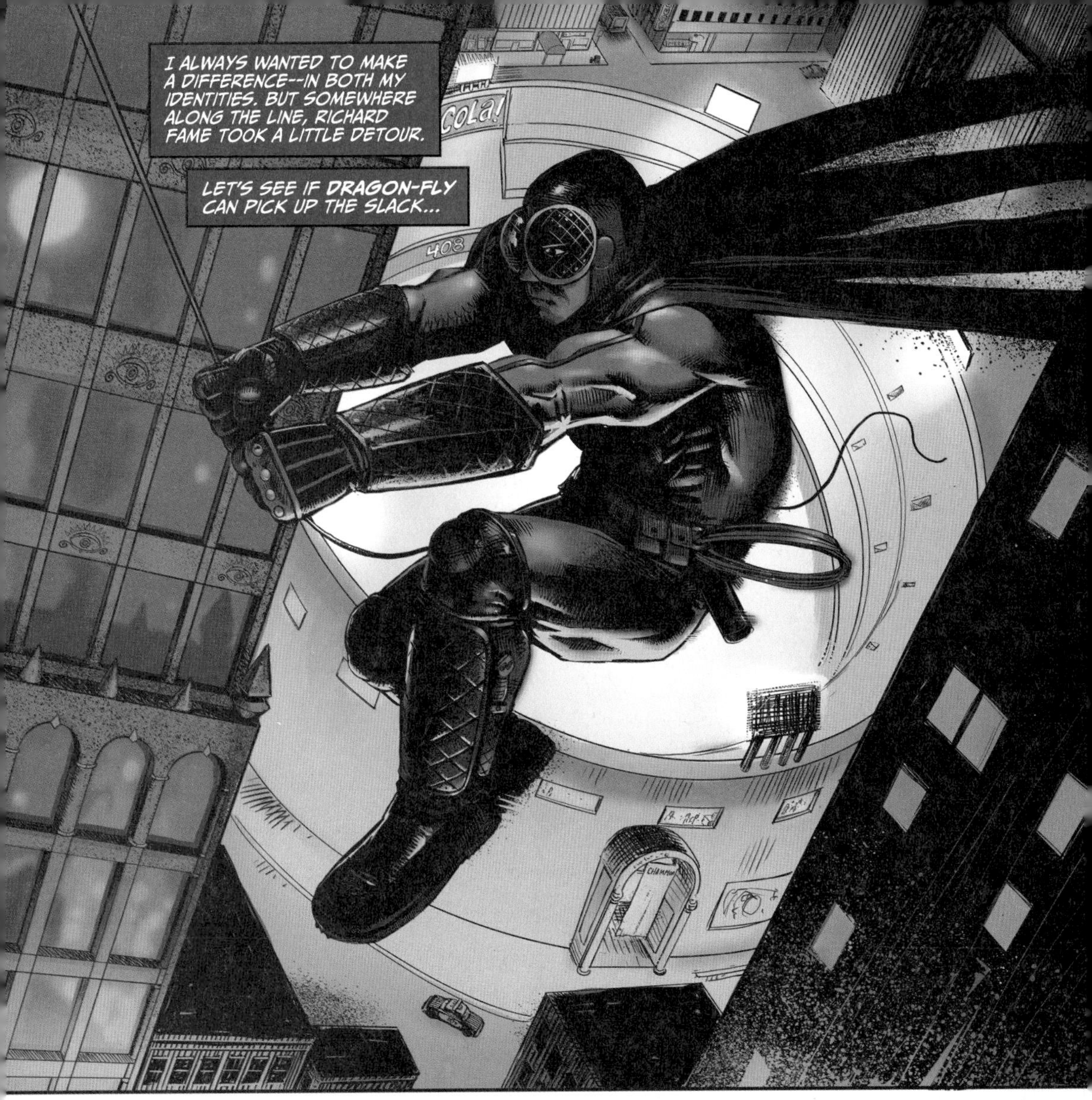
I ALWAYS WANTED TO MAKE A DIFFERENCE--IN BOTH MY IDENTITIES. BUT SOMEWHERE ALONG THE LINE, RICHARD FAME TOOK A LITTLE DETOUR.
LET'S SEE IF DRAGON-FLY CAN PICK UP THE SLACK...
Cola!
408

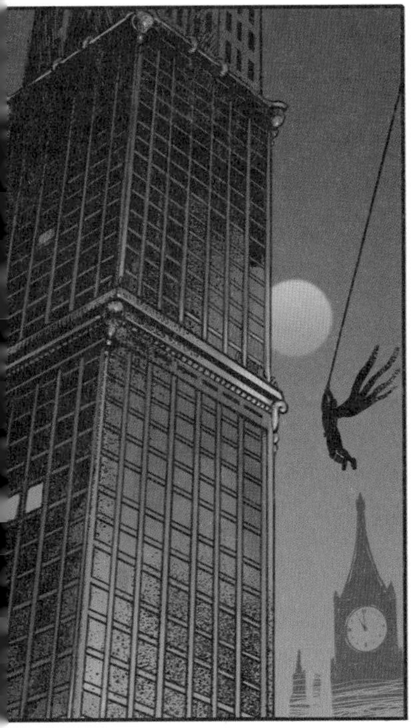

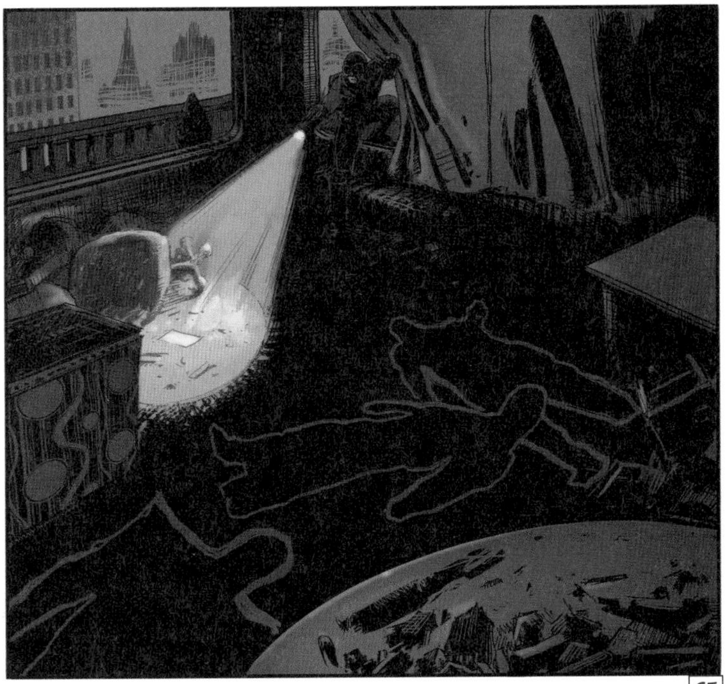

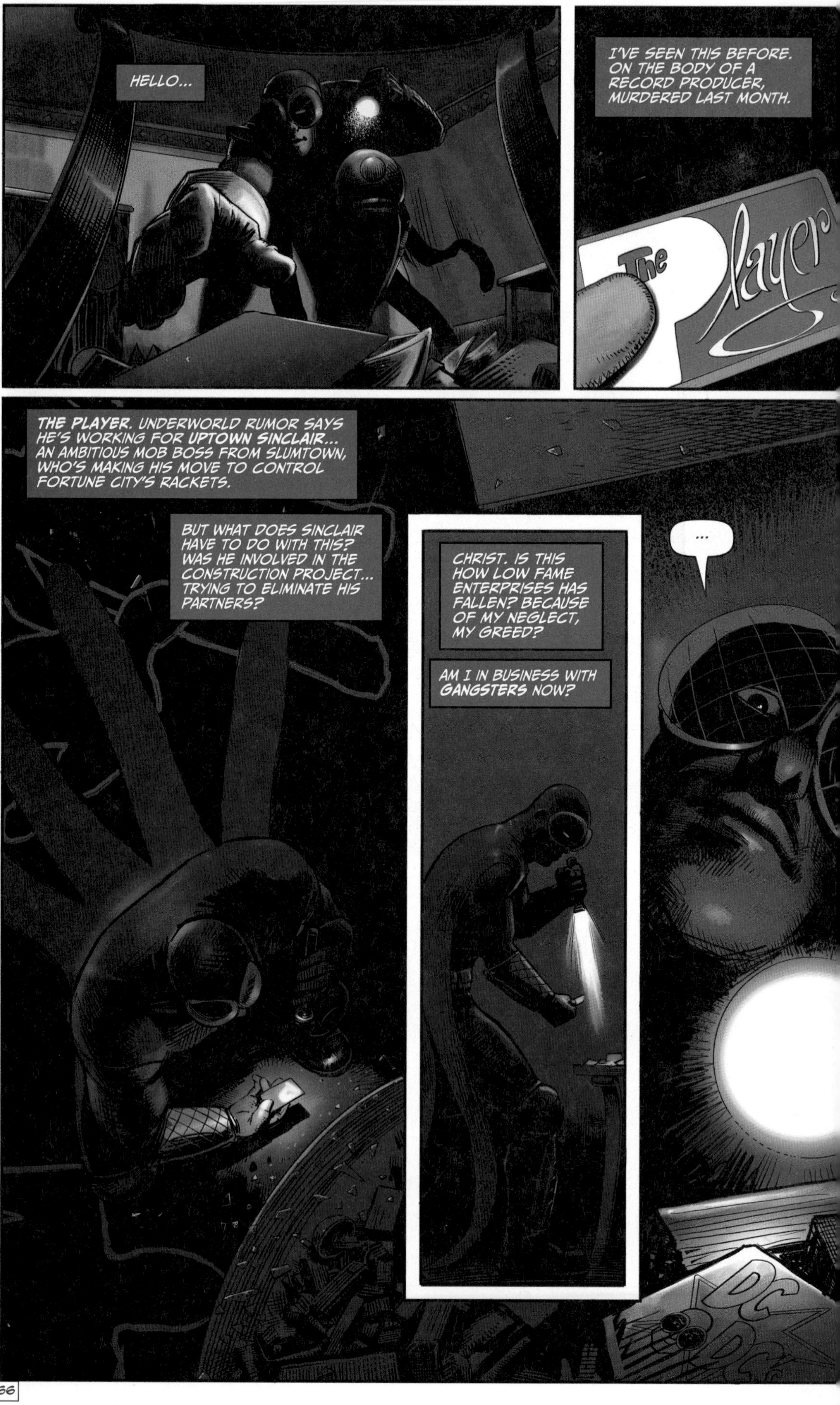

HELLO...
I'VE SEEN THIS BEFORE. ON THE BODY OF A RECORD PRODUCER, MURDERED LAST MONTH.
The Player
THE PLAYER. UNDERWORLD RUMOR SAYS HE'S WORKING FOR UPTOWN SINCLAIR... AN AMBITIOUS MOB BOSS FROM SLUMTOWN, WHO'S MAKING HIS MOVE TO CONTROL FORTUNE CITY'S RACKETS.
BUT WHAT DOES SINCLAIR HAVE TO DO WITH THIS? WAS HE INVOLVED IN THE CONSTRUCTION PROJECT... TRYING TO ELIMINATE HIS PARTNERS?
CHRIST. IS THIS HOW LOW FAME ENTERPRISES HAS FALLEN? BECAUSE OF MY NEGLECT, MY GREED?
AM I IN BUSINESS WITH GANGSTERS NOW?
...

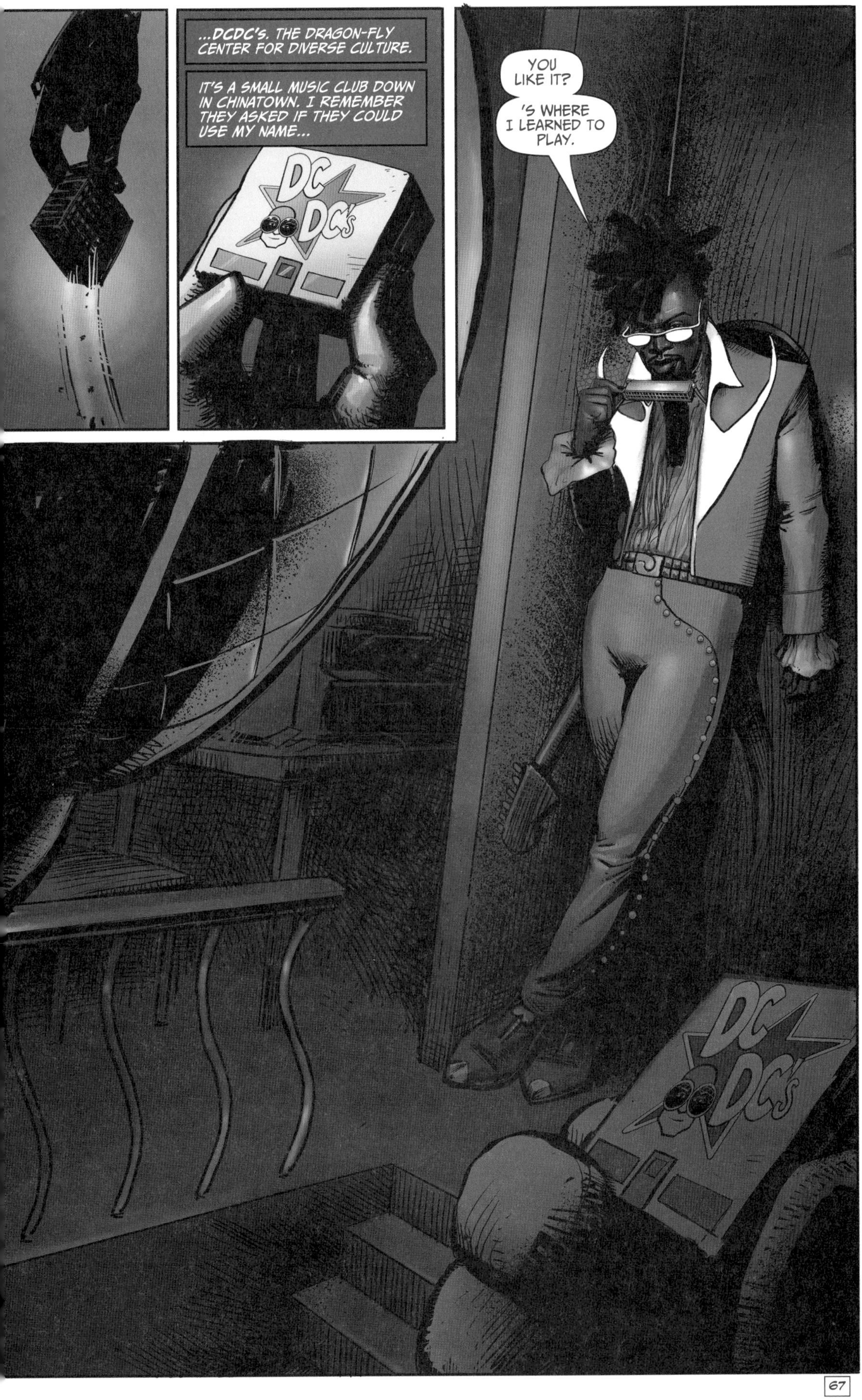
...DCDC's, THE DRAGON-FLY CENTER FOR DIVERSE CULTURE.
IT'S A SMALL MUSIC CLUB DOWN IN CHINATOWN. I REMEMBER THEY ASKED IF THEY COULD USE MY NAME...
DC DC's
YOU LIKE IT?
'S WHERE I LEARNED TO PLAY.
DC DC's

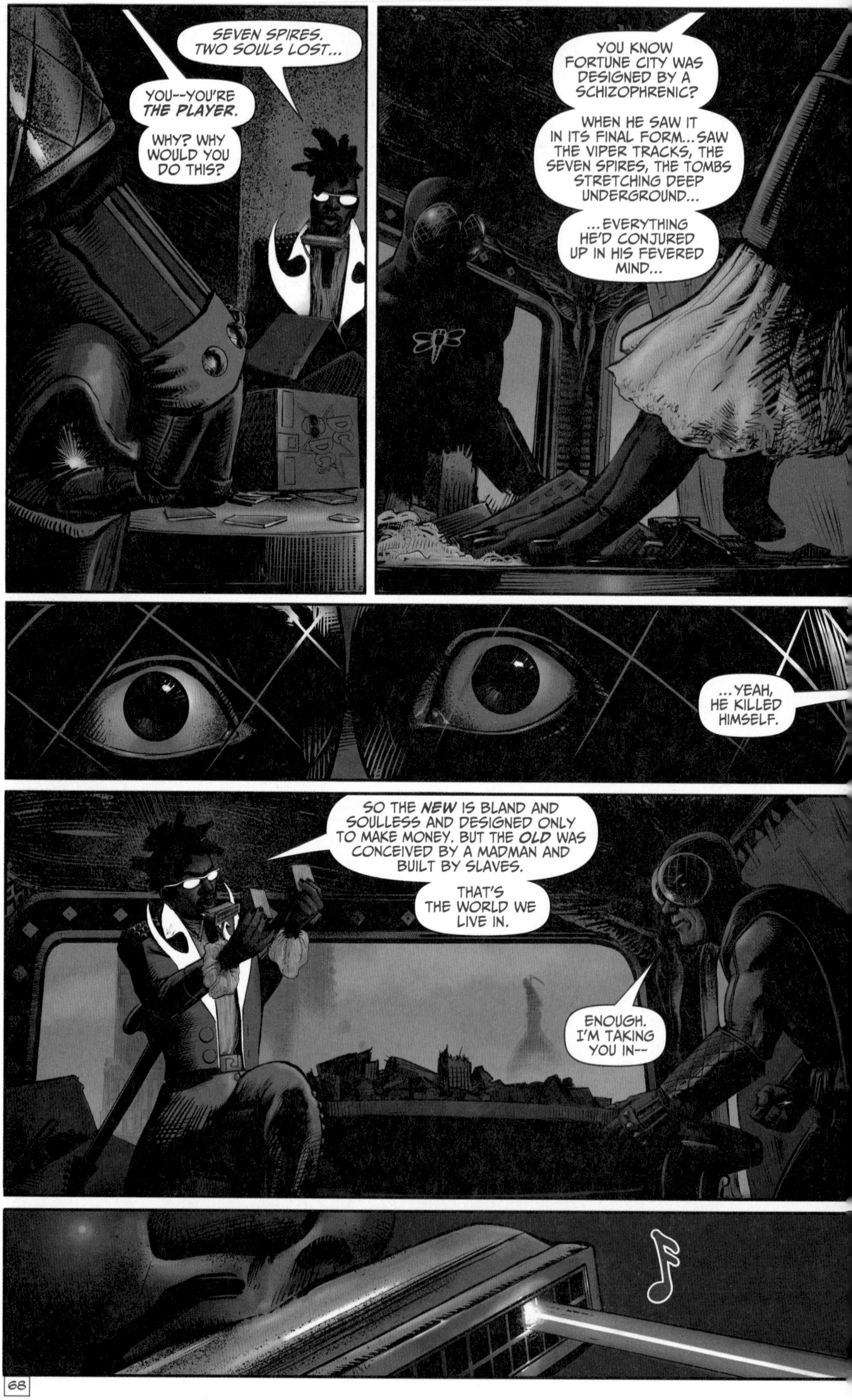
SEVEN SPIRES. TWO SOULS LOST...
YOU--YOU'RE THE PLAYER.
WHY? WHY WOULD YOU DO THIS?
YOU KNOW FORTUNE CITY WAS DESIGNED BY A SCHIZOPHRENIC?
WHEN HE SAW IT IN ITS FINAL FORM...SAW THE VIPER TRACKS, THE SEVEN SPIRES, THE TOMBS STRETCHING DEEP UNDERGROUND...
...EVERYTHING HE'D CONJURED UP IN HIS FEVERED MIND...
...YEAH, HE KILLED HIMSELF.
SO THE NEW IS BLAND AND SOULLESS AND DESIGNED ONLY TO MAKE MONEY. BUT THE OLD WAS CONCEIVED BY A MADMAN AND BUILT BY SLAVES.
THAT'S THE WORLD WE LIVE IN.
ENOUGH. I'M TAKING YOU IN--

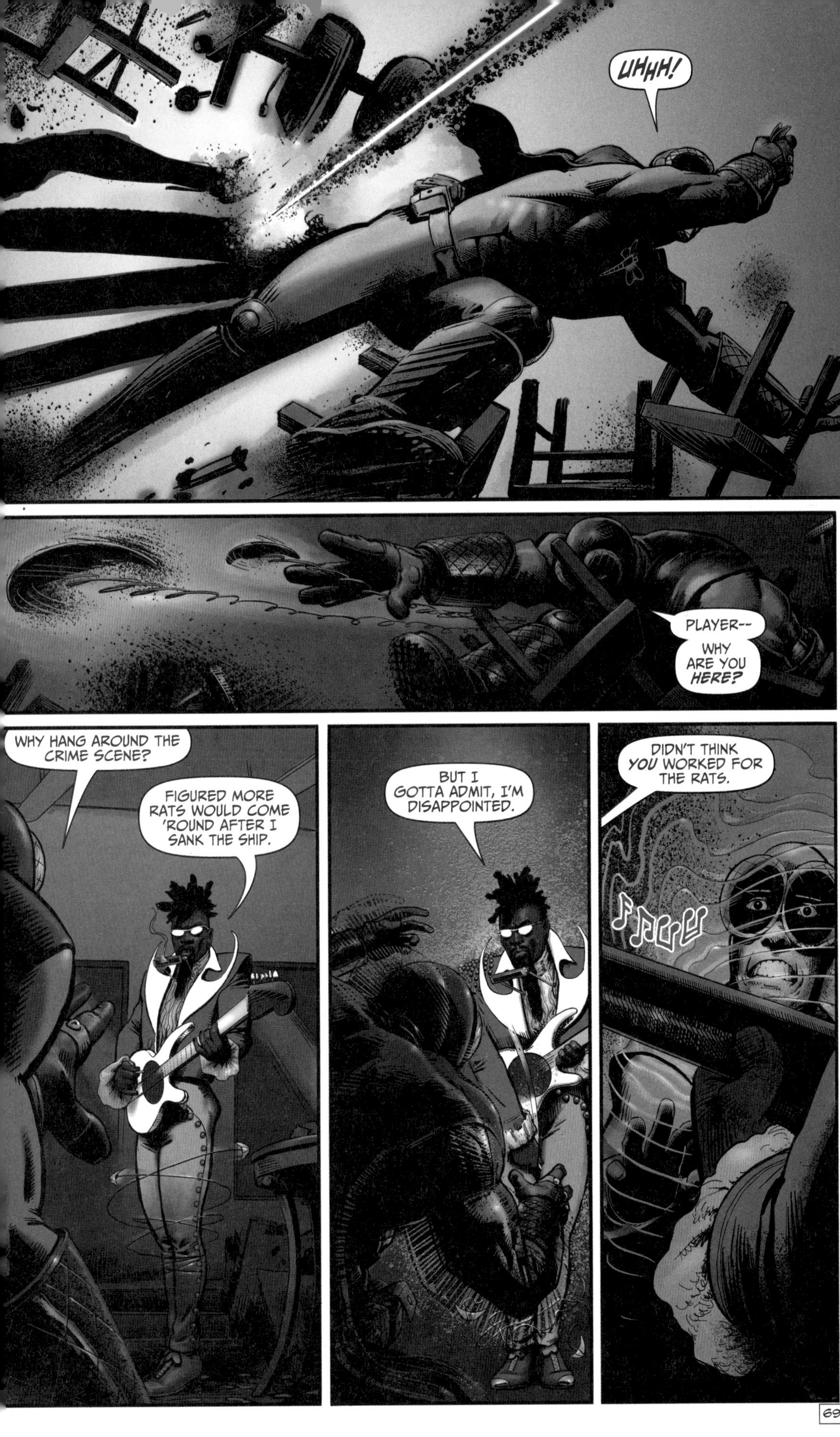
UHHH!
PLAYER--
WHY ARE YOU *HERE?*
WHY HANG AROUND THE CRIME SCENE?
FIGURED MORE RATS WOULD COME 'ROUND AFTER I SANK THE SHIP.
BUT I GOTTA ADMIT, I'M DISAPPOINTED.
DIDN'T THINK *YOU* WORKED FOR THE RATS.

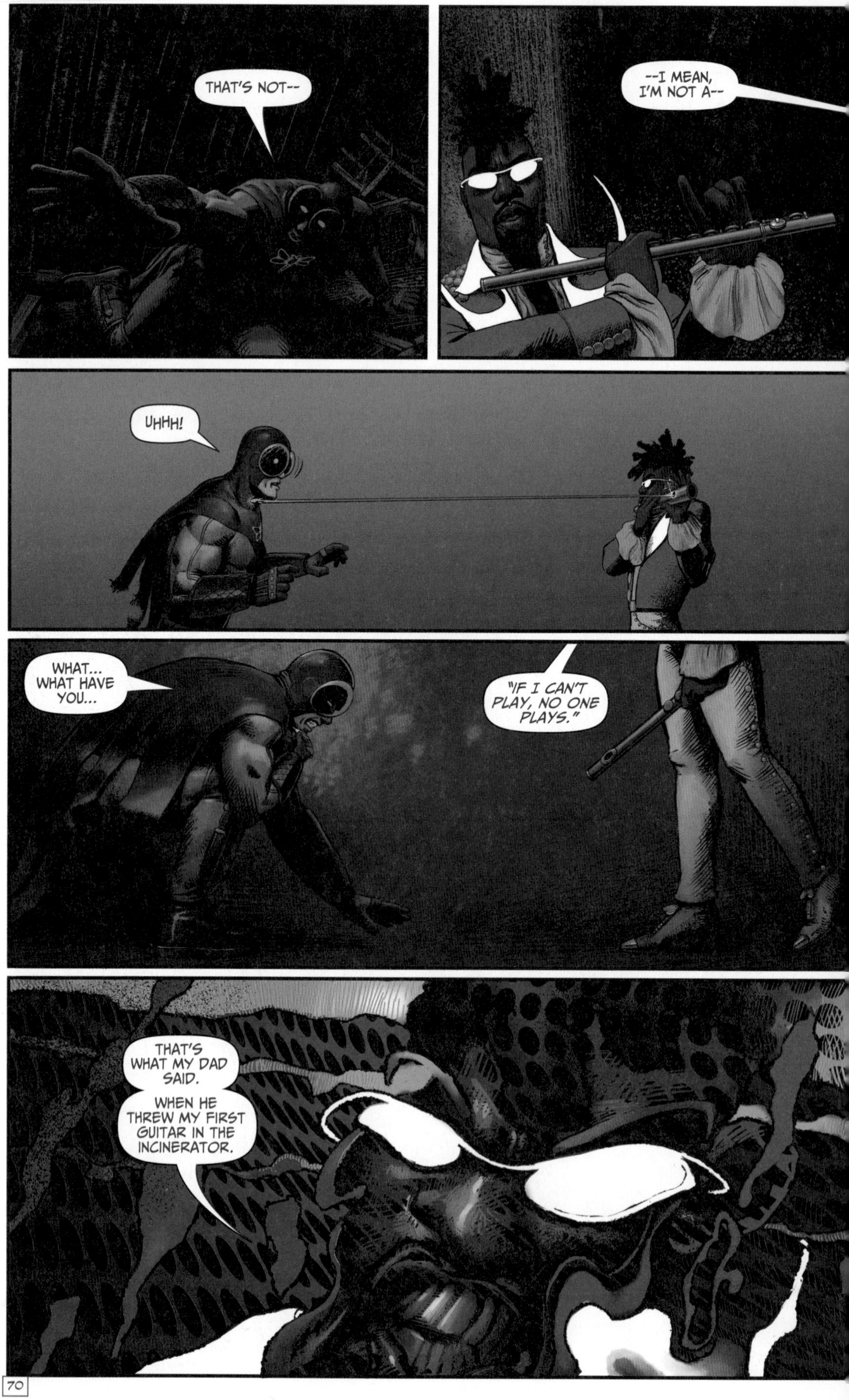
THAT'S NOT--
--I MEAN, I'M NOT A--
UHHH!
WHAT... WHAT HAVE YOU...
"IF I CAN'T PLAY, NO ONE PLAYS."
THAT'S WHAT MY DAD SAID.
WHEN HE THREW MY FIRST GUITAR IN THE INCINERATOR.

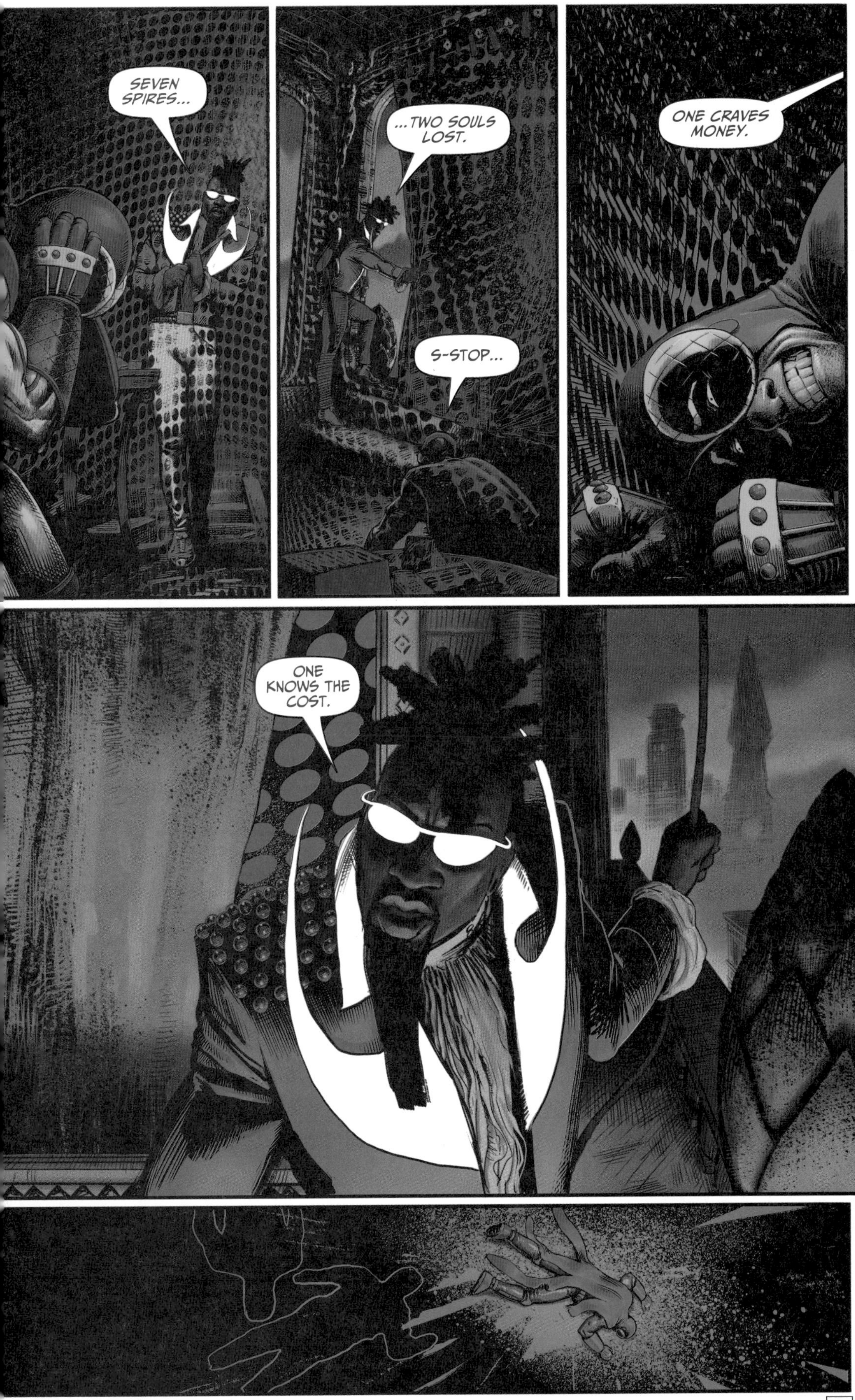
SEVEN SPIRES...
...TWO SOULS LOST.
S-STOP...
ONE CRAVES MONEY.
ONE KNOWS THE COST.

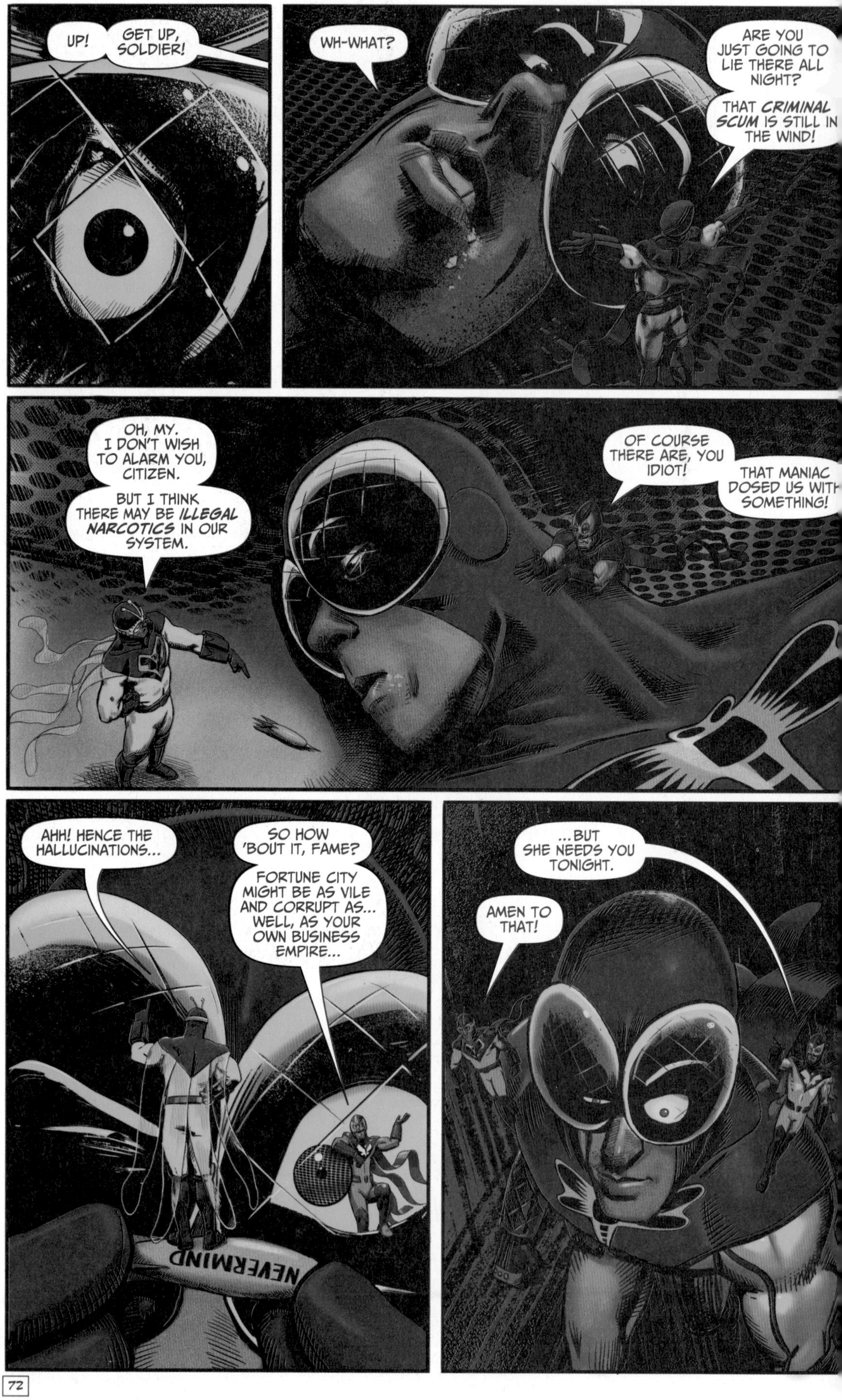

UP!
GET UP, SOLDIER!
WH-WHAT?
ARE YOU JUST GOING TO LIE THERE ALL NIGHT?
THAT CRIMINAL SCUM IS STILL IN THE WIND!
OH, MY. I DON'T WISH TO ALARM YOU, CITIZEN.
BUT I THINK THERE MAY BE ILLEGAL NARCOTICS IN OUR SYSTEM.
OF COURSE THERE ARE, YOU IDIOT!
THAT MANIAC DOSED US WITH SOMETHING!
AHH! HENCE THE HALLUCINATIONS...
SO HOW 'BOUT IT, FAME?
FORTUNE CITY MIGHT BE AS VILE AND CORRUPT AS... WELL, AS YOUR OWN BUSINESS EMPIRE...
NEVERMIND
...BUT SHE NEEDS YOU TONIGHT.
AMEN TO THAT!

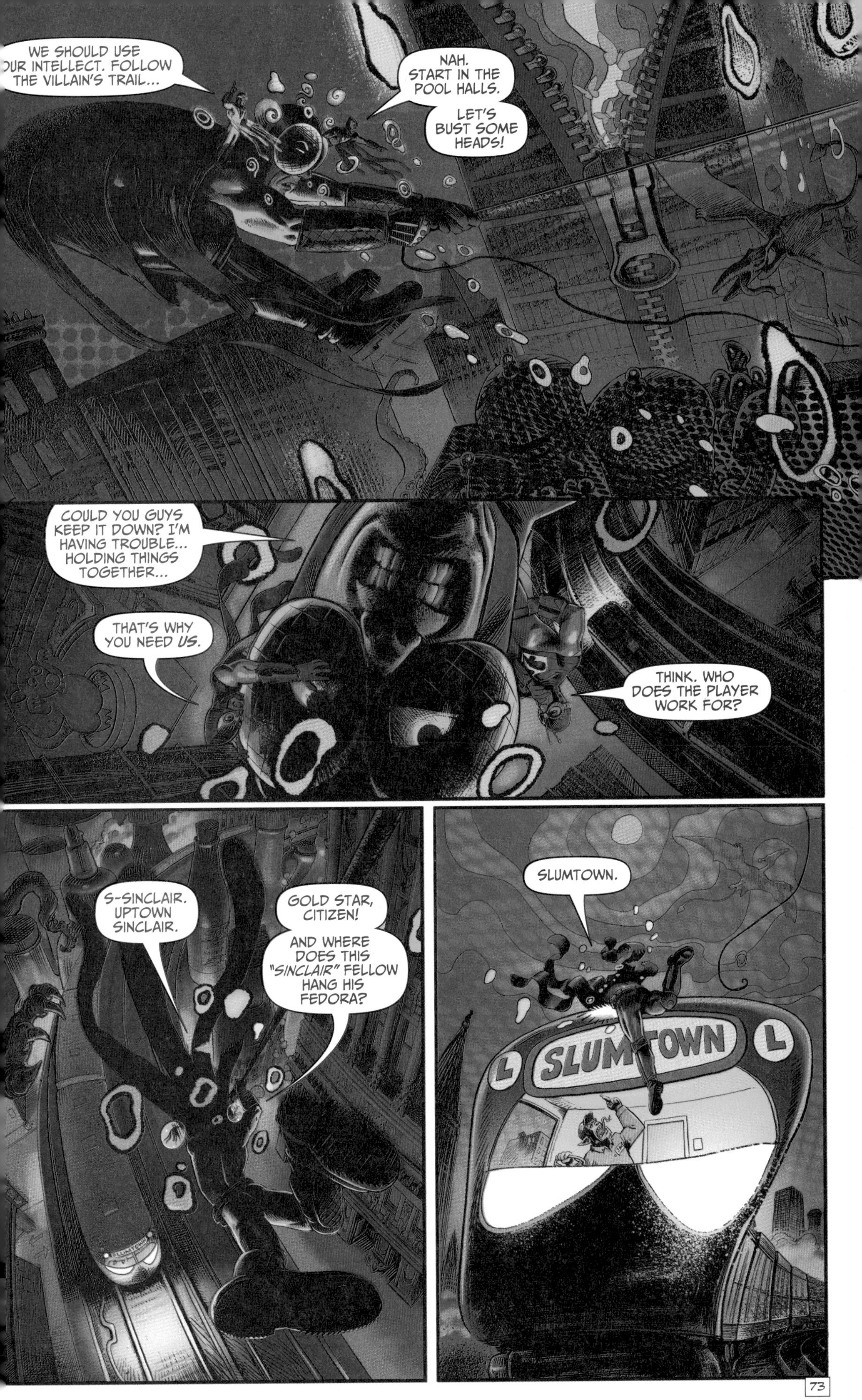

WE SHOULD USE OUR INTELLECT. FOLLOW THE VILLAIN'S TRAIL...
NAH. START IN THE POOL HALLS.
LET'S BUST SOME HEADS!
COULD YOU GUYS KEEP IT DOWN? I'M HAVING TROUBLE... HOLDING THINGS TOGETHER...
THAT'S WHY YOU NEED US.
THINK. WHO DOES THE PLAYER WORK FOR?
S-SINCLAIR. UPTOWN SINCLAIR.
GOLD STAR, CITIZEN!
AND WHERE DOES THIS "SINCLAIR" FELLOW HANG HIS FEDORA?
SLUMTOWN.
SLUMTOWN

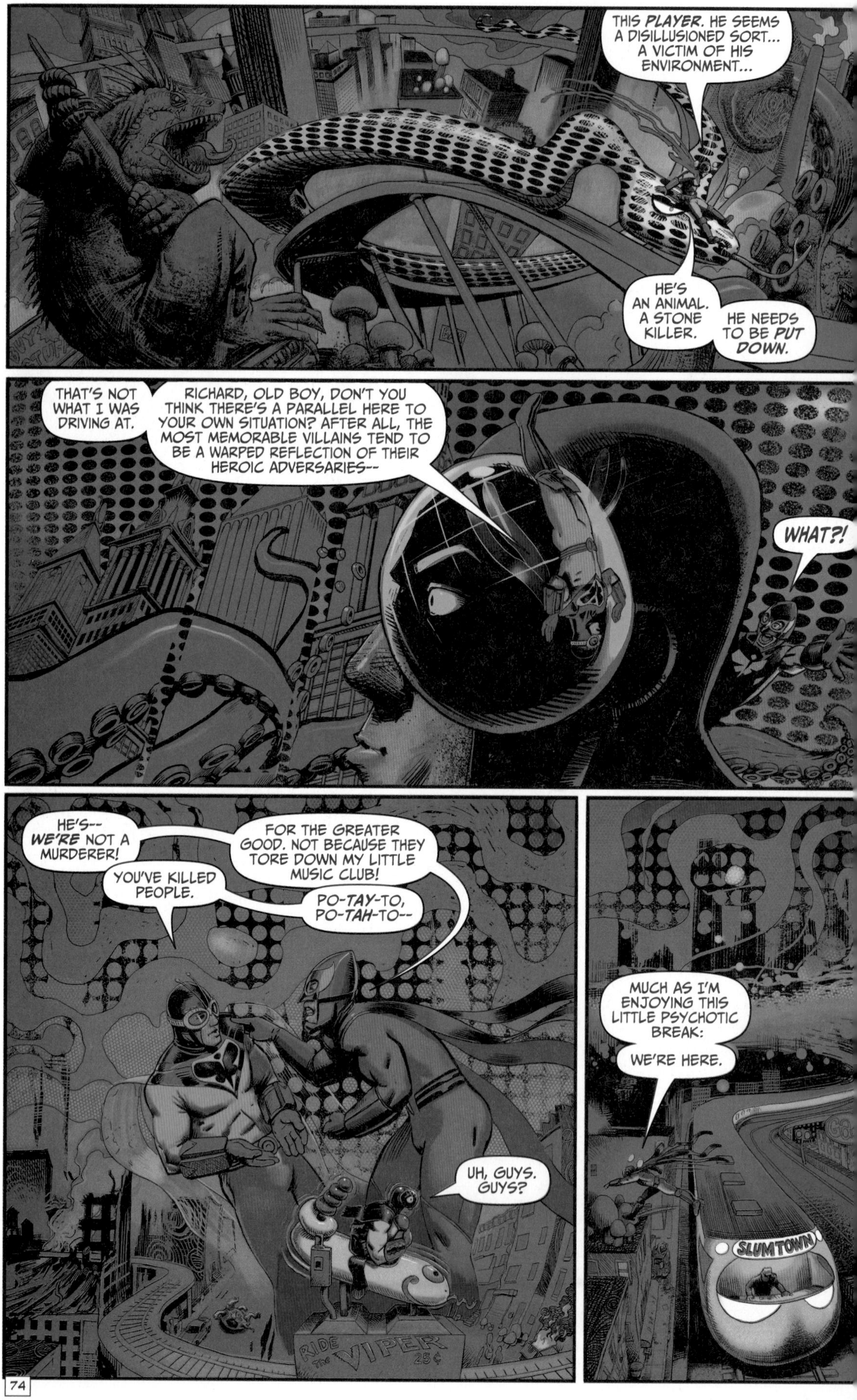
THIS PLAYER. HE SEEMS A DISILLUSIONED SORT... A VICTIM OF HIS ENVIRONMENT...
HE'S AN ANIMAL. A STONE KILLER.
HE NEEDS TO BE PUT DOWN.
THAT'S NOT WHAT I WAS DRIVING AT.
RICHARD, OLD BOY, DON'T YOU THINK THERE'S A PARALLEL HERE TO YOUR OWN SITUATION? AFTER ALL, THE MOST MEMORABLE VILLAINS TEND TO BE A WARPED REFLECTION OF THEIR HEROIC ADVERSARIES--
WHAT?!
HE'S-- WE'RE NOT A MURDERER!
FOR THE GREATER GOOD. NOT BECAUSE THEY TORE DOWN MY LITTLE MUSIC CLUB!
YOU'VE KILLED PEOPLE.
PO-TAY-TO, PO-TAH-TO--
UH, GUYS. GUYS?
RIDE The VIPER 25¢
MUCH AS I'M ENJOYING THIS LITTLE PSYCHOTIC BREAK:
WE'RE HERE.
SLUMTOWN

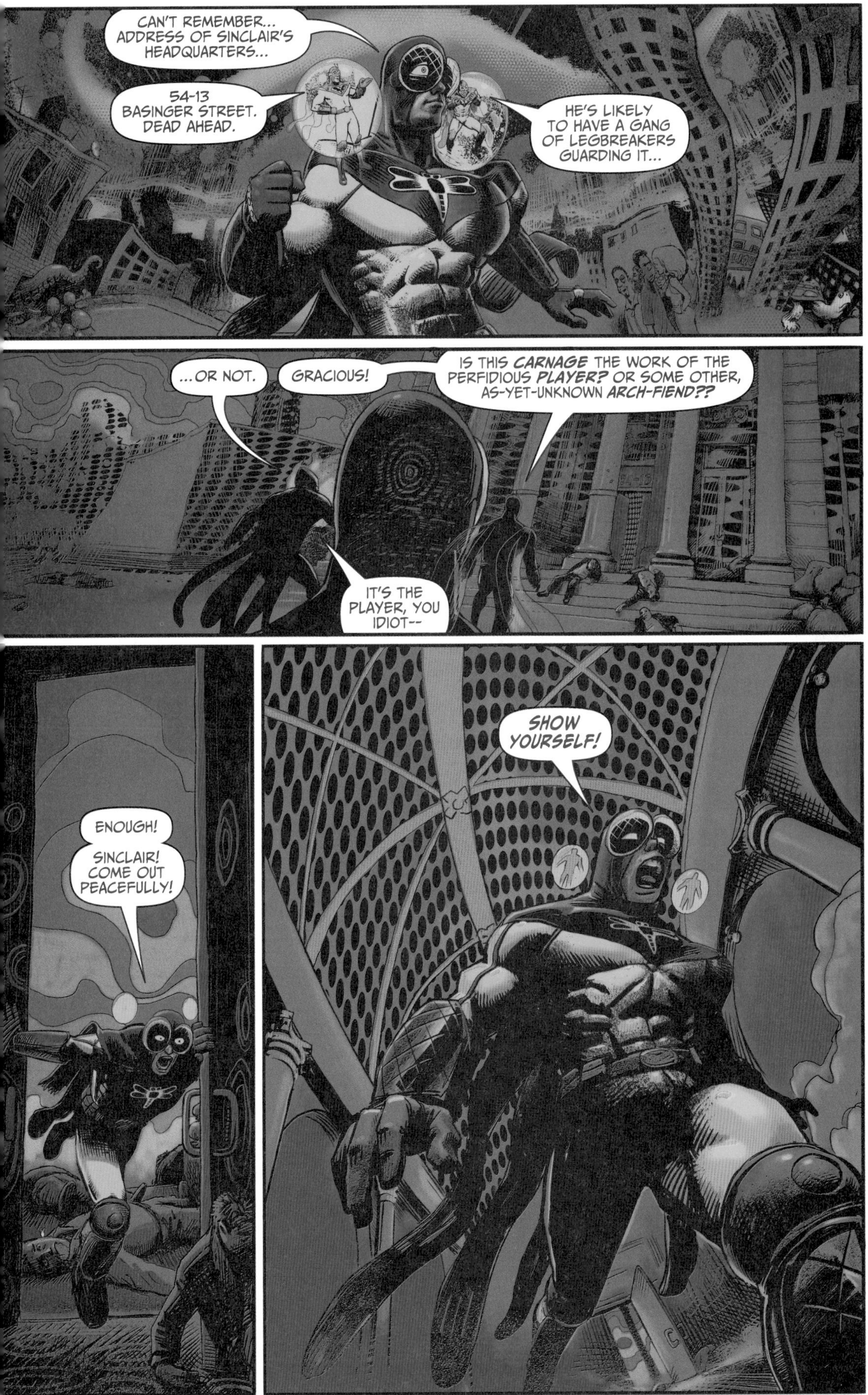

CAN'T REMEMBER... ADDRESS OF SINCLAIR'S HEADQUARTERS...
54-13 BASINGER STREET. DEAD AHEAD.
HE'S LIKELY TO HAVE A GANG OF LEGBREAKERS GUARDING IT...
...OR NOT.
GRACIOUS!
IS THIS CARNAGE THE WORK OF THE PERFIDIOUS PLAYER? OR SOME OTHER, AS-YET-UNKNOWN ARCH-FIEND??
IT'S THE PLAYER, YOU IDIOT--
ENOUGH!
SINCLAIR! COME OUT PEACEFULLY!
SHOW YOURSELF!

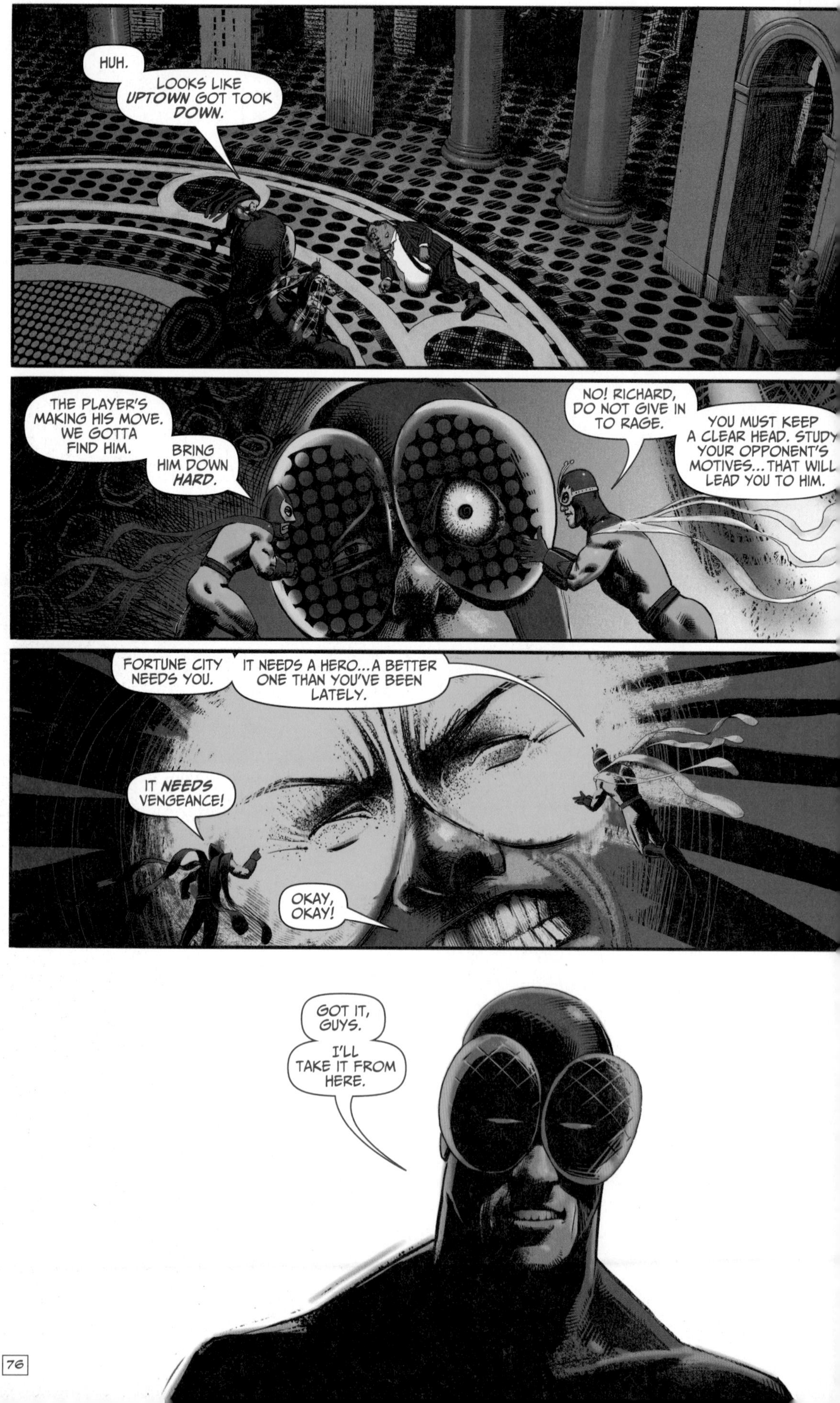
HUH.
LOOKS LIKE UPTOWN GOT TOOK DOWN.
THE PLAYER'S MAKING HIS MOVE. WE GOTTA FIND HIM.
BRING HIM DOWN HARD.
NO! RICHARD, DO NOT GIVE IN TO RAGE.
YOU MUST KEEP A CLEAR HEAD. STUDY YOUR OPPONENT'S MOTIVES...THAT WILL LEAD YOU TO HIM.
FORTUNE CITY NEEDS YOU.
IT NEEDS A HERO...A BETTER ONE THAN YOU'VE BEEN LATELY.
IT NEEDS VENGEANCE!
OKAY, OKAY!
GOT IT, GUYS.
I'LL TAKE IT FROM HERE.

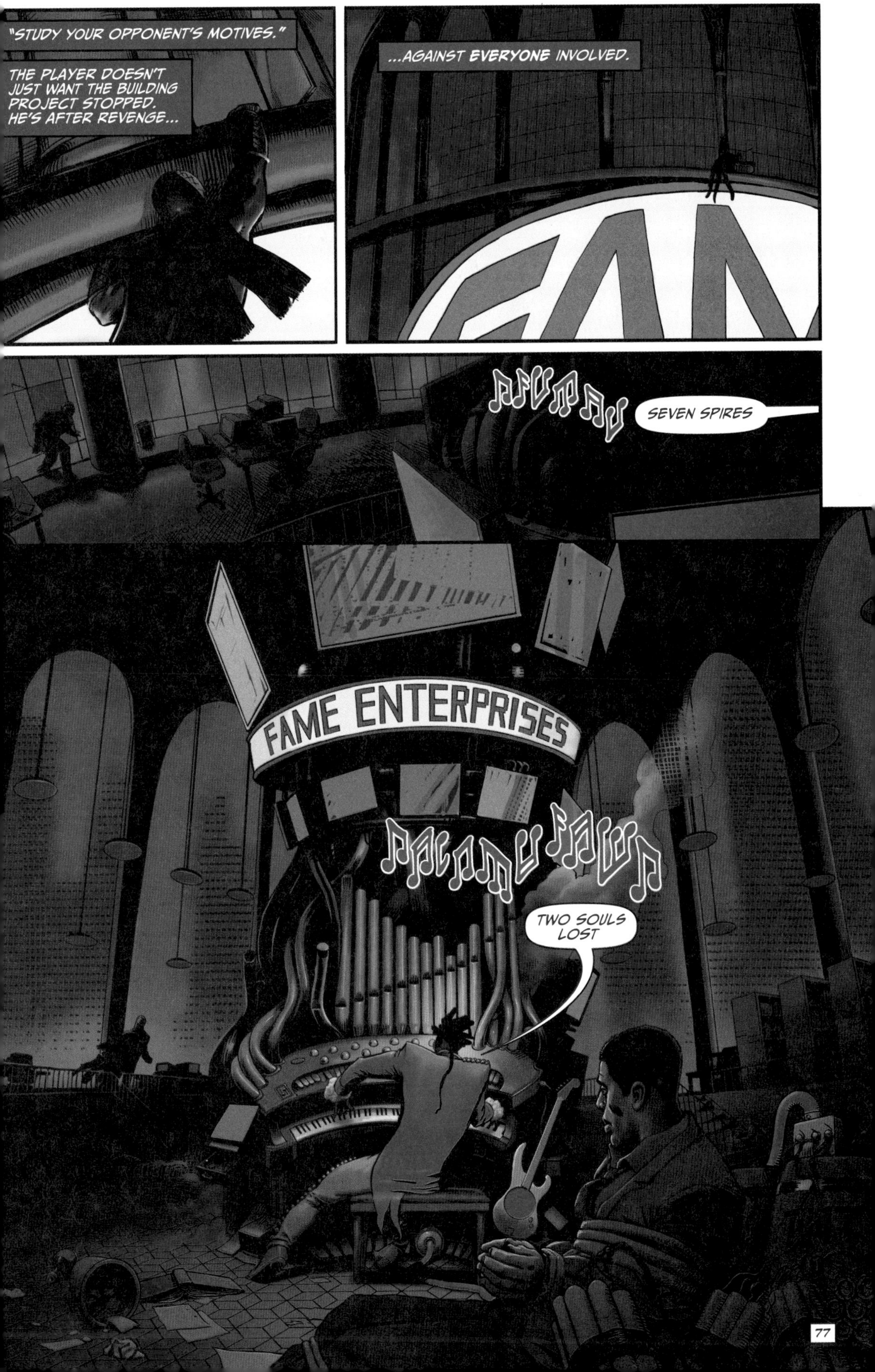
"STUDY YOUR OPPONENT'S MOTIVES."
THE PLAYER DOESN'T JUST WANT THE BUILDING PROJECT STOPPED. HE'S AFTER REVENGE...
...AGAINST EVERYONE INVOLVED.
SEVEN SPIRES
FAME ENTERPRISES
TWO SOULS LOST

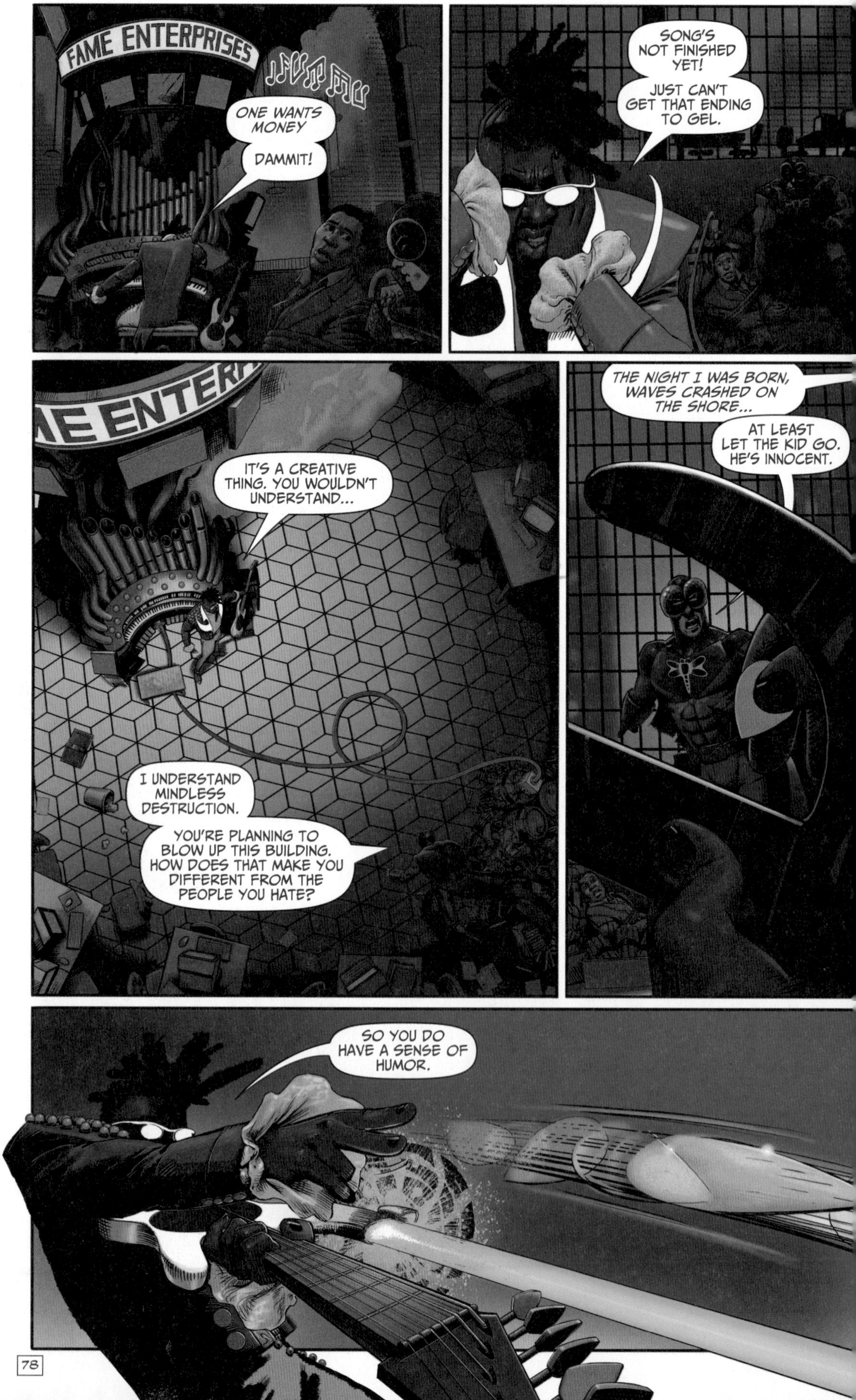
FAME ENTERPRISES
ONE WANTS MONEY
DAMMIT!
SONG'S NOT FINISHED YET!
JUST CAN'T GET THAT ENDING TO GEL.
IT'S A CREATIVE THING. YOU WOULDN'T UNDERSTAND...
I UNDERSTAND MINDLESS DESTRUCTION.
YOU'RE PLANNING TO BLOW UP THIS BUILDING. HOW DOES THAT MAKE YOU DIFFERENT FROM THE PEOPLE YOU HATE?
THE NIGHT I WAS BORN, WAVES CRASHED ON THE SHORE...
AT LEAST LET THE KID GO. HE'S INNOCENT.
SO YOU DO HAVE A SENSE OF HUMOR.

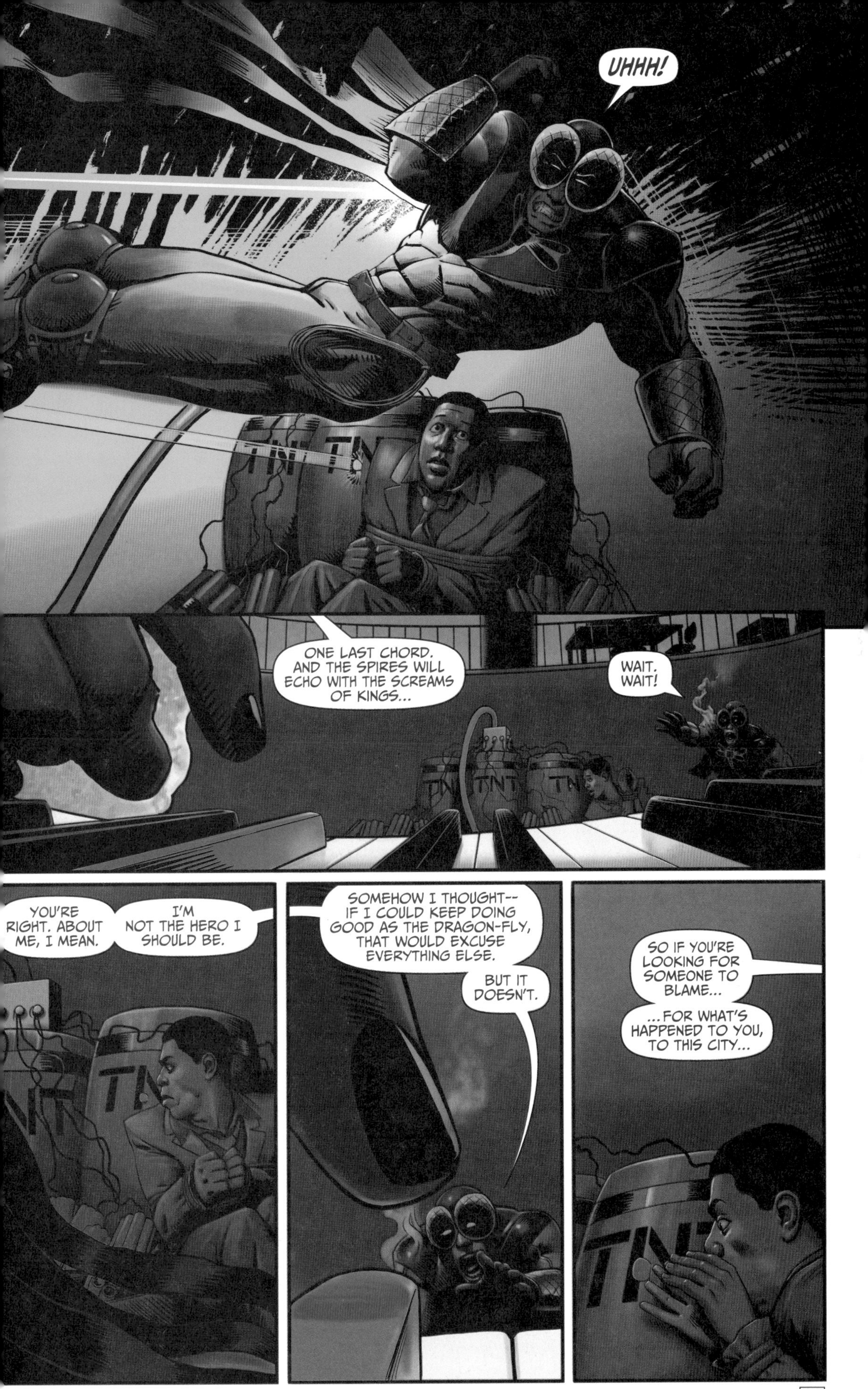
UHHH!
ONE LAST CHORD. AND THE SPIRES WILL ECHO WITH THE SCREAMS OF KINGS...
WAIT. WAIT!
YOU'RE RIGHT. ABOUT ME, I MEAN.
I'M NOT THE HERO I SHOULD BE.
SOMEHOW I THOUGHT-- IF I COULD KEEP DOING GOOD AS THE DRAGON-FLY, THAT WOULD EXCUSE EVERYTHING ELSE.
BUT IT DOESN'T.
SO IF YOU'RE LOOKING FOR SOMEONE TO BLAME...
...FOR WHAT'S HAPPENED TO YOU, TO THIS CITY...

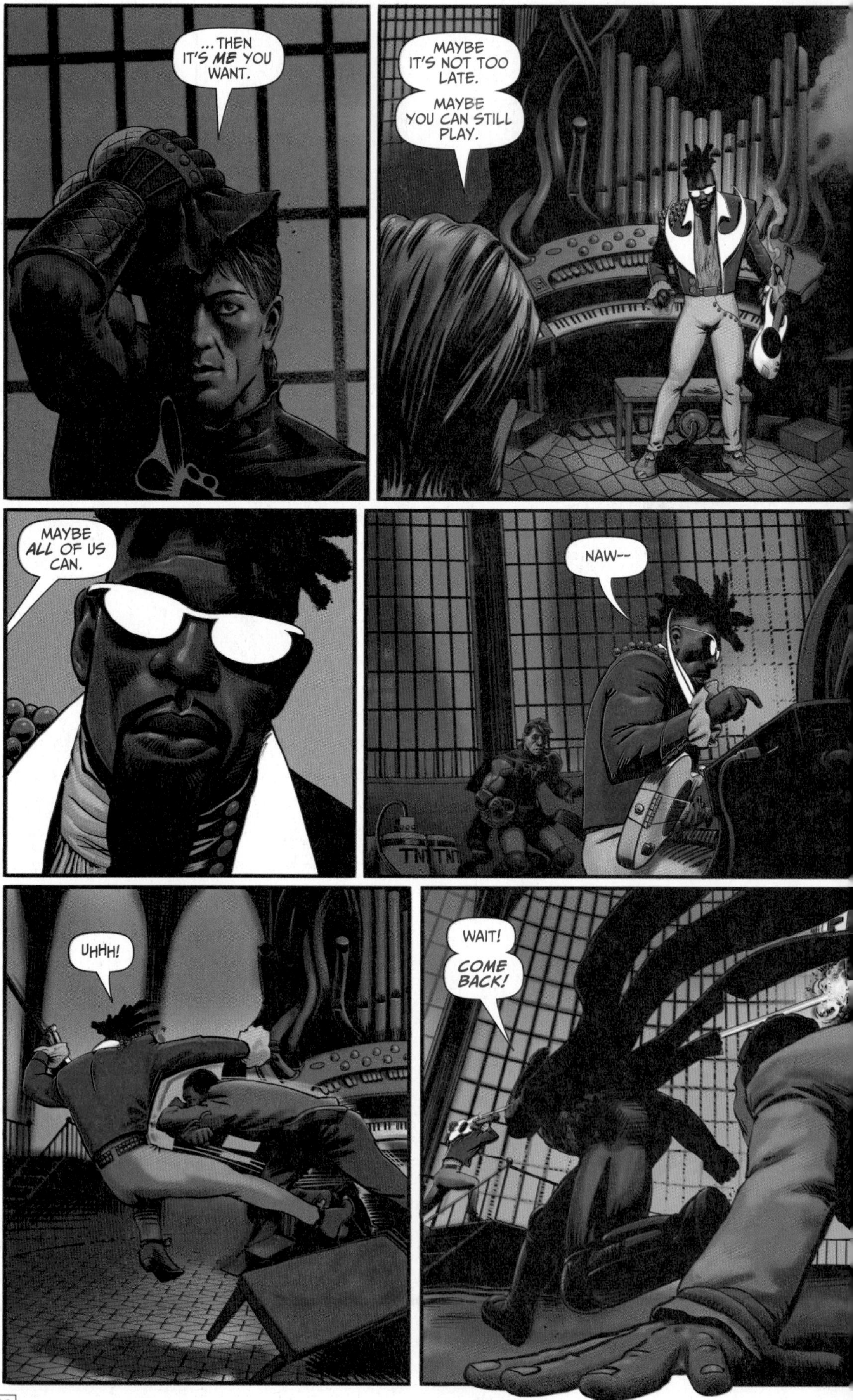

...THEN IT'S *ME* YOU WANT.
MAYBE IT'S NOT TOO LATE.
MAYBE YOU CAN STILL PLAY.
MAYBE *ALL* OF US CAN.
NAW--
TNT TNT
UHHH!
WAIT!
COME BACK!

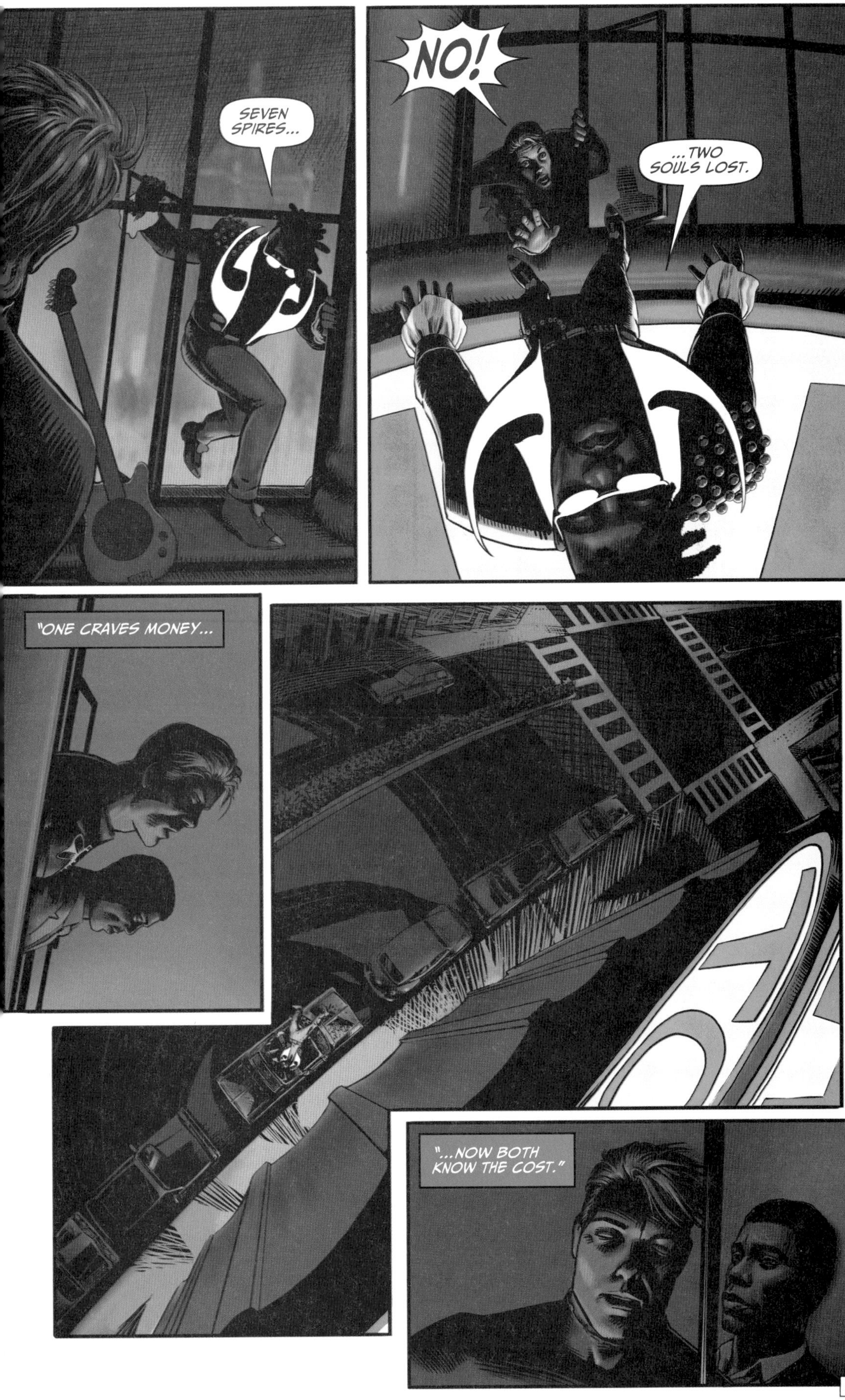
SEVEN SPIRES...
NO!
...TWO SOULS LOST.
"ONE CRAVES MONEY...
"...NOW BOTH KNOW THE COST."

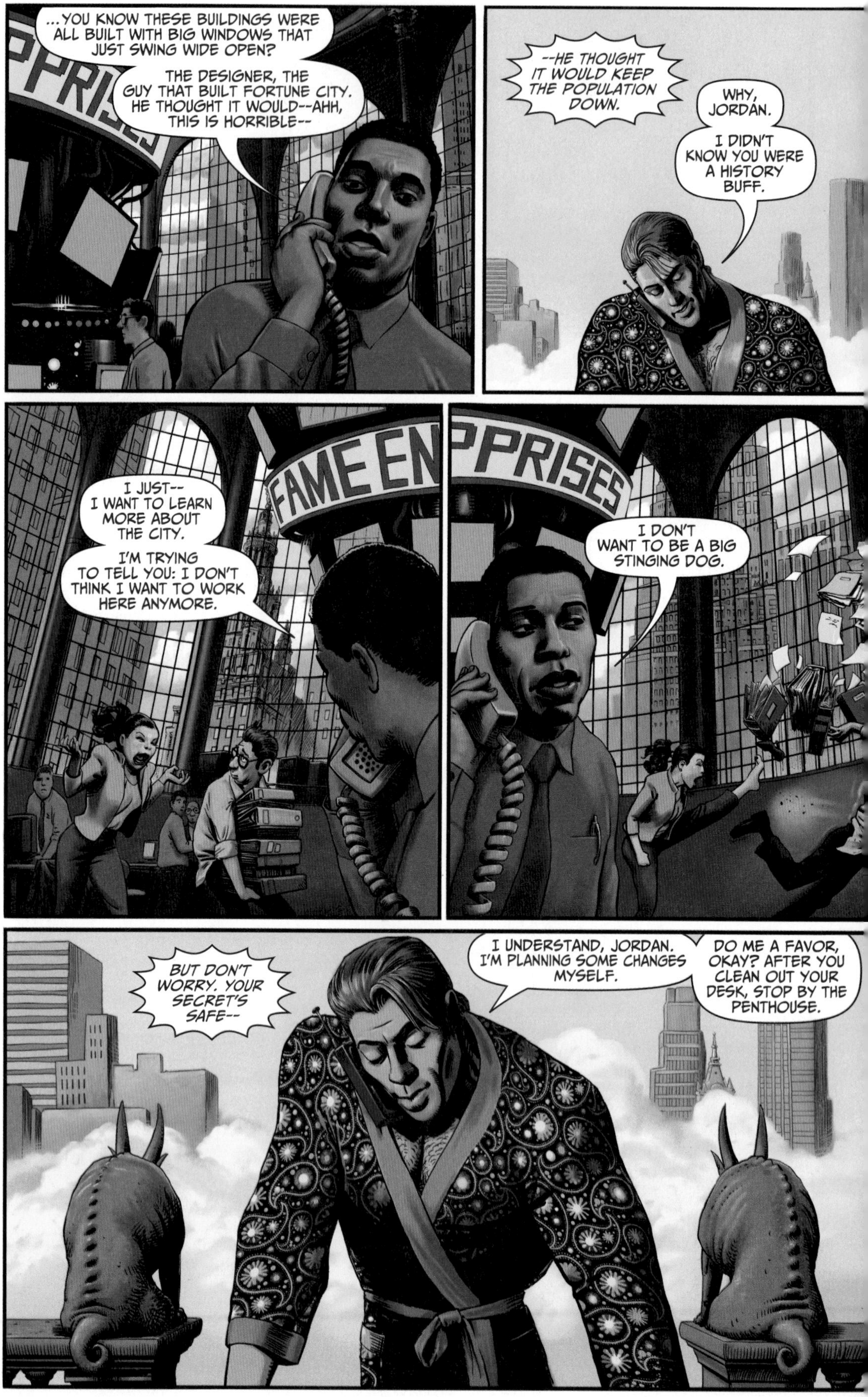
...YOU KNOW THESE BUILDINGS WERE ALL BUILT WITH BIG WINDOWS THAT JUST SWING WIDE OPEN?
PPRISES
THE DESIGNER, THE GUY THAT BUILT FORTUNE CITY. HE THOUGHT IT WOULD--AHH, THIS IS HORRIBLE--
--HE THOUGHT IT WOULD KEEP THE POPULATION DOWN.
WHY, JORDAN.
I DIDN'T KNOW YOU WERE A HISTORY BUFF.
FAME EN
PPRISES
I JUST-- I WANT TO LEARN MORE ABOUT THE CITY.
I'M TRYING TO TELL YOU: I DON'T THINK I WANT TO WORK HERE ANYMORE.
I DON'T WANT TO BE A BIG STINGING DOG.
BUT DON'T WORRY. YOUR SECRET'S SAFE--
I UNDERSTAND, JORDAN. I'M PLANNING SOME CHANGES MYSELF.
DO ME A FAVOR, OKAY? AFTER YOU CLEAN OUT YOUR DESK, STOP BY THE PENTHOUSE.

I MIGHT HAVE A NEW JOB FOR YOU.

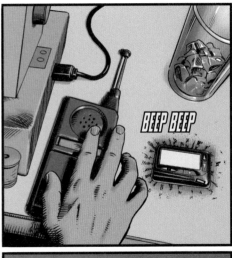

BEEP BEEP

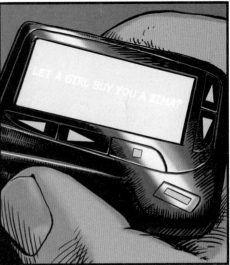

LET A GIRL BUY YOU A ZIMA?

OPERATOR?

SLY MAGAZINE, PLEASE.

THE END

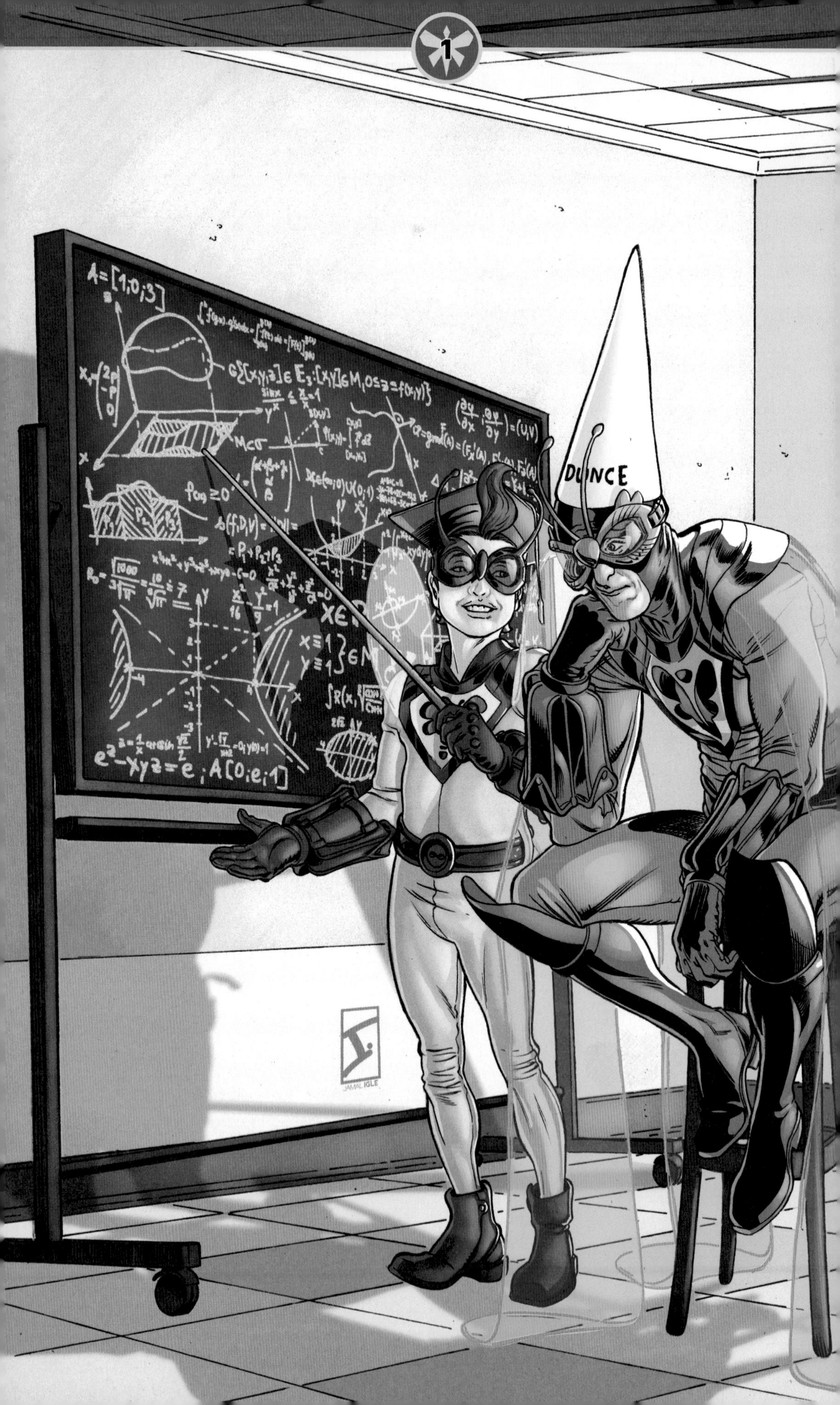
1
DUNCE
JAMAL IGLE

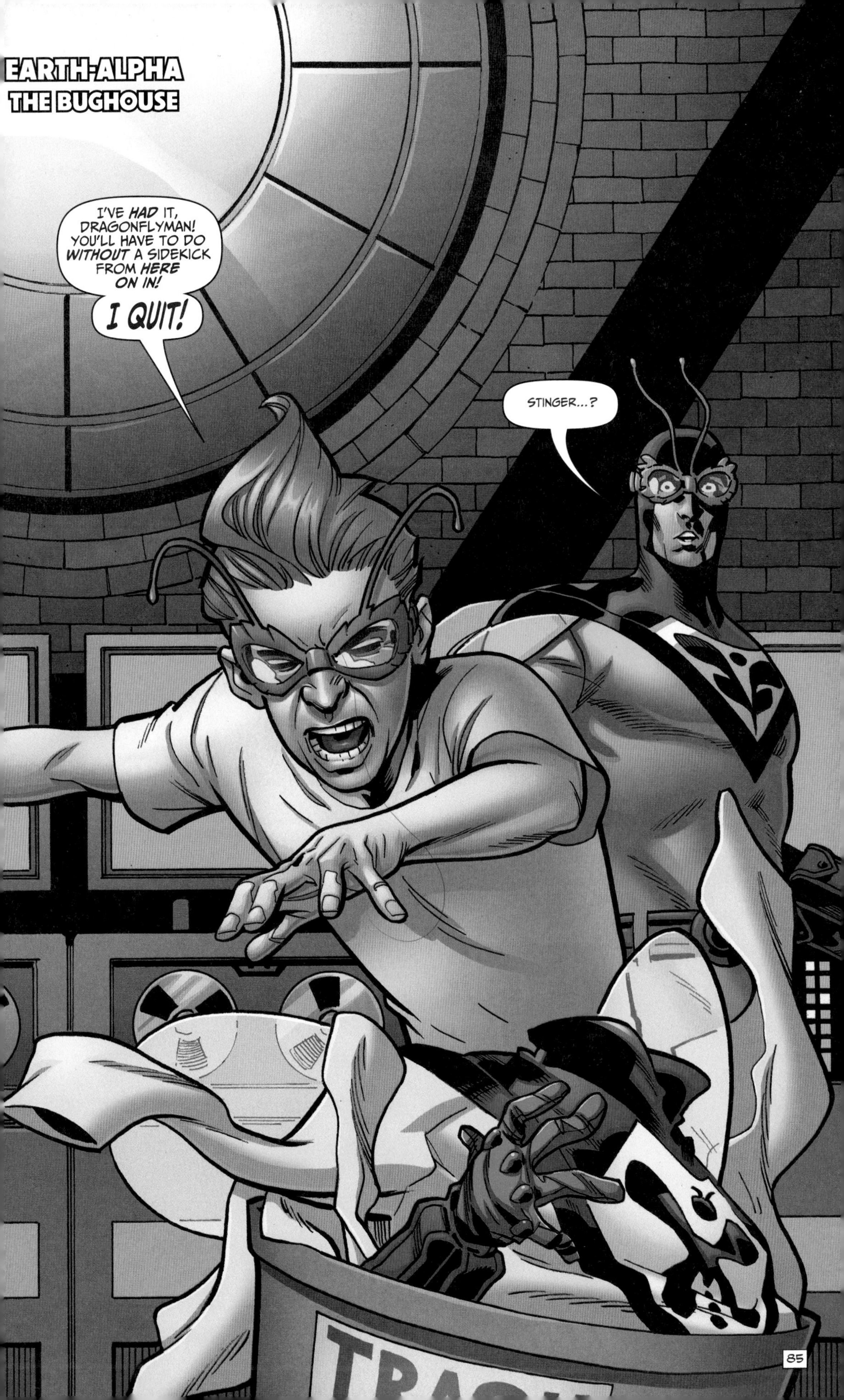
EARTH-ALPHA
THE BUGHOUSE
I'VE HAD IT, DRAGONFLYMAN! YOU'LL HAVE TO DO WITHOUT A SIDEKICK FROM HERE ON IN!
I QUIT!
STINGER...?

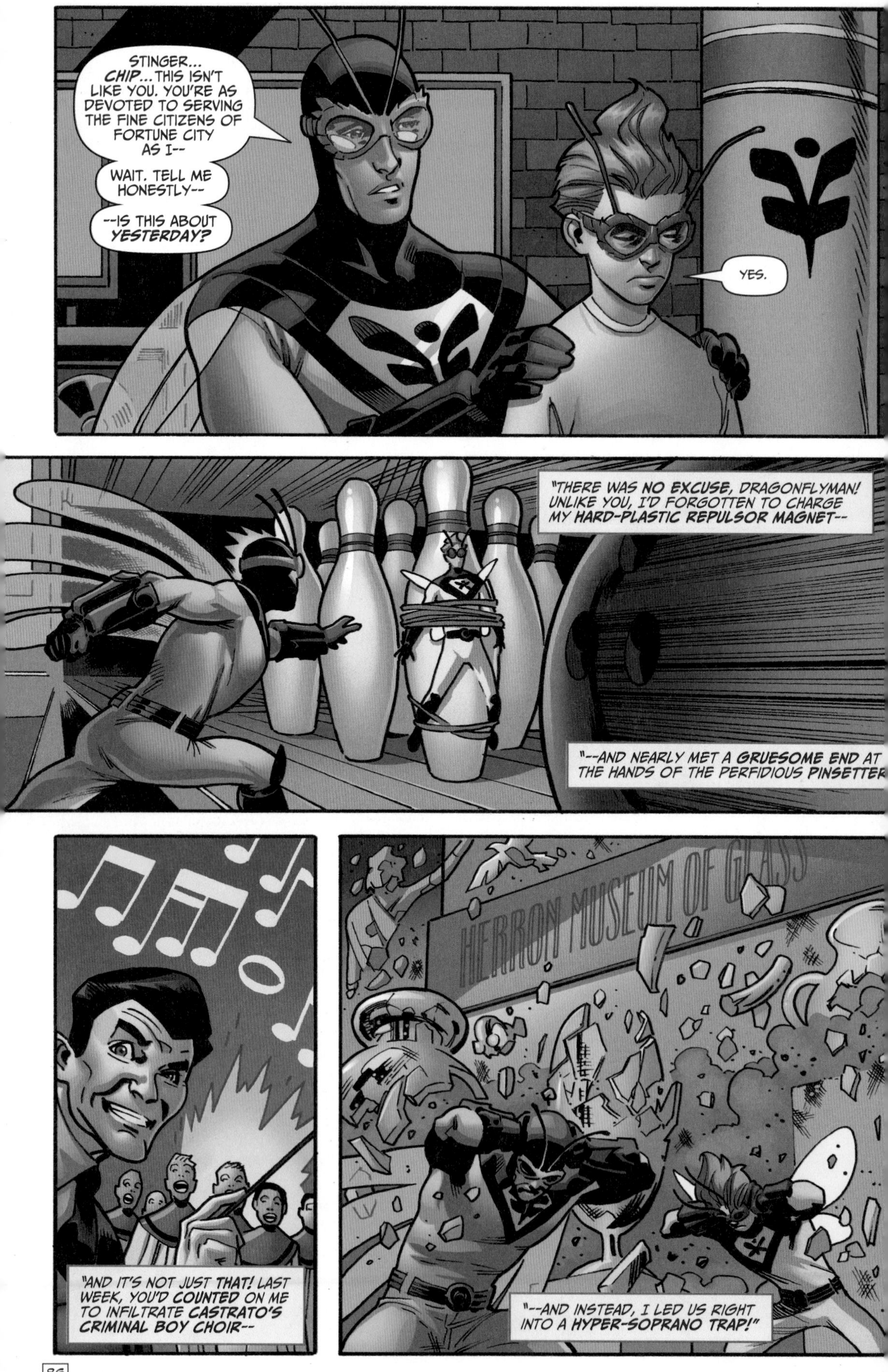
STINGER... CHIP... THIS ISN'T LIKE YOU. YOU'RE AS DEVOTED TO SERVING THE FINE CITIZENS OF FORTUNE CITY AS I--
WAIT. TELL ME HONESTLY--
--IS THIS ABOUT YESTERDAY?
YES.
"THERE WAS NO EXCUSE, DRAGONFLYMAN! UNLIKE YOU, I'D FORGOTTEN TO CHARGE MY HARD-PLASTIC REPULSOR MAGNET--
"--AND NEARLY MET A GRUESOME END AT THE HANDS OF THE PERFIDIOUS PINSETTER
"AND IT'S NOT JUST THAT! LAST WEEK, YOU'D COUNTED ON ME TO INFILTRATE CASTRATO'S CRIMINAL BOY CHOIR--
HERRON MUSEUM OF GLASS
"--AND INSTEAD, I LED US RIGHT INTO A HYPER-SOPRANO TRAP!"

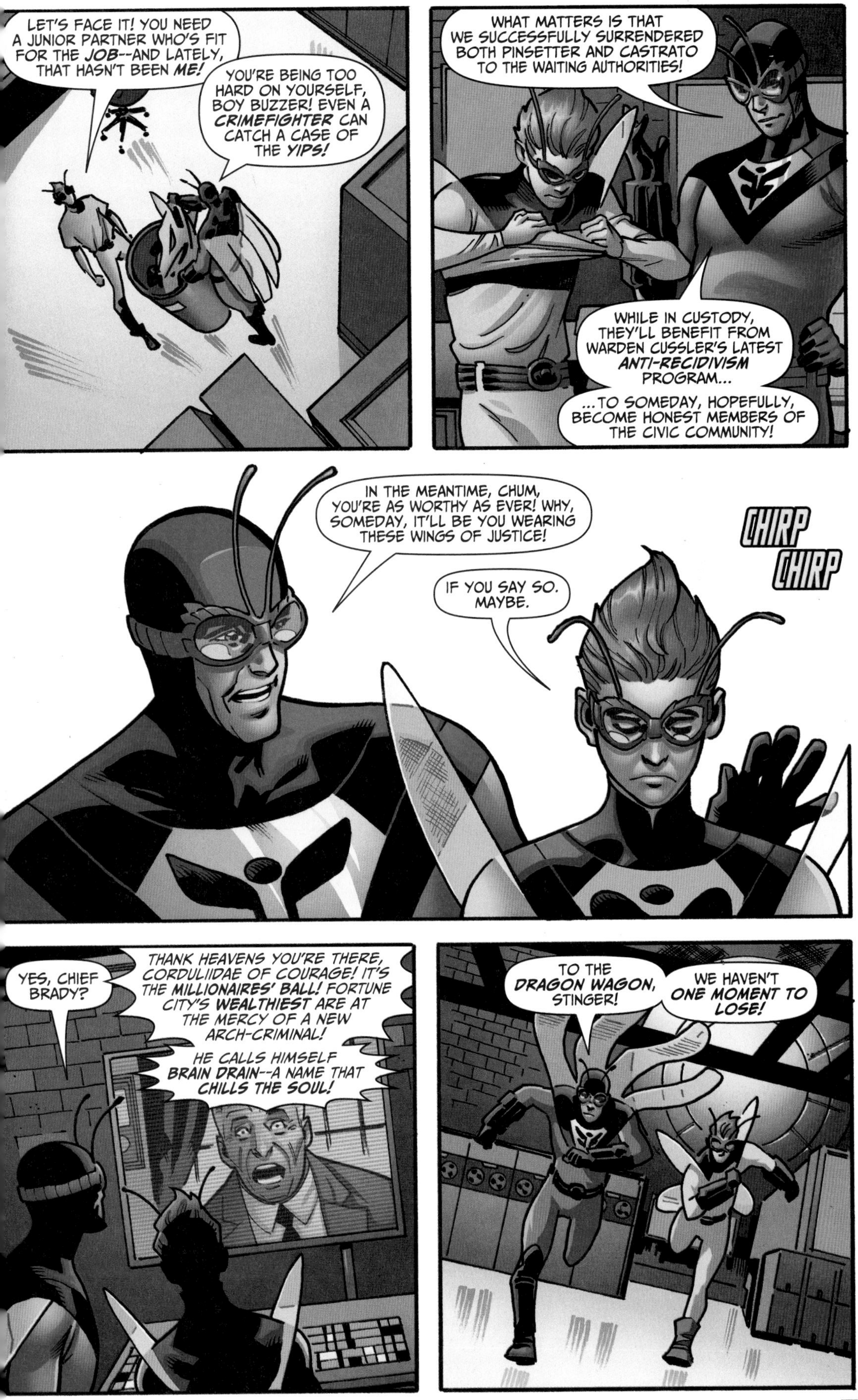
LET'S FACE IT! YOU NEED A JUNIOR PARTNER WHO'S FIT FOR THE JOB--AND LATELY, THAT HASN'T BEEN ME!
YOU'RE BEING TOO HARD ON YOURSELF, BOY BUZZER! EVEN A CRIMEFIGHTER CAN CATCH A CASE OF THE YIPS!
WHAT MATTERS IS THAT WE SUCCESSFULLY SURRENDERED BOTH PINSETTER AND CASTRATO TO THE WAITING AUTHORITIES!
WHILE IN CUSTODY, THEY'LL BENEFIT FROM WARDEN CUSSLER'S LATEST ANTI-RECIDIVISM PROGRAM...
...TO SOMEDAY, HOPEFULLY, BECOME HONEST MEMBERS OF THE CIVIC COMMUNITY!
IN THE MEANTIME, CHUM, YOU'RE AS WORTHY AS EVER! WHY, SOMEDAY, IT'LL BE YOU WEARING THESE WINGS OF JUSTICE!
IF YOU SAY SO. MAYBE.
CHIRP
CHIRP
YES, CHIEF BRADY?
THANK HEAVENS YOU'RE THERE, CORDULIIDAE OF COURAGE! IT'S THE MILLIONAIRES' BALL! FORTUNE CITY'S WEALTHIEST ARE AT THE MERCY OF A NEW ARCH-CRIMINAL!
HE CALLS HIMSELF BRAIN DRAIN--A NAME THAT CHILLS THE SOUL!
TO THE DRAGON WAGON, STINGER!
WE HAVEN'T ONE MOMENT TO LOSE!

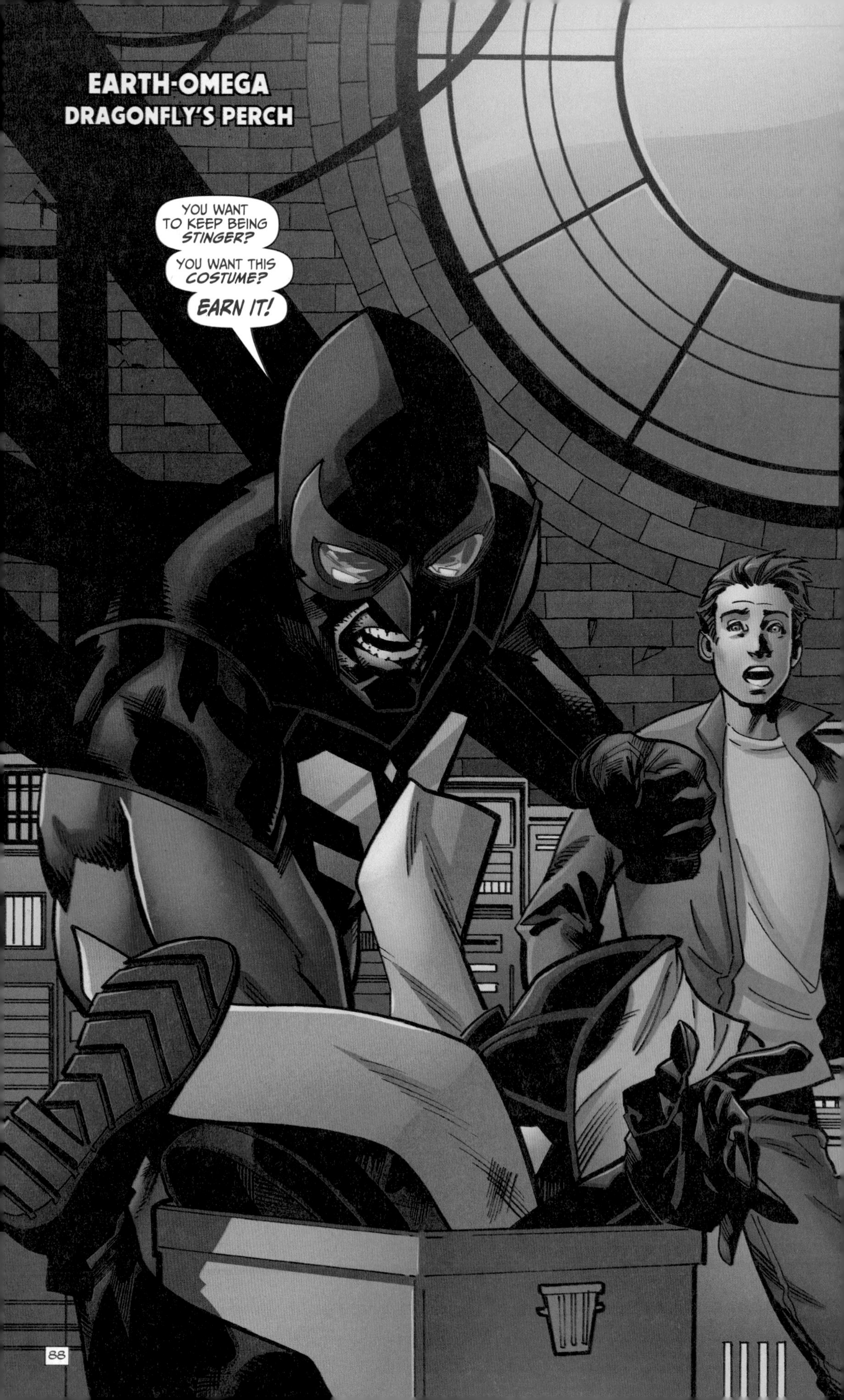
EARTH-OMEGA
DRAGONFLY'S PERCH
YOU WANT TO KEEP BEING STINGER?
YOU WANT THIS COSTUME?
EARN IT!

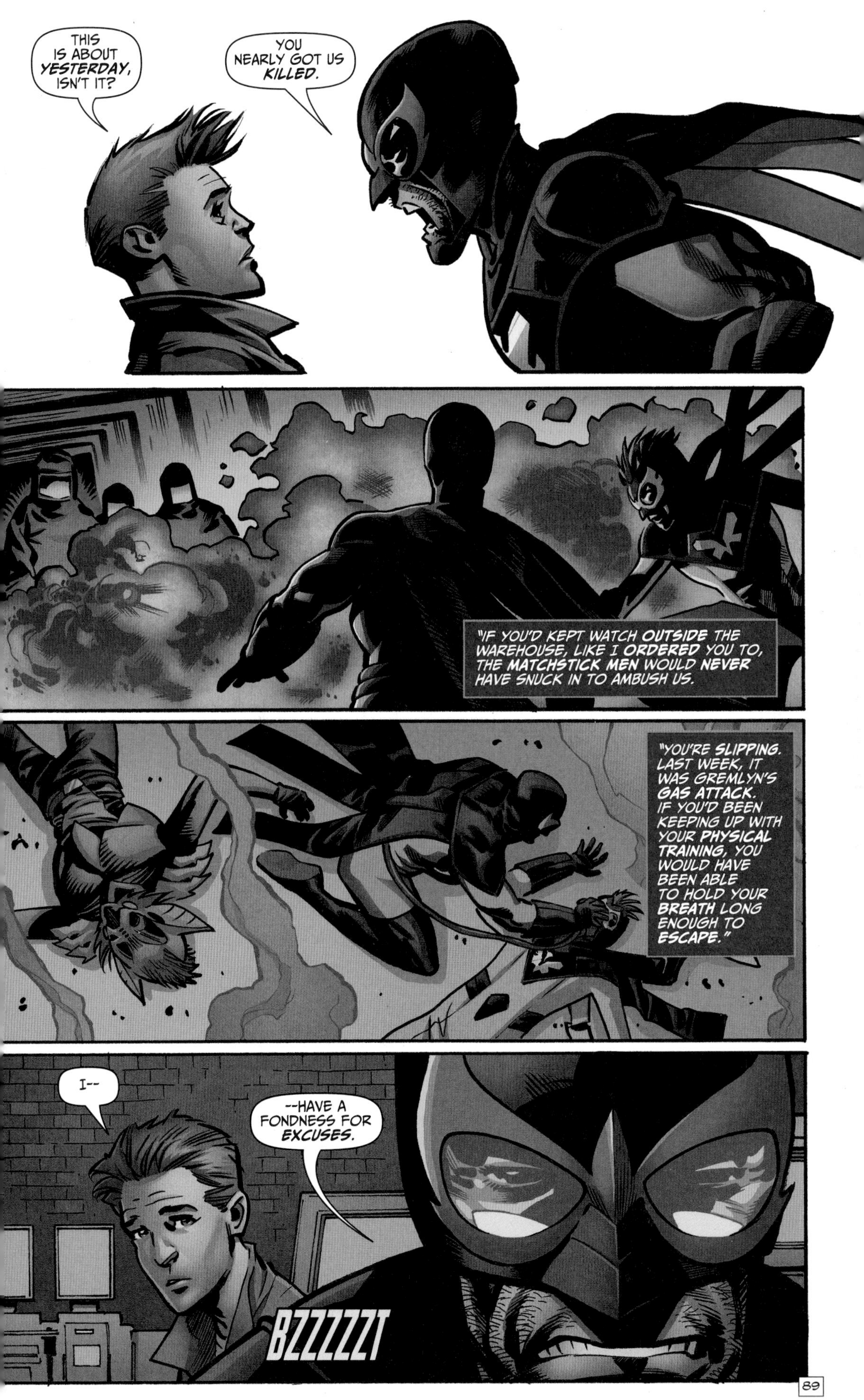
THIS IS ABOUT YESTERDAY, ISN'T IT?
YOU NEARLY GOT US KILLED.
"IF YOU'D KEPT WATCH OUTSIDE THE WAREHOUSE, LIKE I ORDERED YOU TO, THE MATCHSTICK MEN WOULD NEVER HAVE SNUCK IN TO AMBUSH US.
"YOU'RE SLIPPING. LAST WEEK, IT WAS GREMLYN'S GAS ATTACK. IF YOU'D BEEN KEEPING UP WITH YOUR PHYSICAL TRAINING, YOU WOULD HAVE BEEN ABLE TO HOLD YOUR BREATH LONG ENOUGH TO ESCAPE."
I--
--HAVE A FONDNESS FOR EXCUSES.
BZZZZZT

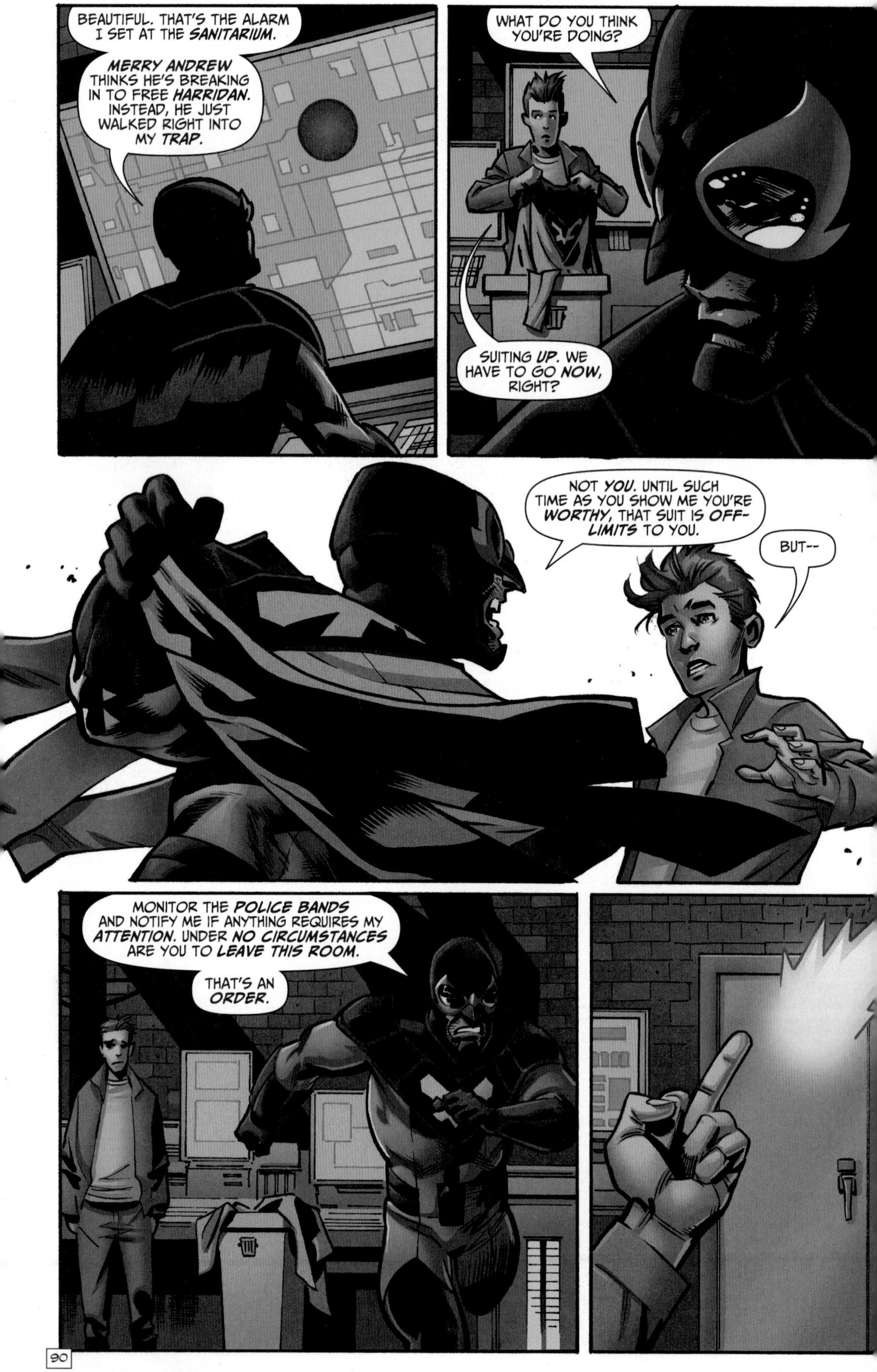
BEAUTIFUL. THAT'S THE ALARM I SET AT THE SANITARIUM.
MERRY ANDREW THINKS HE'S BREAKING IN TO FREE HARRIDAN. INSTEAD, HE JUST WALKED RIGHT INTO MY TRAP.
WHAT DO YOU THINK YOU'RE DOING?
SUITING UP. WE HAVE TO GO NOW, RIGHT?
NOT YOU. UNTIL SUCH TIME AS YOU SHOW ME YOU'RE WORTHY, THAT SUIT IS OFF-LIMITS TO YOU.
BUT--
MONITOR THE POLICE BANDS AND NOTIFY ME IF ANYTHING REQUIRES MY ATTENTION. UNDER NO CIRCUMSTANCES ARE YOU TO LEAVE THIS ROOM.
THAT'S AN ORDER.

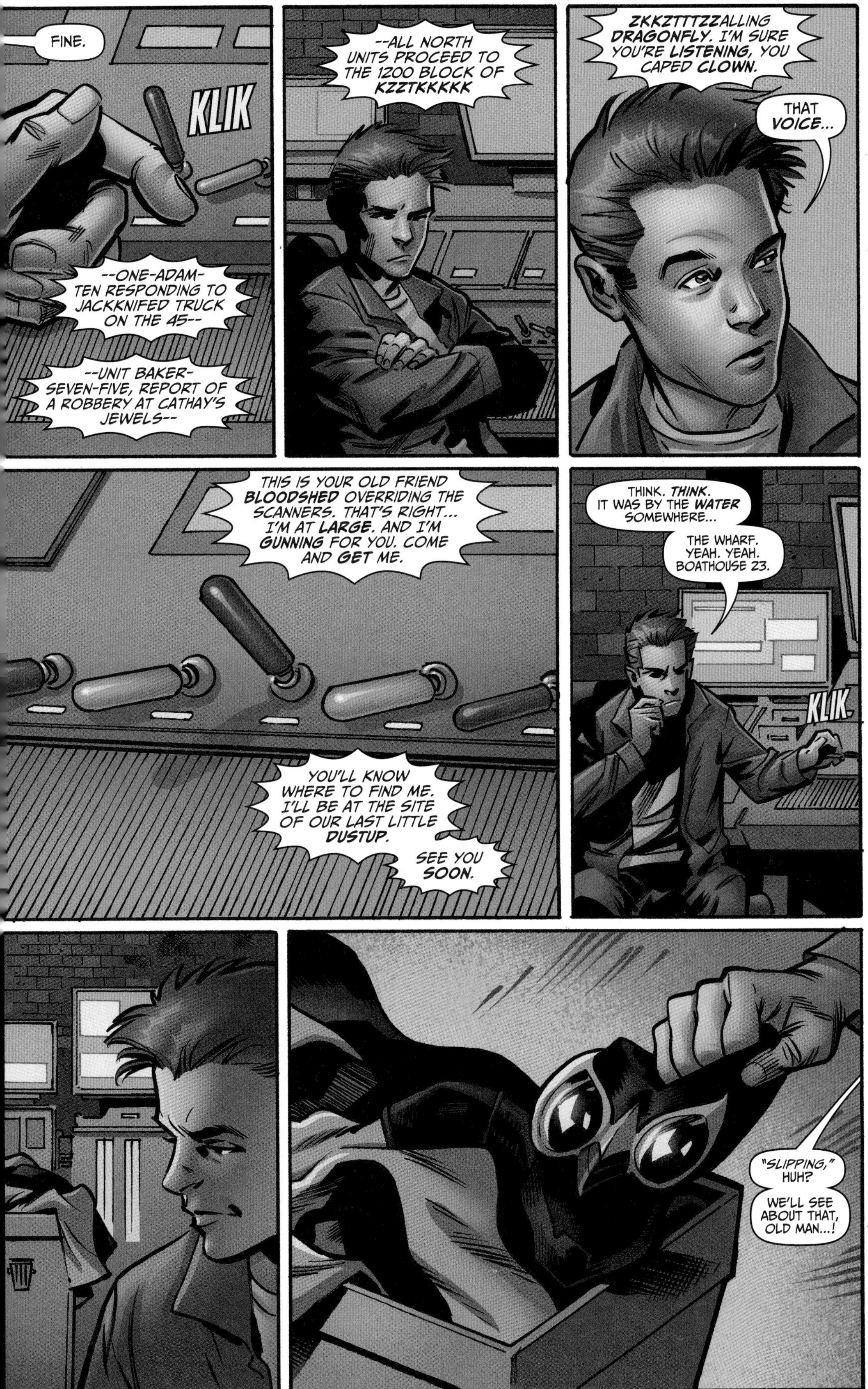
FINE.
KLIK
--ONE-ADAM-TEN RESPONDING TO JACKKNIFED TRUCK ON THE 45--
--UNIT BAKER-SEVEN-FIVE, REPORT OF A ROBBERY AT CATHAY'S JEWELS--
--ALL NORTH UNITS PROCEED TO THE 1200 BLOCK OF KZZTKKKKK
ZKKZTTTZZALLING DRAGONFLY. I'M SURE YOU'RE LISTENING, YOU CAPED CLOWN.
THAT VOICE...
THIS IS YOUR OLD FRIEND BLOODSHED OVERRIDING THE SCANNERS. THAT'S RIGHT... I'M AT LARGE. AND I'M GUNNING FOR YOU. COME AND GET ME.
YOU'LL KNOW WHERE TO FIND ME. I'LL BE AT THE SITE OF OUR LAST LITTLE DUSTUP.
SEE YOU SOON.
THINK. THINK. IT WAS BY THE WATER SOMEWHERE...
THE WHARF. YEAH. YEAH. BOATHOUSE 23.
KLIK
"SLIPPING," HUH?
WE'LL SEE ABOUT THAT, OLD MAN...!

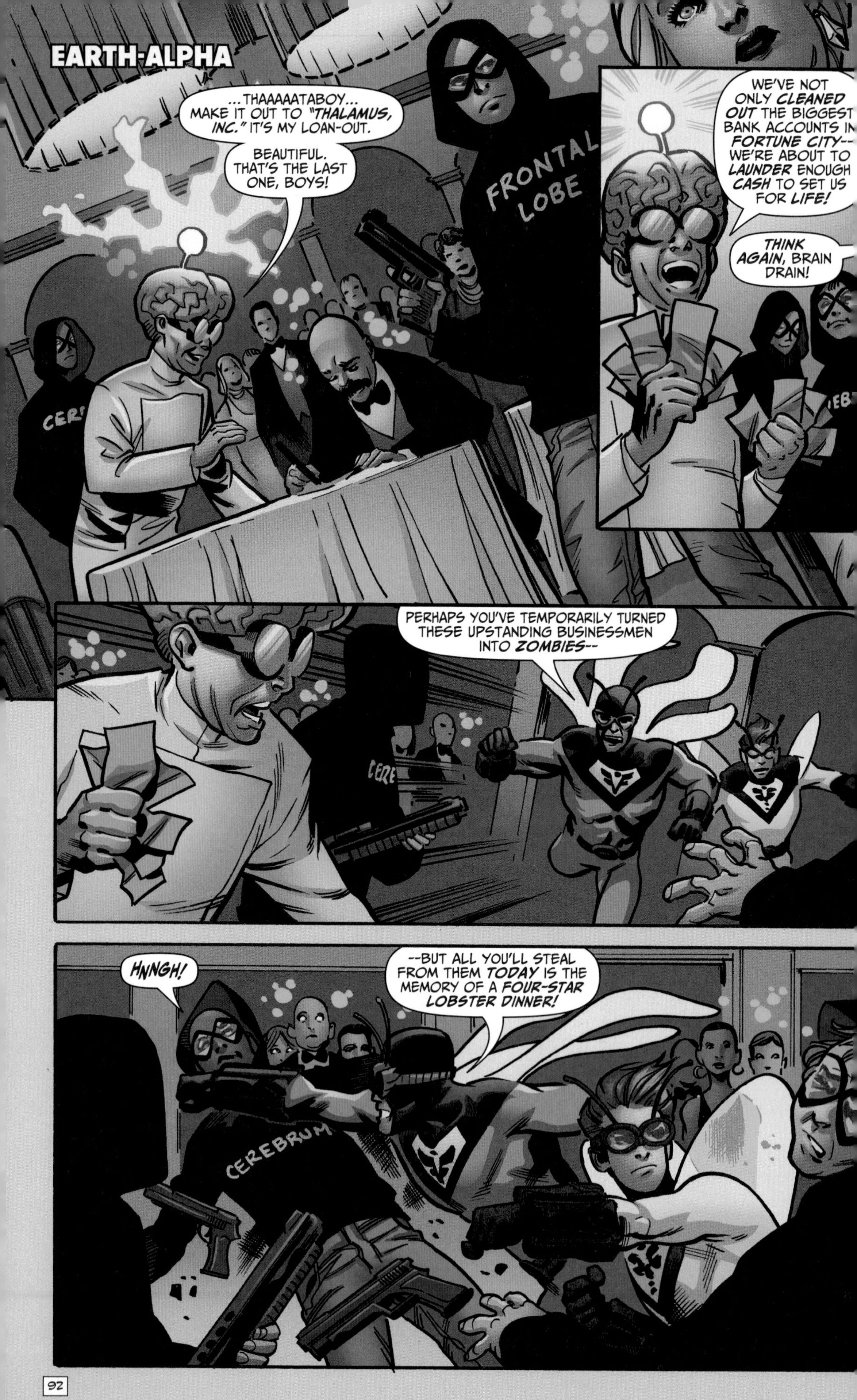

EARTH-ALPHA
...THAAAAATABOY... MAKE IT OUT TO "THALAMUS, INC." IT'S MY LOAN-OUT.
BEAUTIFUL. THAT'S THE LAST ONE, BOYS!
FRONTAL LOBE
CERE
WE'VE NOT ONLY CLEANED OUT THE BIGGEST BANK ACCOUNTS IN FORTUNE CITY-- WE'RE ABOUT TO LAUNDER ENOUGH CASH TO SET US FOR LIFE!
THINK AGAIN, BRAIN DRAIN!
PERHAPS YOU'VE TEMPORARILY TURNED THESE UPSTANDING BUSINESSMEN INTO ZOMBIES--
CERE
HNNGH!
--BUT ALL YOU'LL STEAL FROM THEM TODAY IS THE MEMORY OF A FOUR-STAR LOBSTER DINNER!
CEREBRUM

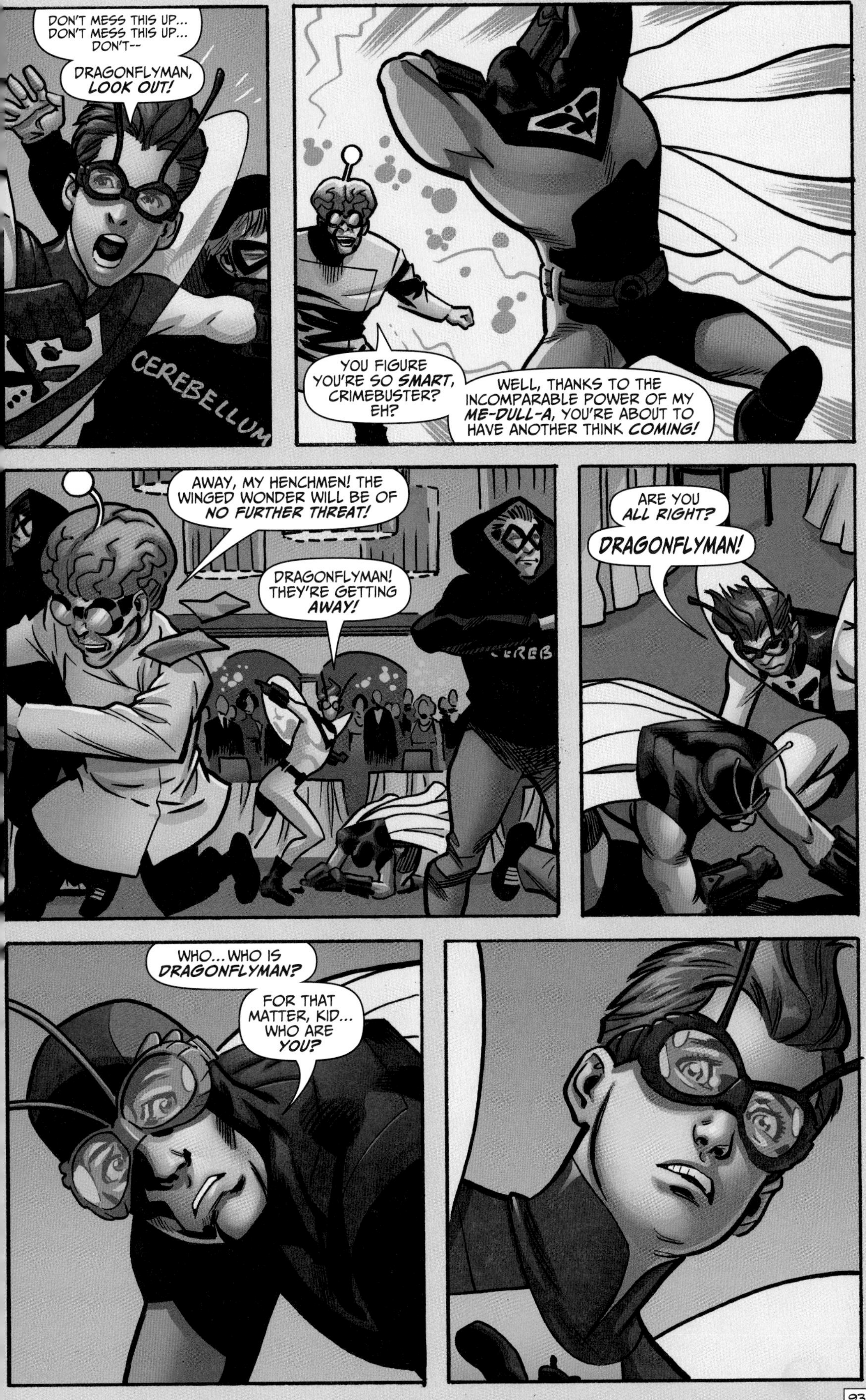
DON'T MESS THIS UP... DON'T MESS THIS UP... DON'T--
DRAGONFLYMAN, LOOK OUT!
CEREBELLUM
YOU FIGURE YOU'RE SO SMART, CRIMEBUSTER? EH?
WELL, THANKS TO THE INCOMPARABLE POWER OF MY ME-DULL-A, YOU'RE ABOUT TO HAVE ANOTHER THINK COMING!
AWAY, MY HENCHMEN! THE WINGED WONDER WILL BE OF NO FURTHER THREAT!
DRAGONFLYMAN! THEY'RE GETTING AWAY!
CEREB
ARE YOU ALL RIGHT?
DRAGONFLYMAN!
WHO...WHO IS DRAGONFLYMAN?
FOR THAT MATTER, KID... WHO ARE YOU?

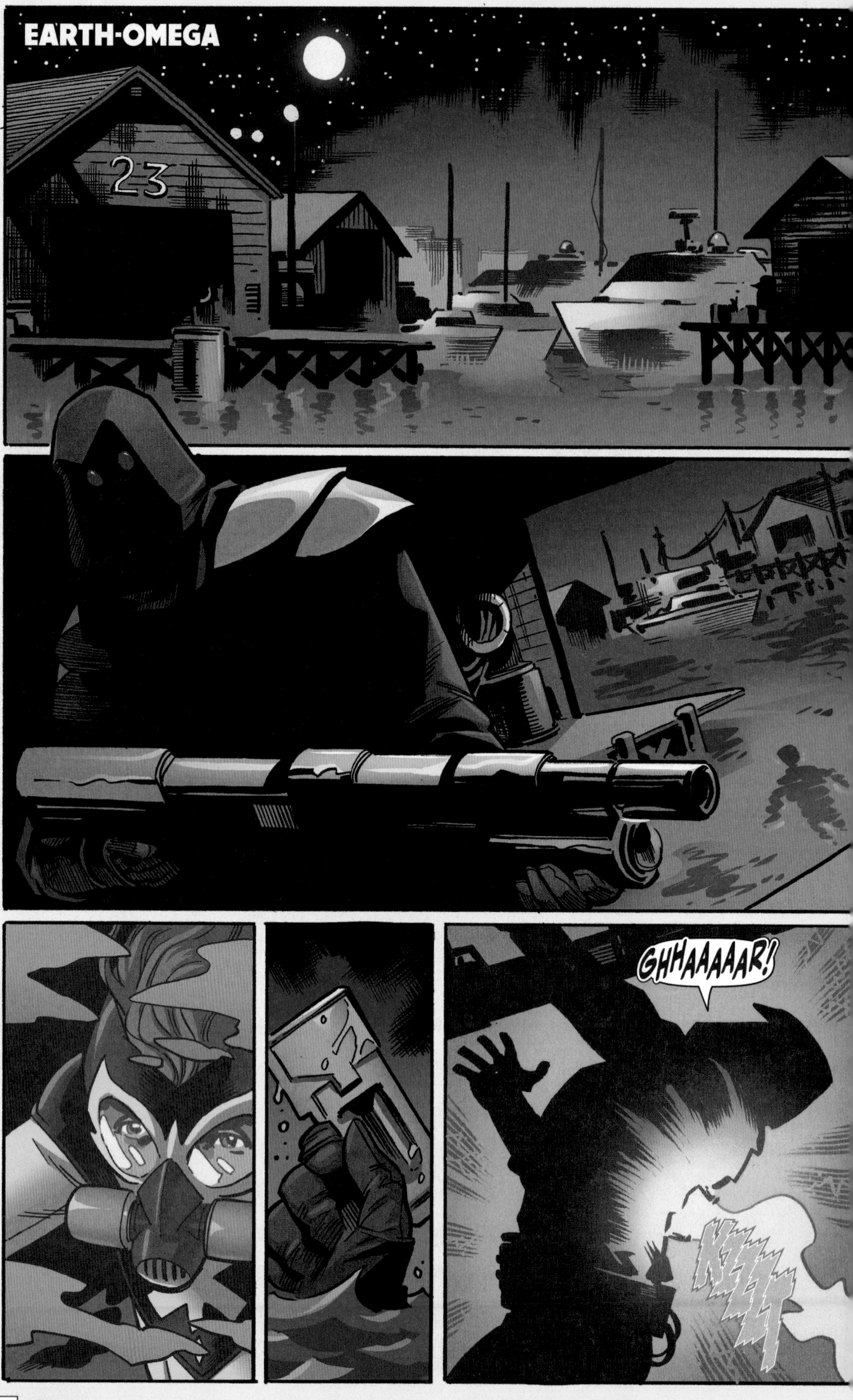
EARTH-OMEGA
23
GHHAAAAAR!
KZZT

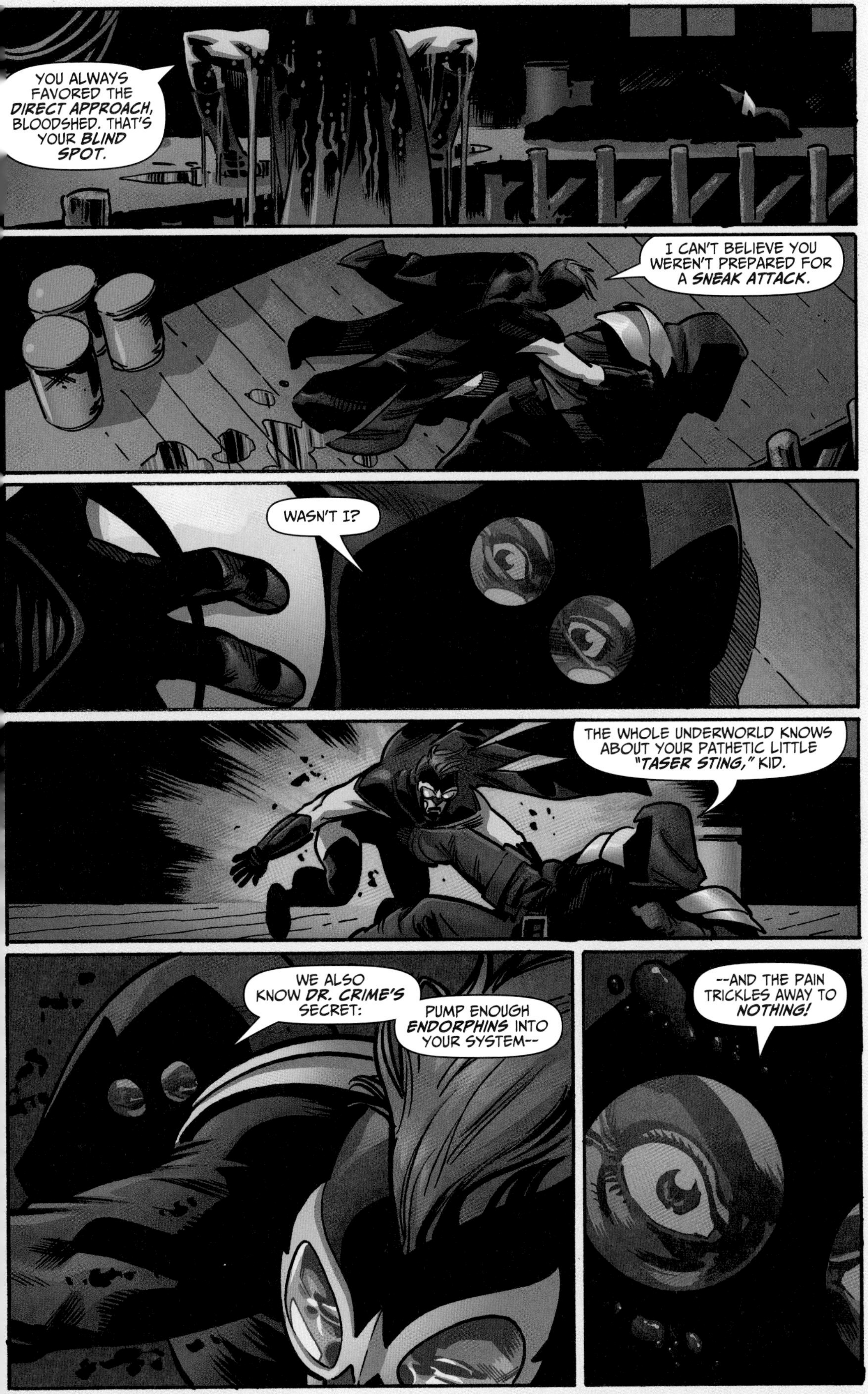
YOU ALWAYS FAVORED THE DIRECT APPROACH, BLOODSHED. THAT'S YOUR BLIND SPOT.
I CAN'T BELIEVE YOU WEREN'T PREPARED FOR A SNEAK ATTACK.
WASN'T I?
THE WHOLE UNDERWORLD KNOWS ABOUT YOUR PATHETIC LITTLE "TASER STING," KID.
WE ALSO KNOW DR. CRIME'S SECRET:
PUMP ENOUGH ENDORPHINS INTO YOUR SYSTEM--
--AND THE PAIN TRICKLES AWAY TO NOTHING!

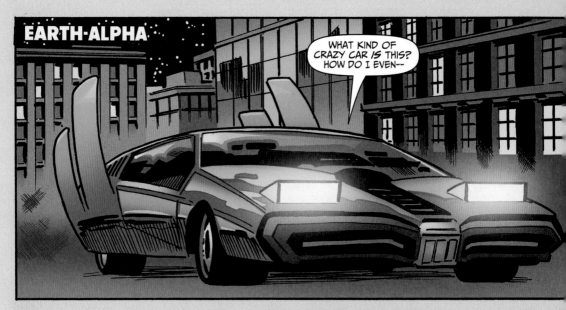

WHAT KIND OF *CRAZY CAR IS* THIS? HOW DO I EVEN--

JUST PUT IT INTO GEAR AND DON'T TOUCH THE *TURBO-BOOST!* I'LL *NAVIGATE--*

--BUT FIRST, WE FOLLOW *PROCEDURE!*

IMMEDIATE PROTOCOL IS *ALWAYS* TO ENGAGE THE *MULTICOLOR LIGHT-TRACER BEAM!*

BEFORE WE ENTERED, I ADJUSTED IT TO THE SPECIFIC *PAINT COLOR* OF WHAT I ASSUMED-- *CORRECTLY--* WAS BRAIN DRAIN'S *GETAWAY VAN!*

WE SHOULD BE ABLE TO *TRACK IT!*

GOOD THINKING, KID. BUT SHOULDN'T WE JUST CALL THE *POLICE?*

AND TELL THEM DRAGONFLYMAN IS OUT OF COMMISSION? THERE'LL BE MASS PANIC!

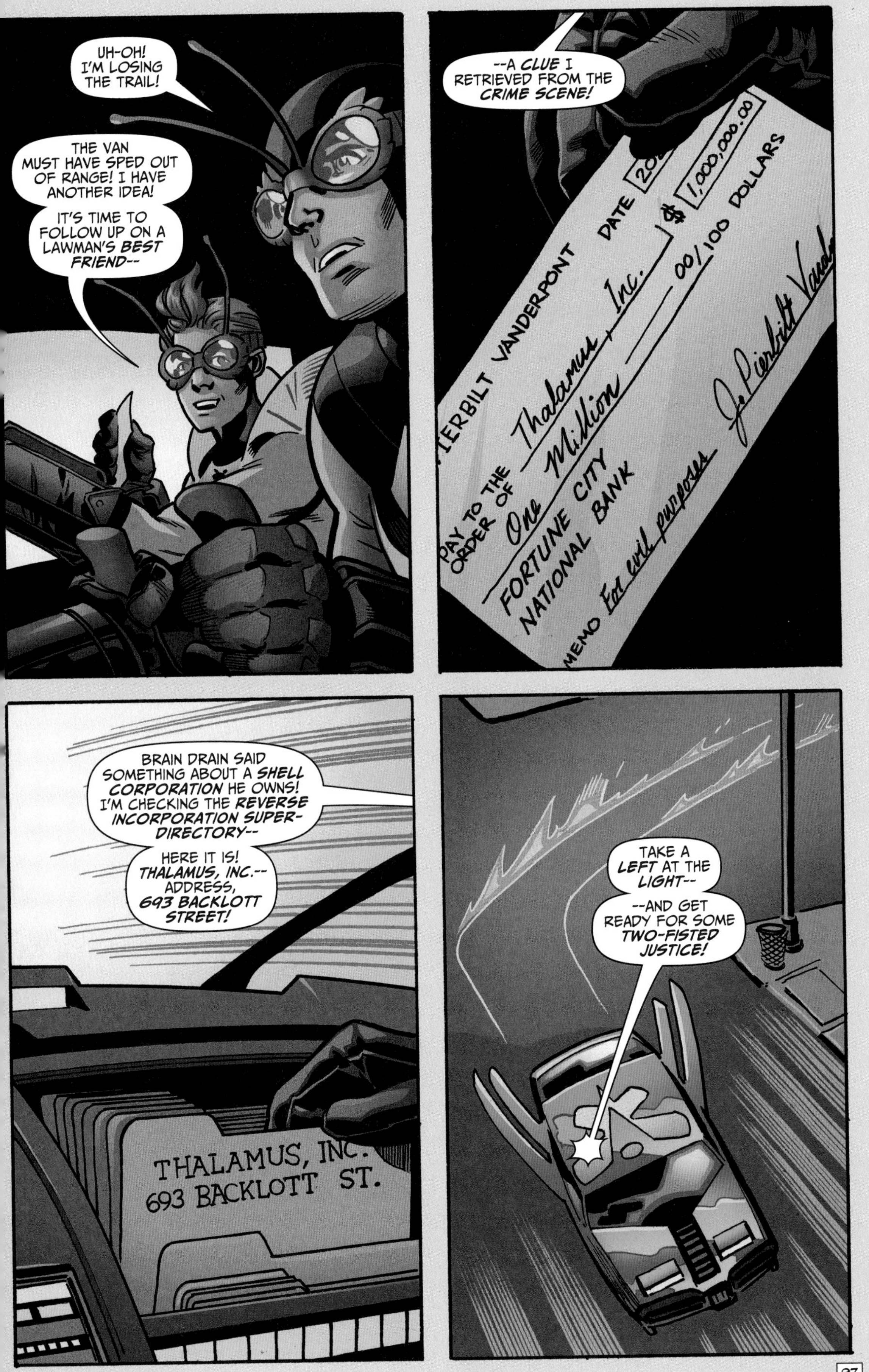
UH-OH! I'M LOSING THE TRAIL!
THE VAN MUST HAVE SPED OUT OF RANGE! I HAVE ANOTHER IDEA!
IT'S TIME TO FOLLOW UP ON A LAWMAN'S BEST FRIEND--
--A CLUE I RETRIEVED FROM THE CRIME SCENE!
DATE
$ 1,000,000.00
PAY TO THE ORDER OF Thalamus, Inc.
One Million 00/100 DOLLARS
FORTUNE CITY NATIONAL BANK
MEMO For evil purposes
BRAIN DRAIN SAID SOMETHING ABOUT A SHELL CORPORATION HE OWNS! I'M CHECKING THE REVERSE INCORPORATION SUPER-DIRECTORY--
HERE IT IS! THALAMUS, INC.-- ADDRESS, 693 BACKLOTT STREET!
THALAMUS, INC.
693 BACKLOTT ST.
TAKE A LEFT AT THE LIGHT--
--AND GET READY FOR SOME TWO-FISTED JUSTICE!

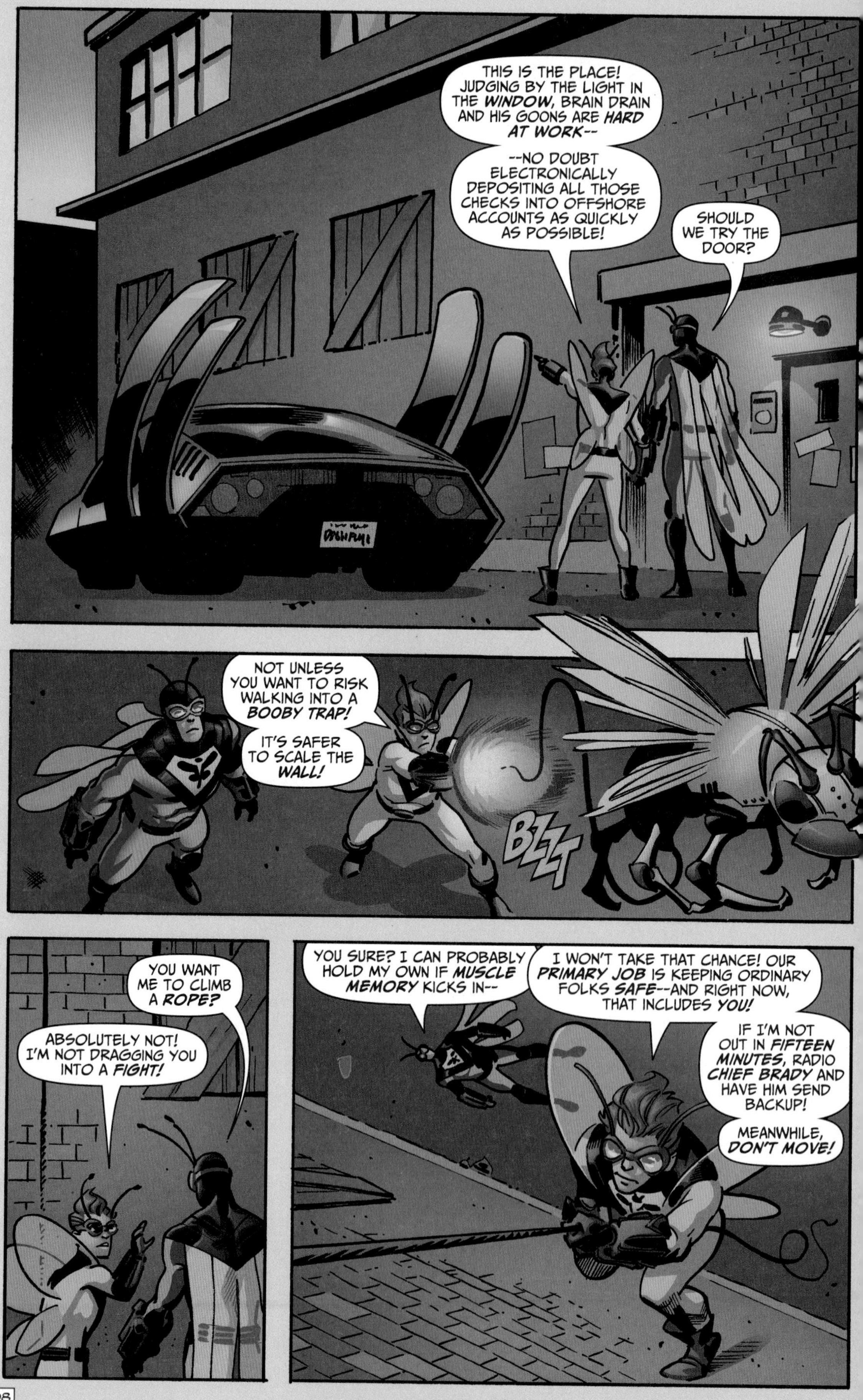

THIS IS THE PLACE! JUDGING BY THE LIGHT IN THE *WINDOW*, BRAIN DRAIN AND HIS GOONS ARE *HARD AT WORK*--
--NO DOUBT ELECTRONICALLY DEPOSITING ALL THOSE CHECKS INTO OFFSHORE ACCOUNTS AS QUICKLY AS POSSIBLE!
SHOULD WE TRY THE DOOR?
NOT UNLESS YOU WANT TO RISK WALKING INTO A *BOOBY TRAP!*
IT'S SAFER TO SCALE THE *WALL!*
BZZT
YOU WANT ME TO CLIMB A *ROPE?*
ABSOLUTELY NOT! I'M NOT DRAGGING YOU INTO A *FIGHT!*
YOU SURE? I CAN PROBABLY HOLD MY OWN IF *MUSCLE MEMORY* KICKS IN--
I WON'T TAKE THAT CHANCE! OUR *PRIMARY JOB* IS KEEPING ORDINARY FOLKS *SAFE*--AND RIGHT NOW, THAT INCLUDES *YOU!*
IF I'M NOT OUT IN *FIFTEEN MINUTES*, RADIO *CHIEF BRADY* AND HAVE HIM SEND BACKUP!
MEANWHILE, *DON'T MOVE!*

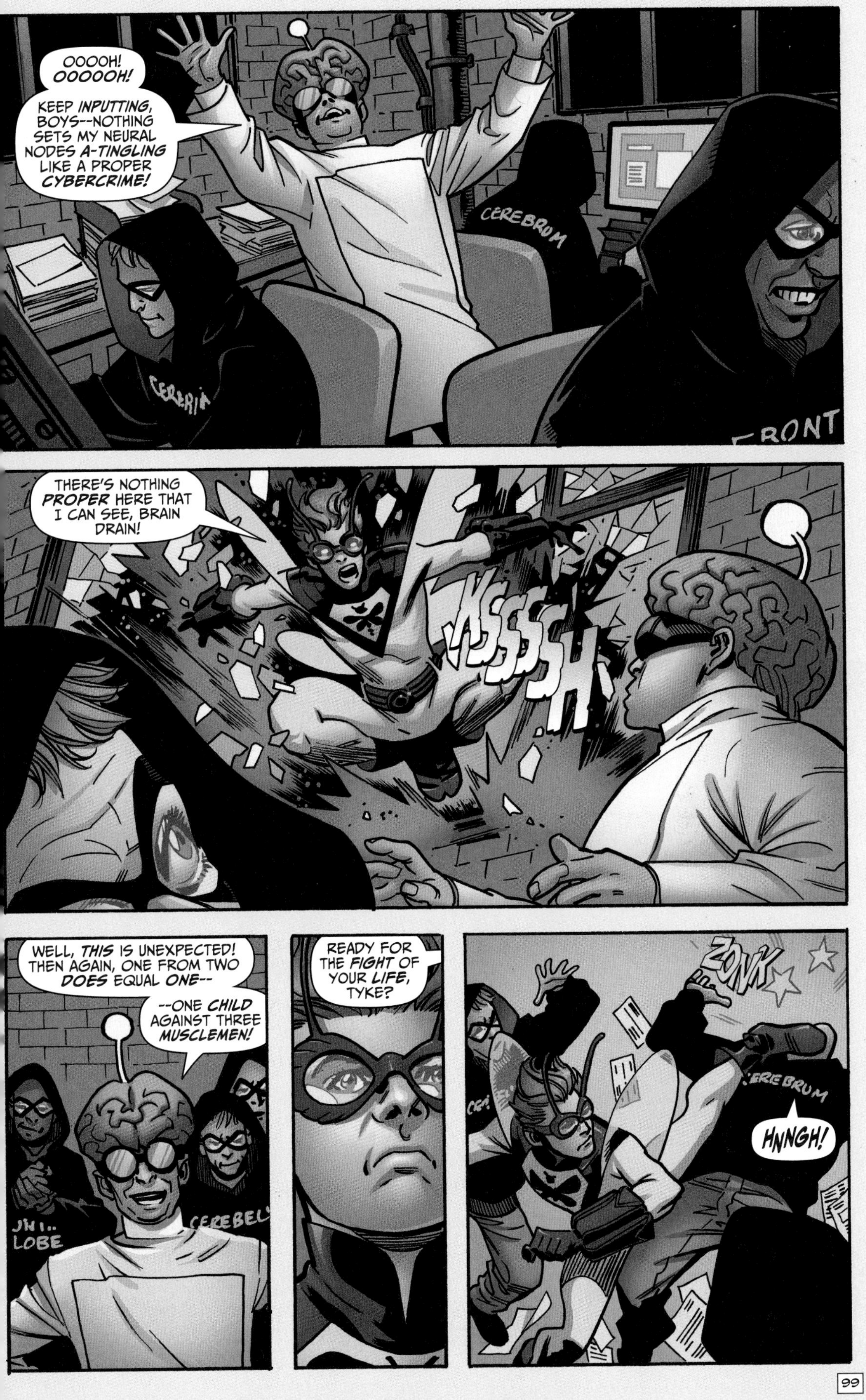
OOOOH! OOOOOH!
KEEP INPUTTING, BOYS--NOTHING SETS MY NEURAL NODES A-TINGLING LIKE A PROPER CYBERCRIME!
CEREBRUM
FRONT
THERE'S NOTHING PROPER HERE THAT I CAN SEE, BRAIN DRAIN!
KSSSSH
WELL, THIS IS UNEXPECTED! THEN AGAIN, ONE FROM TWO DOES EQUAL ONE--
--ONE CHILD AGAINST THREE MUSCLEMEN!
LOBE
READY FOR THE FIGHT OF YOUR LIFE, TYKE?
ZONK
CEREBRUM
HNNGH!

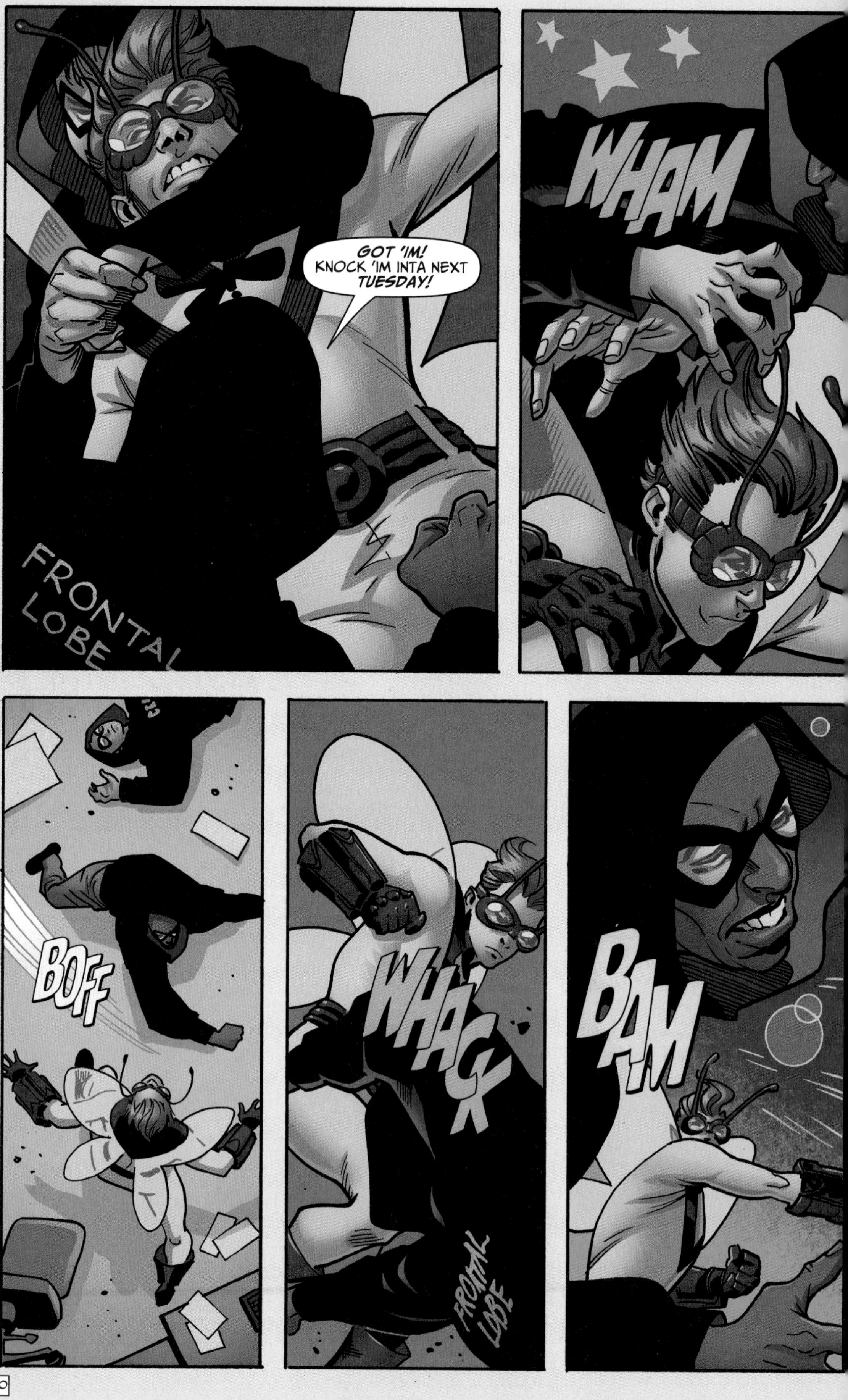
GOT 'IM!
KNOCK 'IM INTA NEXT
TUESDAY!
FRONTAL
LOBE
WHAM
BOFF
WHACK
FRONTAL
LOBE
BAM

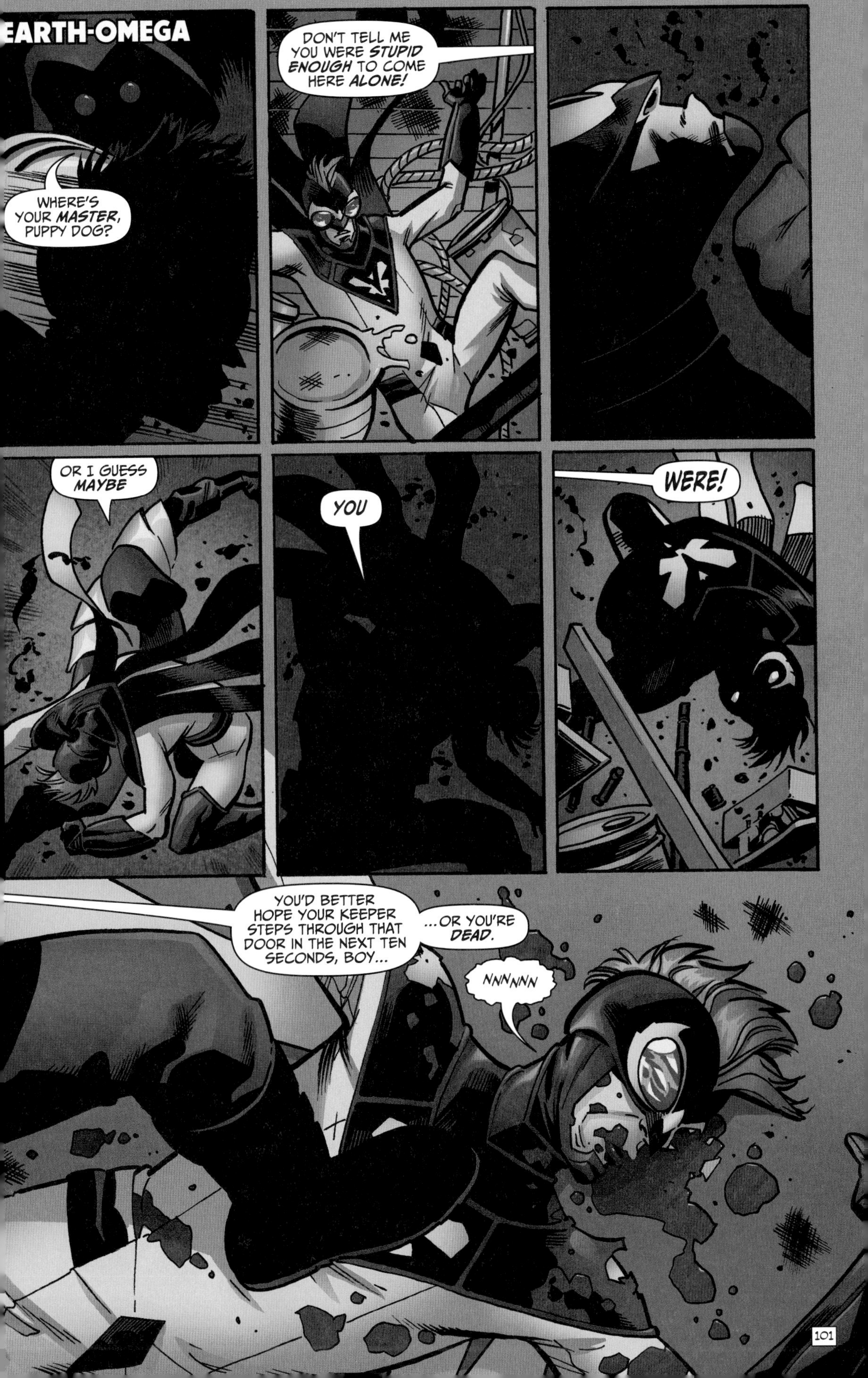
EARTH-OMEGA
WHERE'S YOUR MASTER, PUPPY DOG?
DON'T TELL ME YOU WERE STUPID ENOUGH TO COME HERE ALONE!
OR I GUESS MAYBE
YOU
WERE!
YOU'D BETTER HOPE YOUR KEEPER STEPS THROUGH THAT DOOR IN THE NEXT TEN SECONDS, BOY...
...OR YOU'RE DEAD.
NNNNNN

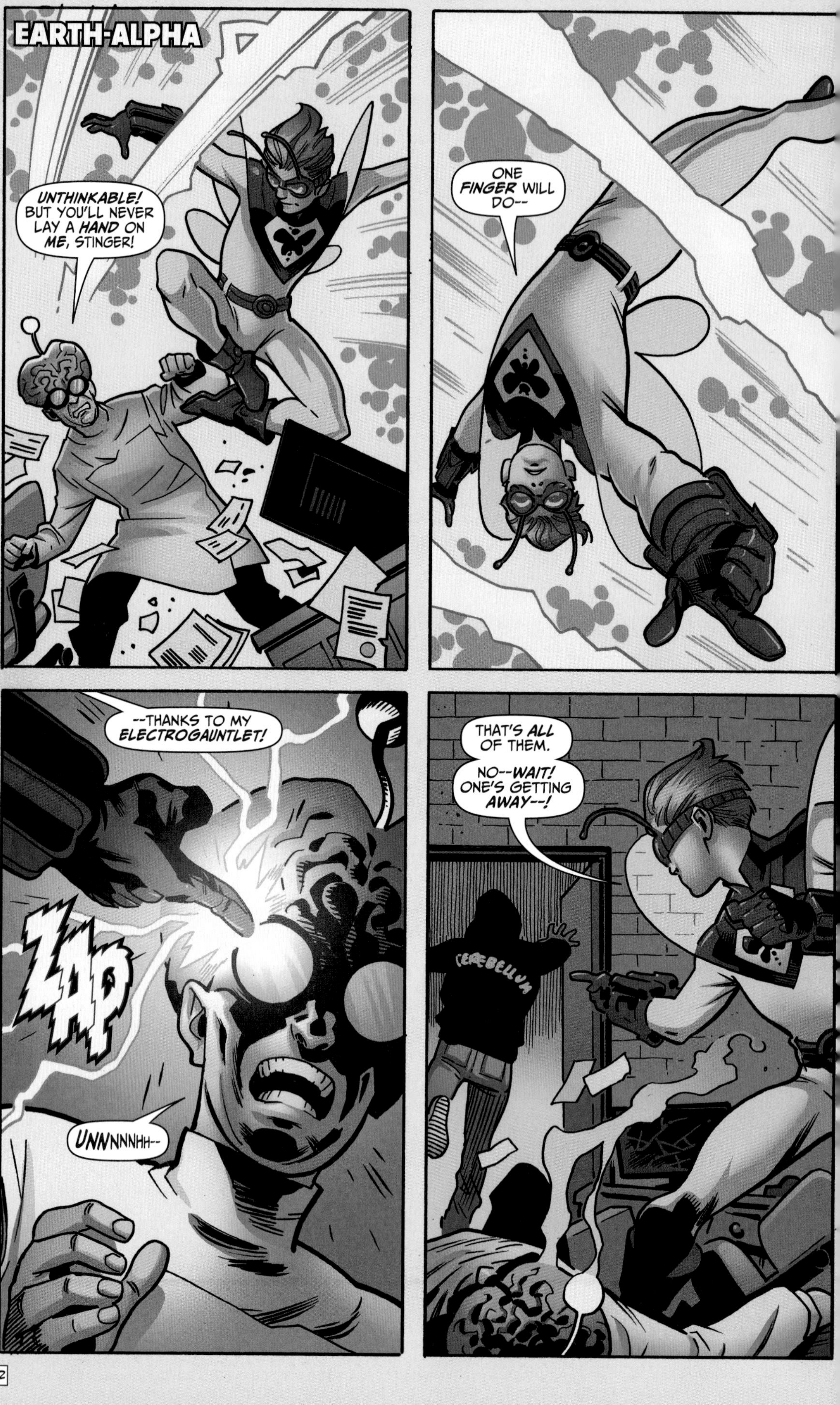
EARTH-ALPHA
UNTHINKABLE! BUT YOU'LL NEVER LAY A HAND ON ME, STINGER!
ONE FINGER WILL DO--
--THANKS TO MY ELECTROGAUNTLET!
ZAP
UNNNNNHH--
THAT'S ALL OF THEM.
NO--WAIT! ONE'S GETTING AWAY--!
CEREBELLUM

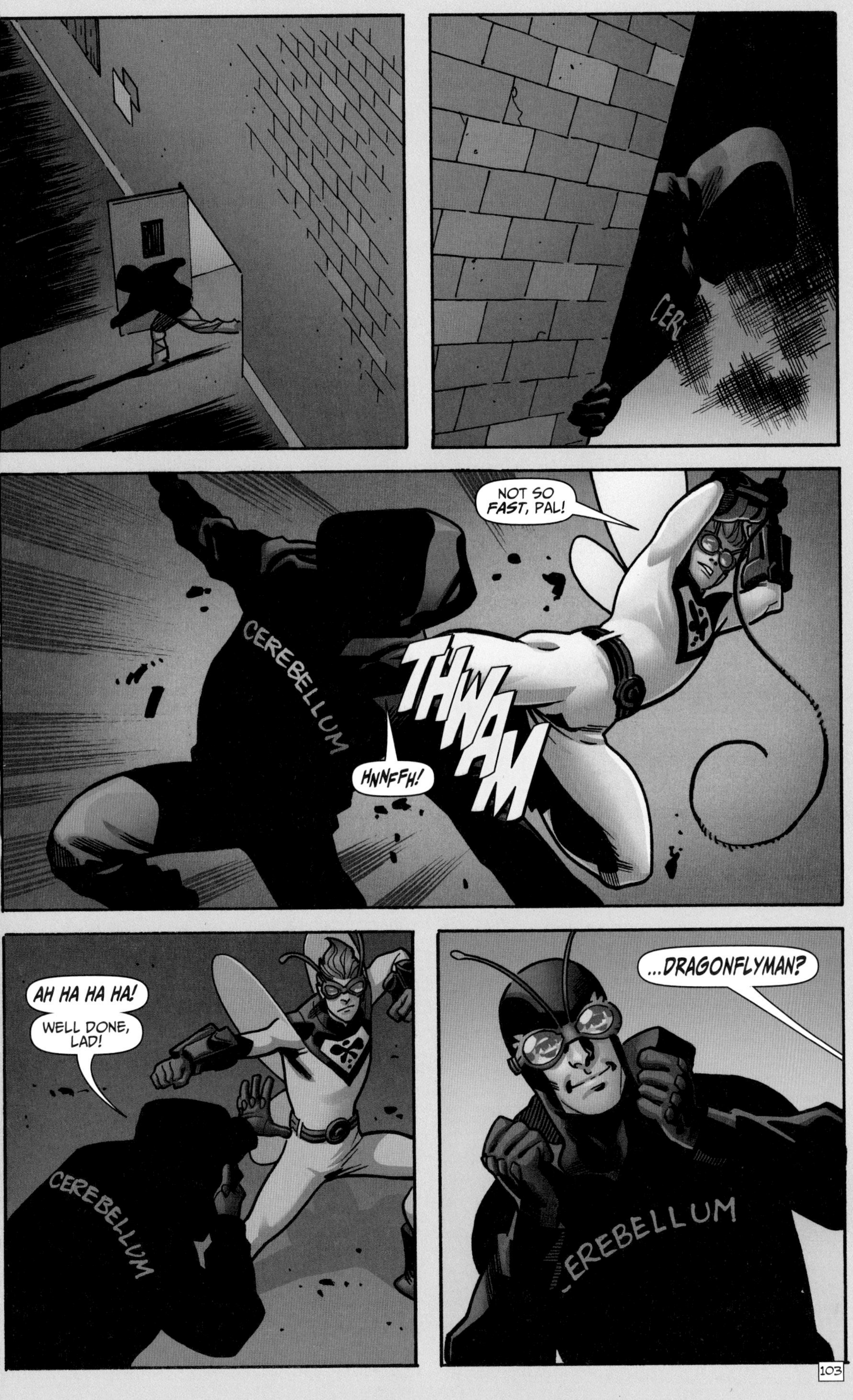
CERE
NOT SO FAST, PAL!
CEREBELLUM
THWAM
HNNFFH!
AH HA HA HA!
WELL DONE, LAD!
CEREBELLUM
...DRAGONFLYMAN?
CEREBELLUM

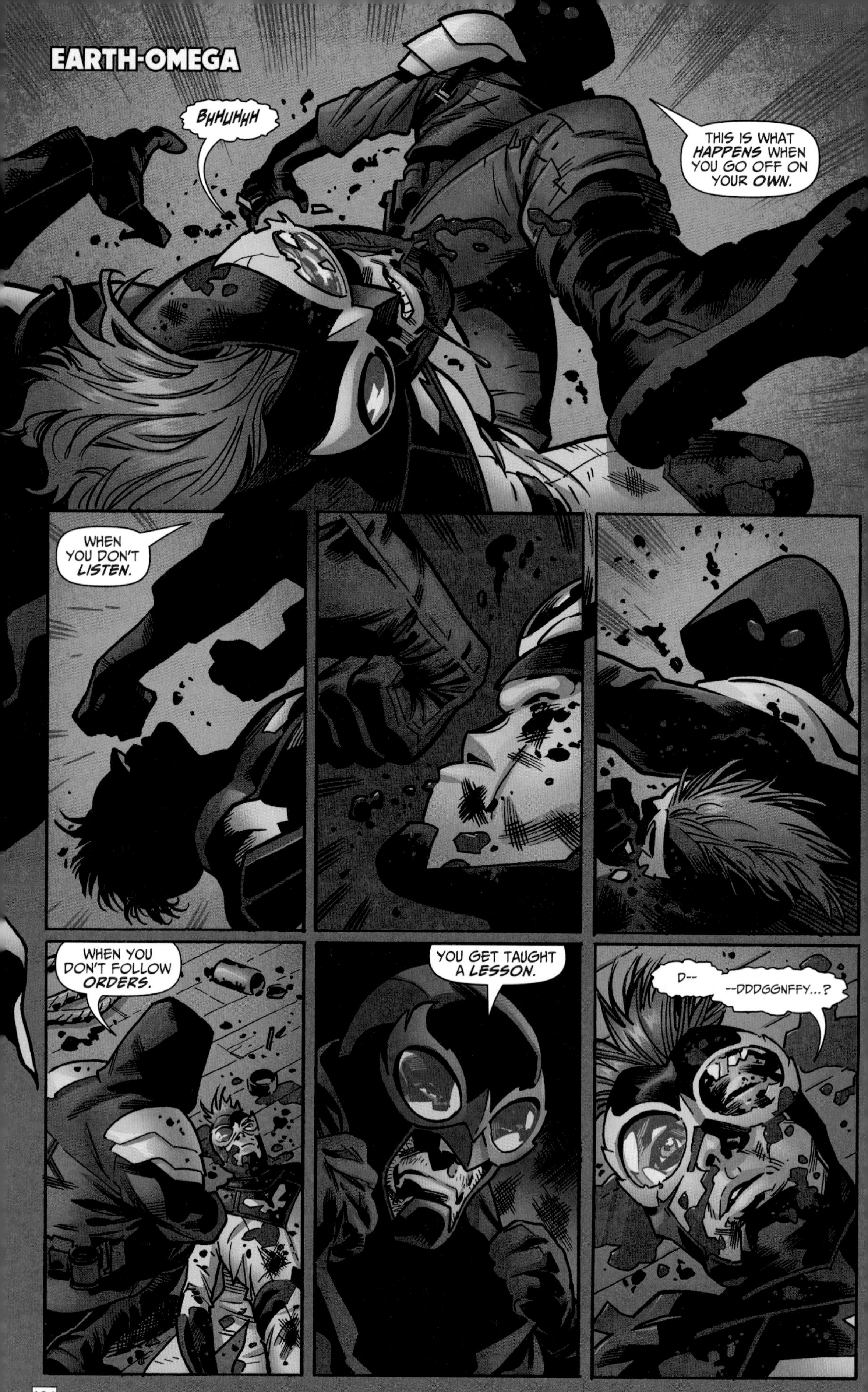
EARTH-OMEGA
BHHUHHH
THIS IS WHAT HAPPENS WHEN YOU GO OFF ON YOUR OWN.
WHEN YOU DON'T LISTEN.
WHEN YOU DON'T FOLLOW ORDERS.
YOU GET TAUGHT A LESSON.
D--
--DDDGGNFFY...?

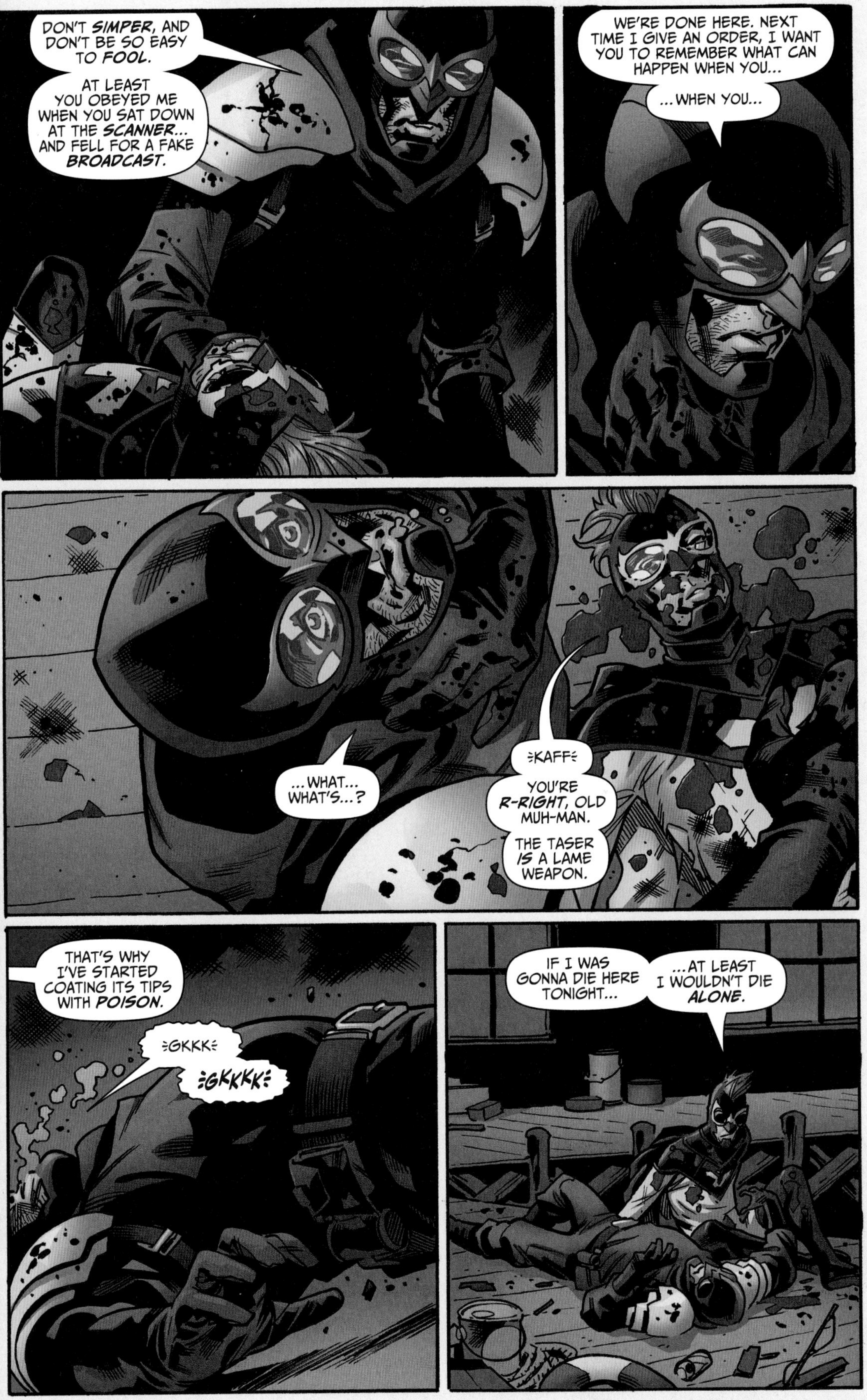
DON'T SIMPER, AND DON'T BE SO EASY TO FOOL.
AT LEAST YOU OBEYED ME WHEN YOU SAT DOWN AT THE SCANNER... AND FELL FOR A FAKE BROADCAST.
WE'RE DONE HERE. NEXT TIME I GIVE AN ORDER, I WANT YOU TO REMEMBER WHAT CAN HAPPEN WHEN YOU...
...WHEN YOU...
...WHAT... WHAT'S...?
KAFF
YOU'RE R-RIGHT, OLD MUH-MAN.
THE TASER IS A LAME WEAPON.
THAT'S WHY I'VE STARTED COATING ITS TIPS WITH POISON.
GKKK
GKKKK
IF I WAS GONNA DIE HERE TONIGHT...
...AT LEAST I WOULDN'T DIE ALONE.

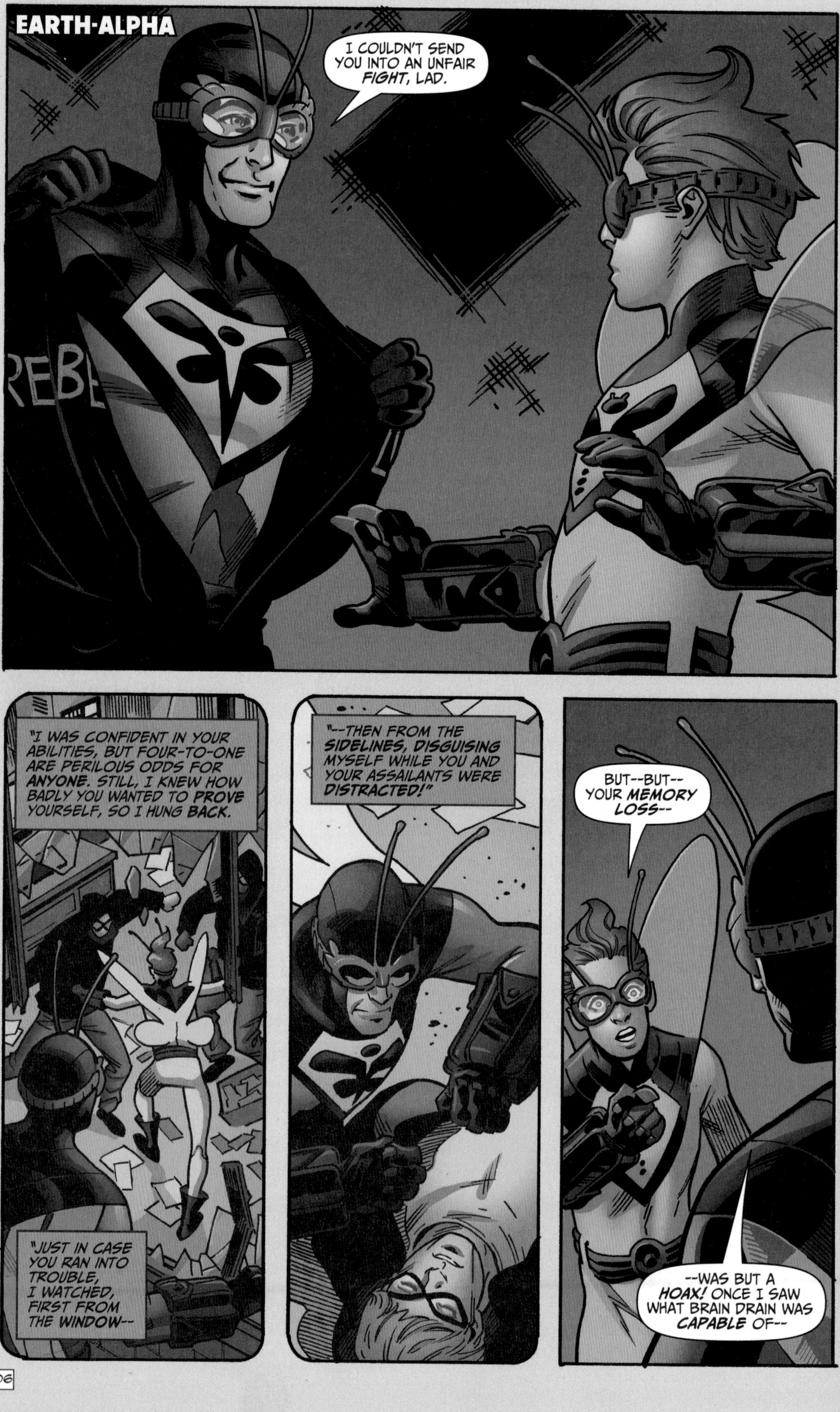
EARTH-ALPHA
I COULDN'T SEND YOU INTO AN UNFAIR FIGHT, LAD.
REBE
"I WAS CONFIDENT IN YOUR ABILITIES, BUT FOUR-TO-ONE ARE PERILOUS ODDS FOR ANYONE. STILL, I KNEW HOW BADLY YOU WANTED TO PROVE YOURSELF, SO I HUNG BACK.
"JUST IN CASE YOU RAN INTO TROUBLE, I WATCHED, FIRST FROM THE WINDOW--
"--THEN FROM THE SIDELINES, DISGUISING MYSELF WHILE YOU AND YOUR ASSAILANTS WERE DISTRACTED!"
BUT--BUT--YOUR MEMORY LOSS--
--WAS BUT A HOAX! ONCE I SAW WHAT BRAIN DRAIN WAS CAPABLE OF--

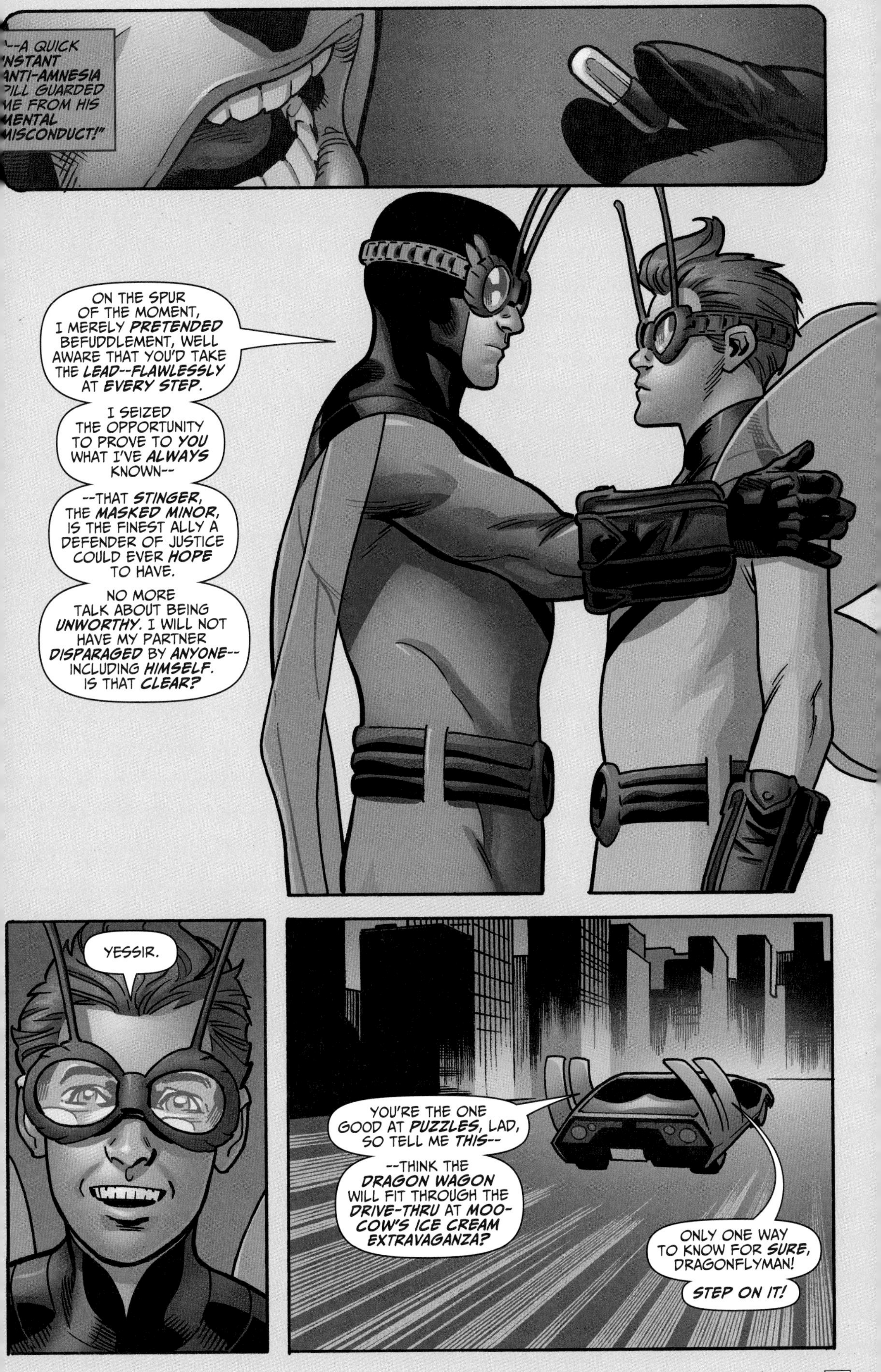
"--A QUICK INSTANT ANTI-AMNESIA PILL GUARDED ME FROM HIS MENTAL MISCONDUCT!"
ON THE SPUR OF THE MOMENT, I MERELY PRETENDED BEFUDDLEMENT, WELL AWARE THAT YOU'D TAKE THE LEAD--FLAWLESSLY AT EVERY STEP.
I SEIZED THE OPPORTUNITY TO PROVE TO YOU WHAT I'VE ALWAYS KNOWN--
--THAT STINGER, THE MASKED MINOR, IS THE FINEST ALLY A DEFENDER OF JUSTICE COULD EVER HOPE TO HAVE.
NO MORE TALK ABOUT BEING UNWORTHY. I WILL NOT HAVE MY PARTNER DISPARAGED BY ANYONE-- INCLUDING HIMSELF. IS THAT CLEAR?
YESSIR.
YOU'RE THE ONE GOOD AT PUZZLES, LAD, SO TELL ME THIS--
--THINK THE DRAGON WAGON WILL FIT THROUGH THE DRIVE-THRU AT MOO-COW'S ICE CREAM EXTRAVAGANZA?
ONLY ONE WAY TO KNOW FOR SURE, DRAGONFLYMAN!
STEP ON IT!

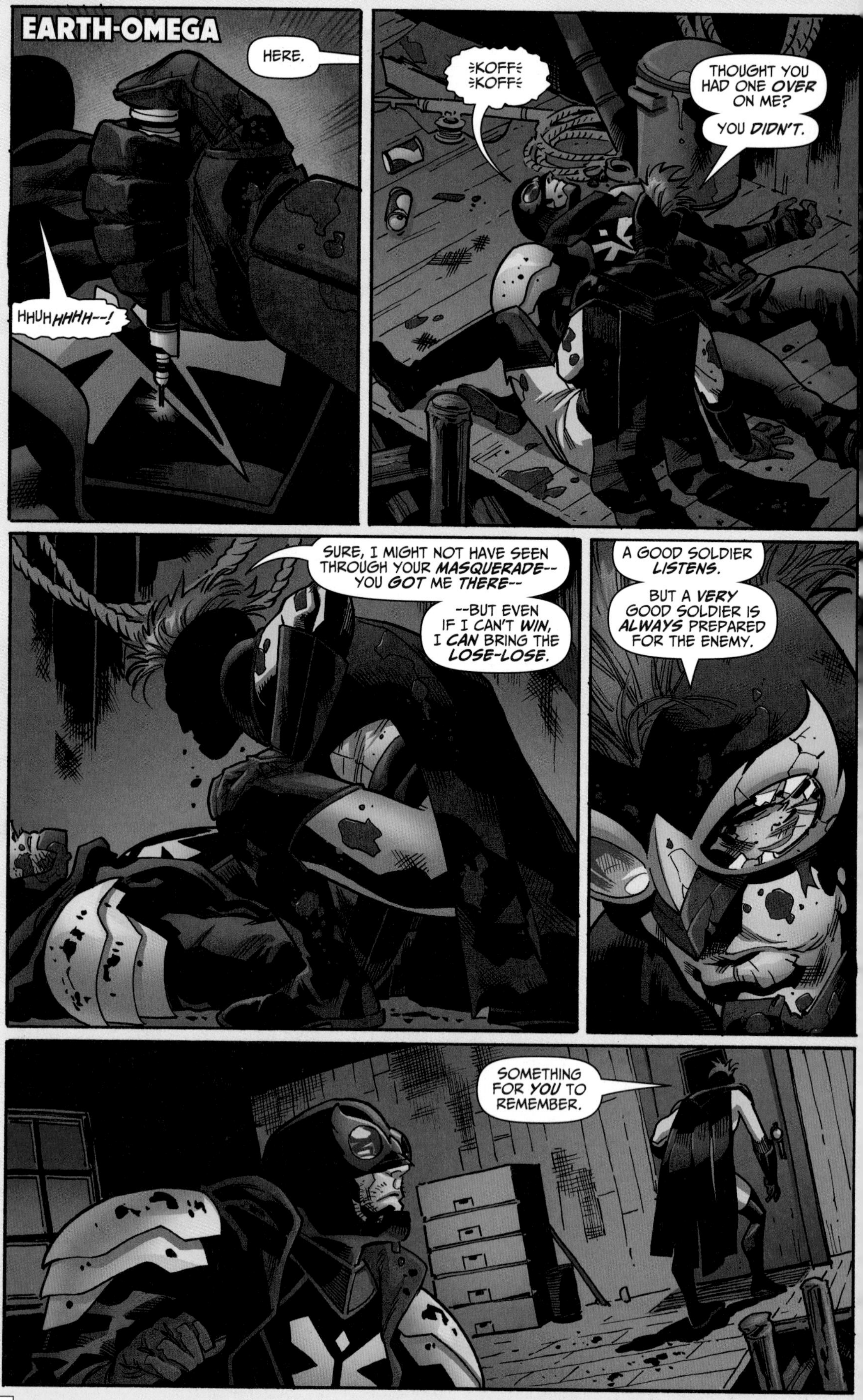
EARTH-OMEGA
HERE.
HHUHHHHH--!
KOFF KOFF
THOUGHT YOU HAD ONE OVER ON ME?
YOU DIDN'T.
SURE, I MIGHT NOT HAVE SEEN THROUGH YOUR MASQUERADE-- YOU GOT ME THERE--
--BUT EVEN IF I CAN'T WIN, I CAN BRING THE LOSE-LOSE.
A GOOD SOLDIER LISTENS.
BUT A VERY GOOD SOLDIER IS ALWAYS PREPARED FOR THE ENEMY.
SOMETHING FOR YOU TO REMEMBER.

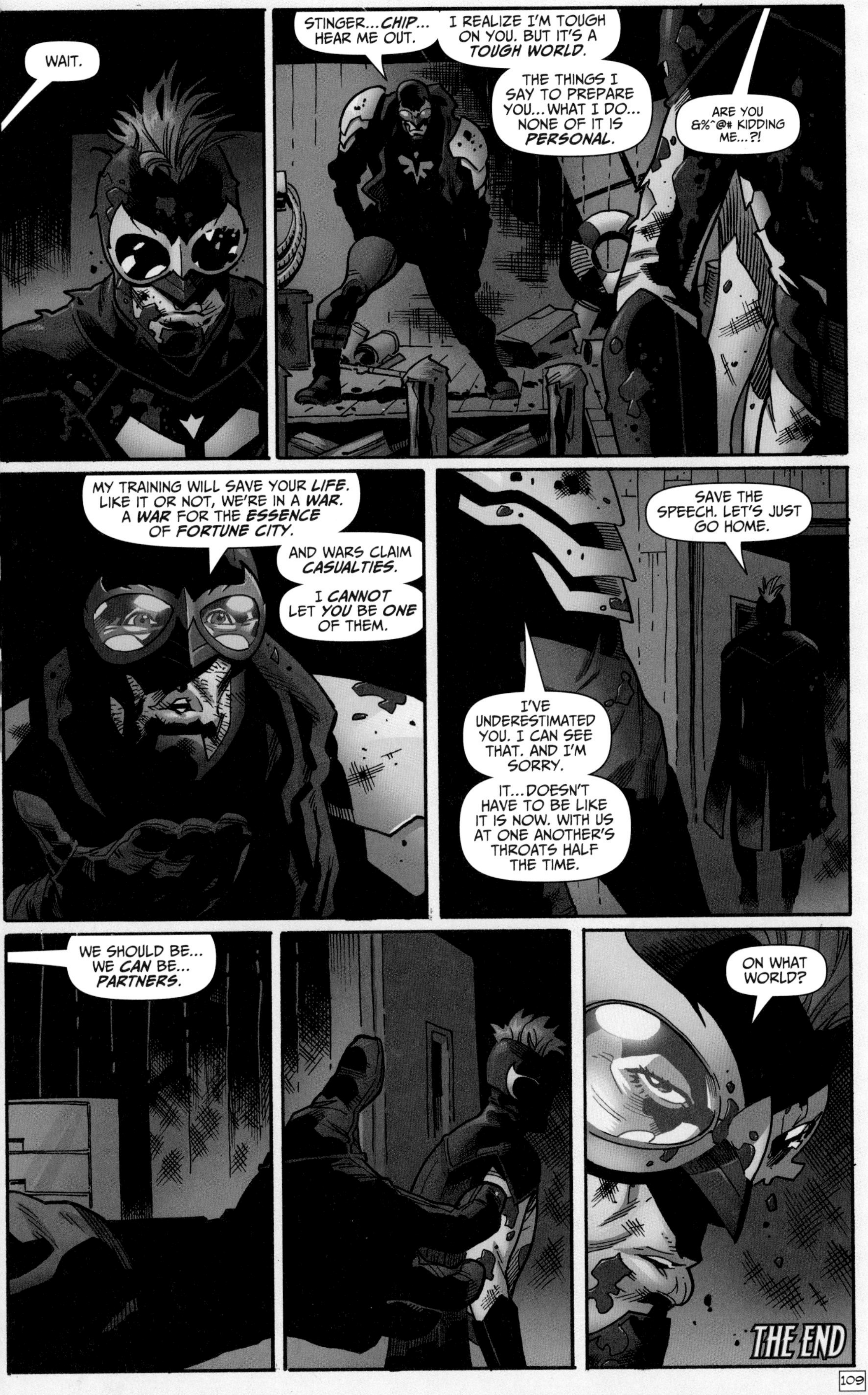
WAIT.
STINGER...CHIP... HEAR ME OUT.
I REALIZE I'M TOUGH ON YOU. BUT IT'S A TOUGH WORLD.
THE THINGS I SAY TO PREPARE YOU...WHAT I DO... NONE OF IT IS PERSONAL.
ARE YOU &%^@# KIDDING ME...?!
MY TRAINING WILL SAVE YOUR LIFE. LIKE IT OR NOT, WE'RE IN A WAR. A WAR FOR THE ESSENCE OF FORTUNE CITY.
AND WARS CLAIM CASUALTIES.
I CANNOT LET YOU BE ONE OF THEM.
SAVE THE SPEECH. LET'S JUST GO HOME.
I'VE UNDERESTIMATED YOU. I CAN SEE THAT. AND I'M SORRY.
IT...DOESN'T HAVE TO BE LIKE IT IS NOW. WITH US AT ONE ANOTHER'S THROATS HALF THE TIME.
WE SHOULD BE... WE CAN BE... PARTNERS.
ON WHAT WORLD?
THE END

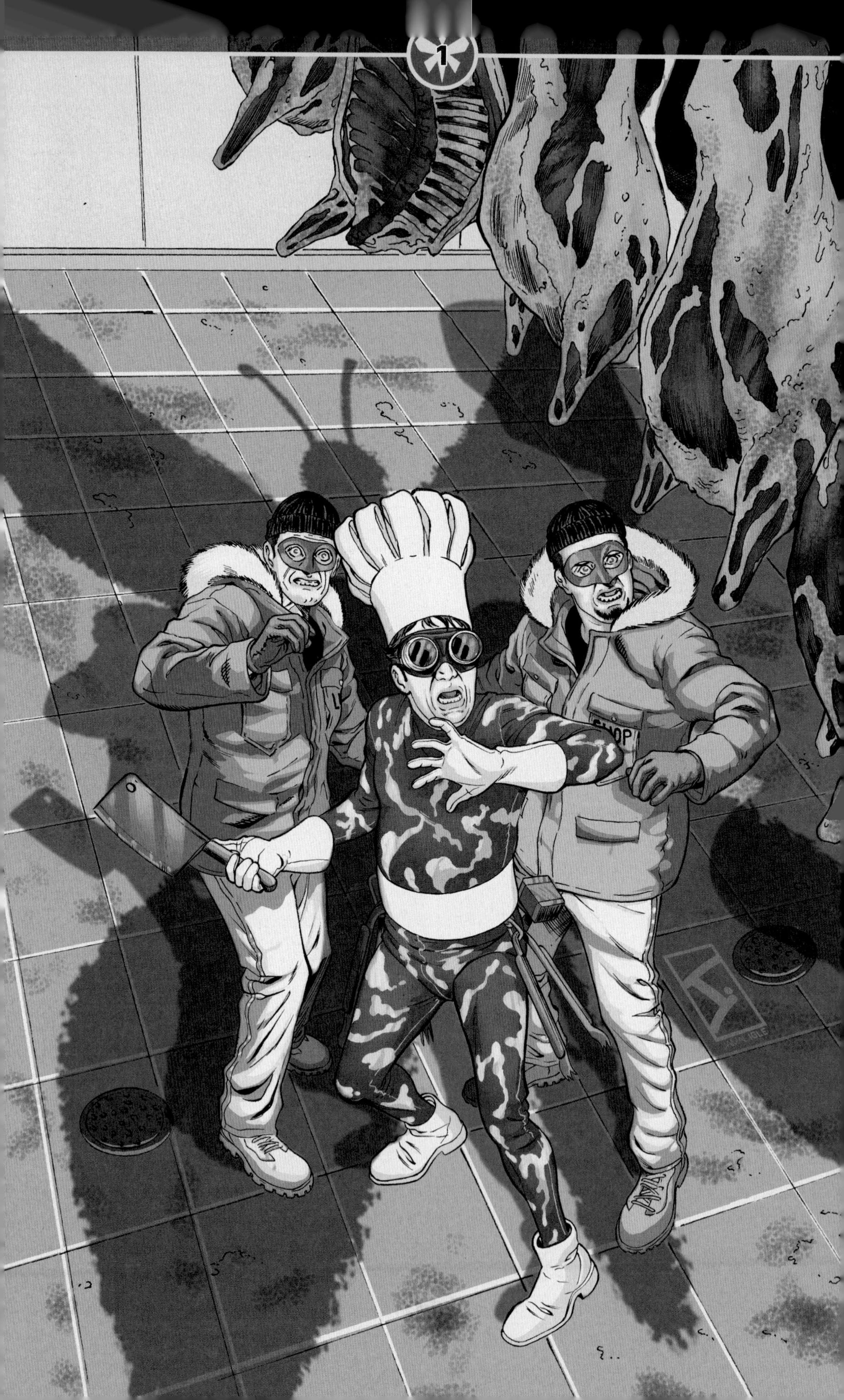
1

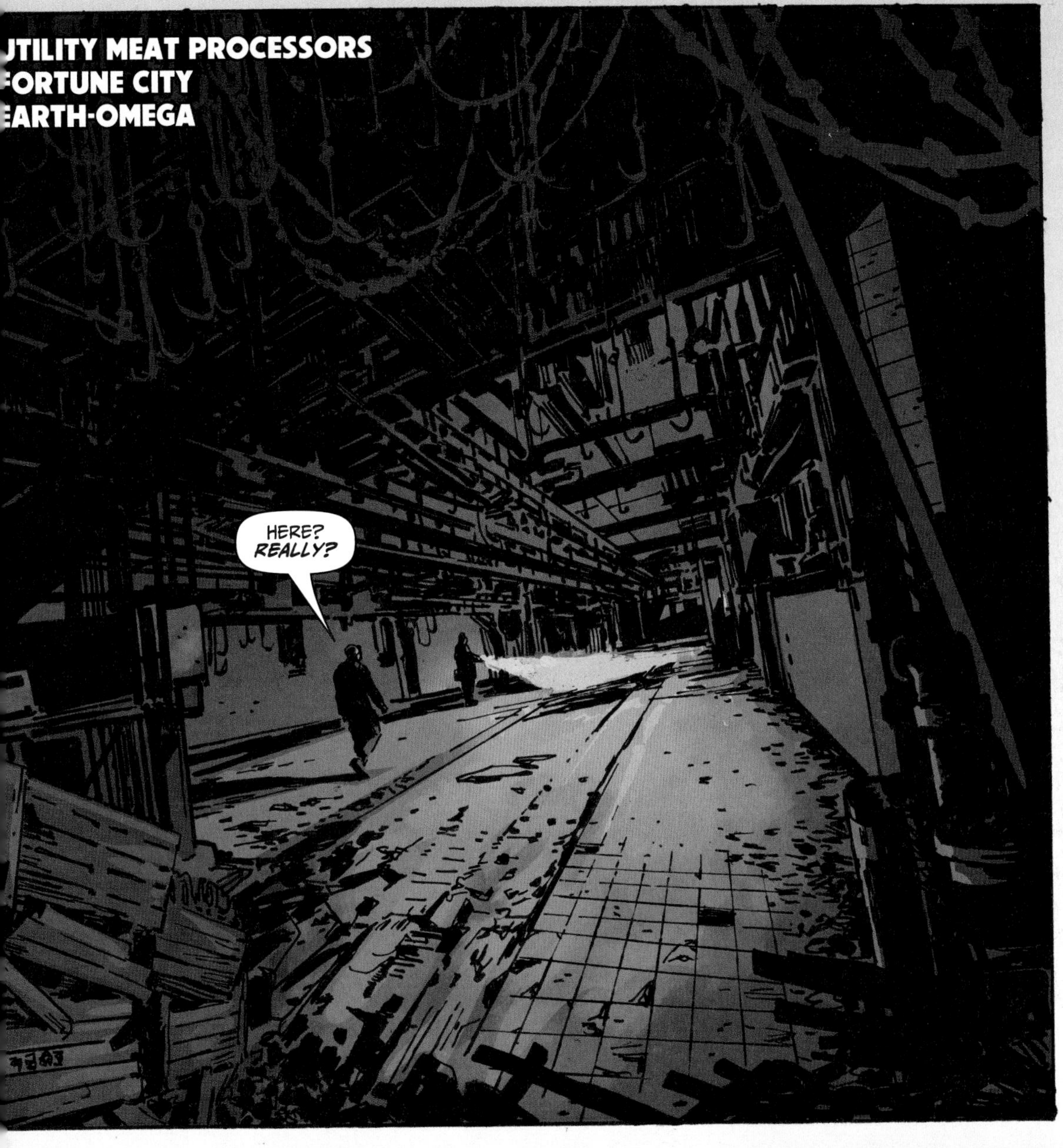
UTILITY MEAT PROCESSORS
FORTUNE CITY
EARTH-OMEGA
HERE? REALLY?

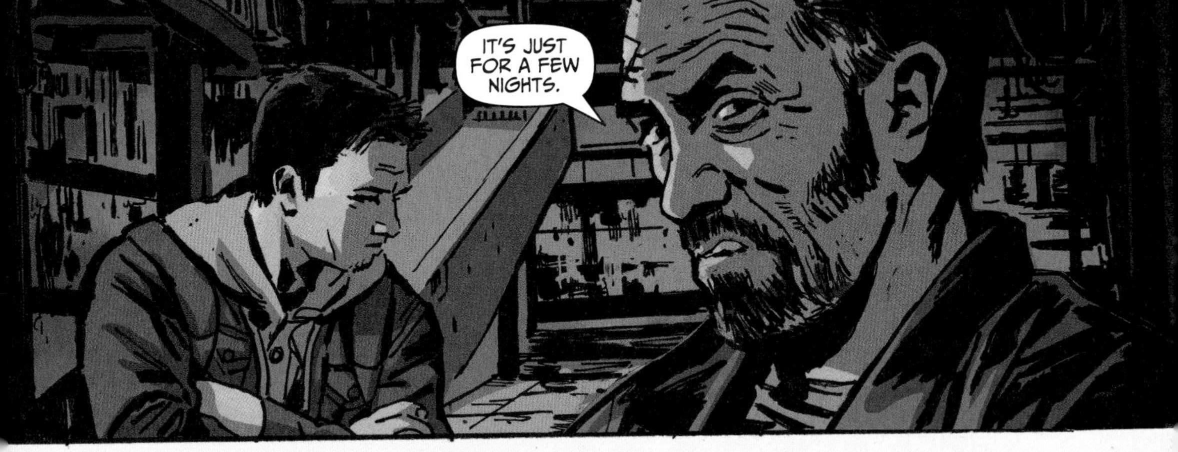
IT'S JUST FOR A FEW NIGHTS.

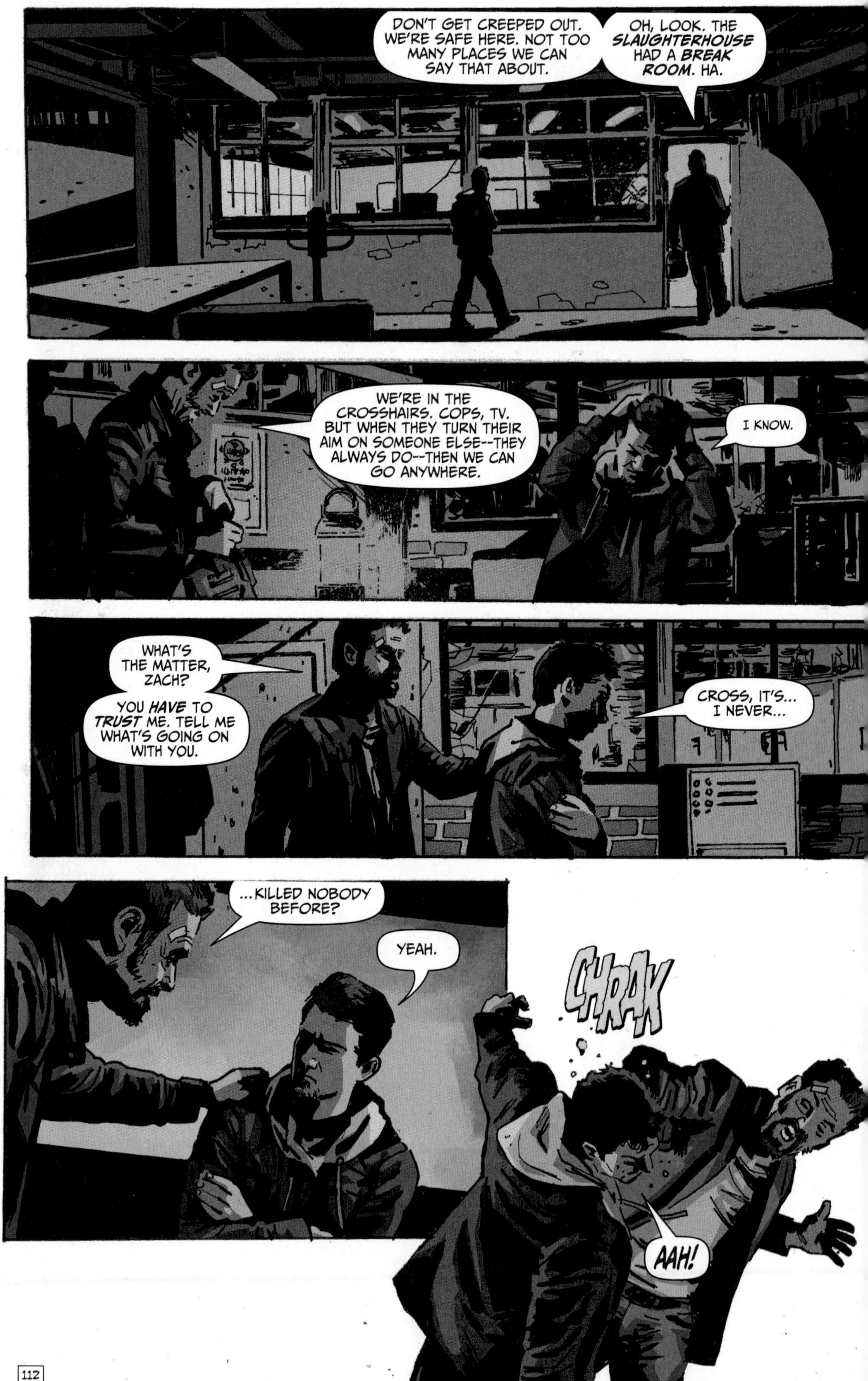
DON'T GET CREEPED OUT. WE'RE SAFE HERE. NOT TOO MANY PLACES WE CAN SAY THAT ABOUT.
OH, LOOK. THE *SLAUGHTERHOUSE* HAD A *BREAK ROOM*. HA.
WE'RE IN THE CROSSHAIRS. COPS, TV. BUT WHEN THEY TURN THEIR AIM ON SOMEONE ELSE--THEY ALWAYS DO--THEN WE CAN GO ANYWHERE.
I KNOW.
WHAT'S THE MATTER, ZACH?
YOU *HAVE* TO *TRUST* ME. TELL ME WHAT'S GOING ON WITH YOU.
CROSS, IT'S... I NEVER...
...KILLED NOBODY BEFORE?
YEAH.
CHRAK
AAH!

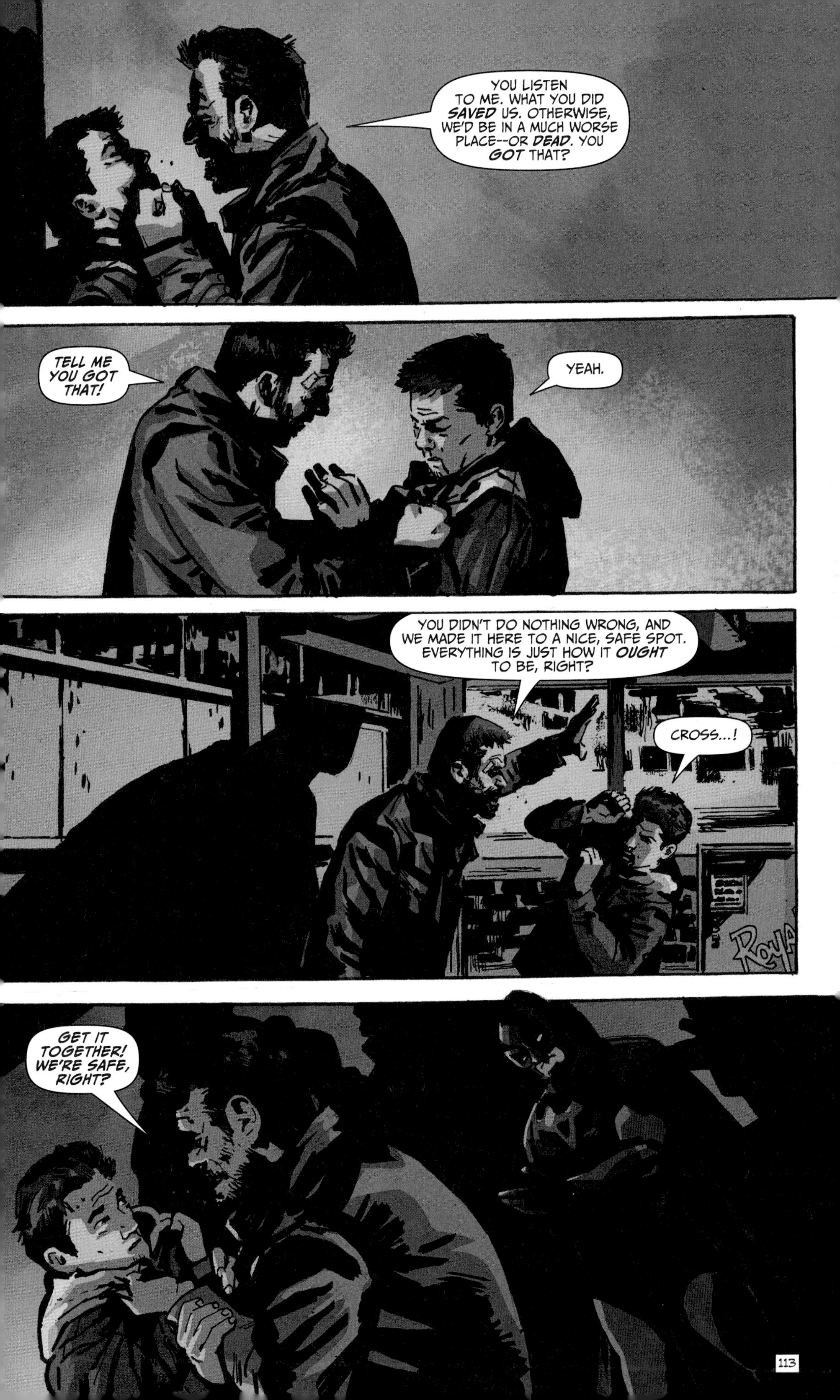
YOU LISTEN TO ME. WHAT YOU DID SAVED US. OTHERWISE, WE'D BE IN A MUCH WORSE PLACE--OR DEAD. YOU GOT THAT?
TELL ME YOU GOT THAT!
YEAH.
YOU DIDN'T DO NOTHING WRONG, AND WE MADE IT HERE TO A NICE, SAFE SPOT. EVERYTHING IS JUST HOW IT OUGHT TO BE, RIGHT?
CROSS...!
GET IT TOGETHER! WE'RE SAFE, RIGHT?

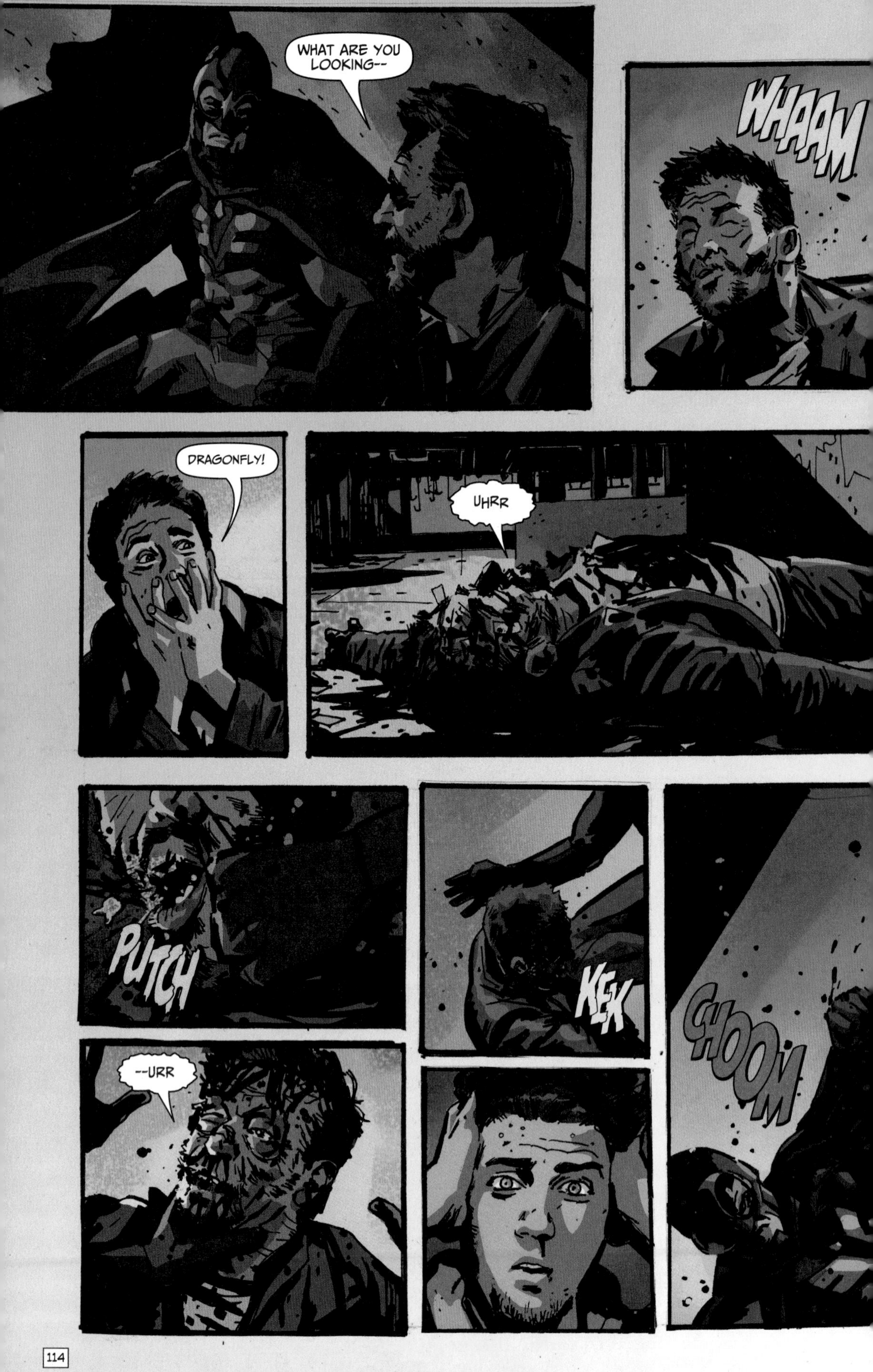
WHAT ARE YOU LOOKING--
WHAAM
DRAGONFLY!
UHRR
PUTCH
KEK
CHOOM
--URR

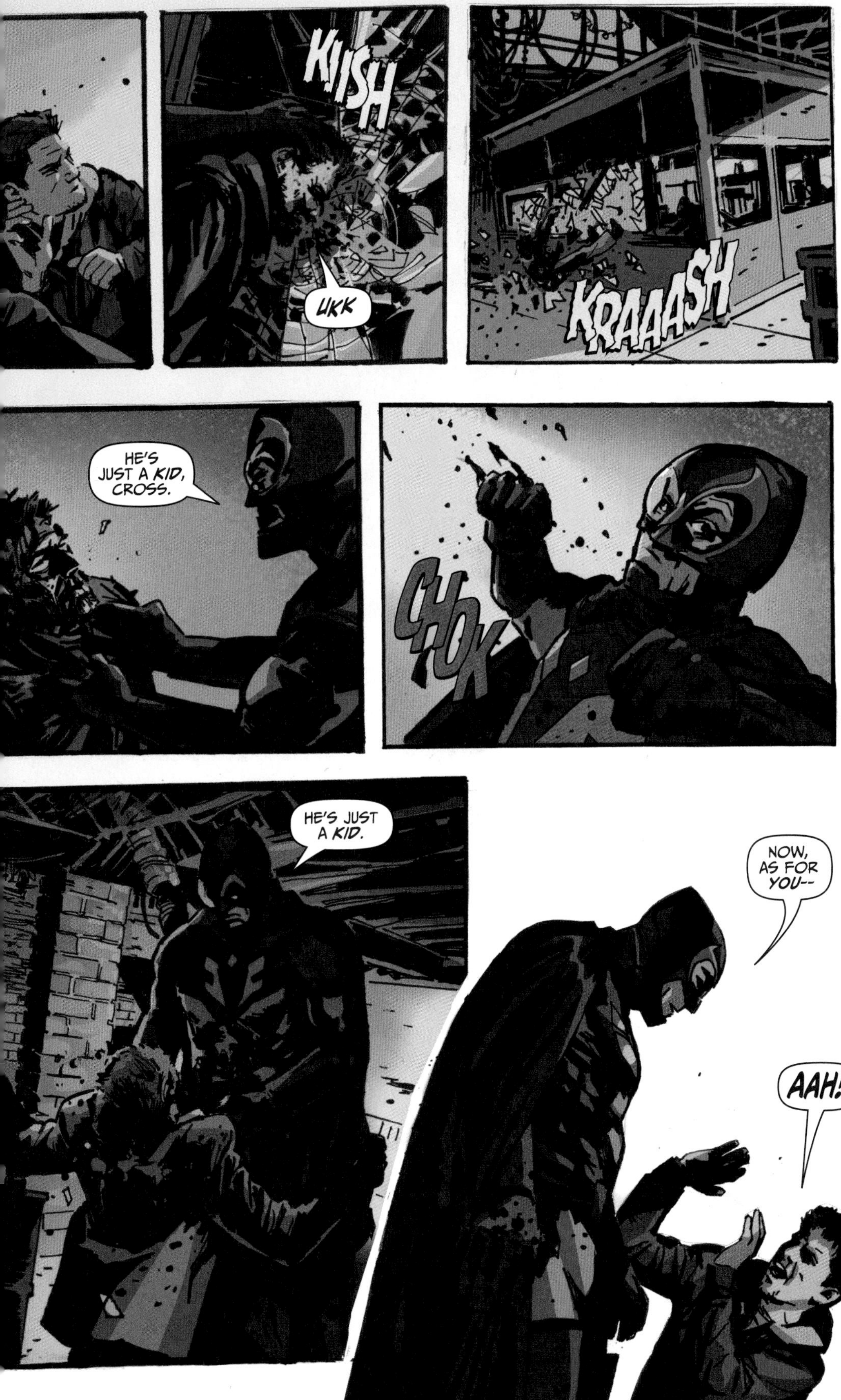
KIISH
UKK
KRAAASH
HE'S JUST A KID, CROSS.
CHOK
HE'S JUST A KID.
NOW, AS FOR YOU--
AAH!

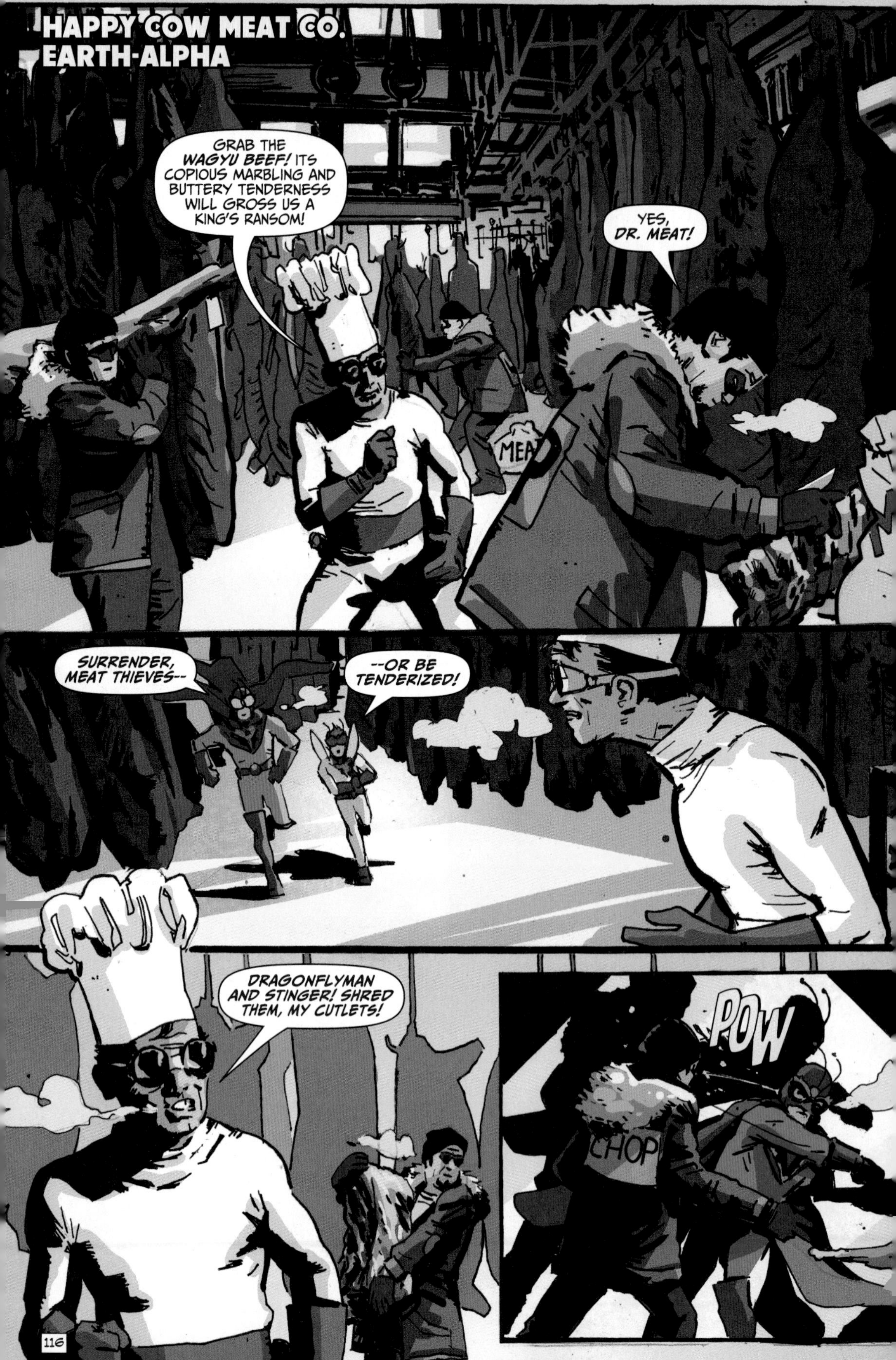
HAPPY COW MEAT CO.
EARTH-ALPHA
GRAB THE WAGYU BEEF! ITS COPIOUS MARBLING AND BUTTERY TENDERNESS WILL GROSS US A KING'S RANSOM!
YES, DR. MEAT!
MEAT
SURRENDER, MEAT THIEVES--
--OR BE TENDERIZED!
DRAGONFLYMAN AND STINGER! SHRED THEM, MY CUTLETS!
POW
CHOP

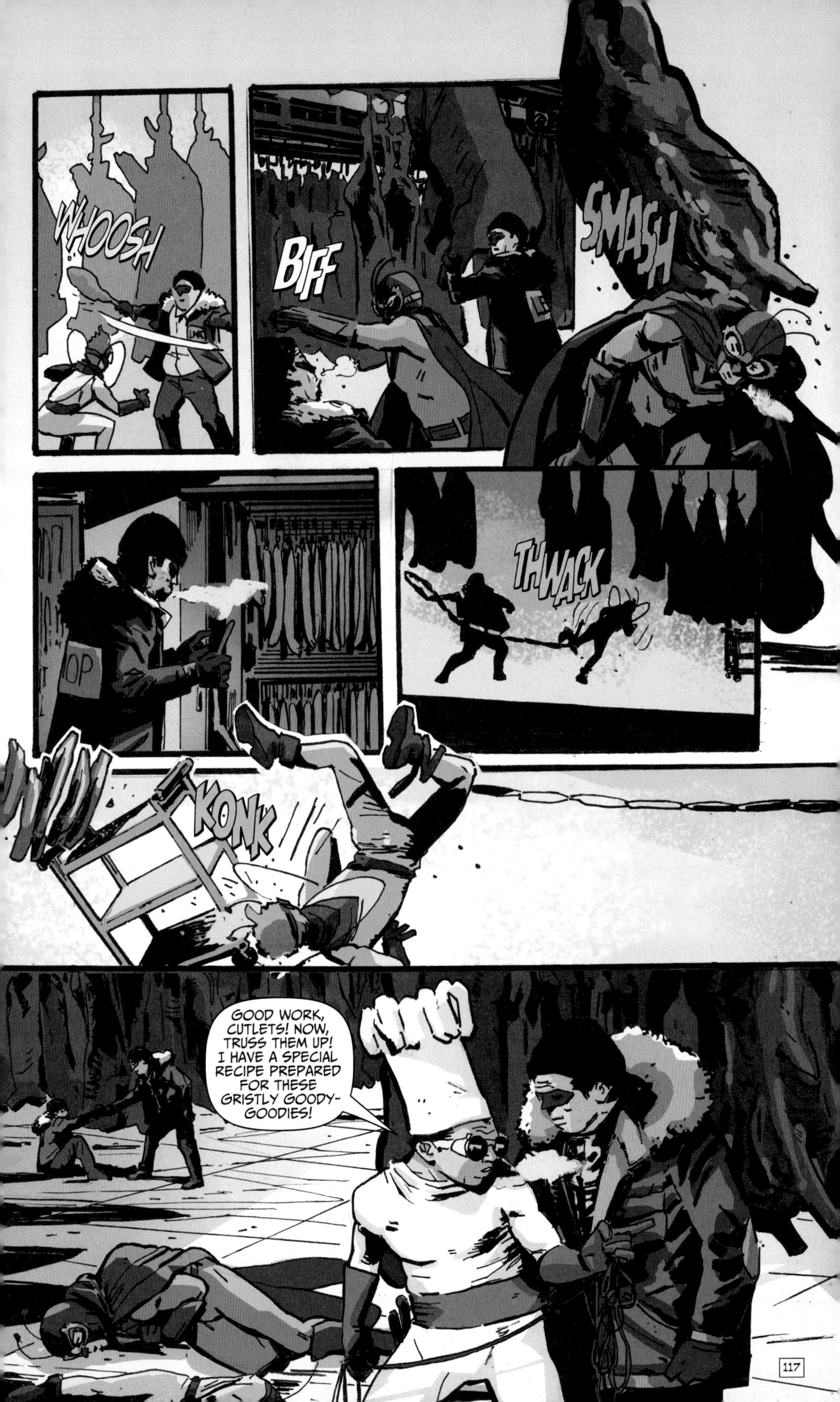
WHOOSH
BIFF
SMASH
THWACK
KONK
GOOD WORK, CUTLETS! NOW, TRUSS THEM UP! I HAVE A SPECIAL RECIPE PREPARED FOR THESE GRISTLY GOODY-GOODIES!

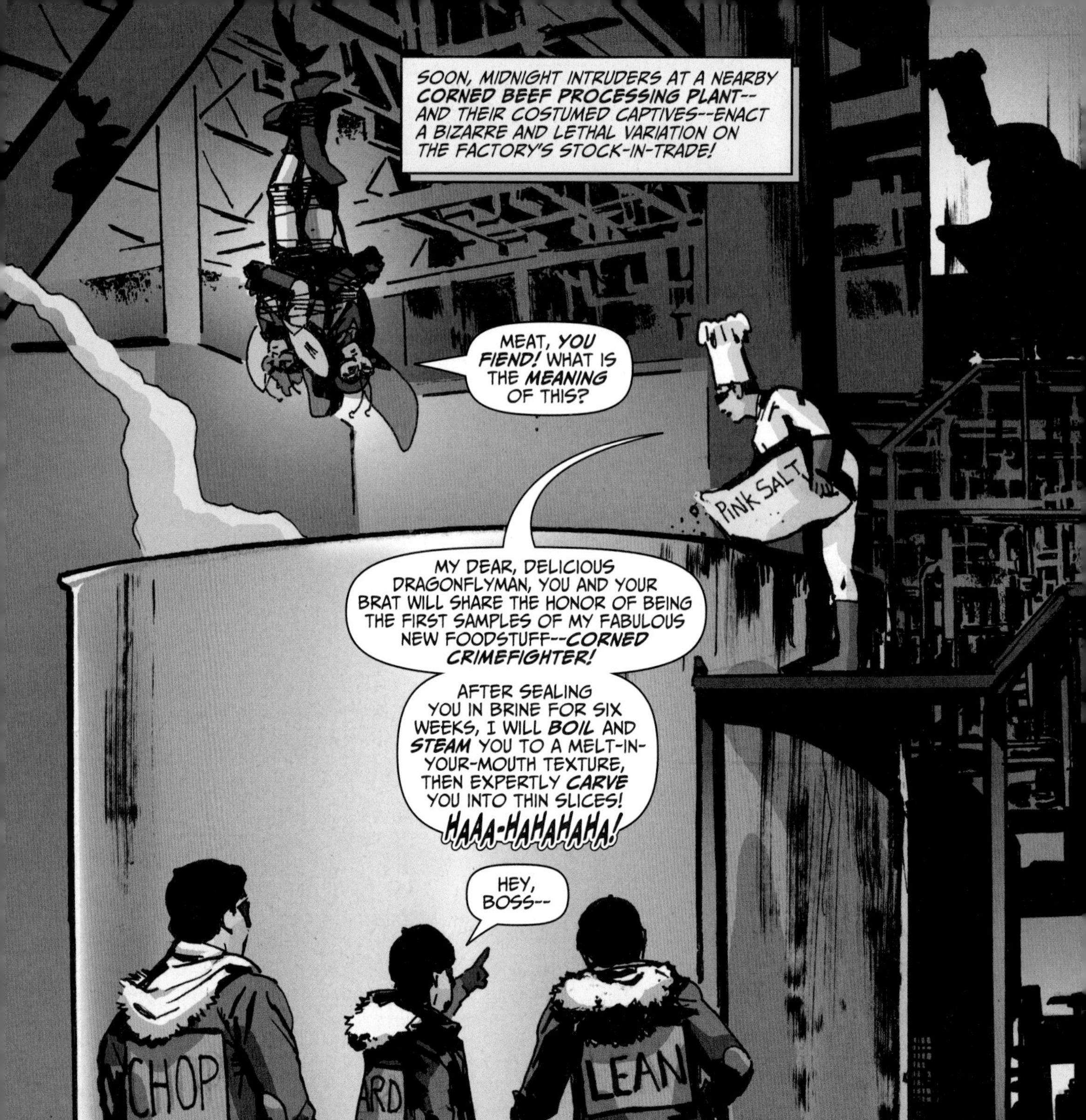
SOON, MIDNIGHT INTRUDERS AT A NEARBY CORNED BEEF PROCESSING PLANT--AND THEIR COSTUMED CAPTIVES--ENACT A BIZARRE AND LETHAL VARIATION ON THE FACTORY'S STOCK-IN-TRADE!
MEAT, YOU FIEND! WHAT IS THE MEANING OF THIS?
PINK SALT
MY DEAR, DELICIOUS DRAGONFLYMAN, YOU AND YOUR BRAT WILL SHARE THE HONOR OF BEING THE FIRST SAMPLES OF MY FABULOUS NEW FOODSTUFF--CORNED CRIMEFIGHTER!
AFTER SEALING YOU IN BRINE FOR SIX WEEKS, I WILL BOIL AND STEAM YOU TO A MELT-IN-YOUR-MOUTH TEXTURE, THEN EXPERTLY CARVE YOU INTO THIN SLICES!
HAAA-HAHAHAHA!
HEY, BOSS--
CHOP
ARD
LEAN
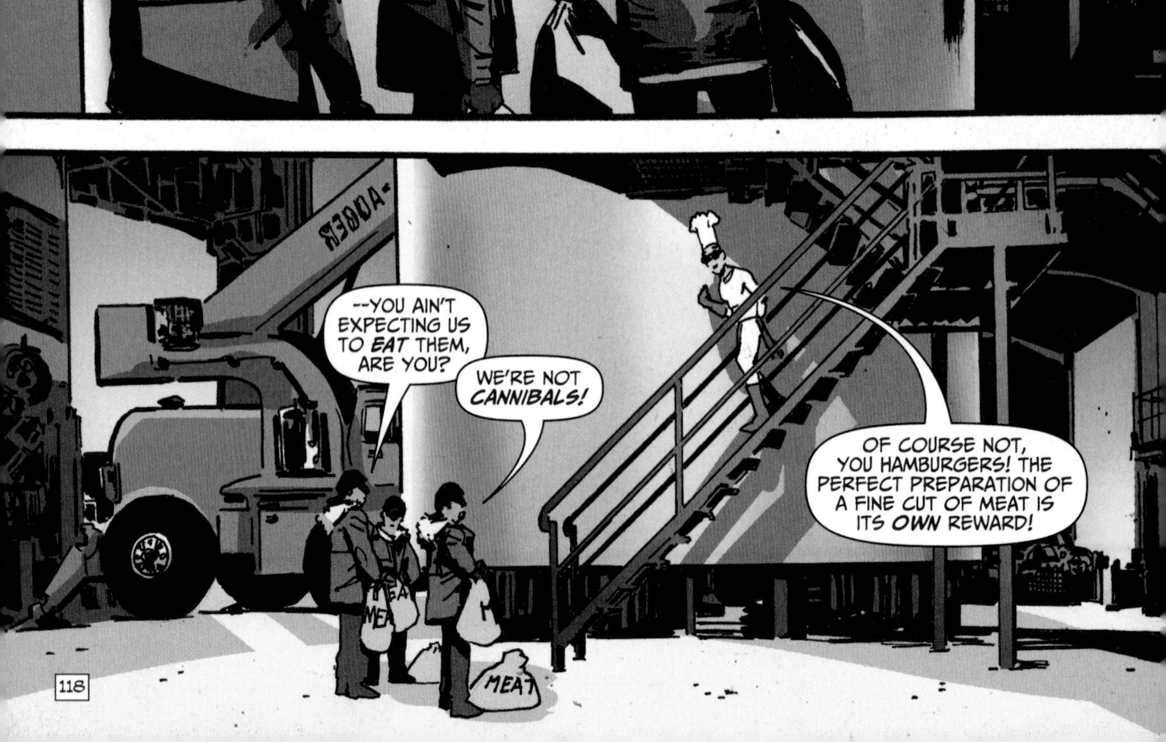
--YOU AIN'T EXPECTING US TO EAT THEM, ARE YOU?
WE'RE NOT CANNIBALS!
OF COURSE NOT, YOU HAMBURGERS! THE PERFECT PREPARATION OF A FINE CUT OF MEAT IS ITS OWN REWARD!
MEAT
MEAT

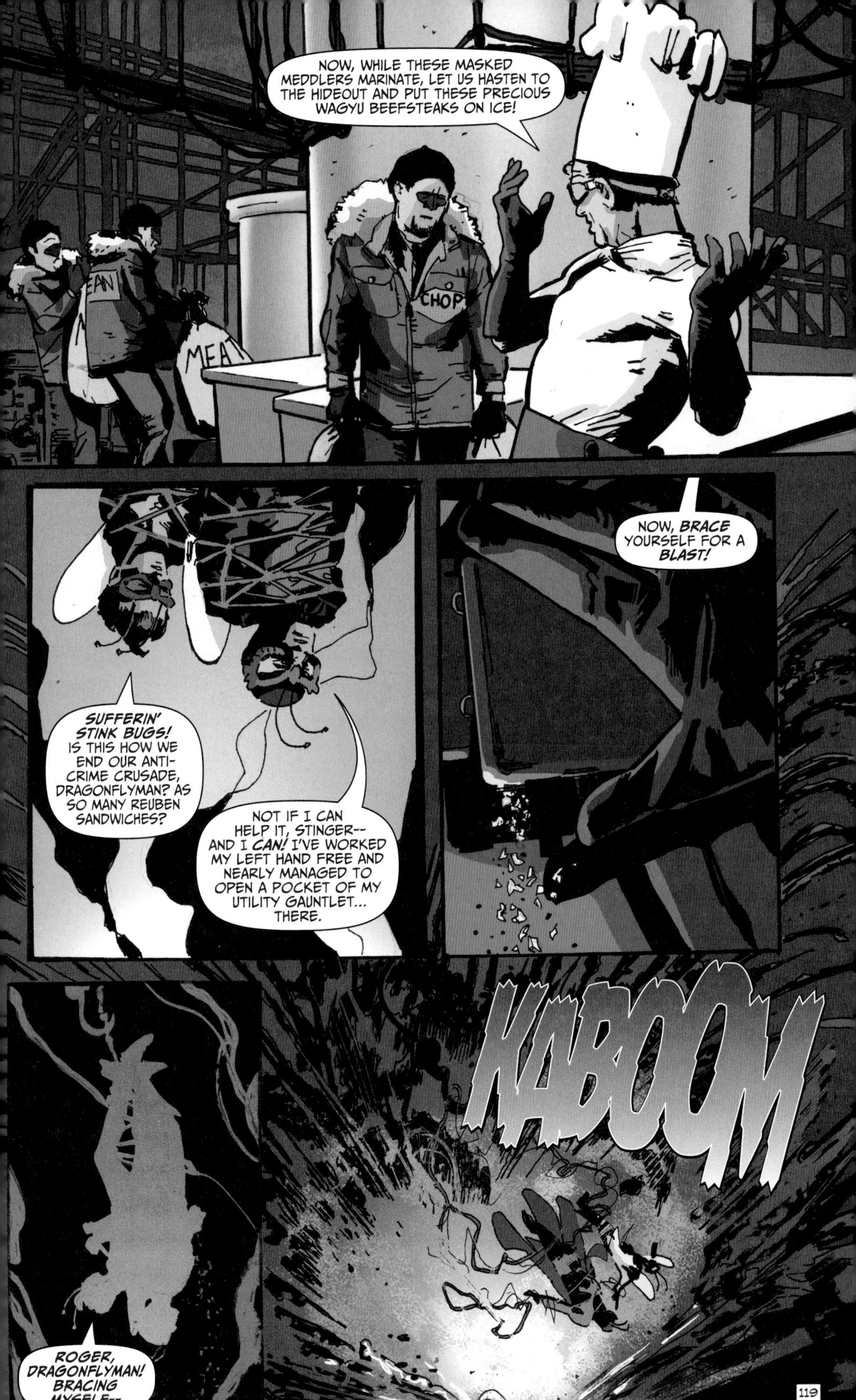
NOW, WHILE THESE MASKED MEDDLERS MARINATE, LET US HASTEN TO THE HIDEOUT AND PUT THESE PRECIOUS WAGYU BEEFSTEAKS ON ICE!
CHOP
MEAT
SUFFERIN' STINK BUGS! IS THIS HOW WE END OUR ANTI-CRIME CRUSADE, DRAGONFLYMAN? AS SO MANY REUBEN SANDWICHES?
NOT IF I CAN HELP IT, STINGER-- AND I CAN! I'VE WORKED MY LEFT HAND FREE AND NEARLY MANAGED TO OPEN A POCKET OF MY UTILITY GAUNTLET... THERE.
NOW, BRACE YOURSELF FOR A BLAST!
ROGER, DRAGONFLYMAN! BRACING MYSELF--
KABOOM

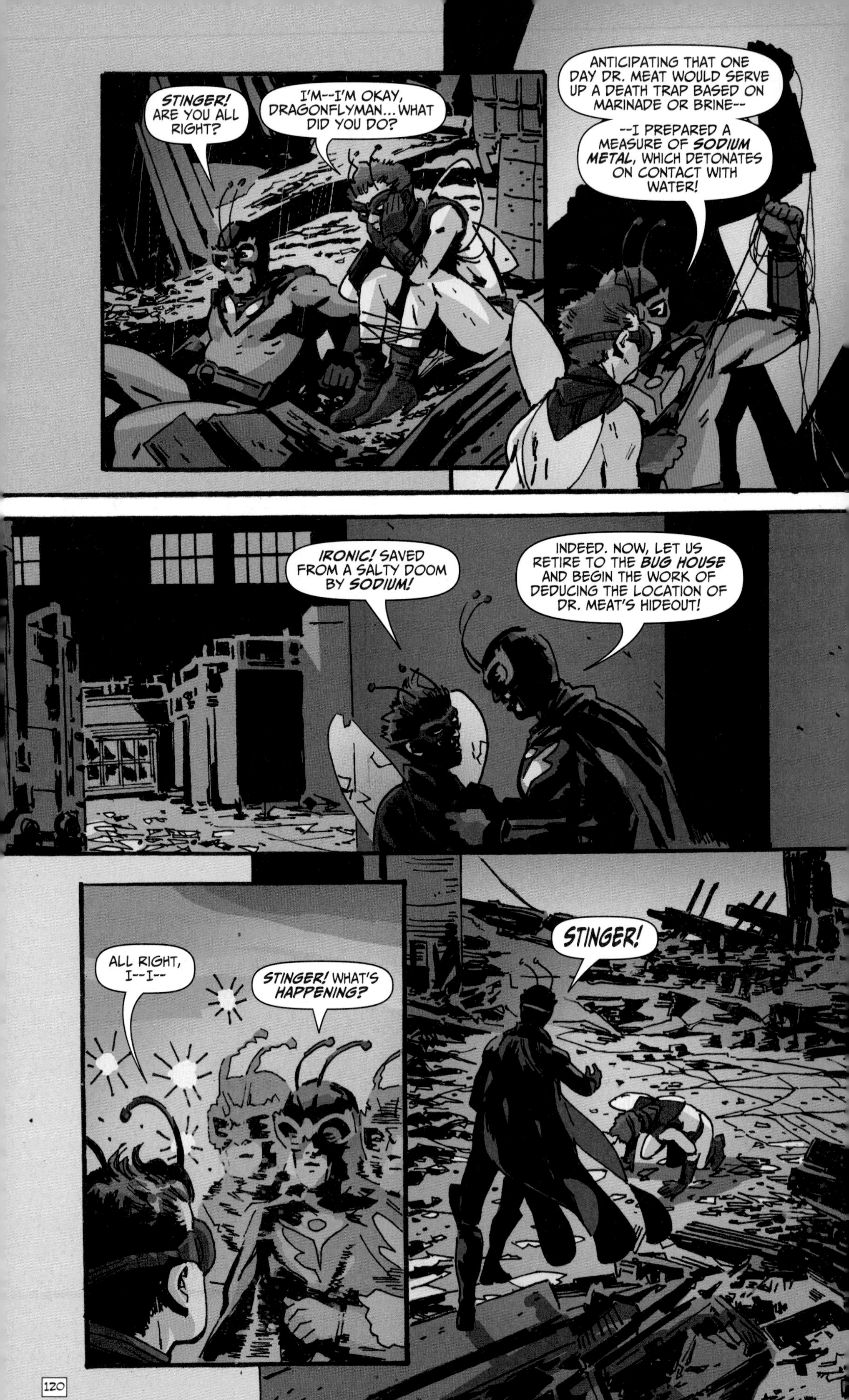
STINGER! ARE YOU ALL RIGHT?
I'M--I'M OKAY, DRAGONFLYMAN... WHAT DID YOU DO?
ANTICIPATING THAT ONE DAY DR. MEAT WOULD SERVE UP A DEATH TRAP BASED ON MARINADE OR BRINE--
--I PREPARED A MEASURE OF SODIUM METAL, WHICH DETONATES ON CONTACT WITH WATER!
IRONIC! SAVED FROM A SALTY DOOM BY SODIUM!
INDEED. NOW, LET US RETIRE TO THE BUG HOUSE AND BEGIN THE WORK OF DEDUCING THE LOCATION OF DR. MEAT'S HIDEOUT!
ALL RIGHT, I--I--
STINGER! WHAT'S HAPPENING?
STINGER!

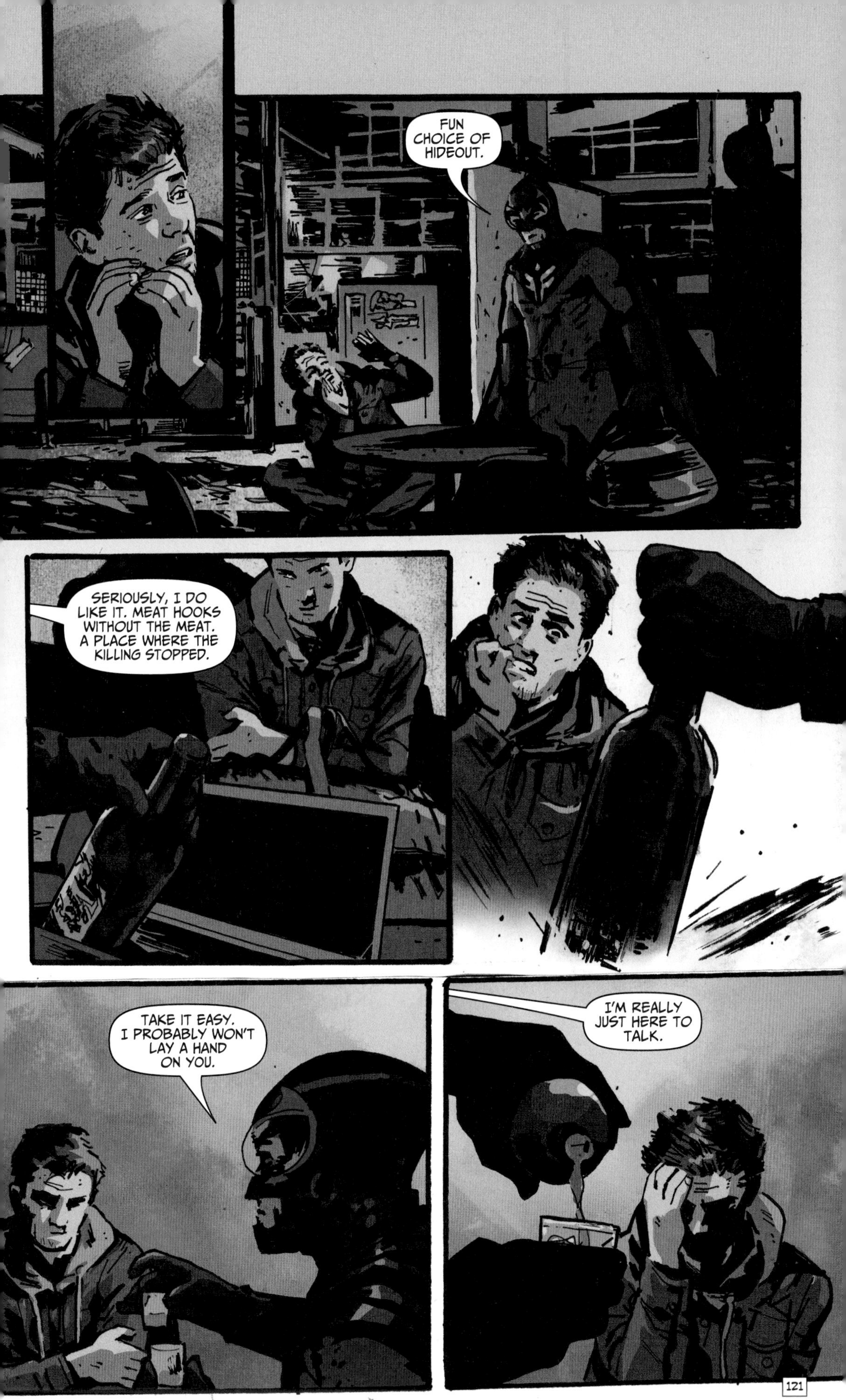
FUN CHOICE OF HIDEOUT.
SERIOUSLY, I DO LIKE IT. MEAT HOOKS WITHOUT THE MEAT. A PLACE WHERE THE KILLING STOPPED.
TAKE IT EASY. I PROBABLY WON'T LAY A HAND ON YOU.
I'M REALLY JUST HERE TO TALK.

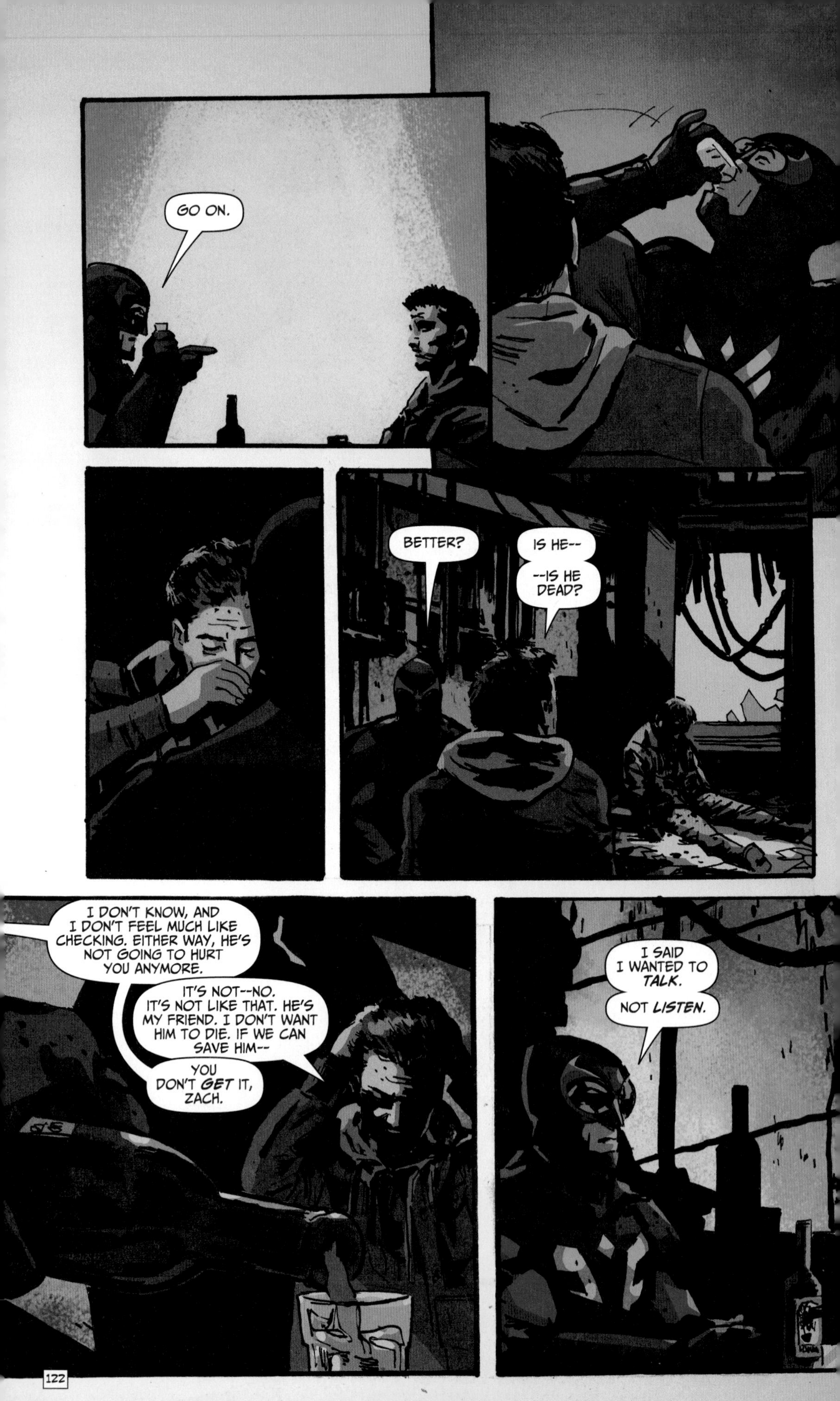
GO ON.
BETTER?
IS HE--
--IS HE DEAD?
I DON'T KNOW, AND I DON'T FEEL MUCH LIKE CHECKING. EITHER WAY, HE'S NOT GOING TO HURT YOU ANYMORE.
IT'S NOT--NO. IT'S NOT LIKE THAT. HE'S MY FRIEND. I DON'T WANT HIM TO DIE. IF WE CAN SAVE HIM--
YOU DON'T *GET* IT, ZACH.
I SAID I WANTED TO *TALK*.
NOT *LISTEN*.

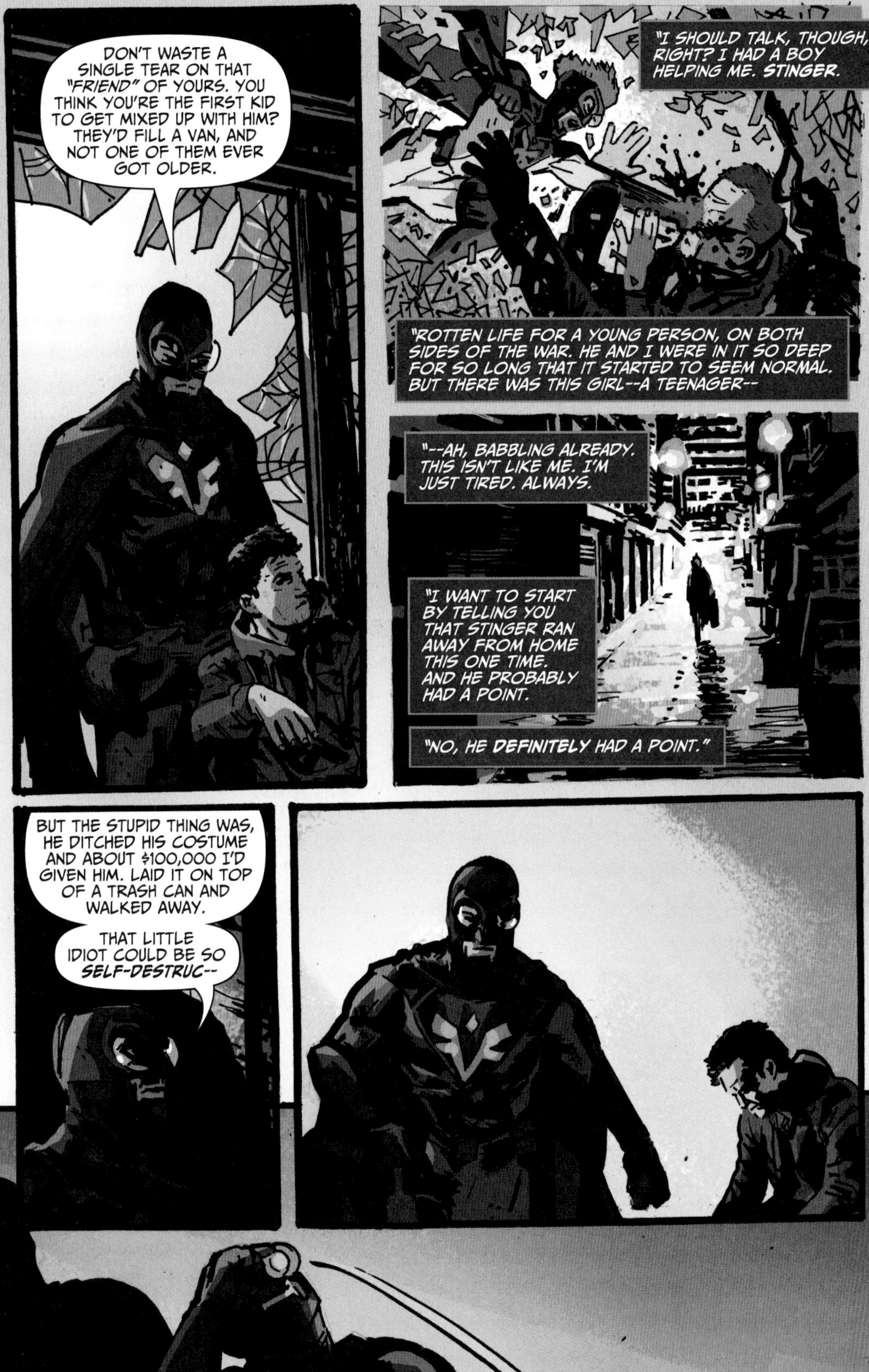
DON'T WASTE A SINGLE TEAR ON THAT "FRIEND" OF YOURS. YOU THINK YOU'RE THE FIRST KID TO GET MIXED UP WITH HIM? THEY'D FILL A VAN, AND NOT ONE OF THEM EVER GOT OLDER.
"I SHOULD TALK, THOUGH, RIGHT? I HAD A BOY HELPING ME. STINGER.
"ROTTEN LIFE FOR A YOUNG PERSON, ON BOTH SIDES OF THE WAR. HE AND I WERE IN IT SO DEEP FOR SO LONG THAT IT STARTED TO SEEM NORMAL. BUT THERE WAS THIS GIRL--A TEENAGER--
"--AH, BABBLING ALREADY. THIS ISN'T LIKE ME. I'M JUST TIRED. ALWAYS.
"I WANT TO START BY TELLING YOU THAT STINGER RAN AWAY FROM HOME THIS ONE TIME. AND HE PROBABLY HAD A POINT.
"NO, HE DEFINITELY HAD A POINT."
BUT THE STUPID THING WAS, HE DITCHED HIS COSTUME AND ABOUT $100,000 I'D GIVEN HIM. LAID IT ON TOP OF A TRASH CAN AND WALKED AWAY.
THAT LITTLE IDIOT COULD BE SO SELF-DESTRUC--

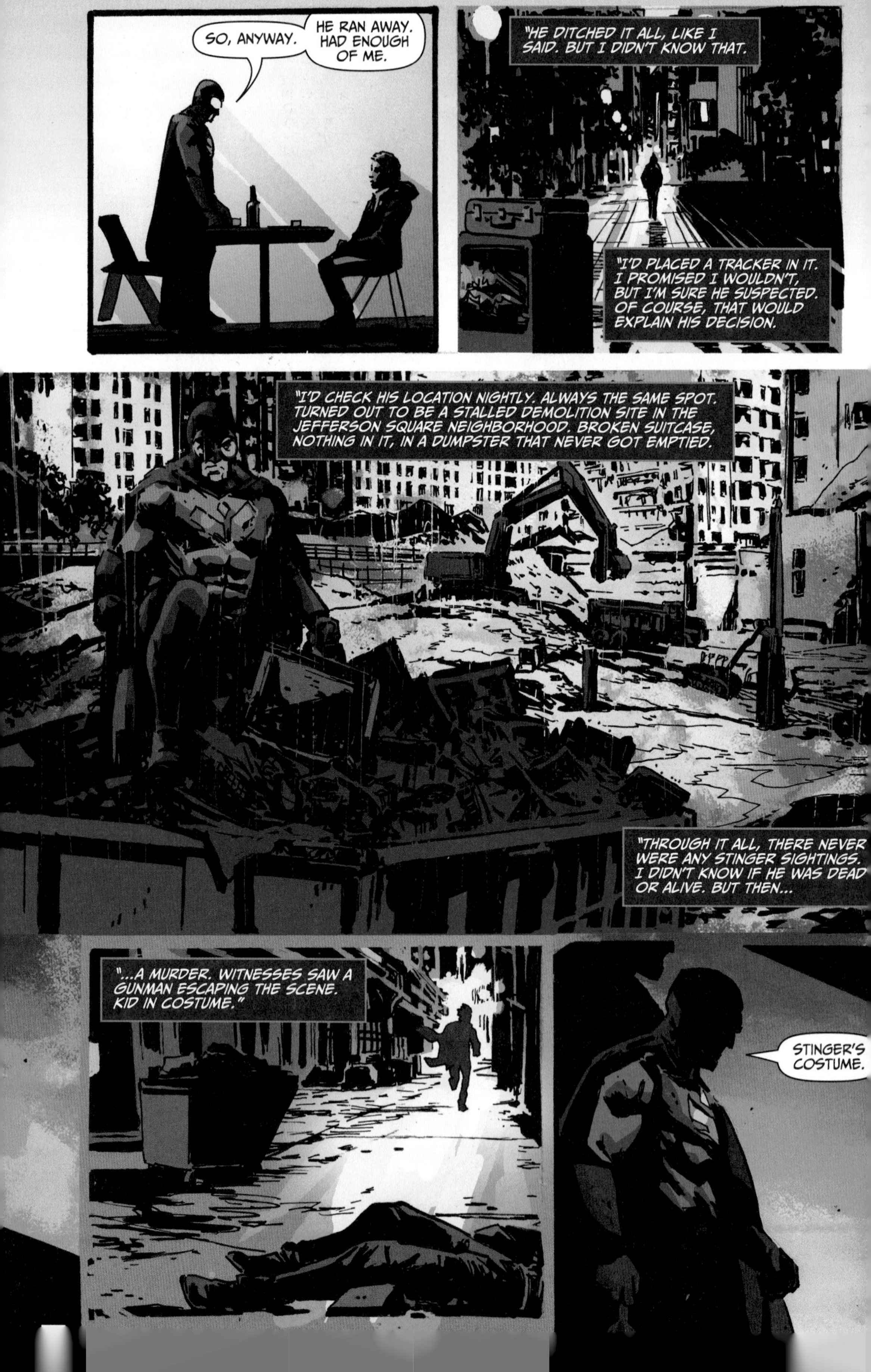
SO, ANYWAY.
HE RAN AWAY. HAD ENOUGH OF ME.
"HE DITCHED IT ALL, LIKE I SAID. BUT I DIDN'T KNOW THAT.
"I'D PLACED A TRACKER IN IT. I PROMISED I WOULDN'T, BUT I'M SURE HE SUSPECTED. OF COURSE, THAT WOULD EXPLAIN HIS DECISION.
"I'D CHECK HIS LOCATION NIGHTLY. ALWAYS THE SAME SPOT. TURNED OUT TO BE A STALLED DEMOLITION SITE IN THE JEFFERSON SQUARE NEIGHBORHOOD. BROKEN SUITCASE, NOTHING IN IT, IN A DUMPSTER THAT NEVER GOT EMPTIED.
"THROUGH IT ALL, THERE NEVER WERE ANY STINGER SIGHTINGS. I DIDN'T KNOW IF HE WAS DEAD OR ALIVE. BUT THEN...
"...A MURDER. WITNESSES SAW A GUNMAN ESCAPING THE SCENE. KID IN COSTUME."
STINGER'S COSTUME.

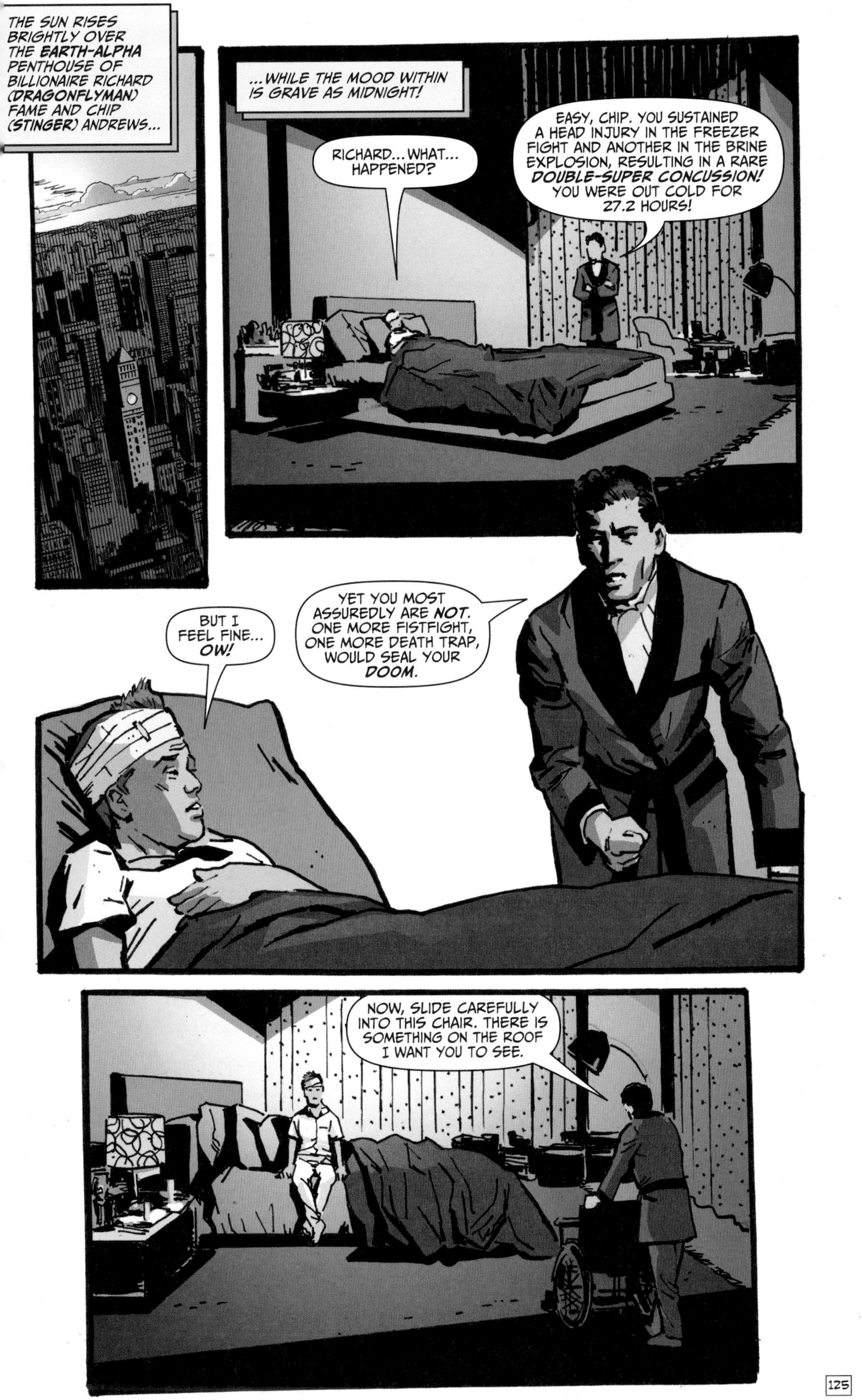
THE SUN RISES BRIGHTLY OVER THE EARTH-ALPHA PENTHOUSE OF BILLIONAIRE RICHARD (DRAGONFLYMAN) FAME AND CHIP (STINGER) ANDREWS...
...WHILE THE MOOD WITHIN IS GRAVE AS MIDNIGHT!
RICHARD... WHAT... HAPPENED?
EASY, CHIP. YOU SUSTAINED A HEAD INJURY IN THE FREEZER FIGHT AND ANOTHER IN THE BRINE EXPLOSION, RESULTING IN A RARE DOUBLE-SUPER CONCUSSION! YOU WERE OUT COLD FOR 27.2 HOURS!
BUT I FEEL FINE... OW!
YET YOU MOST ASSUREDLY ARE NOT. ONE MORE FISTFIGHT, ONE MORE DEATH TRAP, WOULD SEAL YOUR DOOM.
NOW, SLIDE CAREFULLY INTO THIS CHAIR. THERE IS SOMETHING ON THE ROOF I WANT YOU TO SEE.

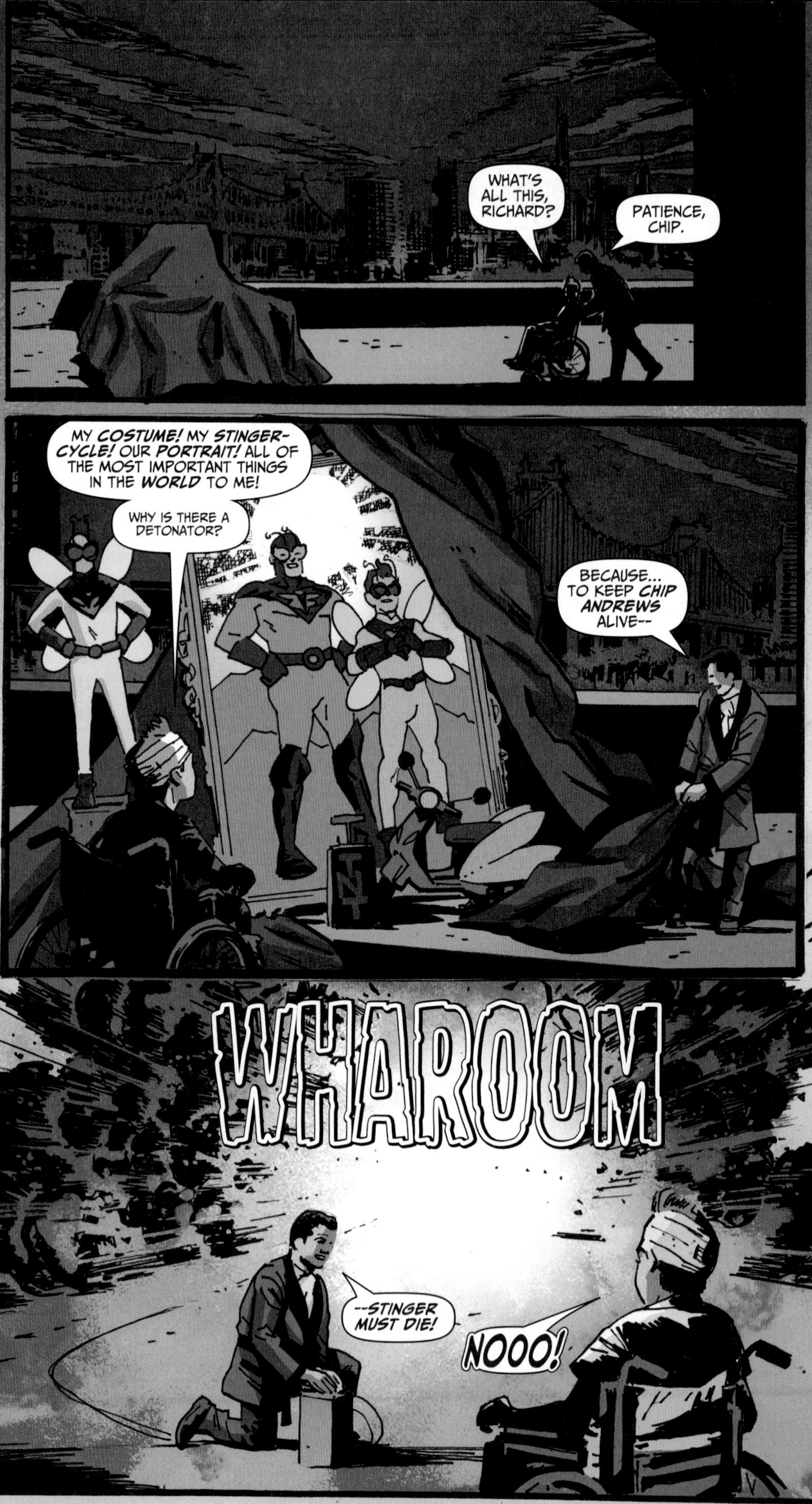
WHAT'S ALL THIS, RICHARD?
PATIENCE, CHIP.
MY COSTUME! MY STINGER-CYCLE! OUR PORTRAIT! ALL OF THE MOST IMPORTANT THINGS IN THE WORLD TO ME!
WHY IS THERE A DETONATOR?
BECAUSE... TO KEEP CHIP ANDREWS ALIVE--
WHAROOM
--STINGER MUST DIE!
NOOO!

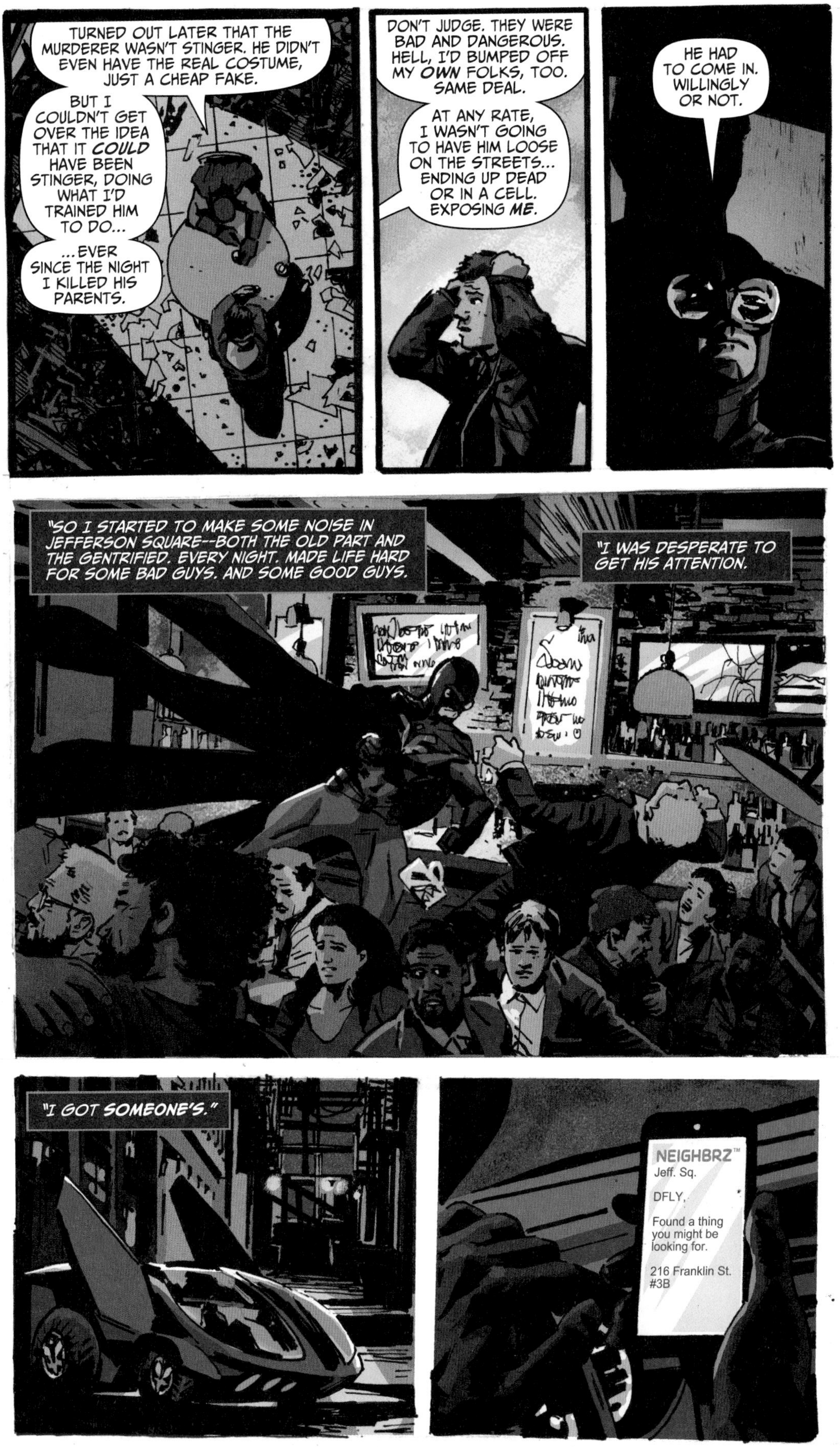
TURNED OUT LATER THAT THE MURDERER WASN'T STINGER. HE DIDN'T EVEN HAVE THE REAL COSTUME, JUST A CHEAP FAKE.
BUT I COULDN'T GET OVER THE IDEA THAT IT COULD HAVE BEEN STINGER, DOING WHAT I'D TRAINED HIM TO DO...
...EVER SINCE THE NIGHT I KILLED HIS PARENTS.
DON'T JUDGE. THEY WERE BAD AND DANGEROUS. HELL, I'D BUMPED OFF MY OWN FOLKS, TOO. SAME DEAL.
AT ANY RATE, I WASN'T GOING TO HAVE HIM LOOSE ON THE STREETS... ENDING UP DEAD OR IN A CELL. EXPOSING ME.
HE HAD TO COME IN. WILLINGLY OR NOT.
"SO I STARTED TO MAKE SOME NOISE IN JEFFERSON SQUARE--BOTH THE OLD PART AND THE GENTRIFIED. EVERY NIGHT. MADE LIFE HARD FOR SOME BAD GUYS. AND SOME GOOD GUYS.
"I WAS DESPERATE TO GET HIS ATTENTION.
"I GOT SOMEONE'S."
NEIGHBRZ™
Jeff. Sq.
DFLY,
Found a thing you might be looking for.
216 Franklin St. #3B

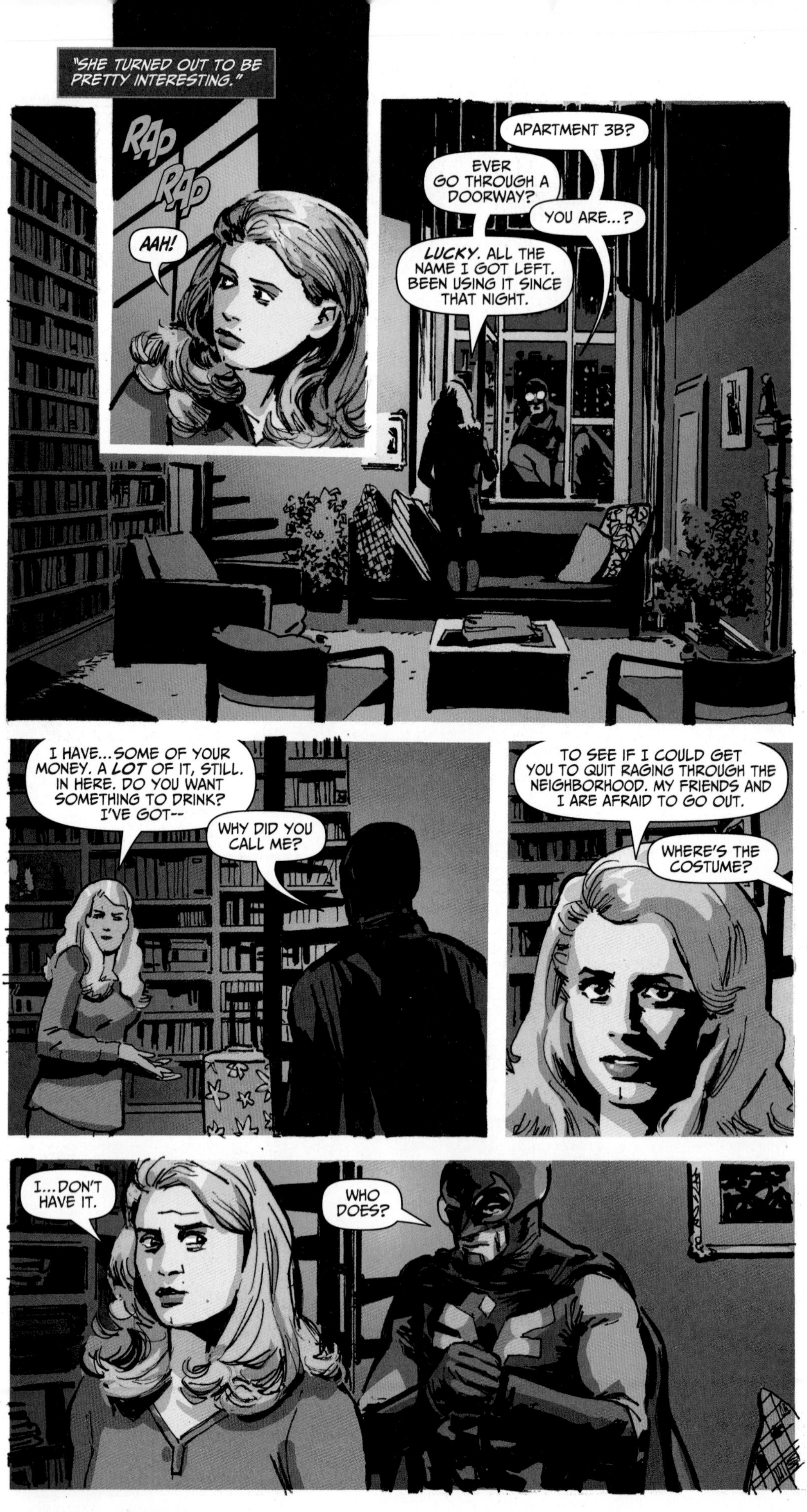
"SHE TURNED OUT TO BE PRETTY INTERESTING."
RAP RAP
AAH!
APARTMENT 3B?
EVER GO THROUGH A DOORWAY?
YOU ARE...?
LUCKY. ALL THE NAME I GOT LEFT. BEEN USING IT SINCE THAT NIGHT.
I HAVE...SOME OF YOUR MONEY. A LOT OF IT, STILL. IN HERE. DO YOU WANT SOMETHING TO DRINK? I'VE GOT--
WHY DID YOU CALL ME?
TO SEE IF I COULD GET YOU TO QUIT RAGING THROUGH THE NEIGHBORHOOD. MY FRIENDS AND I ARE AFRAID TO GO OUT.
WHERE'S THE COSTUME?
I...DON'T HAVE IT.
WHO DOES?

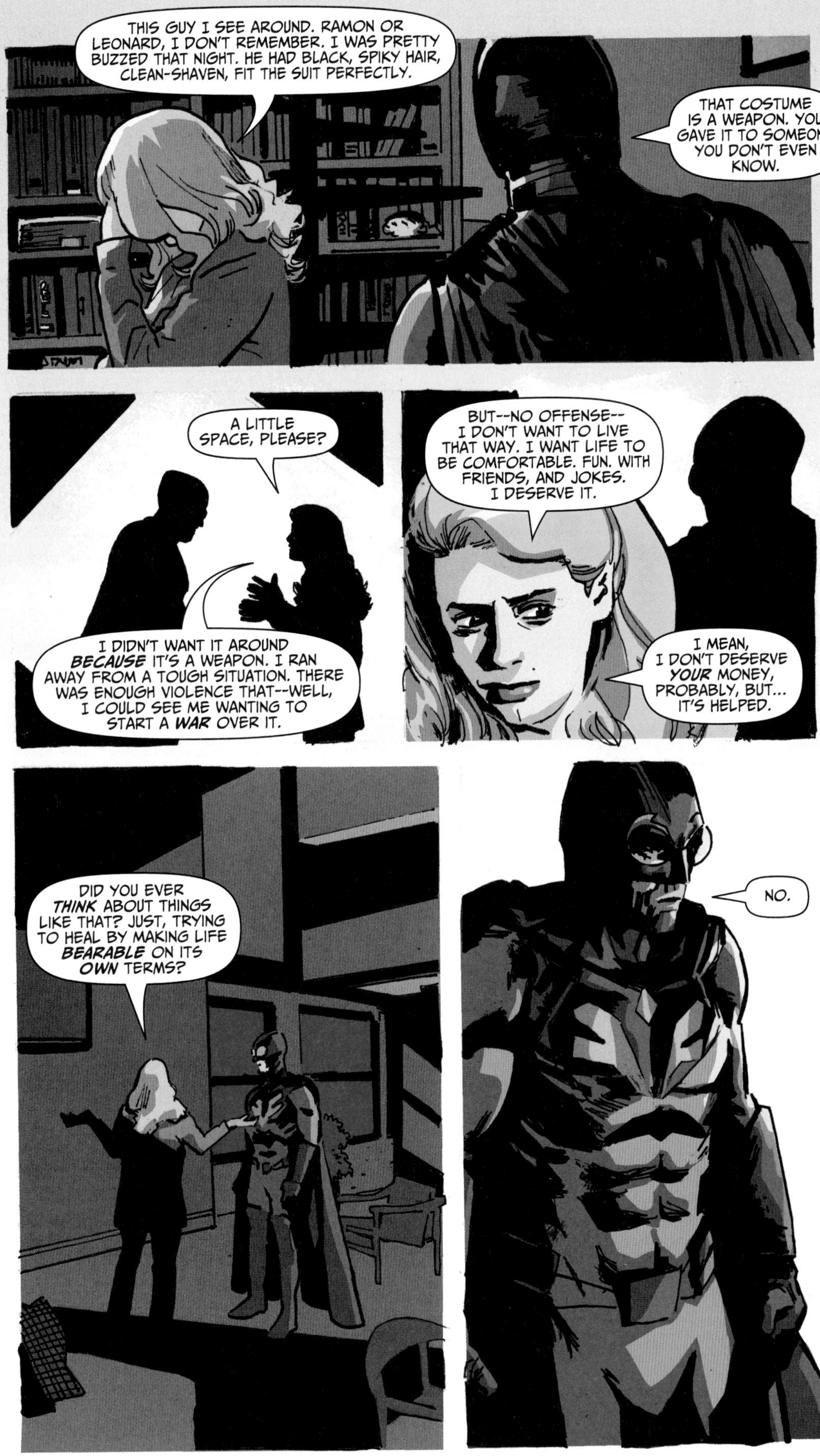
THIS GUY I SEE AROUND. RAMON OR LEONARD, I DON'T REMEMBER. I WAS PRETTY BUZZED THAT NIGHT. HE HAD BLACK, SPIKY HAIR, CLEAN-SHAVEN, FIT THE SUIT PERFECTLY.
THAT COSTUME IS A WEAPON. YOU GAVE IT TO SOMEONE YOU DON'T EVEN KNOW.
A LITTLE SPACE, PLEASE?
I DIDN'T WANT IT AROUND *BECAUSE* IT'S A WEAPON. I RAN AWAY FROM A TOUGH SITUATION. THERE WAS ENOUGH VIOLENCE THAT--WELL, I COULD SEE ME WANTING TO START A *WAR* OVER IT.
BUT--NO OFFENSE-- I DON'T WANT TO LIVE THAT WAY. I WANT LIFE TO BE COMFORTABLE. FUN. WITH FRIENDS, AND JOKES. I DESERVE IT.
I MEAN, I DON'T DESERVE *YOUR* MONEY, PROBABLY, BUT... IT'S HELPED.
DID YOU EVER *THINK* ABOUT THINGS LIKE THAT? JUST, TRYING TO HEAL BY MAKING LIFE *BEARABLE* ON ITS *OWN* TERMS?
NO.

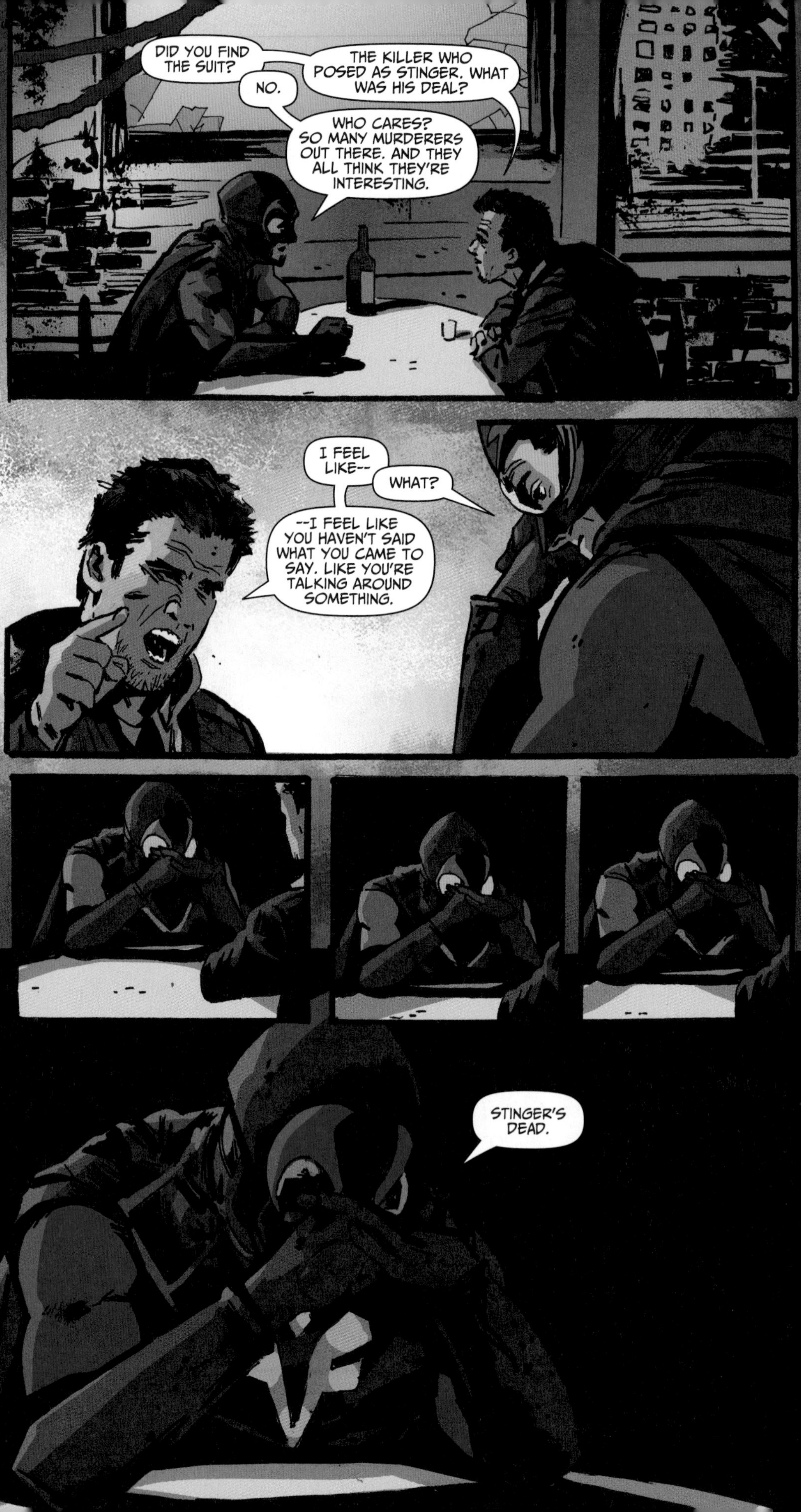
DID YOU FIND THE SUIT?
NO.
THE KILLER WHO POSED AS STINGER. WHAT WAS HIS DEAL?
WHO CARES? SO MANY MURDERERS OUT THERE. AND THEY ALL THINK THEY'RE INTERESTING.
I FEEL LIKE--
WHAT?
--I FEEL LIKE YOU HAVEN'T SAID WHAT YOU CAME TO SAY. LIKE YOU'RE TALKING AROUND SOMETHING.
STINGER'S DEAD.

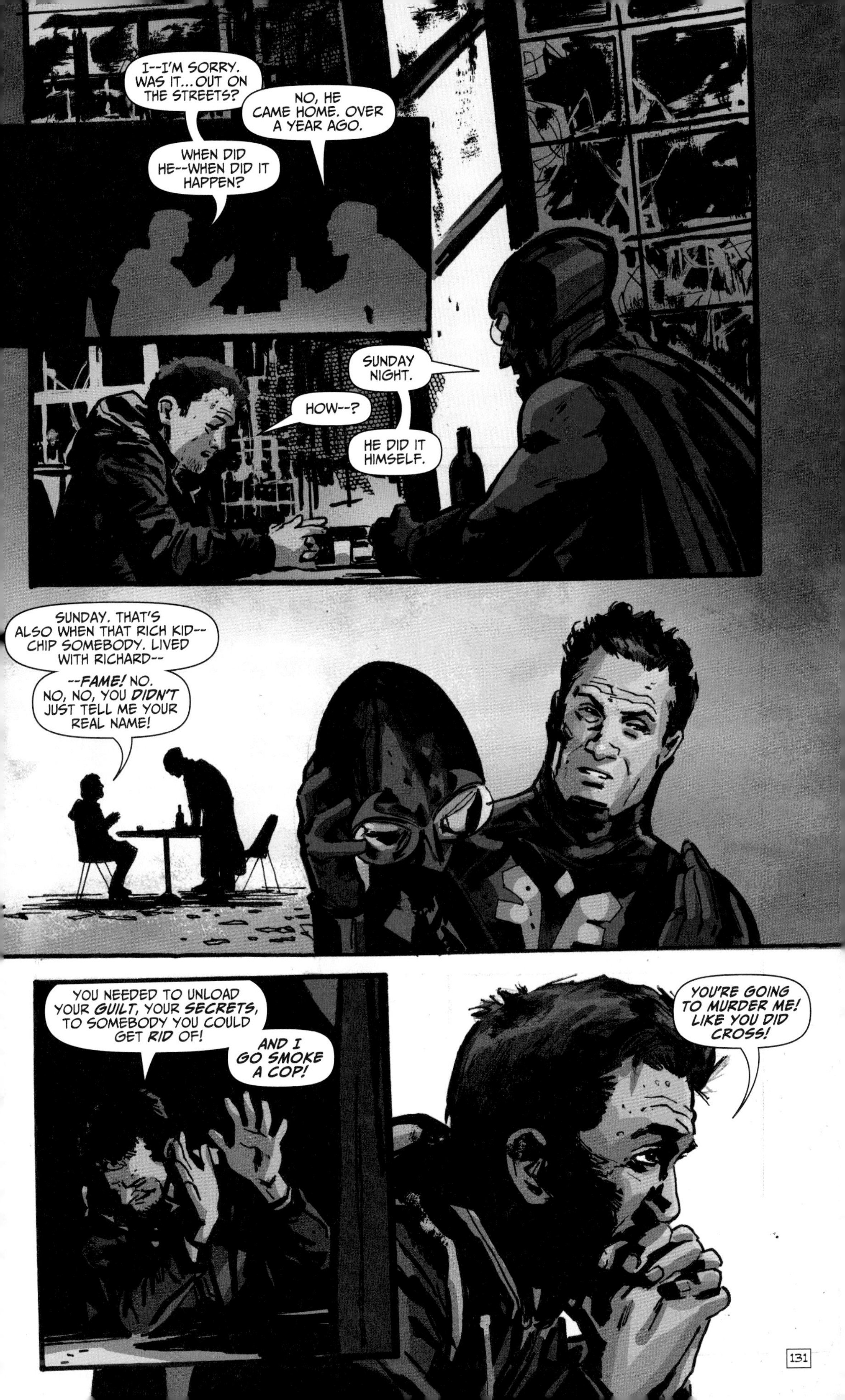
I--I'M SORRY. WAS IT...OUT ON THE STREETS?
NO, HE CAME HOME. OVER A YEAR AGO.
WHEN DID HE--WHEN DID IT HAPPEN?
SUNDAY NIGHT.
HOW--?
HE DID IT HIMSELF.
SUNDAY. THAT'S ALSO WHEN THAT RICH KID--CHIP SOMEBODY. LIVED WITH RICHARD--
--FAME! NO. NO, NO, YOU DIDN'T JUST TELL ME YOUR REAL NAME!
YOU NEEDED TO UNLOAD YOUR GUILT, YOUR SECRETS, TO SOMEBODY YOU COULD GET RID OF!
AND I GO SMOKE A COP!
YOU'RE GOING TO MURDER ME! LIKE YOU DID CROSS!

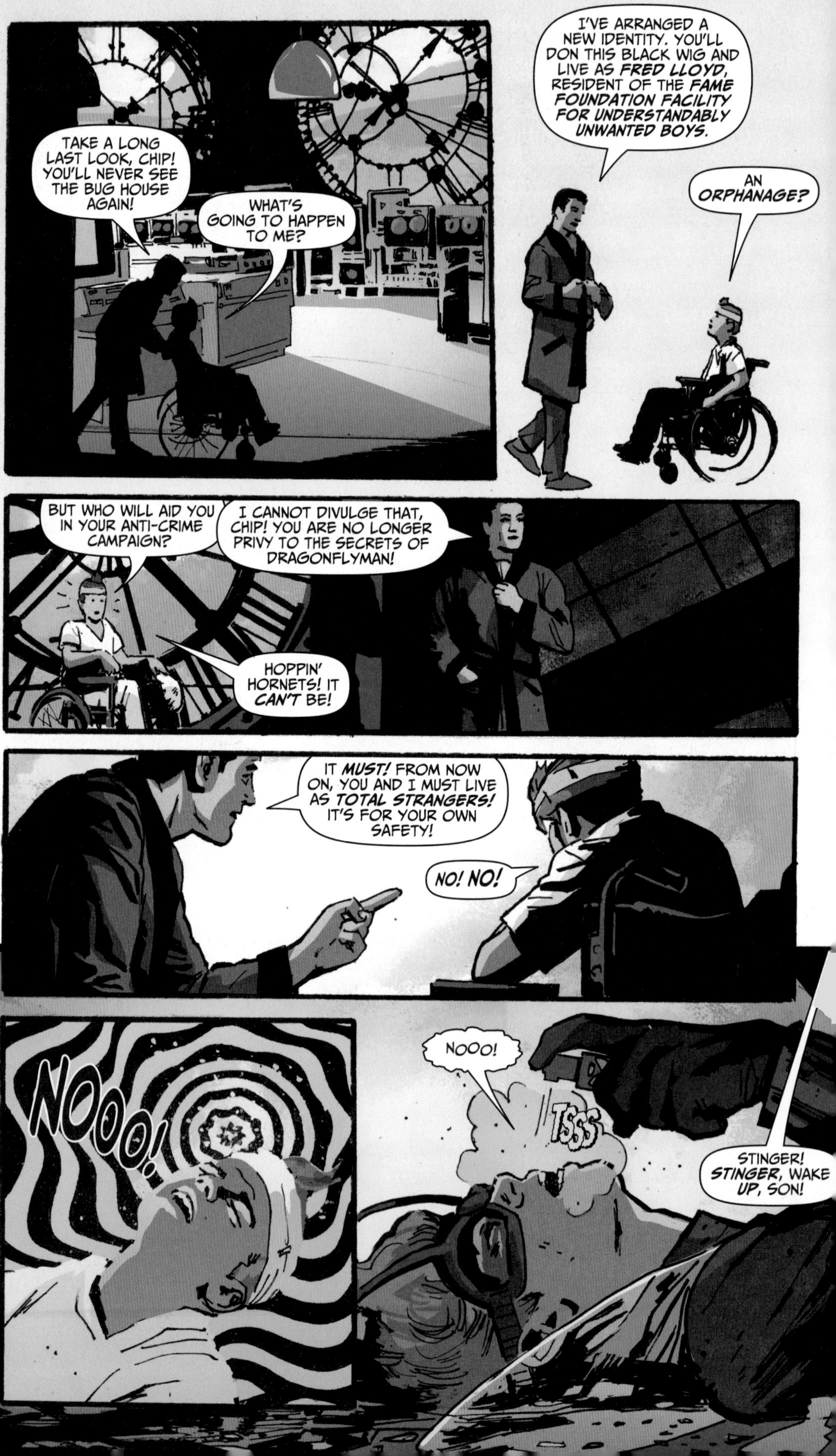
TAKE A LONG LAST LOOK, CHIP! YOU'LL NEVER SEE THE BUG HOUSE AGAIN!
WHAT'S GOING TO HAPPEN TO ME?
I'VE ARRANGED A NEW IDENTITY. YOU'LL DON THIS BLACK WIG AND LIVE AS ***FRED LLOYD***, RESIDENT OF THE ***FAME FOUNDATION FACILITY FOR UNDERSTANDABLY UNWANTED BOYS***.
AN ***ORPHANAGE?***
BUT WHO WILL AID YOU IN YOUR ANTI-CRIME CAMPAIGN?
I CANNOT DIVULGE THAT, CHIP! YOU ARE NO LONGER PRIVY TO THE SECRETS OF DRAGONFLYMAN!
HOPPIN' HORNETS! IT ***CAN'T*** BE!
IT ***MUST!*** FROM NOW ON, YOU AND I MUST LIVE AS ***TOTAL STRANGERS!*** IT'S FOR YOUR OWN SAFETY!
NO! NO!
NOOO!
NOOO!
TSSS
STINGER! ***STINGER***, WAKE ***UP***, SON!

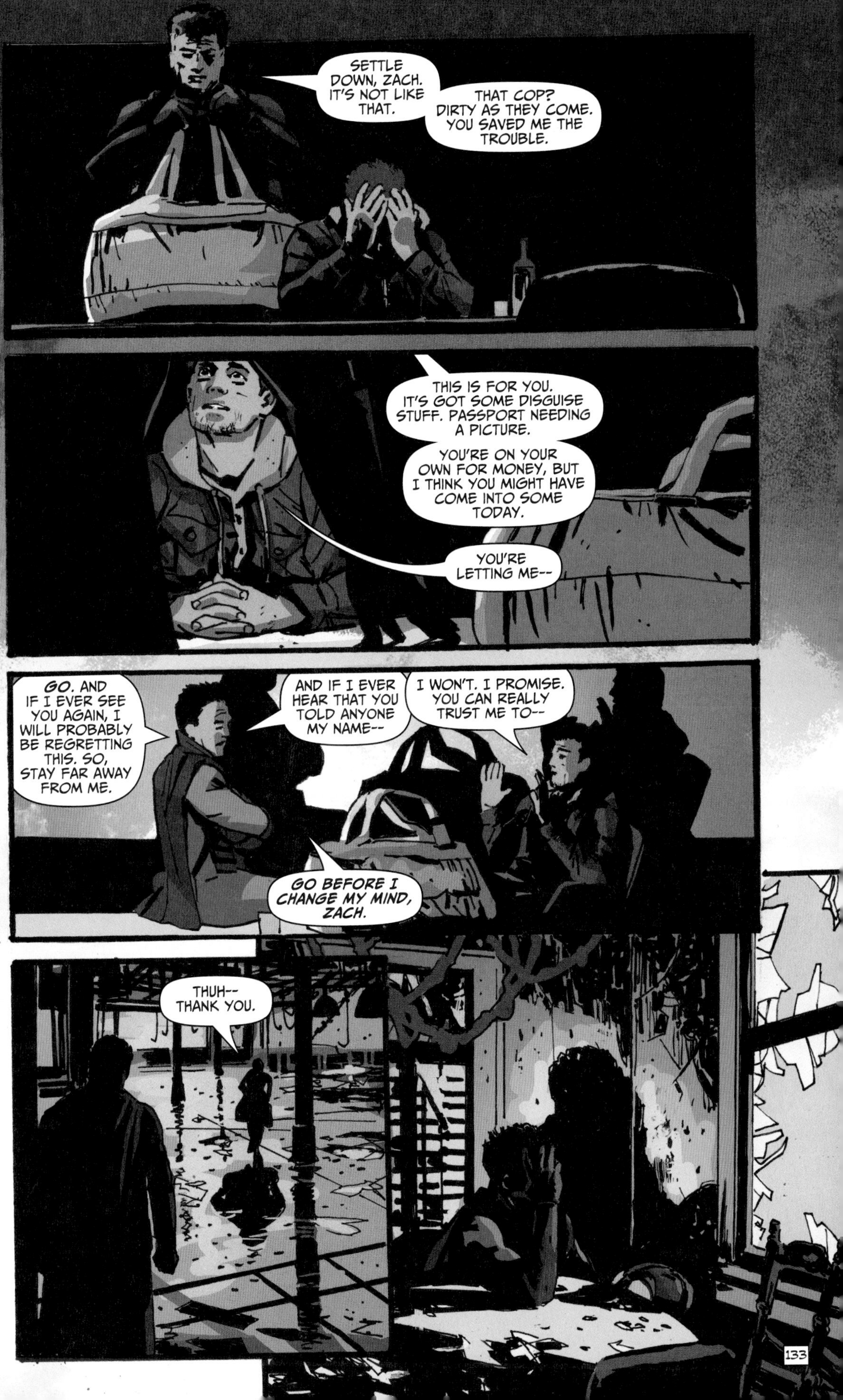
SETTLE DOWN, ZACH. IT'S NOT LIKE THAT.
THAT COP? DIRTY AS THEY COME. YOU SAVED ME THE TROUBLE.
THIS IS FOR YOU. IT'S GOT SOME DISGUISE STUFF. PASSPORT NEEDING A PICTURE.
YOU'RE ON YOUR OWN FOR MONEY, BUT I THINK YOU MIGHT HAVE COME INTO SOME TODAY.
YOU'RE LETTING ME--
GO. AND IF I EVER SEE YOU AGAIN, I WILL PROBABLY BE REGRETTING THIS. SO, STAY FAR AWAY FROM ME.
AND IF I EVER HEAR THAT YOU TOLD ANYONE MY NAME--
I WON'T. I PROMISE. YOU CAN REALLY TRUST ME TO--
GO BEFORE I CHANGE MY MIND, ZACH.
THUH-- THANK YOU.

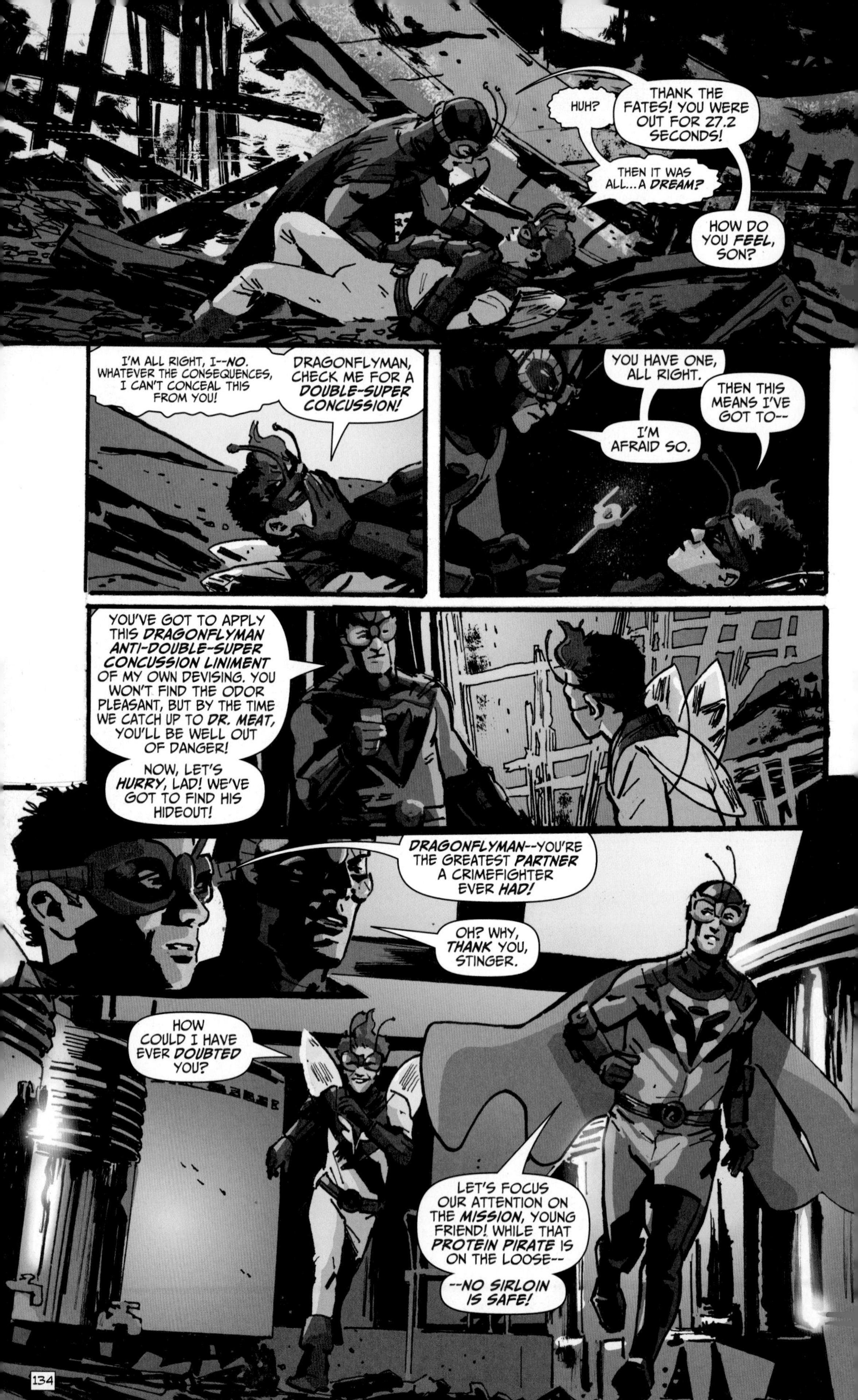
THANK THE FATES! YOU WERE OUT FOR 27.2 SECONDS!
HUH?
THEN IT WAS ALL... A DREAM?
HOW DO YOU FEEL, SON?
I'M ALL RIGHT, I--NO. WHATEVER THE CONSEQUENCES, I CAN'T CONCEAL THIS FROM YOU!
DRAGONFLYMAN, CHECK ME FOR A DOUBLE-SUPER CONCUSSION!
YOU HAVE ONE, ALL RIGHT.
THEN THIS MEANS I'VE GOT TO--
I'M AFRAID SO.
YOU'VE GOT TO APPLY THIS DRAGONFLYMAN ANTI-DOUBLE-SUPER CONCUSSION LINIMENT OF MY OWN DEVISING. YOU WON'T FIND THE ODOR PLEASANT, BUT BY THE TIME WE CATCH UP TO DR. MEAT, YOU'LL BE WELL OUT OF DANGER!
NOW, LET'S HURRY, LAD! WE'VE GOT TO FIND HIS HIDEOUT!
DRAGONFLYMAN--YOU'RE THE GREATEST PARTNER A CRIMEFIGHTER EVER HAD!
OH? WHY, THANK YOU, STINGER.
HOW COULD I HAVE EVER DOUBTED YOU?
LET'S FOCUS OUR ATTENTION ON THE MISSION, YOUNG FRIEND! WHILE THAT PROTEIN PIRATE IS ON THE LOOSE--
--NO SIRLOIN IS SAFE!

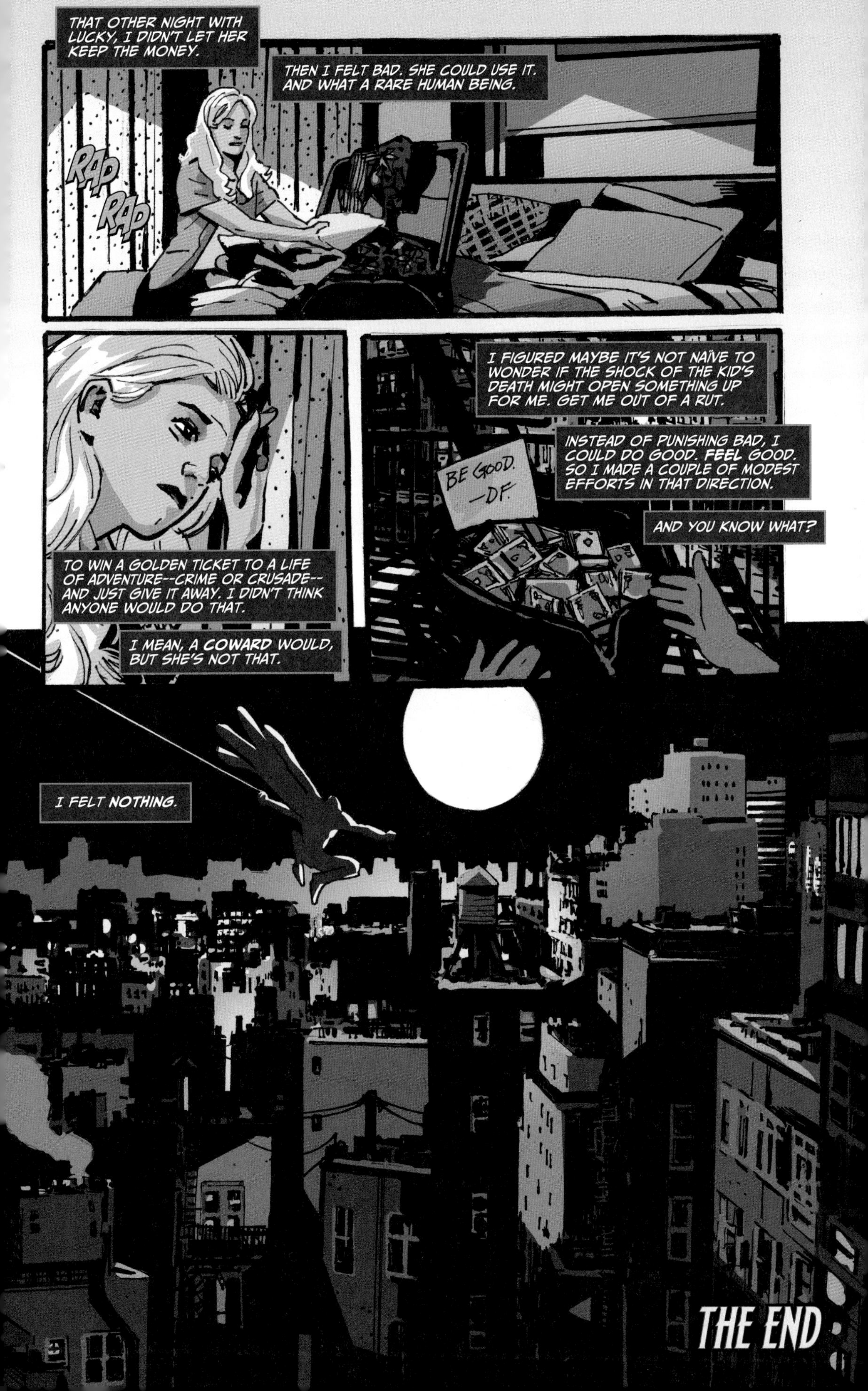

THAT OTHER NIGHT WITH LUCKY, I DIDN'T LET HER KEEP THE MONEY.
THEN I FELT BAD. SHE COULD USE IT. AND WHAT A RARE HUMAN BEING.
RAP RAP
TO WIN A GOLDEN TICKET TO A LIFE OF ADVENTURE--CRIME OR CRUSADE--AND JUST GIVE IT AWAY. I DIDN'T THINK ANYONE WOULD DO THAT.
I MEAN, A **COWARD** WOULD, BUT SHE'S NOT THAT.
I FIGURED MAYBE IT'S NOT NAÏVE TO WONDER IF THE SHOCK OF THE KID'S DEATH MIGHT OPEN SOMETHING UP FOR ME. GET ME OUT OF A RUT.
INSTEAD OF PUNISHING BAD, I COULD DO GOOD. **FEEL** GOOD. SO I MADE A COUPLE OF MODEST EFFORTS IN THAT DIRECTION.
BE GOOD. -DF
AND YOU KNOW WHAT?
I FELT **NOTHING**.
THE END

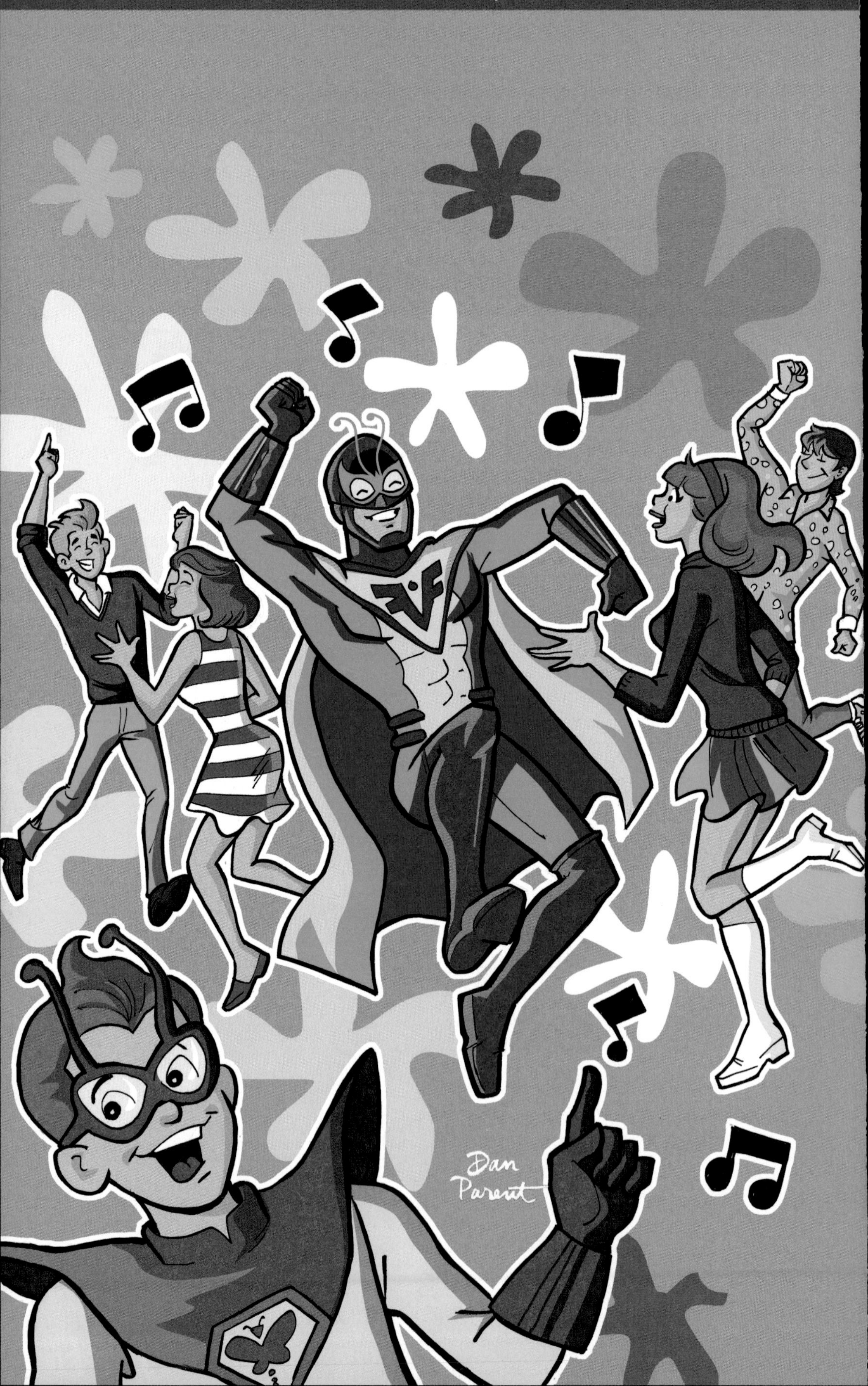
Dan
Parent

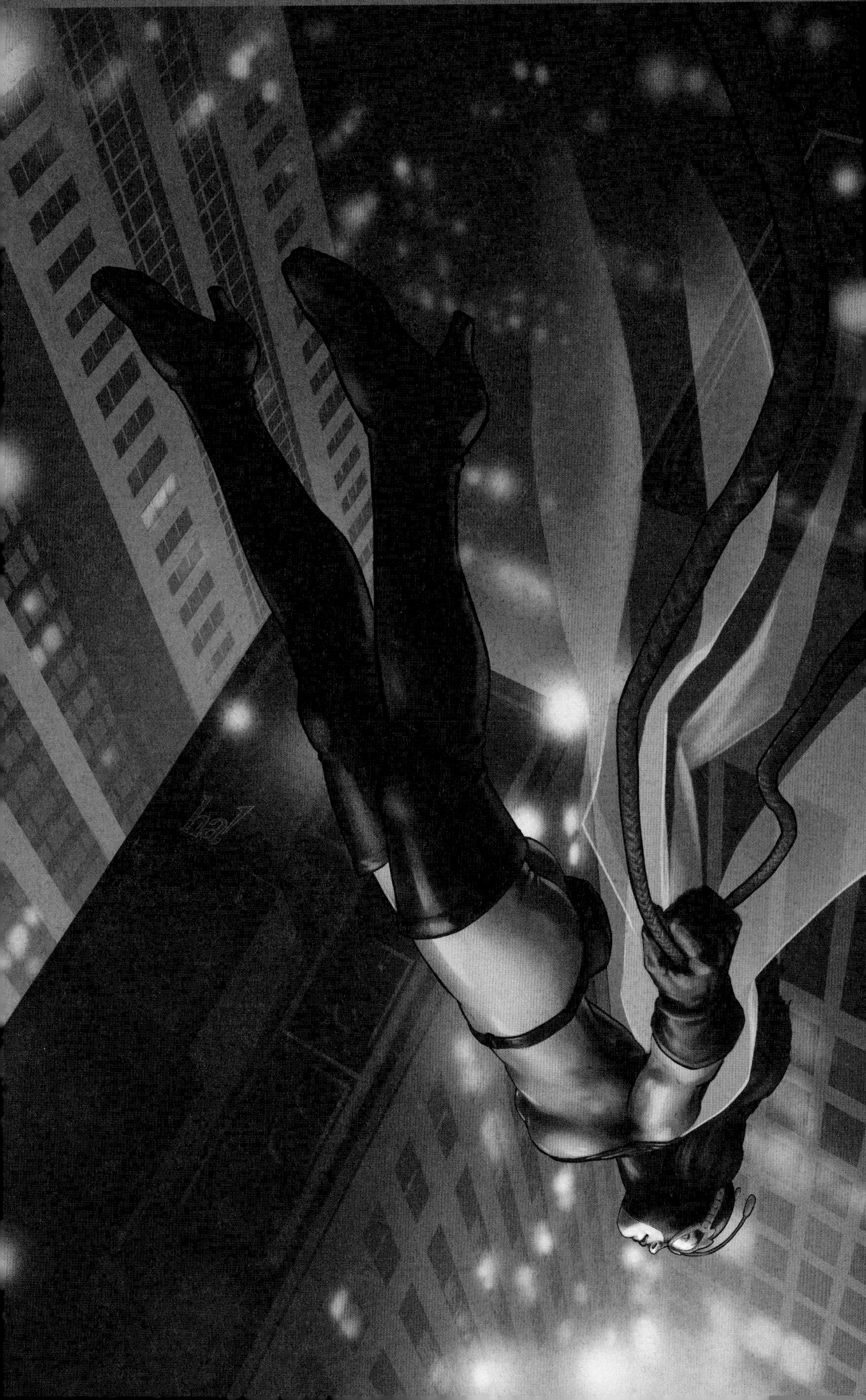
ha!

THE WRONG EARTH: TRAPPED ON TEEN PLANET #1 VARIANT COVER by Gene Ha

THE WRONG EARTH: FAME & FORTUNE #1 VARIANT COVER by Michael Montenat

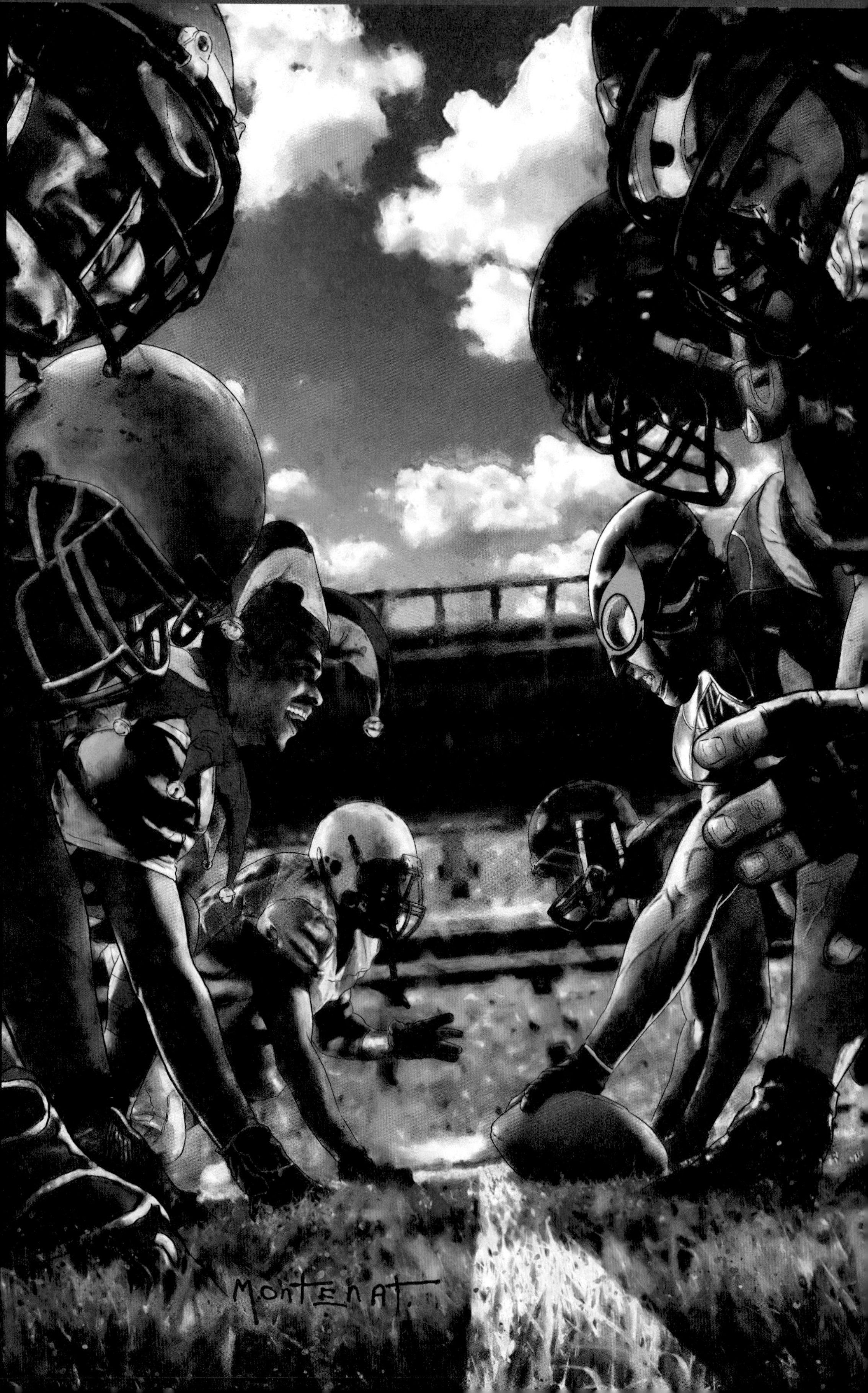
MONTENAT.

THE WRONG EARTH: FAME & FORTUNE #1 VARIANT COVER by Gene Ha

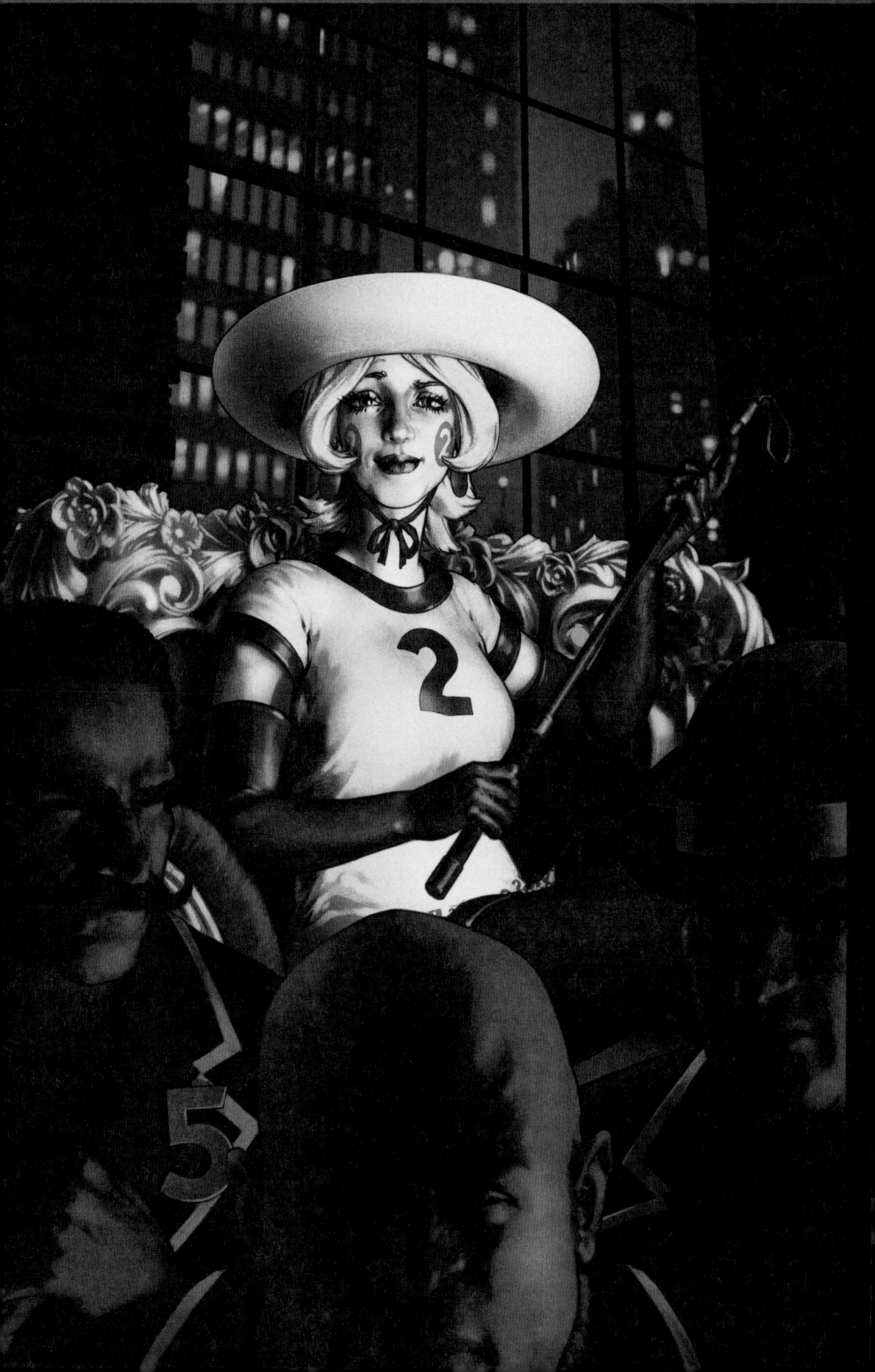
2
5

WRONG EARTH: PURPLE #1 VARIANT COVER by Jerry Ordway

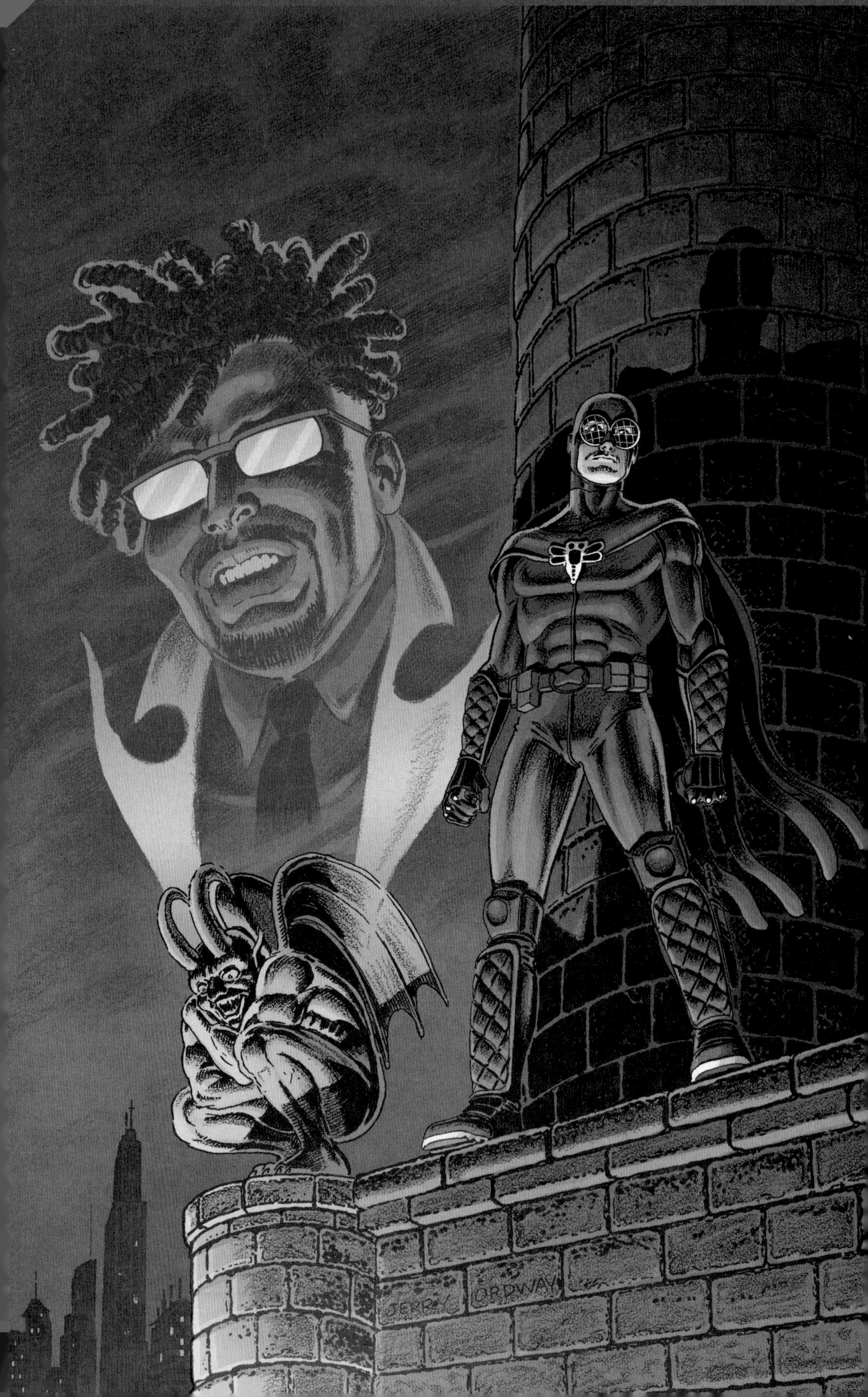
JERRY ORDWAY

THE WRONG EARTH: PURPLE #1 VARIANT COVER by Gene Ha

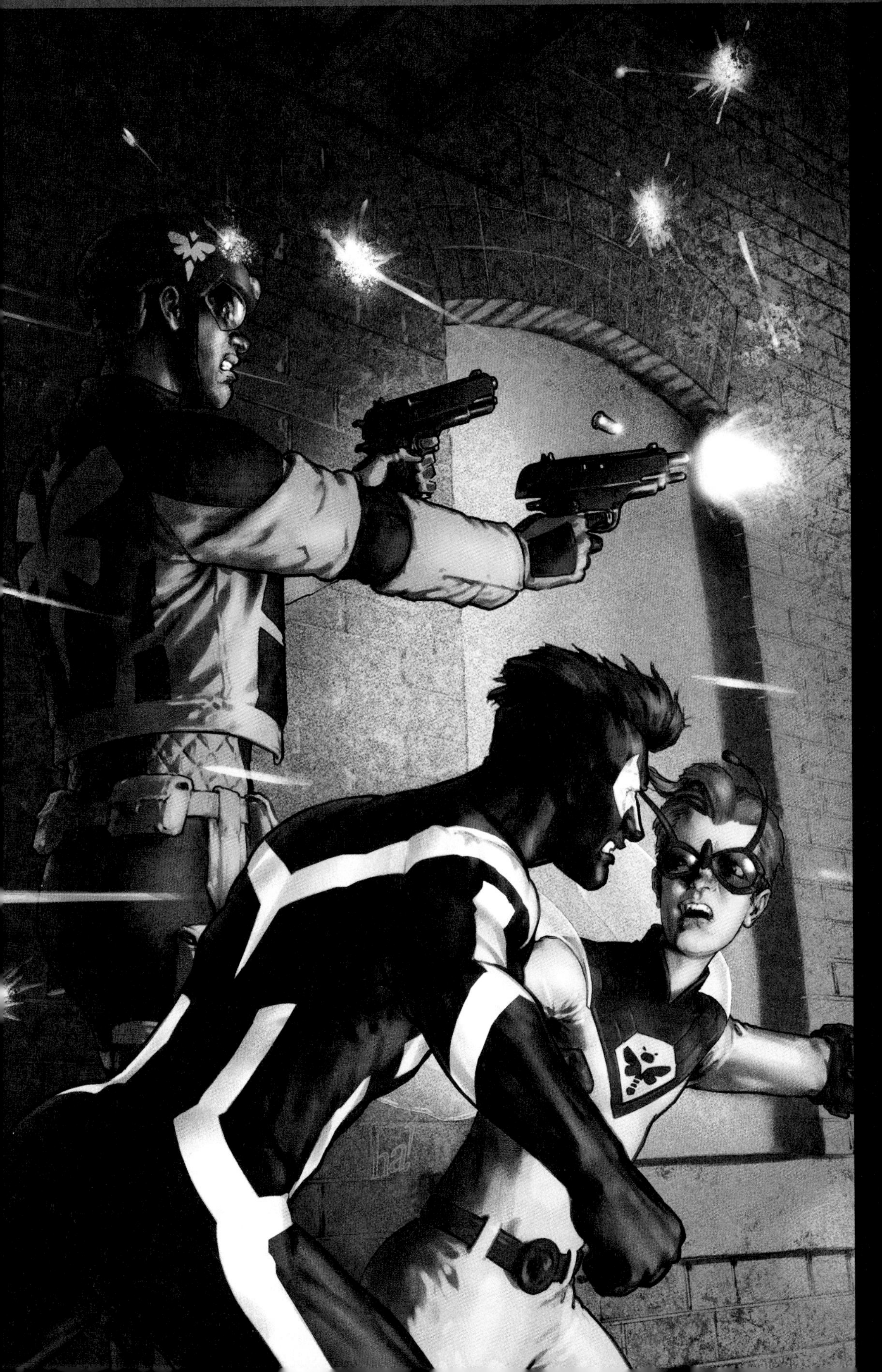

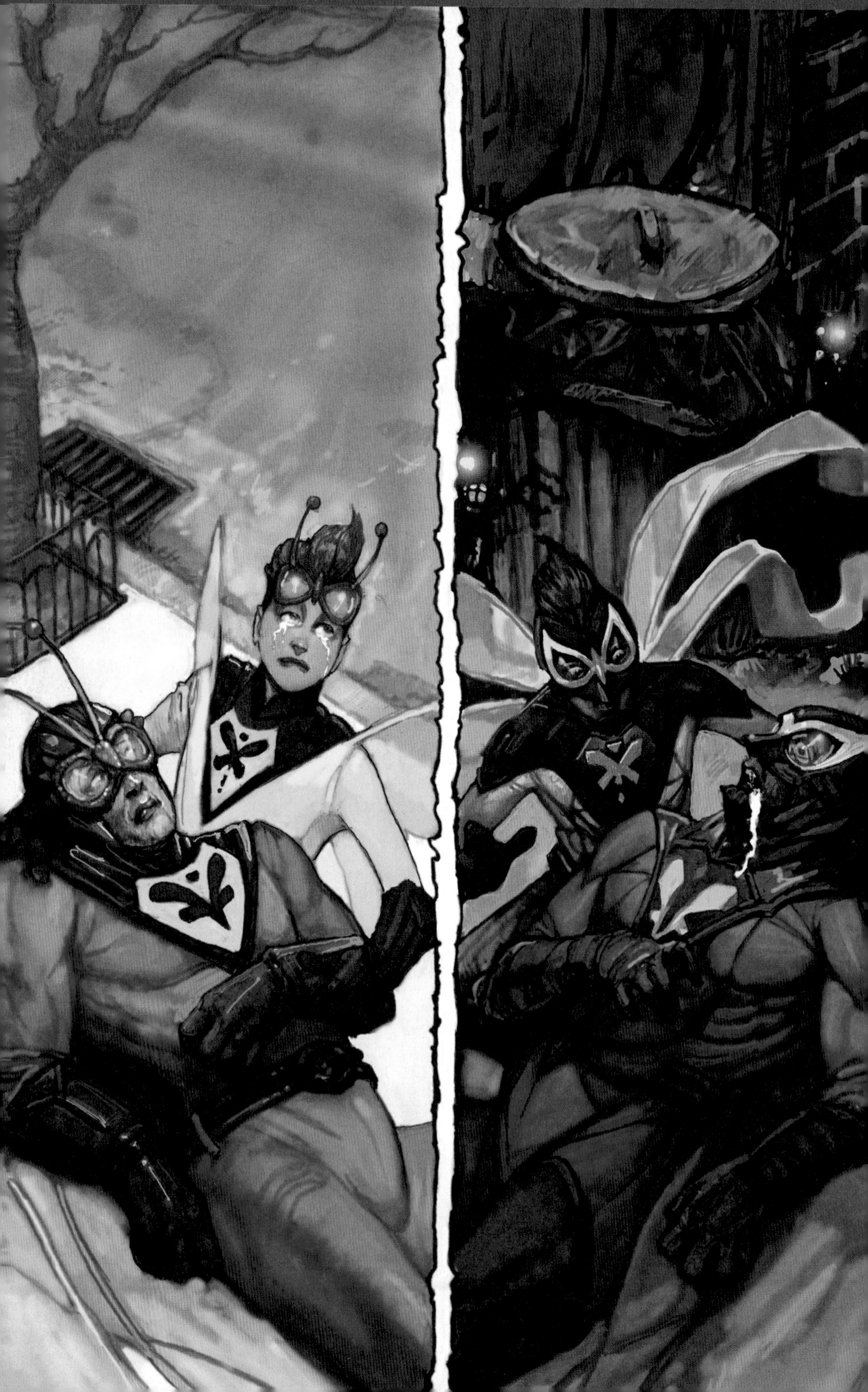

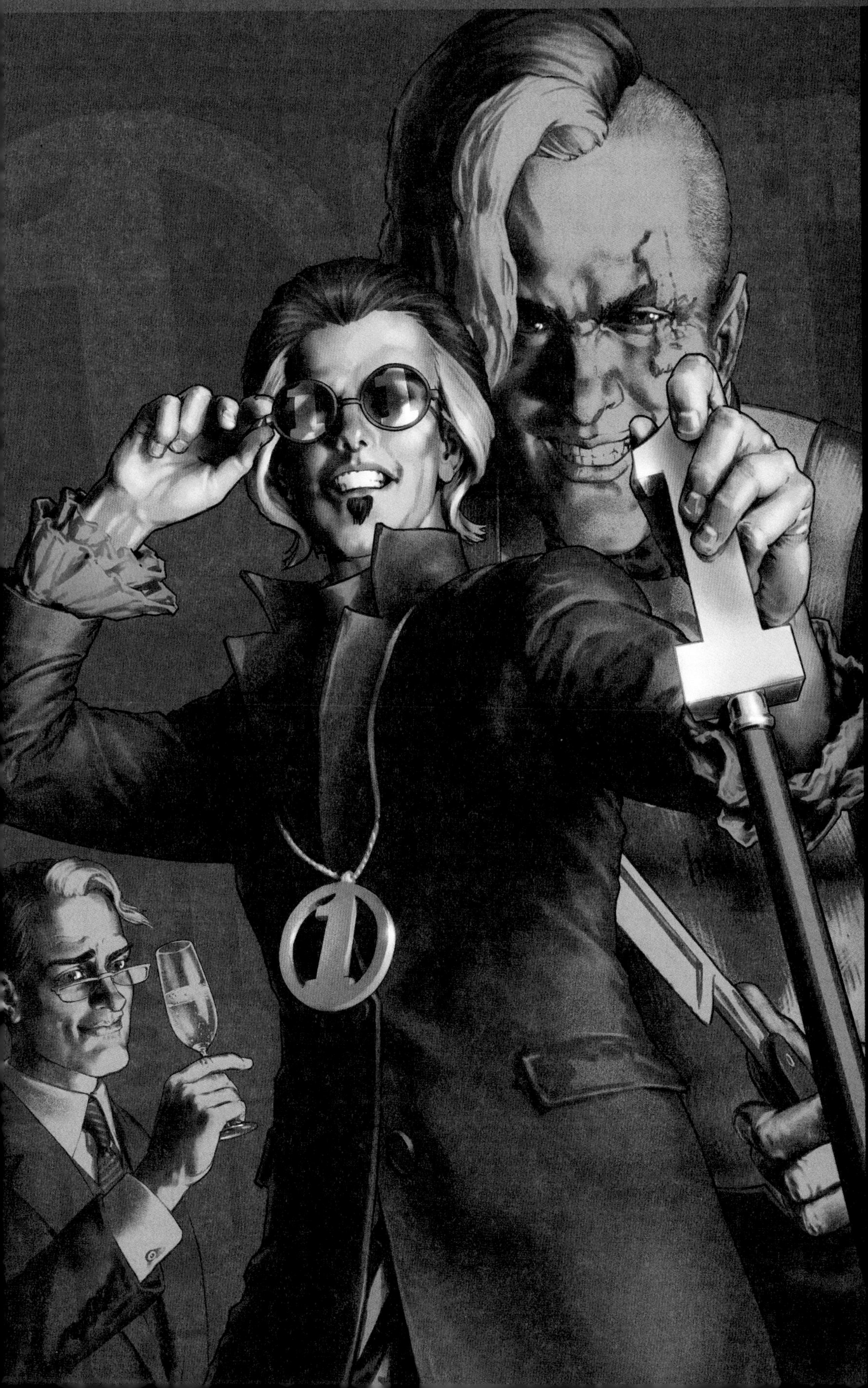

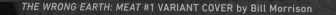

THE WRONG EARTH: MEAT #1 VARIANT COVER by Bill Morrison

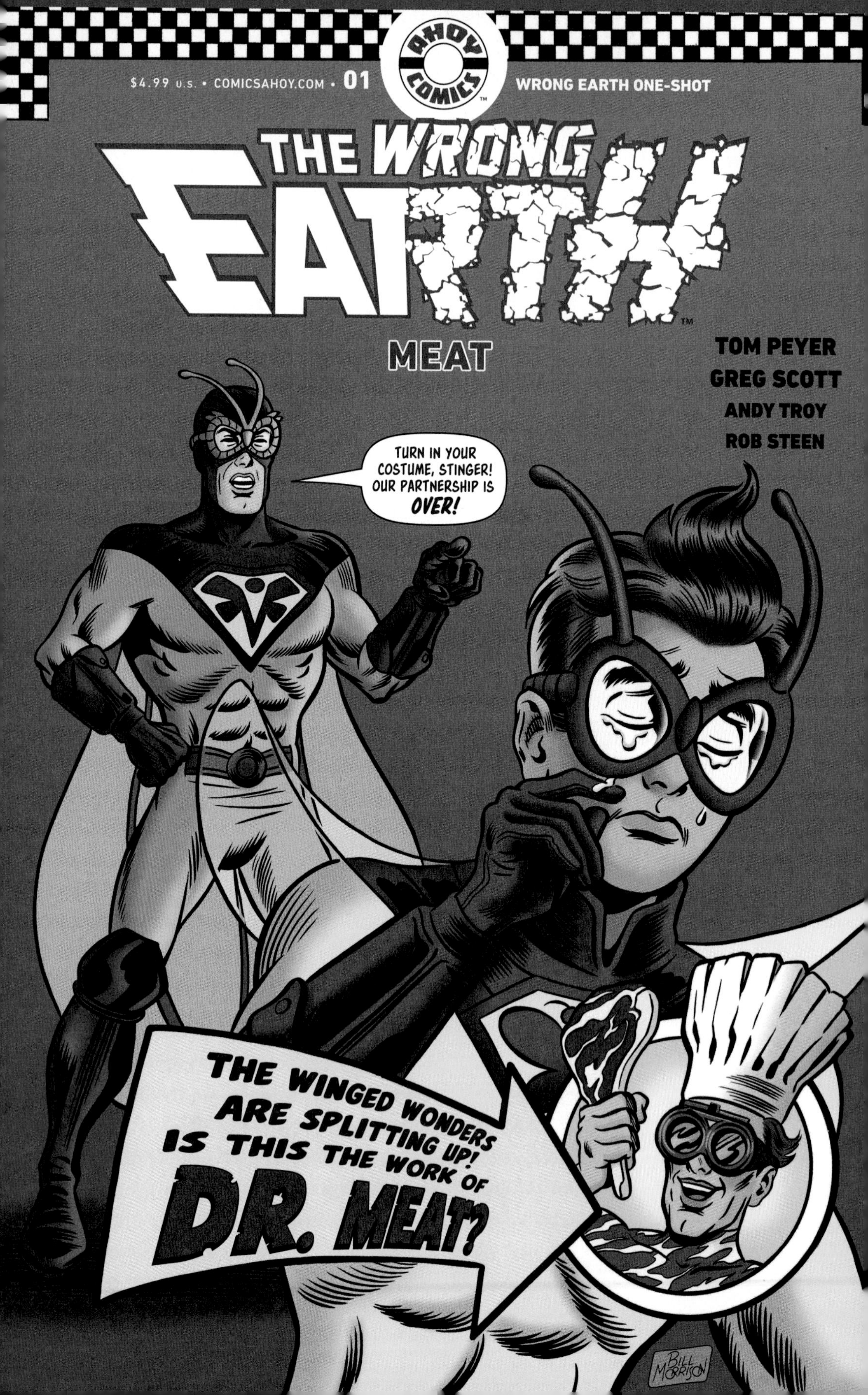

AHOY COMICS
$4.99 U.S. • COMICSAHOY.COM • 01
WRONG EARTH ONE-SHOT
THE WRONG EARTH
MEAT
TOM PEYER
GREG SCOTT
ANDY TROY
ROB STEEN
TURN IN YOUR COSTUME, STINGER! OUR PARTNERSHIP IS OVER!
THE WINGED WONDERS ARE SPLITTING UP! IS THIS THE WORK OF D.R. MEAT?
BILL MORRISON

THE WRONG EARTH: MEAT #1 VARIANT COVER by Gene Ha

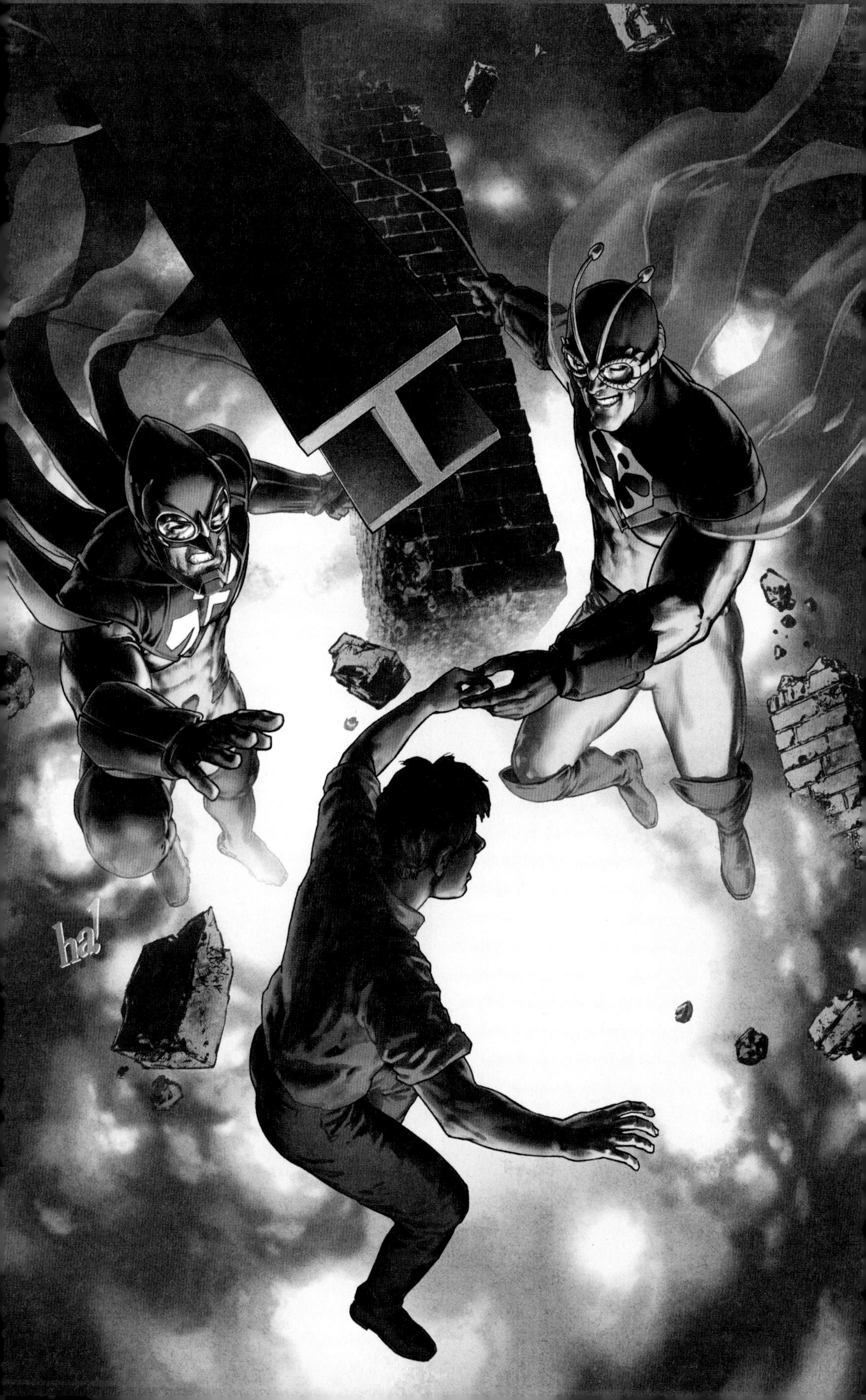
ha!

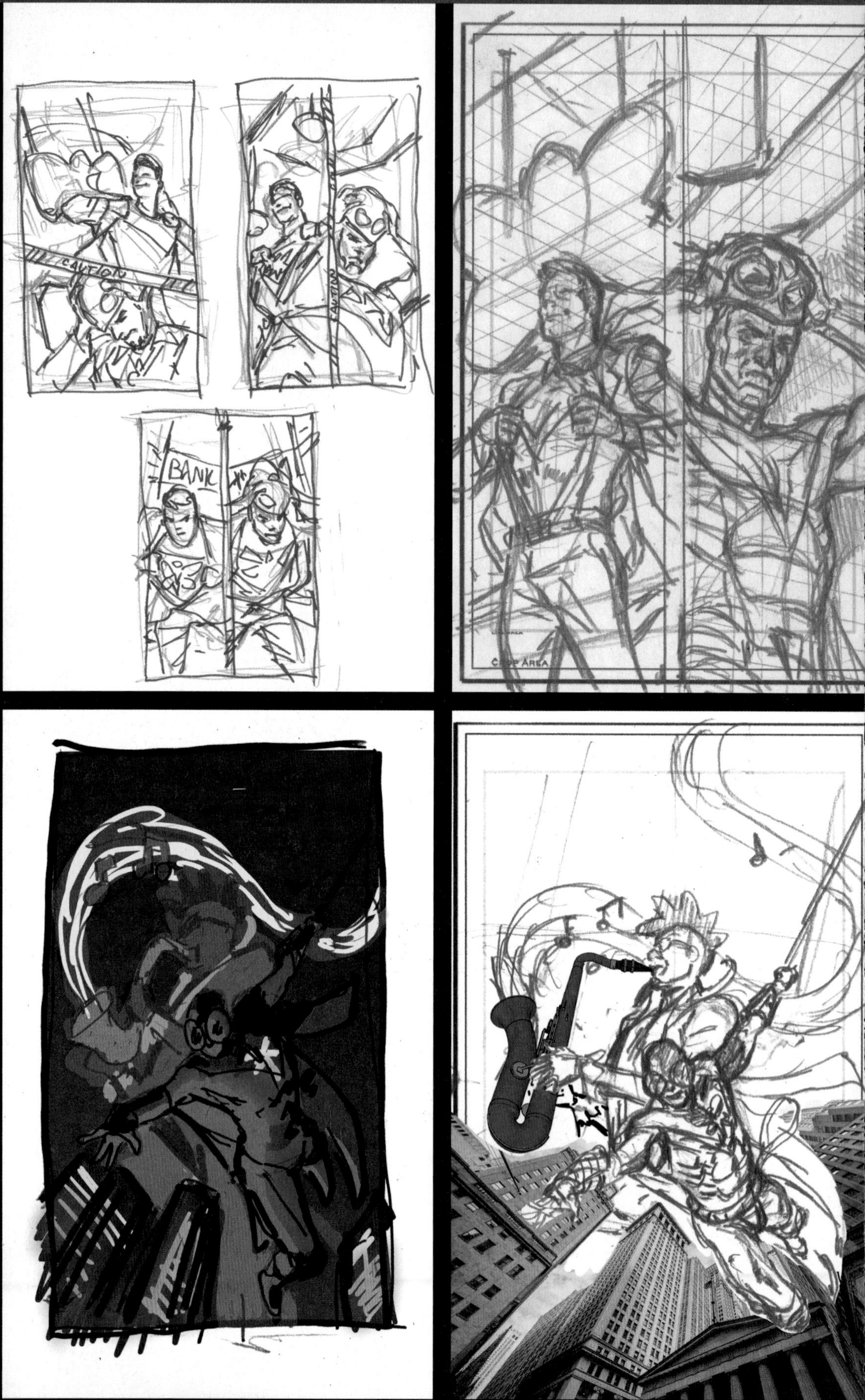
CAUTION
BANK

BOTTOM TIER: ***THE WRONG EARTH: PURPLE*** **#1 COVER ART PROCESS by Jamal Igle**

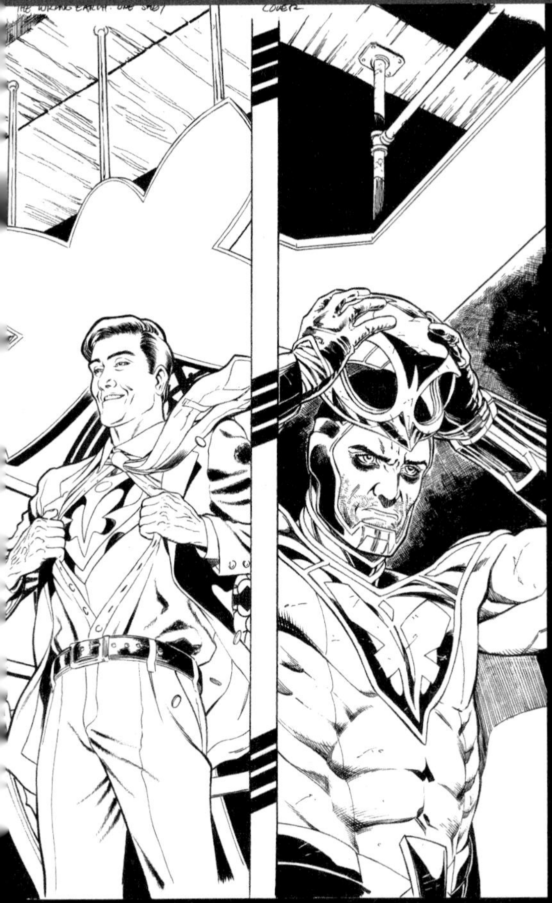

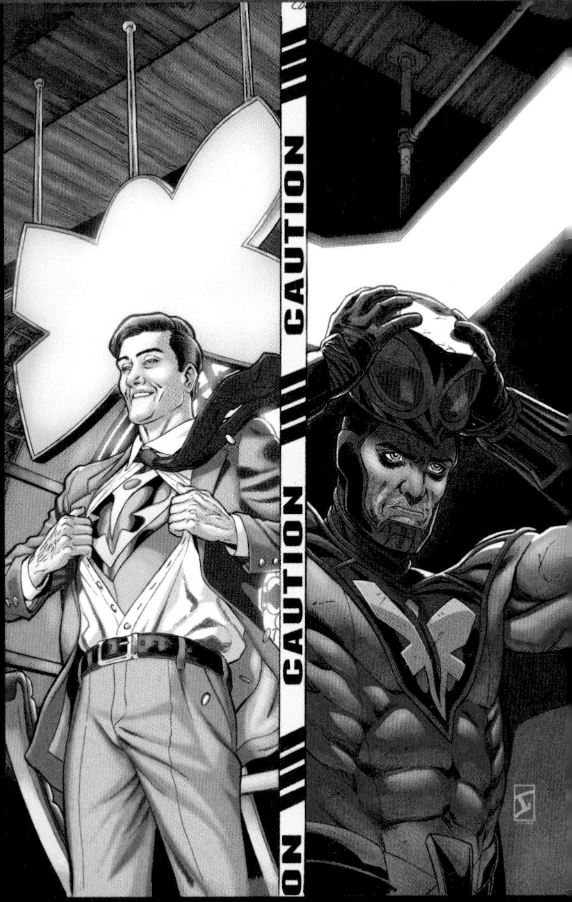

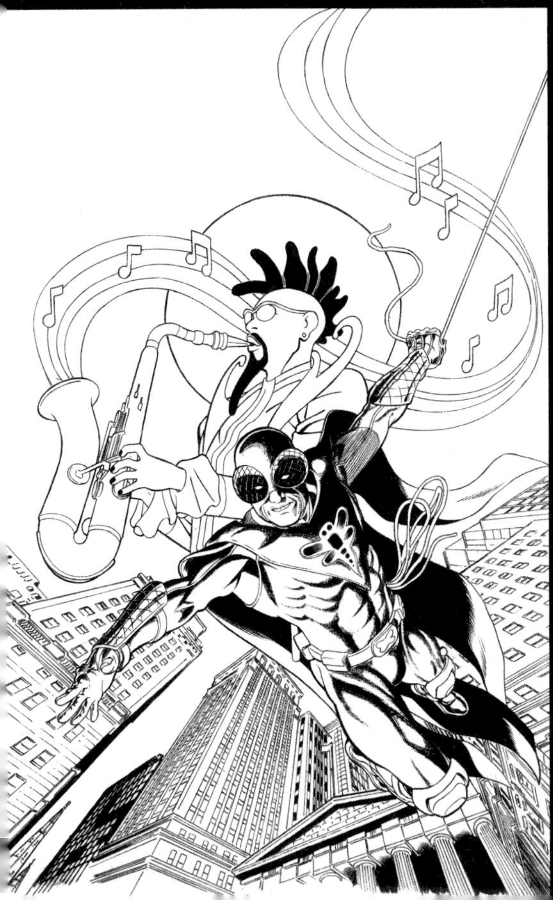

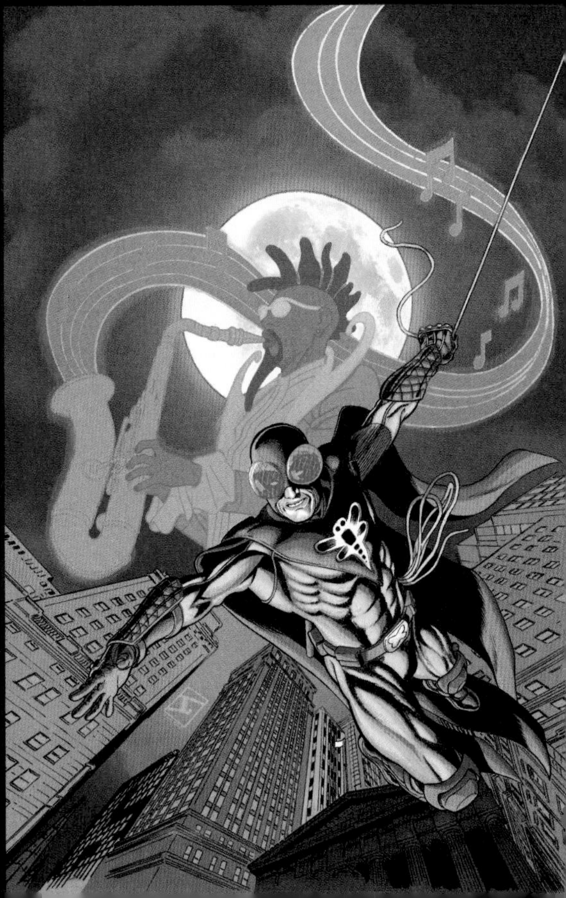

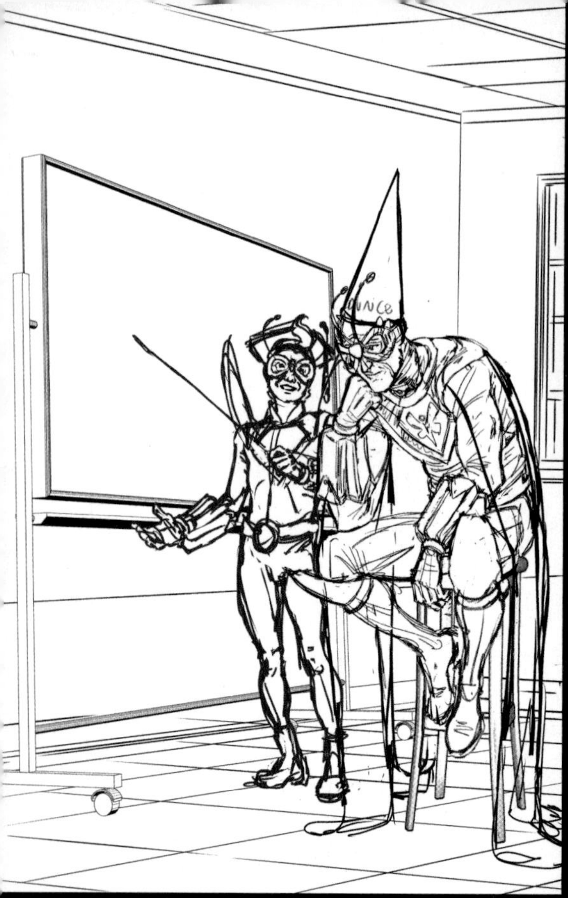
DUNCE

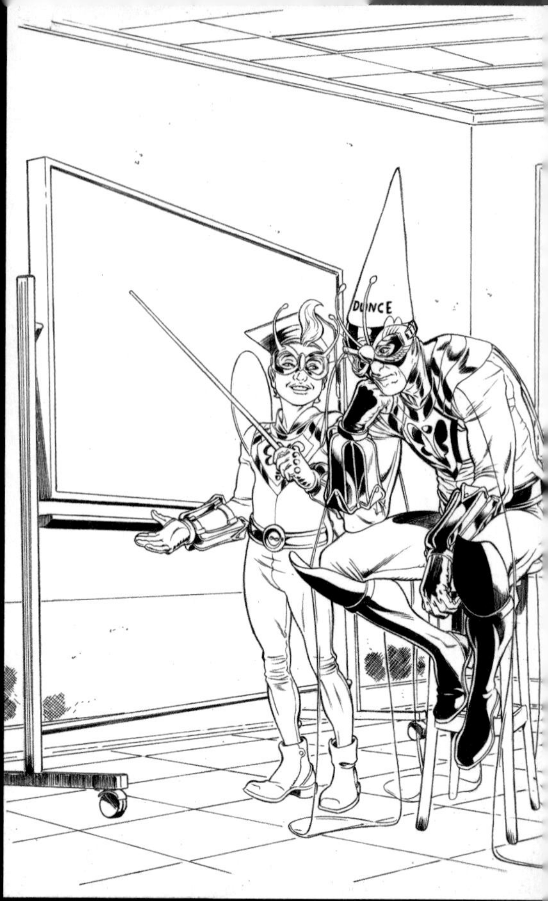
DUNCE

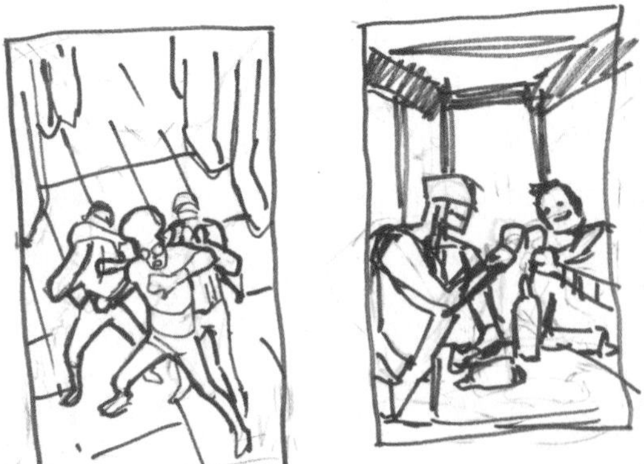

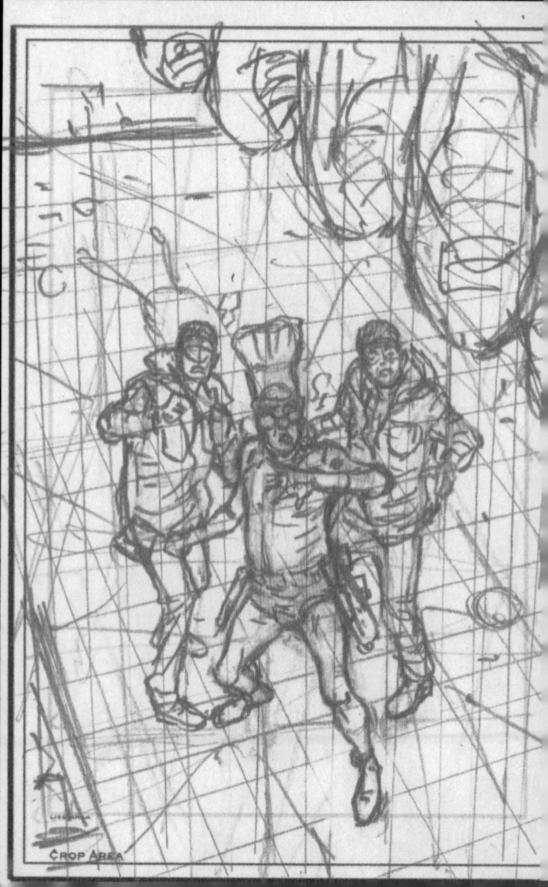
CROP AREA

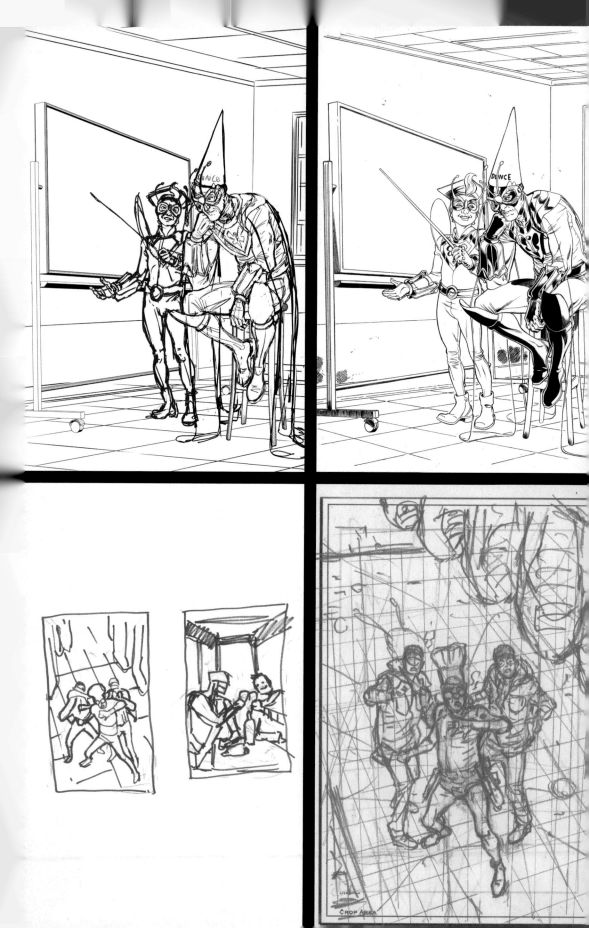

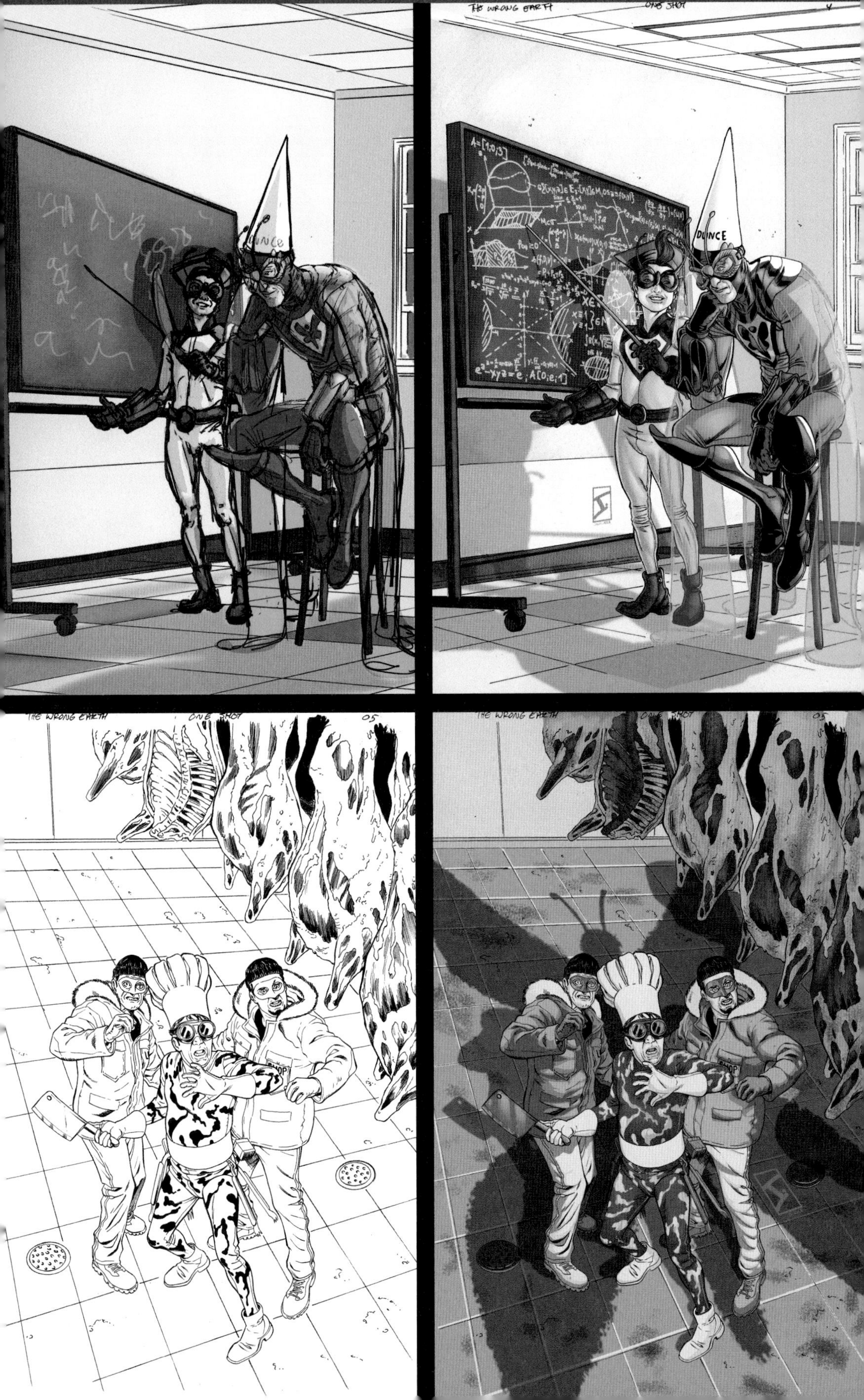
THE WRONG EARTH
ONE SHOT
DUNCE
THE WRONG EARTH
ONE SHOT
05
THE WRONG EARTH
ONE SHOT
05

B I O G R A P H I E S

Brazilian artist **WALTER GEOVANI** was born to be a rock star but he decided for the comic book career because he never liked to take the easier way. He has worked on *Red Sonja, Vampirella, Doctor Who, Clean Room, Red Sonja/ Tarzan* and *THE WRONG EARTH: TRAPPED ON TEEN PLANET*. He still wonders about becoming a rock star, but he's not so sure now because he ain't got enough hair on the head to follow that path.

JAMAL IGLE is the writer/artist/creator of *Molly Danger* for Action Lab Entertainment; the co-creator of *Venture* with writer Jay Faerber; the artist of the series *Black* from Black Mask Studios; and your penciller here on *THE WRONG EARTH*. In 2011, he received a richly deserved Inkpot Award for outstanding achievement in comic art.

GENE HA is best known on this Earth as the artist on Alan Moore's *Top 10* and Kelly Sue DeConnick's *Wonder Woman Historia*. During his long career he has won four Eisners. Gene is the writer and artist on *Mae*, who follows her long missing sister Abbie to a world of mad science and mystery. On Earth-Alpha he's the infamous Taco Taker, a villain who only works on Tuesdays.

LEONARD KIRK began his comic book career with Malibu Comics. He has drawn numerous titles for Marvel and DC, including *Fantastic Four, Star Wars* and extended collaborations with Peter David on *Supergirl* and *X-Factor*. He, wisely, lives north of the border and recently drew a revival of the Canadian comics icon Captain Canuck and a return to the post-apocalyptic world of *Marvel Zombies*.

FRED HARPER has illustrated stories for DC Comics and Marvel Comics. Most memorable (at least to Fred) would be penciling for *Animal Man* at DC Vertigo. He started out with *Savage Sword of Conan, Ghost Rider*, and *Doctor Strange* at Marvel Comics. He went on to do illustrations for White Wolf and Magic the Gathering as he transitioned to magazine illustrations for *The New York Times, The Wall Street Journal, Time, The Week, SPORT, The Sporting News, Muscle and Fitness, Men's Health, Muscular Development,* and *Sports Illustrated*... to name a few. Fred currently resides in an apartment where he conducts experiments about the effects of copious amounts of espresso on an artist's brain. Results have been inconclusive, but sometimes secrets take time for the beans to spill.

ROB LEAN once found a bottle of magic inks. He then began his quest to find magic brushes and pens so he could finally start his comic book career as an inker! But then he woke up and realized that all he needed was regular inks, regular pens and a lot of practice. Lean's true quest began in the early 2000s, and he has worked for publishers including Chaos, DC, Dark Horse, Marvel and Avatar Press and the most magical of them all, AHOY.

PAUL LITTLE is a Canadian colorist who has contributed hues to a bevy of titles from publishers including Image Comics (*Morning Glories, Five Weapons*), BOOM! Studios (*Sons of Anarchy, Palmiotti and Brady's The Big Con Job*), Joe Books (*Darkwing Duck, Disney Princess*), and many more. He lives in the honeymoon capital of the world and is one of the few people who can honestly claim to see Niagara Falls from his living room.

MICHAEL MONTENAT is a digital illustrator and nerd whose work always tells a story, whether it be through comics or single illustrations. Montenat's work adds a gritty realism and texture to new characters as well as ones we all know and love. He has illustrated work for clients as varied as IDW, Top Cow, Legendary, Amazon's Jet City, Darby Pop, Boom!, Panel Syndicate and AHOY Comics' *HAPPY HOUR*. He has also done work for the Dallas Holocaust and Human Rights Museum, country music star Zac Brown, military war veteran and news contributor Johnny Joey Jones, and Universal Studios Japan.

STUART MOORE is a writer, a book editor, and an award- winning comics editor. His recent comics writing includes *Deadpool the Duck* (Marvel), *EGOs* (Image), and *HIGHBALL* (AHOY). His novels include three volumes of *The Zodiac Legacy*, a bestselling Disney Press series created and cowritten by Stan Lee, *Thanos: Death Sentence* (Marvel), and *Target: Kree* (Aconyte). Stuart also handles Publishing Ops for AHOY on a freelance basis from his home in Brooklyn, New York, where he lives with two of the most spoiled cats on this or any other planet.

Then there's **BILL MORRISON**. Movie poster artist (*House, The Little Mermaid*), co-founder, writer, artist, and editor of Bongo Comics (*Simpsons Comics, Futurama Comics*), Editor-in-Chief of *MAD Magazine* (hilarious trash) and psychedelic animated film adaptor (*The Beatles Yellow Submarine*). Bill signed on with AHOY thinking he would finally fulfill his career-long dream of drawing boating safety comics. Though disappointed at first, he loves drawing Dragonfly and enjoys the company policy of talking like a pirate.

JERRY ORDWAY has written and illustrated comics since the early 1980s, earning acclaim as one of the defining Superman creators of his generation. His groundbreaking work includes the "Death of Superman" storyline and Clark Kent's proposal to Lois Lane. Ordway also reintroduced Captain Marvel in *The Power of Shazam!* and illustrated the adaptation of the blockbuster 1989 *Batman* film.

DAN PARENT is a 35 year veteran in the comics industry, writing and drawing primarily for Archie Comics. Dan has also worked for Dynamite, DC, Valiant, IDW and more. He's also co-creator of the successful *Die Kitty Die!* series. Check him out on Instagram @parentdaniel and at www. danparent.com.

TOM PEYER is cofounder and editor-in-chief of AHOY Comics. His recent writing projects include *THE WRONG EARTH, DRAGONFLY & DRAGONFLYMAN, PENULTIMAN, HASHTAG: DANGER*, and *HIGH HEAVEN*. In the before-time he wrote *Hourman* and *Legion of Super-Heroes* for DC Comics and was one of the original editors at Vertigo.

MARK RUSSELL is the author of not one, but two, books about the Bible: *God Is Disappointed in You* and *Apocrypha Now*. In addition, he is the writer behind AHOY's *SECOND COMING, BILLIONAIRE ISLAND* and "The Monster Serials" in *EDGAR ALLAN POE'S SNIFTER OF TERROR*, as well as various DC comic books including *Prez*, *The Flintstones*, and *Exit Stage Left: The Snagglepuss Chronicles*. His series *Not All Robots*, co-created with Mike Deodato, won the Eisner Award for Best Humor Publication. He lives in obscurity with his family in Portland, Oregon.

ANDY TROY has colored for Marvel Comics, DC Comics, Extreme Studios, and others, working on such characters as *Spawn*, *Batman*, *Captain America*, and *Iron Fist*. He lives and works in Huntsville, AL, where he used to play in the metal band Diamond White.

GREG SCOTT is a comic book artist who pencils and inks his own work. He has drawn such titles as *X-Files*, *Black Hood*, *Steve McQueen*, and *Area 51*. He broke into comics through espionage: learning the time of day Marvel editors went outside for a cigarette break, he passed them art samples and was quickly given an assignment.

MARK WAID has written nearly two thousand comics, including the best-selling *Kingdom Come* and *Superman: Birthright*. He and AHOY's Tom Peyer communicate daily and almost exclusively in a stream of references that would befuddle even the most learned of linguists unless they were equally conversant in both the geography of Krypton and the incomparable dramaturgy of Neil Hamilton, superhero TV's finest thespian.

GAIL SIMONE has written some things and some stuff that has sold bunches of copies. People like her work lots, but they seem to like *Birds of Prey*, *Wonder Woman*, *Batgirl* and *Red Sonja* mostest.

ROB STEEN is the illustrator of *Flanimals*, the best-selling series of children's books written by Ricky Gervais, and *Erf*, a children's book written by Garth Ennis.

RICHARD WILLIAMS' illustration work has appeared in many national magazines, most notably *MAD*, for which he was the cover artist during the 1980s. He has also illustrated children's books (*The Legend of the Christmas Rose, Lewis and Clark: Explorers of the American West*) and painted covers for many young adult books such as *Encyclopedia Brown*. His paintings have been purchased by Steven Spielberg, George Lucas, and Howard Stern and are in the collections of the Society of Illustrators and the Library of Congress.